HIS FIRST HERO WAS HIS HALF-JEWISH GODFATHER. HIS SECOND HERO WAS ADOLF HITLER.

Hermann Goering grew up worshiping the brilliant, half-Jewish aristocrat who not only was his godfather but was the lover of his mother. Despite all later taunts, Goering never turned his back on this man.

Then, in the bitter aftermath of World War I defeat, Goering met Adolf Hitler. In Goering, Hitler found what he most needed—a famed war hero who was at once a sophisticated man of the world and a superlative political infighter. In Hitler, Goering found a person who gave meaning to his shattered life and purpose to his tremendous energies and love of danger.

Thus this man of so much courage and so little conscience, so much personal loyalty and so little regard for humanity, started on the course that would lead him to stand beside Hitler on the dizzying summit of power, and to the prison cell where a vial of poison was his final act of defiance. . . .

"Not only the story of Hermann Goering, but of the Nazi party . . . a masterful work!"—*Abilene Reporter News*

THE
REICH
MARSHAL
A BIOGRAPHY OF
HERMANN GOERING

Leonard Mosley

A DELL BOOK

Published by
DELL PUBLISHING CO., INC.
1 Dag Hammarskjold Plaza
New York, New York 10017

CONTENTS

CONTENTS

Acknowledgments

In the Notes which will be found at the end of this book there in a full and detailed documentation of all statements which have been made in the course of this biography. Here I would simply like to make a few acknowledgments to those to whom I am especially grateful for helping me to fill in the gaps in Hermann Goering's life.

First and foremost, I suppose, I should name Emmy Goering, his second wife. I first met her at Carin Hall in 1939, when I was the Berlin correspondent of a British newspaper group. I saw and talked to her several times from 1945 onward, first of all at Sackdilling, in Franconia, shortly after her release from jail, then at Nuremberg, and afterward at her denazification trial in Garmisch Partenkirchen. I last spoke to her in Munich shortly before she died in 1973. She was hardly impartial about her husband, of course, but she replied frankly to all questions, did not try to conceal Goering's weaknesses, and seemed genuinely contemptuous of the Nazi bigwigs with whom life with Goering forced her to come in contact.

I also spent seven days in the last weeks of his life with Goering's stepson, Thomas von Kantzow, who died at his home in Stockholm shortly before Emmy Goering. Von Kantzow was a man sick of an ailment that was as much emotional as physical, and I was with him when he was most anxious to relieve himself of the *Angsts* which had burdened him most of his life, particularly concerning his mother and her entanglement with Goering. Just before I saw him into hospital (he died on May 27, 1973), he carefully and meticulously answered all the questions I put to him about Goering, and, with his nurse, went through his papers and photographs to find those which would best help me in my project. Thomas von Kantzow was one of the saddest men I have ever met, and he died a disappointed man at the end of a ruined life; but I hope the aid he gave me in building up a picture of his mother and stepfather will give him (posthumous though it is) the justification for his existence for which he was looking.

I am greatly indebted to these others who went out of their way to help me:

General Adolf Galland, once Germany's greatest fighter pilot, today a powerful air expert, who talked to me at length about his encounters all through World War II with Hermann Goering;

Herr Albert Speer, who was no friend of the Reich Marshal during the last months of his life, but insisted during our talks on giving a full and balanced picture of him;

General Erhard Milch, who, before his death, coldly and calculatingly catalogued for me his former chief's vices and gave me invaluable information about where to find out more;

General Josef Kammhuber, the creator of Germany's night fighter force, who gave me graphic pictures of life in his native Munich immediately after World War I, as well as his meetings with Goering;

General Karl Bodenschatz, the permanent adjutant (no matter what his rank) of the Luftwaffe from 1916 to 1945, who became an adoring fan of Goering in 1918, and, in spite of everything, never ceased to admire him;

My good friend, General Paul Stehlin, now a much-respected member of the French Chamber of Deputies, who was with me in Berlin when I was a very young correspondent and he was a very young secret agent, for giving me many details of the domestic life of Goering's family;

Dr. Robert Kempner, Doctor Werner Krausnick, Mr. Rolf Wartenberg, Mr. Howard Triest, Mr. Walter H. Rapp, Mr. Morton E. Rome, Mr. Owen Cunningham, Herr and Frau Harry Wiegand of Munich, the older villagers of Veldenstein and Mauterndorf (for their memories of Goering and his godfather), the relatives and friends of the late Professor Hans Thirring, Dr. Carl J. Burckhardt, all of whom have helped to provide me with information and background for this narrative.

Finally, I should like to acknowledge my debt, as always, to the cool head and calm assessment of the one who is always my precious companion and researcher on these projects.

Foreword

One of the favorite gathering places of diplomats and newspaper correspondents in Berlin just before the outbreak of World War II was a small, raffish night club called the Kabarett der Komiker, and it was because I was given a birthday party there in 1938 that I first met Hermann Goering.

The Kabarett der Komiker's resident comedian was an indestructible character named Werner Finck, whose specialty was making fun of the Nazis. He would open his act by rushing on to the tiny stage and lifting his hand in the Hitler salute and then saying: "That's how high my dog can jump!" He would close it by saluting once more and saying: "Heil . . . er . . . er. Now what *is* that fellow's name?" And in between, he would tell the latest jokes that were going around Berlin about the Nazi Party leaders.

It was no moment for a comedian to make his career out of satirizing Hitler and his gang, for almost all of them were high on *amour propre* and low on sense of humor. Finck had been badly beaten several times by Brownshirt bullies and jailed for "insulting" the Fuehrer. But he bounced back with Brechtian braggadocio, and continued to mock the men who now had the fate of the Third Reich in their hands.

One of the regular targets of his jokes was Hermann Goering. It was Finck who first suggested that the fat field marshal had had a set of rubber medals made, so that he could wear them in his bath, and he also liked to tell the story of the baby elephant at the circus which spied Goering in the audience and trumpeted at him: "Papa! Papa!" Finck later said that Goering was the only Nazi leader who never made an official complaint against him, though he must have come extremely close to it at the time when his wife, Emmy, revealed that she was pregnant.

"Do you know what Goering's going to call his firstborn
if it's a boy?" Werner Finck asked his audience, shortly
after the news became known. "Hamlet. Yes, Hamlet! And
do you know why?" At which point the comedian took up
the stance of the Gloomy Dane and began to recite: *"Sein
oder nicht sein, dass ist die Frage!"* *

Goering was outraged that anyone should suggest, even
as a joke, that his beloved Emmy was carrying a child not
fathered by himself, and thereafter he sent his adjutant and
collaborator, General Karl Bodenschatz, to the Kabarett
der Komiker at regular intervals to make sure that Werner
Finck's patter kept away from the subject of his family
life.

It was Bodenschatz who joined my birthday table in
1938 (Werner Finck was already there) and, on learning
that my accreditation as a correspondent was not yet
through, and that I was therefore barred from "official"
occasions, invited me personally to a Goering press luncheon three days later. It was there that I was introduced to
the blond giant Ernst Udet, who had flown with Goering in
World War I and was now the technical director of the
German air arm; to Erhard Milch, the hard-driving second-
in-command of the Luftwaffe; and finally to Hermann
Goering himself.

When it suited him, Goering could be the most charming and attentive of hosts. He liked being with newspapermen, though this was obviously mainly because they gave
him the world publicity which he so much loved. I also got
the feeling that he rather liked their company and their
conversation, which must have been a pleasant change
from the stultifyingly boring talk which he had to listen to
in Hitler's circle. He took the trouble to know the names
and backgrounds of most members of the foreign press in
Berlin, and he had usually read—and was ready to argue
about—their latest dispatches. But given a breath of an
excuse, he would turn away from the grim political situation of the day and begin talking about his two favorite
subjects: his art collection, or the animal and plant con-

---

* Which, in German, can mean either the first line of Hamlet's
soliloquy: "To be or not to be, that is the question" or "His or
not his, that is the question."

servation projects in which he was engaged around Carin
Hall, in Northeast Prussia.

I remember coming away from my first meeting asking
myself the question: How had such a worldly, cultivated
man got himself mixed up with such a sleazy and murder-
ous gang as the Nazis? I was somewhat chastened shortly
afterward when I went to one of his meetings and saw on
the platform not the charming art and animal lover I had
first encountered but a ranting, raving anti-Semite mouthing all the shibboleths of the Party, a quivering mass of
hate and rancor.

I was to meet him several times before I finally left
Berlin on the outbreak of World War II, and each encounter made me more conscious of the contradictions of
his nature. Which was the real Hermann Goering? The self-
proclaimed friend of Britain who seemed to be sincerely
and genuinely trying to prevent an Anglo-German war in
1939? The family man, the ecologist, the lover of art and
beauty? The Party hack and Hitler's fawning slave? The
peacock, the bully, the cunning deceiver of foreign statesmen?

By the time I left Berlin, I had still not made up my
mind. The last time I saw Hermann Goering, he was so
confident that his efforts to prevent World War II would
succeed that he bet me a bottle of champagne that Britain
would not fight Germany.† Was it a brave effort on his
part to frustrate Hitler's plans, or was it merely a trick?

In some ways, this book could be described as the search
for the answer to those questions. Certainly it is not another history of the Third Reich seen through the eyes of
one of its chief protagonists. It is not a political biography.
It is not an excuse for retelling the story of the Battle of
Britain, the war against Russia, life in Adolf Hitler's
bunker, or the rise and fall of the National Socialist Party.
It is, instead, the study of the man who happened to be
involved in all those things, and the search for his true
identity.

I hope I have achieved my purpose, and that the real
Hermann Goering will step out from the pages of this
book.

† He paid up by delivering a case of Dom Perignon to my room in
the Amstel Hotel, Amsterdam, Holland, two weeks after war had
begun.

THE
REICH
MARSHAL

I. FATHER FIGURE

In the last decade of the nineteenth century the convalescent home known as the Marienbad Sanitarium was situated a little way out of the small town of Rosenheim, some forty miles south of Munich on the main railroad line to Salzburg, in Austria. It was run by a doctor and matron, both Austrians, who had formerly worked in the spas of the Sudetenland at Carlsbad, Franzensbad, and Marienbad, and their skillful care had made their establishment so well known that patients came from all over Germany and the Austro-Hungarian Empire to recuperate there from illnesses and depressions.

The sanitarium sat in its own well-wooded grounds on an eminence overlooking the town, and from its windows and terraces there was a breath-taking panoramic view across South Bavaria to the snowclad peaks of the Obersalzberg and the Austrian Alps. It catered mainly to weak-chested and convalescent patients, but since it was a moment in history when all good Germans were being urged to breed for the Fatherland, and since this was a remarkably fecund region anyway, the director had also engaged two midwives and opened a maternity section.

It was here, early in January 1893, that Frau Franziszka Goering came to bear her fourth child.

Twenty-seven years old in 1893, Fanny Goering was a broad-shouldered, full-breasted blonde whose pretty peasant face (she came from Bavarian and Austrian farming stock) was transformed by one feature—the blazing beauty of her astonishingly vivid blue eyes. It was her eyes which had caught and held the man who was now her husband, when he had first met her eight years before. Heinrich Ernst Goering was a senior official of the German consular service, forty-five years old and recently widowed, the father of five motherless children by his dead wife. He was looking for a replacement. He was due to sail in a few months' time for the new German colony in Southwest Africa and he needed a wife not only capable of coping with the pioneering life in the new settlement at Windhoek but of caring for his children as well. The young, cheerful, nineteen-year-old Fanny Tiefenbrunn gave every promise of being a devoted stepmother, and one not likely to be daunted by the rigors of life in a strange, rough land. But in addition to that, there was a quality in those extraordinary blue eyes that hinted that her husband would not be stinted of affection, either.

An arrangement was made with her parents and the couple left in the spring of 1885 for London, where Heinrich Goering was to take a crash course from the British in colonial administration. It was in London that they were married, and by the time they sailed for Africa, where Chancellor Bismarck had appointed Heinrich the new Minister-Resident at Windhoek, his bride was already pregnant. Despite her sturdy appearance, it was to prove a difficult first birth. Conditions in the new German colony were primitive indeed: water was short, the heat and dust appalling, and the local Germans not particularly friendly toward the family of the official representative of Berlin.* It seems possible that Fanny would have died or been permanently invalided had it not been for the intervention of a young German doctor who arrived at the residency and took charge. Soon he had brought Fanny's firstborn, Karl, squealing into the world. Then he turned his attention to the pained and distressed young mother, and he did not leave the residency until he had seen the lids close over those blue eyes and she had drifted off into a peaceful sleep.

The doctor, a plump, dark-haired Berliner with a well-trimmed mustache only half hiding a full, sensual mouth, was named Ritter Hermann von Epenstein (his title had been granted by Kaiser Wilhelm II a few years previously). He was to become a close friend and strong influence on the Goering family, especially upon one of the sons as yet unborn. By the time she had recovered suffi-

---

* Bismarck, not really interested in colonies, insisted that all expenses in Southwest Africa be paid by the chartered companies and not by the state, and this was resented by the German merchants.

ciently to get up from her bed, Fanny was already under his spell. He had appeared in her hour of need and saved her life, and she would remain everlastingly grateful to him, determined one day to repay him. As indeed she did.

Now, seven years and three children later, she was about to give birth again. Much had happened to the Goering family in the intervening years. Heinrich, after years of arduous but successful administration in Southwest Africa, had been back to Germany and then accepted an appointment as consul general on the island of Haiti. But both he and Fanny had maintained contact with Ritter von Epenstein, and it was on his advice that she had been sent to the Marienbad Sanitarium at Rosenheim for her fourth pregnancy. Afterward she was to tell her children that it was a pure coincidence that, while Heinrich remained on duty in Haiti, Von Epenstein just happened to be on leave in Austria, a few hours away by train, when she arrived at the sanitarium. On the morning of January 12, 1893, she gave birth to her fourth child and second son. A few hours later, a horse-drawn sleigh arrived at the door of the Marienbad Sanitarium and Ritter von Epenstein was announced.

Fanny gestured to the bundle in the cot beside her bed and proudly announced:

"This is Hermann Goering." She had determined to name the child after Von Epenstein if it was a boy.†
"Look," she added, "he has blue eyes just like mine."

Von Epenstein brusquely pointed out that nearly all babies were born with blue eyes, and that they would change later.

"No," said Fanny with conviction, "not Hermann's eyes. They will always be blue."

She could see that Von Epenstein was touched by the gesture over the name. He stayed in Rosenheim for the next few days, visiting her each afternoon, before taking the train back to Austria to resume his leave. From there he wrote to both Fanny and Heinrich to announce that he had made up his mind, and, providing they approved, he would appoint himself godfather of Hermann Wilhelm Goering.

† In fact he was christened Hermann Wilhelm Goering, the Wilhelm being for Emperor Wilhelm II.

In the spring of 1893, Fanny Goering weaned the three-month-old Hermann and left Germany to rejoin her husband and the rest of her family in Haiti. It was three years before they returned to Germany. During that time Hermann was left with a family in the Bavarian town of Fürth, and was brought up with the two young daughters of the house; they were afterward to remember him as a child given to fits of tears and tantrums, which were invariably followed by gifts and gestures of affection. He was obviously a lonely child and nothing that his surrogate parents did for him seemed capable of making up for the absence of his real parents. "It is the cruelest thing that can happen to a child, to be torn from his mother in his formative years," Hermann Goering was to say many years later. His older sister, Olga, remembered that when Herr and Frau Goering eventually returned from the Caribbean and he was taken to the railroad station to meet them, the three-year-old Hermann deliberately turned his back as the train steamed into the platform. When his mother took him in her arms and embraced him, he responded by beating her about the face and chest and then bursting into tears. The stranger who was his father he ignored completely.

Heinrich Goering deserved well of the Fatherland, for he had toiled hard and successfully for it under the most arduous conditions. Had Bismarck not been so unenthusiastic about Germany's colonial empire the work which this devoted consular official had done in Southwest Africa would almost certainly have received the recognition it deserved. He had arrived when the colony was only twelve months old and the natives were suspicious and unfriendly. He had reconciled the hostile Hereros and Hottentots to the arrival of the white man in their midst, and insisted that the Germans under his jurisdiction should treat them with civilization and understanding; and it was only after his departure that the tribes rose against his brutal and unimaginative successors. He had met and talked on equal terms with Cecil Rhodes and other architects of British influence in southern Africa, and had foreseen the coming clash between Britain and the Boers which could have been prevented had his advice been followed. In his consular office in Haiti he had made Germany's name respected by trying to bring medicine and enlightenment to that benighted, superstition-ridden island.

But by the time Heinrich Goering came back to Berlin, in 1896, a current of anti-liberalism was running through the political life of Germany, and anyone who talked of the natives of Africa as human beings, as Heinrich did, was looked upon with the gravest suspicion and dubbed an incipient Socialist, and Socialists were the bogeymen of the day. It was soon evident that there would be no advancement for him. His experiences in Africa and the Caribbean had aged him prematurely, and he looked considerably more than fifty-six years old. Moreover, prematurely retired, dogged by a sense of failure, he began to seek solace from alcohol. He became a drunk, a quiet, even-tempered one, but a drunk nevertheless, and he was usually speechless or inarticulate by midevening. Hermann Goering, who had never known his father in his heyday, can hardly be blamed for regarding him with an affectionate contempt about which he was to have strong guilt feelings in the years to come.

His respect was hardly increased by the frequent appearance at their home, in a quiet suburb of Berlin, of his godfather, Ritter von Epenstein. He too had by this time retired from government service but otherwise there was scant similarity between him and the crumbling proconsul, for he had burgeoned with the years, and gone on to better things. He had always been rich, he was still a bachelor, and on the fringes of the Court circles in Berlin and Vienna he had begun to acquire a reputation both as an eligible catch for daughters of the minor aristocracy and as the successful lover of several of their more personable mothers. He was of only medium height and much given to fleshiness, against which he regularly took the cure at Carlsbad, Spa, and Vichy, but he wore his clothes with a dash and assumed an arrogant manner of speech and gesture which overawed most people with whom he came in contact. To the Goering family his sudden arrival from exotic places like Cairo, Constantinople, Naples, or St. Petersburg brought the smell of adventure into an otherwise drab and fraying household.

For Hermann Goering, already dazzled by military uniforms, obsessed in his childhood games by medieval battles and knightly chivalry, his godfather was a shining hero to be emulated in dress, in manner, in speech, and in boldness. A few years after Heinrich Goering's retirement, Von

Epenstein appeared in Berlin and announced that he was taking the whole family to Austria, where he had come into possession of a castle at Mauterndorf, in a fold of the Tauern Mountains just below the Bavarian frontier. At Mauterndorf Castle, as Hermann Goering and his brothers and sisters discovered to their delight, Von Epenstein had indulged his own secret yearning for medieval grandeur and pomp. Retainers were dressed in old Court uniforms, meals were called by a blast of a hunting horn, and on festive occasions a group of minstrels and musicians played and sang in the gallery of the great hall. As for Ritter von Epenstein, he behaved as if he were lord of all he surveyed (as indeed he was) and he strode his domain, giving orders, receiving deferential salutes from the men and curtsies from the women, as if he were of royal blood. It was a sight which Hermann Goering was never to forget and one which he dreamed one day of imitating.

When did Von Epenstein and Fanny Goering first become lovers?

Most students of the Goering family history would time it at about a year to nine months before the birth of Hermann's youngest brother, Albert. It was a year in which Heinrich Goering was ill for several months at a time with bronchitis and pneumonia, and shortly after Albert was born, Von Epenstein proposed that the family should move out of Berlin "for the sake of Heinrich's health" and should take up residence in another castle which he had recently purchased. This was Burg Veldenstein, a restoration of an ancient Franconian fortress, built on a cliff overlooking the small beer-brewing town of Neuhaus, on the river Pegnitz. The castle sat amid the rolling hills and lush forests some twenty-five miles north of Nuremberg, and it was within easy reach of Bayreuth, where Von Epenstein, a keen lover of Wagner, liked to go for the opera and music festivals.

With the birth of Albert, Von Epenstein announced that he was adopting all five of Fanny's family as his godchildren. "*Pate*‡ had made Hermann his favorite godchild until then," said his sister Olga in later years, "but after Albert's birth he was always fussing over him." She did not

‡ Godfather.

add that this baby's eyes were definitely not blue but grew to be as doe-brown as Von Epenstein's own, and that as he became older Albert looked uncannily like the family benefactor. She did remark: "Hermann became quite jealous of his younger brother."

He was seven years old by this time, and like everyone else he knew that his mother was his godfather's mistress, though he may not have understood exactly what that meant. At Mauterndorf it was common knowledge that whenever Ritter von Epenstein gave a dinner party, which was almost every night, Fanny acted as his hostess while the rest of her family, Heinrich included, stayed down in one of the lodges in the grounds where they were housed; and at the end of the evening she did not return to join them until breakfast time. At Burg Veldenstein it had been a stipulation of the Goerings' occupancy that one of the principal bedrooms and drawing rooms should always be reserved for their benefactor, especially when the opera season at Bayreuth was in progress; and while he was there Heinrich complaisantly swallowed the fact that his wife would occupy the guest's bed rather than his own for the duration of the visit.

That young Hermann Goering was aware of his mother's liaison with his godfather seems certain.

"We never had any doubt about it," said Professor Hans Thirring later.* "Everyone who stayed at Mauterndorf accepted the situation, and it did not seem to trouble Hermann or the other Goering children at all. Like all the rest of us, they went in fear and trembling of Pate Epenstein. We had to stand to attention while he was talking to us, and we were not allowed to address him without permission. But we all admired him—he was such a dashing, almost swashbuckling kind of man. We would all have hated anyone who said unkind things about him, but it was Hermann who actually fought and badly bloodied the nose of a boy visitor in the village who remarked in his hearing that Pate had won his title from the Kaiser with money, rather than with brave deeds. How Pate came to hear about the incident I never discovered, but next day the boy

* Professor Thirring and his brother were also godchildren of Ritter von Epenstein, who was one of their father's closest friends. It was Thirring senior who had found Mauterndorf for his friend and completed the arrangements for its purchase.

and his parents had disappeared from Mauterndorf and
Hermann was given the special treat of spending the day
alone with his hero, hunting chamois up in the mountains."

It is a measure of Hermann Goering's admiration for his
godfather that it even survived the discovery that he was of
Jewish blood.

Ritter von Epenstein was a Roman Catholic and he
made a great show each Sunday at Mauterndorf or Neuhaus (when he was staying at Veldenstein) of leading his
guests and his godchildren into the village church, where
rows of pews were reserved for them. But in fact his father
was Jewish. A doctor at the court of King Frederick Wilhelm IV of Prussia, he had prospered under royal patronage, made the acquaintance of the daughter of a rich Gen-
tile merchant banker and quietly converted to Roman
Catholicism before marrying her. But the family name
went into the semi-Gotha of the day beside all other titled
German families of Jewish blood, and had Hermann von
Epenstein lived into the regime of Adolf Hitler and the
National Socialists he would undoubtedly have been considered a Jew within the definition of the Nuremberg laws
and treated accordingly.

Hermann Goering found out the truth about his godfather's background when he was sent to a boarding school
at Ansbach, in Franconia, in 1904. He was eleven years
old now, and proud, arrogant, and headstrong, much given
to bossing his brothers and sisters and organizing their
games. At Ansbach he was suddenly a small frog in a very
large pool, faced with fellow pupils as willful and bossy as
himself, only older and stronger. He hated every moment
of his stay in the school. Discipline was strict, the food was
poor, and though his parents had put him down to study
the piano, during music lessons he was forced to take up
the violin, an instrument he loathed because he could never
coax anything but unmusical croaks from its strings. The
last straw came when pupils were told to write an essay on
the subject of "the man I admire most in the world." At
Ansbach it was expected that the boys would produce patriotic essays about Wilhelm II, Bismarck, or Frederick the
Great, or respectful tributes to their fathers. Hermann
Goering's essay paeaned the praises of Ritter von Epenstein. The following day he was called to an interview with
the high master and frigidly informed that Ansbach boys

did not write pieces in praise of Jews, and when Hermann hotly protested that his godfather was a Roman Catholic he was handed a copy of the semi-Gotha and sent away to write out a hundred times "I shall not write essays in praise of Jews" and copy out all the names in the semi-Gotha from A to E.

A few hours later the story had spread through the school and the snickers and insults began, culminating in a fierce battle with three of the boys and a parade around the school grounds, during which Hermann Goering was frog-marched with a placard around his neck saying: MEIN PATE IST EIN JUDE. Early next day he slipped out of bed and made his way to the station, where he spent his last pocket money on a ticket back to Neuhaus. His last act before leaving school was to smash his violin and cut the strings of all the other instruments in the school band.†

There was no persecution of the Jews in the Germany of Kaiser Wilhelm II, and, in fact, many of them rose to fill eminent and important positions in the state; but an under-current of anti-Semitism ran through German life and the Jews were sneered at in public and attacked in the press and there were certain clubs, houses, and social circles into which they were never admitted. But Hermann Goering did not allow the fact that his hero belonged to a race despised by so many of his fellow Germans to color his attitude toward him at any time during his lifetime.

"There was always one thing you could be sure of about Hermann," said Professor Hans Thirring. "Once he had chosen his hero, he would stand by him through thick and thin."

Not that Von Epenstein ever showed any sign of needing the loyalty of his young godson, and such was his over-weening self-confidence and his awe-inspiring manner that it is most unlikely that the amount of blood of one race or another running through his veins ever became a topic of discussion between them. There were Germans or Aus-

† Erich Gritzbach, author of the official biography of Goering, published in Germany in 1938, says Hermann left Ansbach because he was disciplined for leading a strike against the poor quality of the school food, and that he paid his fare home by selling his violin to a fellow pupil. This version comes from his favorite sister, Olga.

trians who made derogatory remarks about Hermann von Epenstein behind his back, but it was a bold man or woman who dared to do so to his face, and they must have been few and far between.

For a time his affections had concentrated upon the youngest of the Goering children, Albert, whose resemblance to him physically became so noticeable that most people who saw them together assumed that this was his own son. But except in physical appearance, Albert showed no signs of possessing his stepfather's qualities; he was a sad boy, apt to whine and to cry before he was hurt. Von Epenstein's favoritism swung back to Hermann Goering, who was developing all the qualities he considered desirable in a German boy. He was bold and resolute and completely without fear. By the time he was ten he had developed such a passion for mountaineering that, to demonstrate to his elders that he was fit to be trusted in the mountains, he scaled the sheersided cliff upon which Burg Veldenstein sits. Three years later, accompanied by a brother-in-law and one other, he made it successfully to the peak of the 12,000-foot Gross Glockner, cutting his way to the top by the most hazardous route, used only rarely and then by professional mountaineers. He put his shoulder out while swinging around an outjutting rock beneath Mont Blanc, calmly reset the joint while dangling from the rope, and continued the climb though in great pain.

"I have no fear of heights. They stimulate me," he said. "Besides, any danger is worth while if, by risking it, you reach the top of the mountain. You know you will have a view few other men will ever see."

Egged on by Fanny, ambitious to see her son succeed, Heinrich Goering and Von Epenstein (both old cavalry men) succeeded in gaining a place for Hermann in the military academy at Karlsruhe. Heinrich Goering had feared that his son's unruliness and reputation for rebelliousness and indiscipline would mitigate against the boy's chances. He need not have worried. The cadet school prided itself on its ability to tame the wildest spirits and welcomed boys with guts and go; he emerged at the age of sixteen with excellent marks in discipline, riding, history, English and French, and music. "Goering has been an exemplary pupil," said his final report, "and he has devel-

oped a quality that should take him far: he is not afraid to
take a risk."

With such a report in his knapsack he had no difficulty
whatsoever in progressing from Karlsruhe to Lichterfelde,
near Berlin, a cadet college for future officers of the German Army. It was as if all his childhood of military
games and play-acting with gaudy uniforms had been but a
preparation for this. The uniforms of the cadets were smart
and colorful, especially on dress occasions; behavior was
based on medieval codes, and in the cadet societies—and
he was elected to one of the most exclusive—there were
rituals to be followed "that make me think I am an inher-
itor of all the chivalry of German knighthood," he wrote
home to his family. There were also times, he confessed to
his sister Olga, that he dreamed of becoming a modern
Siegfried, destined to bring the light back to Germany. He
did not add that there were several much more mundane
but no less enjoyable advantages to being a cadet at Lichterfelde: great beer-drinking revels, racing at Ruhleben,
swimming parties on the Wannsee, and girls. His mother
had been right; his eyes had stayed vivid greenish-blue, and
their effect on the opposite sex was startling.

It could have been the happiest period of his life for
Hermann Wilhelm Goering had it not been for the sudden
surfacing of trouble in the family at Veldenstein. After
fourteen years of being an uncomplaining cuckold, Heinrich Goering began to object to his wife's relationship with
Ritter von Epenstein. He could not have chosen a more
ironic moment. Fanny Goering had never been her lover's
only mistress, and she must have known that though she
shared his bed at Veldenstein and Mauterndorf, when he
was in other places he had other female companions. He
had always been proud of his status as a rich, merry bachelor, and it was one of the reasons why he specialized in
liaisons with married women.

But in 1912, just about the time when Hermann Goering
was graduating from Lichterfelde, a different kind of
woman came into his life, and the result was disaster for
the Goerings.

Hermann Goering had passed through military college
with brilliant results, and his family had every right to be
proud of him. In almost every subject he had emerged
magna cum laude, and the auguries were bright for his

future. At nineteen he was a slim, loose-limbed lady-killer
of great cheerfulness and charm. He was given a commission in the Prinz Wilhelm Regiment No. 112 and posted to
its headquarters at Mülhausen, but before going there he
came home to Burg Veldenstein on leave, proud of the
opportunity to show off his new uniform. To his great
disappointment, Ritter von Epenstein was not there with
the family to greet him on his arrival, though his godfather
had already written him his felicitations and enclosed with
the letter a small purse filled with gold marks.

The young ensign was shocked by the appearance of his
parents. Heinrich Goering had turned into a querulous old
man who spent most of his time shuffling around the corridors of Veldenstein muttering darkly to himself. Fanny
had suddenly become plump and middle-aged and, except
when she was looking proudly at her son, rarely smiled;
she was forty-six years old and seemed much more to
Hermann. When he mentioned his godfather the old man
flared with temper and talked angrily about "betrayal of
friendship" and he saw tears come into his mother's eyes.
But there was a note from Von Epenstein awaiting him,
inviting him to visit Mauterndorf.

Once he arrived there it was clear why his godfather was
staying so close to home. For the first time in his life this
arrogant feudal lord had fallen in love. He was sixty-two
years old, and it had hit him hard. Unfortunately for him,
the girl who had bowled him over was barely in her twenties, but with the seductive skills of a woman twice her age.
Unfazed by Von Epenstein's aristocratic airs and haughty
manner, she touched him, stroked him, brushed him with
her superb little body, flirted outrageously with him and
promised him everything with her eyes, but never allowed
him to do with her what he had done with most other
women he had fancied in his life, that is to take her in his
arms and carry her off to his bed. The girl who was to
become Lilli von Epenstein was determined that no man
was going to go to bed with her until there was a marriage
ring on her finger.

News of Von Epenstein's burning but frustrated passion
was soon the talk of Berlin, Salzburg, and Vienna. In
Mauterndorf the men were taking wagers on who would
succumb first, but among the women, only too aware of
Fräulein Lilli's youth, gaiety and roguish charm, there was

never really any doubt. But it was a fierce battle of the sexes, and of ages, while it lasted.

In the meantime, Von Epenstein's liaison with Fanny Goering simply withered and died. The end came early in 1913, when Von Epenstein arrived at Burg Veldenstein to tell his mistress that he was in love and was going to be married. Heinrich Goering chose the occasion to erupt on the scene with outraged accusations against his old friend, and the result was a bitter quarrel, full of recriminations, which came to an end only when Heinrich informed his startled family that they could no longer stay in the house of a friend who had so wickedly betrayed him and his honor.

Hermann Goering, on duty with his regiment by this time, was aghast when he heard the news, not least because he had boasted to his fellow officers about "our castle" at Veldenstein. But it was too late to do anything. Von Epenstein was back at his courtship of Fräulein Lilli, and soon learned from that determined young woman that lending castles rent-free to friends was not something of which she approved. Whether Heinrich Goering had been serious in his threat to quit Veldenstein no longer mattered, because a curt note from Mauterndorf arrived giving the family a time limit for getting out.

In the late spring of 1913 the Goerings said good-by to Burg Veldenstein, and for Heinrich and Fanny Goering it was the last time they would see together the handsome old castle in which they had spent fifteen years of their life. Heinrich Goering was already seriously ill, and the heart-breaking wrench of leaving what had been his home for twelve years, plus his strained relationship with Fanny, were such that, shortly after arriving in Munich, where the family had rented a house, he took to his bed and died. Hermann Goering came home on compassionate leave from his regiment and spent the day and the night before the funeral helping his mother to go through his father's papers. As he leafed through the faded photographs, the old diaries and letters, and as he listened to his mother reminiscing about the triumphs and disasters in Africa and Haiti, it was as if he realized for the first time the stature of his dead father during the years of his colonial triumphs. He was afterward to say that he experienced an anguished surge of guilt over the way he had failed to establish any real rapport with his father, and his agony of remorse reached its climax next day as the family stood around the grave in Munich's great cemetery, the Waldfriedhof. He knew that it was considered unmanly for an officer in uniform to show emotion, but he could not help it and tears streamed down his face as he watched the coffin being lowered into the grave.

II. WAR

Hermann Goering was twenty-one years old when World War I began, and few young men on either side were more eager to get into the battle. In these days of enlightened disillusionment with war and patriotism it is difficult to understand the pitch of fervor and enthusiasm to which the average German officer had been brought as war came to Europe. So far as Goering was concerned, all family and environmental influences brought to bear on him since babyhood served to add an extra measure to his fever for fulfillment through the fight for the Fatherland's glory.

Though he had no doubts about the rightness of Germany's cause, that was not the main concern. The main concern was war itself, the test of courage and the challenge to manhood—an exciting and dangerous ordeal from which there was a prize to be won by the strong, the brave and the chivalrous. There was nothing in his baptism of fire, in the months of August and September 1914, to dissuade him from this belief.

According to the records of his regiment and to the documents consulted by his official German biographer, Erich Gritzbach, his first contact with the enemy occurred within a few hours of the outbreak of hostilities. The garrison town of the Prinz Wilhelm Regiment was Mülhausen, but once war began it had two strikes against it: it was in Alsace-Lorraine, annexed from the French after the war of 1870, and it was on the wrong side of the river Rhine. So the moment war was declared by France, the troops of the Prinz Wilhelm Regiment retreated across the Rhine to German territory, and forward elements of the French Army under the command of General Paul Pau almost immediately moved in to fill the vacuum. They hoisted the French flag over the town hall and declared the inhabitants French citizens once more. But in the midst of the celebrations a platoon of German troops under Lieutenant Hermann Goering's command steamed back across the Rhine in an armored train, and the French, who were extremely thin on the ground, retreated hastily back to their main positions. Goering personally lowered the French flag, instructed his men to tear down all posters in French which had been affixed to the walls of the town, and returned to German territory just before nightfall bringing with him four cavalry horses which had been left behind by the French in their headlong retreat.

Next day there was no question of bringing a train across, for the French had occupied the railroad lines during the night and poured troops into the city. The tricolor was once more flying from the town hall, and General Pau himself had set up headquarters there. Not to be outdone, Goering organized a seven-man patrol and led them on bicycles across the river and by back roads toward Mülhausen once more. The Germans had the advantage of knowing the topography of the town and its surroundings much more intimately than the enemy, and shortly after dawn, after first overcoming a French outpost on the outskirts, they rode into the center of Mülhausen through deserted streets to a point just short of the main square. There most people of the town had gathered to greet the French troops, and Goering quickly realized that in the center of the fraternizing crowd was none other than the French commander, General Paul Pau. He quickly conceived a daring plan, the details of which he whispered to his men: while they covered him from behind, he would creep forward, take one of the horses tethered on the fringes of the crowd, and mount it. He would then gallop through the throng to the point where General Pau was standing, gather him up and across his saddle (he was a small man), and race back with him to the German positions while his men covered his retreat.

Whether this mad plan would have succeeded will never be known. Just as Goering was about to grasp the reins of the nearest horse one of his platoon nervously fingered the trigger of his rifle and it went off. The horse reared and backed off. The alarm was given. There was nothing else to do but run back, grab his bicycle, and pedal away, followed by his men, French bullets spattering in their wake. Determined to bring something tangible back with him,

Goering ambushed another French outpost on the way home—it had not expected to be attacked from the "wrong" side—and captured four French *poilus*. For this feat Lieutenant Hermann Wilhelm Goering was mentioned in dispatches for the first time and commended for his daring and initiative.

But, as he discovered, there was another side to war, and this one was painful, muddy, cold—and boring. As the first rains of winter fell over the Western Front and the lines of battle began to solidify, the Prinz Wilhelm Regiment moved into the trenches and months of bloodthirsty stalemate followed. Hermann Goering was lucky. After only a few weeks of miserable static warfare he fell ill with a bout of rheumatic fever and was invalided back to a hospital at Freiburg; otherwise he would have had to share with his fellow officers the filthy, useless horrors of the Battle of the Marne.

It was while he was convalescing at Freiburg that he received a visit that was to change the course of his military career, and much else besides.

Among the friends Goering had made while he was stationed at Mülhausen was a young fellow officer named Bruno Loerzer. It was, in fact, a friendship that was to last almost a lifetime, but shortly after war began the two young men had been separated. Now they came together again in Freiburg, for Loerzer had been posted there to the air training school as a potential pilot of the fledgling German Air Force. Goering was delighted to see his friend, but also consumed with envy. He was already disillusioned with infantry warfare and suspected that there would be few wild adventures and little opportunity for individual initiative on the Western Front from now on. Whereas, in the new Air Force . . .

It was a period when the German newspapers were filled with heady stories about the exploits of their pilots operating over the Western Front. A young man named Lieutenant Karl von Hiddessen had become a national hero because, during September 1914, when the Germans were at the gates of Paris, he had several times flown over the French capital and performed aerobatics at a low altitude for the benefit of the awed and infuriated Parisians watching from below. On his final mission he had deliberately flown around and around the Eiffel Tower, defying the

machine gunners stationed on its platforms to shoot him
down. Finally, with bullets exploding all around him, he
had swooped low and scattered the vast crowd in panic by
dropping on them what they thought was a bomb. It was
in fact a sandbag to which was attached the message:
"Surrender! The Germans are at your gates. Tomorrow
you will be ours!"

It was an exploit after Goering's own heart, and the fact
that the Germans never did reach Paris did not detract
anything from it. Now here was his friend Bruno, who,
any moment now, would be participating in equally exciting adventures. He listened enviously as Loerzer revealed
his hopes and ambitions once he had won his wings as a
combat flier, but suddenly he burst into unbelieving laughter as his friend went on:

"I will tell you in confidence that I have made application to be attached to the Brieftauben Abteilung Ostend."

Brieftauben Abteilung means Carrier Pigeon Unit and
the thought that Bruno Loerzer was learning to fly in order
to spend his war operating a pigeon loft was too absurd for
words. But his friend went on to explain that BAO was the
code name for a top-secret unit of picked fliers and special
planes which would be stationed at Ostend, in occupied
Belgium, in preparation for a move to Calais, on the English Channel, once Paris and most of France was overrun.

"And from Calais," said Loerzer, "we will begin the
bombing of England!"

It was a prospect bristling with so many opportunities
for glory that Goering knew that he had to be part of it.
He would apply for a transfer at once. The moment his
friend had disappeared from his room he wrote off to his
commanding officer, asking permission to apply for a place
at the Freiburg flying school. When over two weeks had
passed without any reply, Goering, who had meantime
made a remarkable recovery from his illness, obtained the
necessary papers from a local barracks and filled in and
signed the transfer form. He was confident that permission
would be granted, and if he was to join Bruno Loerzer at
Ostend there was no time to waste. He had already fitted
himself out and started flying as an observer in Loerzer's
plane when the reply arrived from his regiment. Permission
to transfer was definitely refused, and he was ordered to

report to his unit the moment the medical authorities reported him fit.

This was something Hermann Goering had absolutely no intention of doing. He had discovered the joys of flying through the sky, and they were even more exciting than mountain climbing; and the thought that he must now abandon them for the muddy earth of the Western Front was impossible to accept. If to continue flying meant disobeying orders, then he would disobey. He told no one except Bruno Loerzer about the communication from his regiment and meantime spent every hour when there was a plane available up in the air with his friend, learning the job which he had now decided to fill, that of a cameraman-observer. The circumstances were such that if he wished to see action with the German Air Force, there would be no time for him to take a pilot's course.

In the meantime, news had reached his regiment that he had discharged himself from the hospital, and he was ordered to report to his unit forthwith. Goering took no notice. His biographers have glossed over or made light of the situation in which he now found himself, but in reality he was in an extremely grave position. Technically, he had laid himself open to a charge of forging transfer papers and deserting his unit, the latter being the second most serious crime an officer could commit in wartime (the first was desertion under fire). Not only his career but his liberty was now in jeopardy. When news reached him from friends in the regiment that his colonel was furious and was demanding a court-martial for his recalcitrant officer, Goering, more determined than ever to escape from the infantry and the mud of the Somme, telegraphed his godfather. Once more Ritter von Epenstein demonstrated his affection for his favorite godson. Not only did he secure for Lieutenant Goering a medical certificate declaring him unfit for further service in the trenches,* but he also began some discreet lobbying in royal circles, where his influence was still strong. It now became a contest between who would get him first—the military police or the Air Force. In fact a military court had already been established and had begun preliminary hearings on his case when Goering heard from his godfather that his efforts had borne fruit,

---

* It was true; he was unfit; but then, so were hundreds of others.

and he had secured postings for him and for Bruno Loerzer
with an air-force unit.

Whether news of this move reached the court and influenced it, or whether it was Goering's brilliant record and
popularity with his fellow officers, is not clear, but the
charges against him were suddenly reduced to the minor
one of late reporting, and he was sentenced to be brought
back to headquarters and confined to barracks for twenty-
one days. But before the sentence could be implemented,
superior orders supervened. They came from the Crown
Prince himself, no less. Prince Friedrich Wilhelm, the
Kaiser's eldest son, was an enthusiastic supporter of the
new air arm and among his commands was that of the
German Fifth Army's field air detachment, aiding the
troops now battling against the French Army's defenses in
and around Verdun. He asked that Lieutenants Bruno
Loerzer and Hermann Goering be attached to one of the
forward observer units. Goering was afterward to say that
they stole a plane from Freiburg and flew it direct to their
new field headquarters at Stenay, in northern France, in
order to get away before the military policemen could pick
him up and take him back to headquarters to serve his
sentence. Whether true or not, what is certain is that he
was finished with the infantry forever.

It would be an unfair estimation of the young lieutenant's character to say that he had changed roles out of fear
of dying in the slaughter that was beginning in the trenches
along the Western Front. Fear—at least fear of physical
danger—was an emotion to which Hermann Goering
rarely succumbed, and certainly not in the days when he
was twenty-one years old and looking for glory. It was the
dreary boring discomfort of static infantry action which he
had found distasteful, and it was the opportunity for individual enterprise which made his transfer to the air arm so
attractive. That plus the fact that, as he once put it, "I
seem to come alive when I am up in the air and looking
down at the earth. I feel like a little god."

This does not mean to say that he was not pleased that
henceforward he would sleep in a bed every night, untroubled by mud and rats and the thunder of artillery, or
that he felt guilty at having all the food and drink (particularly champagne) he could consume. It was simply that he
had found again the excitements of war which he had

experienced in the first days of hostilities. The next four years were to be the most thrilling of his life, and never again was it to seem so simple and so happy.

By the time Bruno Loerzer and his observer, Hermann Goering, began operating out of Stenay in the spring of 1915 the air war over the battlefields in France was about to undergo a startling revolution. Until this time, it was a rare French or British plane which shot down a German one, or vice versa. At the beginning of the war, enemy planes often passed close to each other in the air without the pilots doing anything about it except wave their hands to their opponents in recognition. There was very little else they could do. True, some pilots and some observers carried revolvers and rifles and took pot shots at the enemy as they passed, but they were few and far between and considered not quite gentlemen; and in any case there was only the remotest chance of scoring a hit.

Since most of the planes were engaged in reconnaissance work for army artillery and headquarters planners below, they left their opponents to their own devices and got on with the job. Most of the danger to themselves came from fire from below as they swooped down to check artillery fire or take photographs of positions, and since there could be as many as several thousand infantrymen and machine gunners firing up at them at the same time there was a considerable chance of getting wounded in the most humiliating places.†

As a cameraman-observer, Goering's job was a particularly tricky one and soon earned him the nickname of the Flying Trapezist. The plane in which he and Loerzer flew was a two-seater Albatros whose lower wing, unfortunately for the observer, came directly under the second seat, so that it was impossible to point a camera over the side and take a shot of the ground. Goering would wait until the plane was approximately over the target, signal Loerzer to go in low, and then climb to his feet. Gripping the sides of the cockpit with his feet and lower limbs, he would hang out over the side and would signal Loerzer to bank the plane and "skid" it at an angle, so that he could get a direct

† After the first casualties, most pilots on both sides flew sitting on metal tea and coffee trays until their seats were reinforced with steel.

shot. In this position, holding on practically by his toes,
with the plane under fire from thousands of guns down
below, he would calmly go on taking pictures, and changing plates for each shot, for minutes at a time.

The German Fifth Army to which Loerzer and Goering
were now attached came under the command of the Crown
Prince Wilhelm, but over-all command of the forces in the
area was in the hands of the chief of the General Staff,
General Erich von Falkenhayn. Von Falkenhayn had a
fixation about the French fortress of Verdun, and he was
convinced that so long as the French held steadfast within
the walls of the fortress his armies would never get through
to the wide open French farmlands beyond.‡ He had
practically ringed the chain of enemy fortresses with his
heavy siege guns, and day and night they poured shells
down upon the beleaguered Frenchmen. Each day Von
Falkenhayn demanded reconnaissance photographs of the
Verdun chain, and such was the concentration of fire inside the walls that they were extremely hard to get. Either
the planes were shot down, the cameras smashed or the
results too distant or too blurred.

Loerzer and Goering volunteered for the job and spent
three days cruising low over the chain of forts, Loerzer
skidding his Albatros while Goering hung over the side,
methodically shooting with his camera. The resulting photographs were so close and so detailed that Crown Prince
Wilhelm exercised his royal privilege and invested Loerzer
and Goering in the field with the Iron Cross, First Class.

The two young airmen drank a local estaminet dry of its
stock of champagne and came back to the airfield, in
Loerzer's words, "with the heaviest heads but the lightest
hearts in the German Air Force." But it had not been a
simple carousal for Hermann Goering. He had been doing
some thinking; and when the Albatros next took off for a
reconnaissance flight, Loerzer discovered that his observer
had lugged a machine gun aboard and rigged it up in the
cockpit. Now when they went out on operations, the sight
was even more extraordinary. In his toehold stance, Goering would, as usual, start taking his pictures, and then
suddenly he would lean down and swing out the machine

‡ He was quite right. Verdun held, and the Germans never did get
through.

gun, and in that half-crouched position, well out of the
plane, he would begin raking with bullets the enemy troops
firing up at him from down below; and though Loerzer
could not hear him, in his mirror he could see that his
observer was roaring with laughter as he watched the men
below scampering for cover.

And then one day in April 1915, the whole nature of the
air war changed. Four Albatros observer planes from a
Fifth Army base were cruising over French territory, on
their way back from a reconnaissance mission. They were
unarmed but since they were flying at 10,000 feet they felt
completely safe from any kind of attack; even those
French planes whose observers had now begun to emulate
Goering and take a machine gun aboard could not possibly
reach this height with such a load in the cockpit. When
one of the Albatros pilots sighted a French monoplane
coming toward them, and signaled the fact to his comrades, no one broke formation and none of them felt any
particular concern. What could one unarmed French
monoplane do to them?

What they could not guess was that not only was the
plane armed but that it was flown by a remarkable Frenchman named Roland Garros who was about to make two of
the German planes the first victims of a new form of aerial
combat. For the first time in aerial warfare, he was trying
out a light machine gun which fired bullets between the
blades of his propeller. The weapon was not completely
synchronized, and in the course of firing Roland Garros
knew that some of the bullets would tear great lumps out
of his props, even though he had reinforced them with
bands of steel. But what did that matter if he could shoot
down a Hun?

He came straight at the enemy quartet and opened fire at
close range, and the plane on the near-side wing crumpled,
caught fire, and fell away at once. As the other three
scattered in terrified confusion, he rounded on them and
shot down another before the remaining two disappeared
into the clouds and his own machine began to yaw wildly.
He had shot one of his props almost completely away. But
that did not faze him, for he had expected it—and cutting
out the engine he turned and began gliding earthward,
back toward his station and a safe place to land.

Next day, with a new propeller fitted, he was up again

and on the hunt. In four combats in the next eighteen days, Garros shot down five German planes. But he did more than that. He spread first disbelief and then panic among German air strategists. How could this happen? How could a monoplane carry a machine gun that seemed to shoot right through its own propellers?

On April 19, eighteen days after the first encounter, they found out. On that day, Garros was on his way toward a new kill when engine trouble stalled his plane and he had to glide down for a forced landing on German territory, where he was taken prisoner before he could set fire to his plane. Garros was taken off to an interrogation center and his plane hauled away for minute examination.

It so happened that one of the men who was designing planes for the German Air Force was a young Dutchman named Anthony Hermann Gerard Fokker, and because the new plane which he had just produced was a monoplane of a type similar to that flown by Garros, he was called in to examine the captured machine and its alarming new weapon. Could he design something like it?

Fokker, who would soon be recognized as one of the world's greatest aircraft designers, knew nothing about guns, but after a cursory examination of the weapon in the captured plane he told the anxious Germans that he could do much better.

This was practically a suicide weapon, he told the Germans. He pointed to the steel-reinforced propellers. "A bullet hitting this as it passed through could tear off a chip big enough to smash the engine or kill the pilot as it flew back at him. Such a gun can only be used when it is really synchronized."

But that wasn't possible, said the Germans.

It was possible, replied Fokker calmly. He remembered his boyhood days in Holland when he and his companions had spent their time trying to throw stones between the flailing arms of the windmills in the fields around Haarlem. There was a trick to it. You waited until the sail was vertical and then you threw straight at it, and by the time the stone reached it there was a space for it to pass through. Somewhere, somehow, there was a lesson in that which could be adapted to a bullet instead of a stone firing through a propeller rather than a windmill sail.

Fokker, a supremely self-confident man, had promised

his skeptical German masters that he would solve the problem and produce a perfected version of the Garros gun
within a week. The remarkable thing is that he brought the
project in ahead of time. Working with three trusted as-
sistants for forty-eight hours straight, he found the secret
of synchronization* and six days later had towed a monoplane equipped with a machine gun to Berlin for a demonstration. The Germans looked at the device and expressed
disbelief that it would work. Fokker gave them a demonstration on the ground. They were still skeptical about its
chances in the air. So Fokker took the plane up to nine
hundred feet, directed the nose at a pile of old debris in a
corner of the field, and opened fire. The bullets not only
slashed the pile to pieces but also ricocheted all over the
field, forcing the German experts to run for their lives.
Fokker had done it deliberately.

"When they took to their heels," Fokker wrote later, "I
decided that they would never forget that the gun shot
from the air as well as from the ground."

Still, the Germans demanded final proof that the new
weapon would work, and that could only be achieved in
actual combat in the air, with the gun actually shooting
down an enemy plane. If Fokker wanted the money he
had been promised for his weapon, it was up to him to
show it would work, and they shrugged their shoulders
when he pointed out that he was Dutch, neutral, and a
civilian.

The upshot was that in mid-May 1915, Anthony Fokker
found himself dressed in the uniform of a German lieutenant, a false identity card in his pocket, taking a buffet
lunch and hock with Crown Prince Wilhelm and a round
table of German pilots at a château close to the airfield at
Douai. Among his lunchtime companions were Hermann
Goering and Bruno Loerzer, both of them excited at the
potentials of the weapon that Fokker was due to demonstrate over the front that afternoon. Goering was eager to
see the performance of the new weapon, which he recognized as a crucial development in air warfare, but it was no
use asking permission to go along. The Albatros in which

* It was not until much later that Fokker learned that a similar
solution to the problem had already been patented (in 1912) by
Franz Schneider, but had been filed away by the Germans and
forgotten.

he and Loerzer flew was too slow for Fokker's monoplane. When he became friends with Fokker in later years, Goering afterward reminded him of that luncheon party and remembered that he had patted him on the back, "because you looked so miserable and hardly touched your food."

"I was miserable," Fokker replied. "I kept wondering how I had got into such a fix. I was a non-combatant and I was going up to make a kill. If I were shot down or landed on enemy territory, I would be executed as a spy. And rightly."

The flight that afternoon was something of an anti-climax, because no enemy planes were sighted. But on the eighth day Fokker was flying over Douai at six thousand feet when he saw a French Farman two-seater. He dived toward him, but the Frenchman, utterly ignorant of the weapon that was now being sighted on him, took no action to get out of the way.

"As the distance narrowed between us," Fokker wrote later, "the plane grew larger in my sights. My imagination could picture my shots puncturing the gasoline tanks . . . Even if my bullets failed to kill the pilot and observer, the ship would fall down in flames. I had my finger on the trigger . . . I had no personal enmity towards the French. I was flying merely to prove that a certain mechanism I had invented would work. By this time I was near enough to open fire, and the French airmen were watching me curiously, wondering no doubt why I was flying up behind them. In another instant it would be all over for them. Suddenly I decided that the whole job could go to hell. It was too much like 'cold meat' to suit me. I had no stomach for the whole business, nor any wish to kill Frenchmen for Germans. Let them do their own killing!"

The Germans were astonished and infuriated, and threats and insults were used to try to persuade him to change his mind. But Fokker was adamant. Finally, it was agreed that he would instruct a German fighter pilot in the use of the gun, and a man who was to become one of Germany's greatest aces, Lieutenant Oswald Boelcke, was picked for the task. He shot down his unsuspecting victim on his third flight, and the German air strategists were convinced at last of the vital importance of the new weapon. Orders were given to fit it into all fighter planes. Lieutenant Max Immelmann, who was to give his name to

a classic maneuver in air combat, was the second pilot to
be given a fixed-gun Fokker monoplane.

"It was an improved model, designated the Fokker E-2
with a hundred horsepower Oberursel engine in place of
the eighty horsepower Argus," writes Aaron Norman.
"Within three or four weeks, half a dozen E-2s were in
service at the front. Immelmann, Boelcke and the other
Fokker pilots—who numbered sixteen by the middle of
June—had only to spot an enemy plane and get above it or
behind it to guarantee the kill. They found that by slightly
wobbling the monoplane's nose in circular fashion they
could emit, instead of a straight stream of bullets, a cone
of fire, trapping their victim in the center, who, no matter
which way he turned to escape, met a curtain of death."

By the summer of 1915, the German Air Force was
master of the skies over the Western Front. But not for
long.

It was inevitable that Hermann Goering should become
a pilot. It will by now have become apparent that he was
always a man of great enthusiasms, but the moment he had
squeezed a new game or a new métier dry of its possibilities, he needed to pass on to new adventures. For a time, as
the famed flying trapezist in the observer's seat, he had
been the talk of every aircraft mess along the Western
Front. But now, with new and dangerous forms of air war
developing, it was the fighter pilot who was becoming the
hero of the day. The names of Immelmann, Boelcke, and
Hess began to crop up in the newspapers as news came
back of the "kills" they were making over the front, and
Goering longed to see his name included with them.

In June 1915, he arrived in Freiburg to begin a course as
a pilot, and not for the first time in his life he excelled
all the rest. He made perfect takeoffs and landings almost
from the start (not unnaturally, since he had seen Loerzer
do them often enough) and, once in the air, speedily
showed an aptitude for aerobatics that impressed his in-
structors and turned his fellow pupils green with envy. He
was afterward to boast that he was the only one to emerge
from the course with an absolutely clean record, never
having crashed a plane from start to finish.

In October 1915, he was posted to Jagdstaffel 5, a fleet
of twin-engined fighter planes which was now going into

operation along the Western Front. He had been flying for
only three weeks when he had his first encounter with the
new giant Handley-Page bomber, which the British had
recently introduced into operations along their sector. Goering, sighting the huge shape as it emerged from a heavy
November cloud, moved in to get a closer look, unmindful
of the fact that the rest of his squadron had broken away.
They knew what Goering seemed to have forgotten, that
the new bombers never moved through the skies without a
fighter escort.

Goering came up close to the big ship and realized that
he was being fired on from the tail and amidships. He
made a tight turn and came in with his guns blazing, and
saw the tail gunner collapse and a wing engine catch fire.
That was the last he saw of the Handley-Page, because he
had now been jumped by a flight of British Sopwith fighters, which came at him from all angles and riddled him
with bullets. He was hit first in the wing and then in his
fuel tank, and then he felt the bullets slam home into his
body. Instinctively, he put his plane into a cloud but could
not control either its spin or its rate of descent. Through
his fast-fading mind passed the thought that he would soon
be over enemy lines, and it was, in fact, the thud of bullets
being fired up at him from the British lines below that
forced him back to consciousness. That and the pain in his
hip.

Steadying the plane as best he could, he managed to
hedge-hop it back toward the German lines, and crash-
landed in what looked like a cemetery but which also
turned out to be the site of an emergency hospital. He was
in luck. Had he crashed anywhere else he would undoubtedly have died from loss of blood; as it was, he was
dragged from the wreck of his plane and rushed to the
operating table, where pieces of bullet and splintered bone
were taken from his thigh. (He did not know it then, of
course, but, to coin a phrase, his wounded thigh was to
prove Hermann Goering's Achilles' heel in the years to
come.)

Shortly afterward he was removed to rear hospital where
he spent several months abed and in pain, before the
wound and the frayed bone began to heal. In the summer
of 1916 he was sent home on convalescent leave, and he

spent most of it at his godfather's castle at Mauterndorf. It
was there that he fell in love for the first time.

Mauterndorf Castle had changed since Lilli von Epenstein, now known to everyone as Baronin Lilli, had taken
over the running of the household. She was a happy and
uninhibited young matron now that she was married, and
though she was still inclined to play the roguish flirt when
her husband was around, she made it plain that she only
did it because she knew he loved it so. She was forty years
his junior and she seemed to take pleasure in indulging
him.

Everywhere throughout the castle and beyond it there
was evidence of her lightness of spirit. She had thinned out
the heavy gothic furniture with which the great rooms were
encumbered and brought light, color, and gaiety into dark
and musty corners. She had also done much to ease the
heavy-handed, feudal manner in which Von Epenstein had
always controlled the lives of the families on the estate,
and moved among the women and their children no doubt
as the lady of the manor, but one wishing to be friendly
and helpful. She had also done something else which her
husband, for snobbish reasons, had always eschewed, and
established friendly connections with the farmers and landowners in the neighboring countryside, inviting them to
meals and celebrations at the castle and to hunts over the
Mauterndorf estate.

It was at one such party that Hermann Goering met
Marianne Mauser, the daughter of a Mauterndorf land-
owner. All his life he had loved parties, and they brought
out the best in him. "I am not like the Englishman," he
once said. "They start a party two drinks under par, I two
over." He had shaken off the effects of his wound, and in
his air-force uniform, the Iron Cross worn proudly on his
chest, he made a gay and attractive figure, and his charm
was strongly enhanced by the remarkable eyes he had inherited from his mother. Marianne Mauser was not the
only girl to be bowled over by them, but she was the only
one to whom he gave his attention. They were so much in
love that during the last days of his stay at the castle he
visited Herr Mauser and formally asked for his daughter's
hand in marriage. Herr Mauser, less impressed by Goering's record than by his family's lack of land or money,

was not enthusiastic, but because he did not wish to offend Von Epenstein by turning down his godson, he temporized, and consented to a secret engagement. He evidently reasoned that life on the Western Front was too short for the arrangement ever to lead to marriage.

Just before returning to the hospital for his discharge and reassignment, the young lieutenant journeyed north with Baronin Lilli for a short stay at Veldenstein. He went reluctantly because it was obvious that memories would be aroused that could hardly be pleasant. But when they arrived, a touching surprise awaited him. His mother was installed there and waiting for them. Lilli von Epenstein had already re-established contact with her, and had indicated in every way possible that she wished to be friends. It was as if she were making amends for the way in which, through her marriage, the Goerings had lost their family home.

Toward the end of Goering's stay, as the three of them stared from the old walls across the thick green forests of Franconia, Lilli (Frau Goering afterward told her daughter Olga) turned to the young lieutenant and pressed his hand.

"One day," she said, "all this will be yours again. And so will Mauterndorf."

"Shall I tell you why she said that?" Olga remarked later. "Lilli von Epenstein was always in love with Hermann. But he never guessed it. He could not possibly think that anyone could prefer him to our legendary godfather."

III. FIGHTER PILOT

The master ace of the German Air Force in the winter of 1916, when Hermann Goering returned to the Western Front, was Baron Manfred von Richthofen. Both German and British newspapers soon began to call him by his nicknames of the Red Baron or Red Knight, though in truth if his plane was painted red there was very little of knightly chivalry in his make-up. These were the days when there were repeated instances during the air battles over Flanders of respect for an enemy and compassion for him when he had been bested in combat and was going down crippled or in flames. There is an entry in Goering's squadron diary in which one of his pilots reports the crippling of a British Sopwith and ends with the words: "He had fought bravely and well but luck was on my side. I did not finish him off but maneuvered him so that he was forced to crashland in our territory." Goering's note in the margin says: "Good."

Richthofen had no time for gallantry of this kind. He was a great collector of "kills" and, some of his fellow pilots grumbled, liked to go in and finish off enemy machines they had already hit, and then claim them as his own. He had a small loving cup engraved with the type of plane and date of its destruction each time he made a "kill" and there were eighty of them on his mantelpiece by the time he was himself shot down.

"One's heart beats faster," he once wrote to his mother, "when the enemy whose face one has just seen, goes down enveloped in flame from an altitude of twelve thousand feet. Naturally nothing was left of the pilot or his plane when they crashed. I salvaged a small fitting as a remembrance. From my second Britisher I have kept the machine gun, the breech of which has been jammed by a bullet."

Goering reported back for duty on November 3, 1916,

on the day that Oswald Boelcke, shot down two days before, was given a great funeral with full military honors. It
was typical of Von Richthofen that he went up before
breakfast, shot down a French fighter, came back, ate,
changed into his dress uniform and stood at the head of
the coffin as Boelcke's principal mourner. Goering was
now attached to Jagdstaffel 26, of which Bruno Loerzer
had been made commander, and their squadron, stationed
at Mülhausen, was too far away to be concerned with the
ceremonials. But Loerzer had decided that Boelcke's burial
should be commemorated by the destruction of some
enemy planes, and Goering found himself in the air and on
the hunt within hours of his arrival. The squadron failed to
find an enemy that day, but in subsequent weeks they more
than made up for the lack.

As a fighter pilot, Goering did not have the dash, the
flair, or perhaps the luck of Von Richthofen (who shot
down twenty-one planes in the space of a single month) or
the recklessness of a laughing giant of a flier named Ernst
Udet (who was the next most successful pilot), but he had
skill and guts, and it would never be said of him that he
failed to accept a challenge or fled from an enemy. By mid-
1917 he had shot down seventeen planes, earned two more
medals to go with his Iron Cross, and so won his spurs that
he was made commander of a new squadron, Jagdstaffel
27, which flew with Loerzer's unit out of Yseghem, on the
Flanders front. The air war was hotting up, and the British
and French, now equipped with new planes and synchronized guns, and some daredevil new pilots from the United
States, had equalized the odds in the air even if they had
not yet wrested back the mastery of it.

Though they now operated two separate squadrons, the
bond between Loerzer and Goering had grown stronger. In
the dogfights over Flanders, each had intervened on the
other's behalf during crucial moments in the battle and
saved his friend from destruction. Goering had one lucky
escape when Loerzer drove off three French fighters and
allowed him to crash-land, his craft riddled with bullets,
but himself unharmed. And Goering once had jumped a
British pilot who was just about to hit Loerzer's plane from
the blind side.

"We are bound together by something stronger than

chains, Loerzer and I," Goering wrote to his sister. "I know that in my hour of need, he will never let me down."

Goering was a good squadron commander. His army training came in useful in the administrative and strategical side of his work, and his unit was tightly and efficiently run. His pilots noted that he was two different persons, according to what he was doing. Off-duty he was a great party-man and ready to share with his subordinates any games or girls that were going. But on the ground and running the squadron, he was a cold, hard, unforgiving martinet who demanded the strictest obedience to military usage; and up in the air he demanded that his pilots fly according to a plan he had worked out for them, with no breaking away for feats of individual derring-do of the kind he himself had indulged in at different periods of the war. He had seen the way the air war was going over Flanders, and had decided that victory would henceforward go to the best-drilled and best-disciplined squadrons. His pilots did not like it, but they discovered that they got a better share of the "kills" and were losing fewer planes to the enemy.

The success with which he ran Jasta 27 can be measured by the fact that though hitherto Germany's highest decoration, the Ordre Pour le Mérite, had been given only to those pilots (like Boelcke, Von Richthofen, and Udet) who had shot down more than twenty-five planes, Goering received his when his score was still only fifteen. It was official recognition of his all-round qualities of leadership and skill.* He went to Berlin to receive his award personally from the Kaiser and while there tasted for the first time the delights of being a hero. His name and picture were in the newspapers, and he was applauded and gushed over by the female guests when he went into a fashionable restaurant. It was heady stuff and he relished every moment of it. He came back to the squadron wearing a large sapphire stone, of a color almost exactly matching his eyes, on a gold chain round his neck, next to his skin, but would not say who had given it to him.

For the great air battles over Flanders the Germans formed their fighter planes into supersquadrons called

---

* His eventual score was twenty-two enemy planes destroyed.

Jagdgeschwaders, No. 1 of which was commanded by the master ace himself and known as "Richthofen's Flying Circus." On the morning of April 20, 1918, Richthofen flew in to the cheers of his mechanics and a celebration in the mess. He had shot down his eightieth plane. "Eighty!" he said, with satisfaction. "That is a decent number," and complacently accepted the toasts from his comrades to "our leader, our teacher and our comrade, the ace of aces."

It was to be his last "kill." Next day a military band marched up and down the parade ground as Von Richthofen's plane was rolled on to the tarmac, its scarlet coloring making the light machines accompanying it look drab and insignificant. The adjutant, Karl Bodenschatz, came down from the observation tower to report to the commander that weather reports were bad, and that an east wind was blowing, which would make it difficult for any crippled German plane to beat its way home. The red plane and its eight satellites took off for a rendezvous over the Somme canal with the remainder of the geschwader. Half an hour later they were involved in a dogfight with great clusters of British Sopwiths, including a flight commanded by a Canadian, Captain Roy Brown. With Brown's flight that day was another Canadian named Wilfred R. May, and for him it was his baptism by fire. On his first operational flight, May had been instructed not to involve himself in any fight he could avoid. He cruised at twelve thousand feet on the fringes of the great battle, but when first one enemy plane and then a second passed underneath him the temptation was too strong, and he dived, firing as he went. However, not only did he miss but he fired for too long and both his guns jammed, and he was by now in the middle of the dogfight. He got out like a scalded cat and was sighing with relief at his escape when he realized that someone was behind him, and firing.

It was in fact Von Richthofen, who had picked him out as an easy prey and was now coming in for the kill. Brown, however, had just come out of a scrap and caught sight of May's machine with a red Fokker on its tail, and realized that the Red Knight was about to strike again. He closed in and swooped down, guns blazing, not expecting to make a hit but hoping to distract Von Richthofen from his prey. They were quite close to the ground now, and British troops had begun firing up at the German plane—and it will always be a question in military history books which fatal shot got the great ace, Brown's or a machine gun from below.

Drifting slowly earthward, the triplane red Fokker slipped for a mile over the green countryside, as if its pilot was still in control, and then it tipped into a shell crater, which tore off its undercarriage, and flipped down on its belly beside the road.

"A standing order forbade the troops in the area from exposing themselves on or near the road, which was under enemy observation," writes Aaron Norman, "but in their curiosity they violated this order and thronged around the wrecked aircraft. An officer ascertained that the pilot was dead, then unhitched the safety harness and, with the help of others, lifted the limp body from the cockpit. The handsome Nordic face, what could be seen of it below the strapped helmet and shattered goggles, was lathered in blood. The body was laid on the ground and searched for papers. 'My God, it's Richthofen!' the officer exclaimed. 'Christ,' a tommy gasped, 'they got the ruddy baron.' "†

It was not until April 23, 1918, that his fellow pilots learned of what had happened to their leader. On that day a British plane flew over the main squadron airfield at Cappy and dropped a metal container attached to a streamer. Enclosed was a photograph of the military funeral which the British had given Von Richthofen and a note:

To the German Flying Corps
Rittmeister Baron Manfred von Richthofen was killed in aerial combat on April 21, 1918. He has been buried with all due military honours.
From the British Royal Air Force.

When Hermann Goering heard of the master ace's death he was as stunned as anyone in Germany at the news, but he had no idea that it was going to affect him personally. He too had been in action with his squadron on the day of the tragedy, and he had lost four of his pilots during the day; it was for them as much as for Von Richthofen that he led a memorial service on April 24, 1918, to laud the

† *The Great Air War.*

memory of the airmen who had given their lives for the Fatherland. That same afternoon his squadron was back in business, and Goering had the satisfaction of shooting down a Sopwith of the same type which had destroyed his own pilots as well as the Red Knight.

Von Richthofen had left a last will and testament behind him, to be read in case of his death, and the adjutant of Jagdgeschwader No. 1, Karl Bodenschatz, had opened it on the morning of April 22, when it became obvious that the commander of the superunit was not coming back to them. To the surprise of everyone in the Flying Circus, Von Richthofen had named Captain Wilhelm Reinhardt as his successor as commander of J.G. 1.

Reinhardt was the oldest man in the superunit at twenty-seven, but that was not the reason for his fellow pilots' stupefaction; it was, in fact, his generally recognized maturity of judgment which had probably influenced Von Richthofen in naming him. But though he had solidity, courage, and great professionalism, he lacked one quality which the Flying Circus needed if it was to go on being the formidable scourge of the Allied air arm over Flanders. He had no flexibility. He was strictly a textbook flier who went entirely by the rules, and anyone who operated accordingly over the battlefield these days was unlikely to achieve any of the spectacular successes which Germany was now demanding of its fliers.

It did not help Reinhardt's leadership that he recognized his own weakness, and almost always when battle was joined with the enemy immediately delegated the tactics for the dogfight to one or other of the pilots under him. He wrote in his daybook after one of his men had been shot down in battle:

"He had the makings of an outstanding leader, and in the air I yielded to his guidance."

It was only thanks to this modest delegation of authority that the Flying Circus (it had now been officially dubbed J. G. Richthofen No. 1) had some notable successes during the first weeks of May, and on the fifteenth of that month it shot no fewer than thirteen British bombers and fighters out of the sky. On May 20 the supersquadron received orders to leave its headquarters at Cappy and fly into Guise, in preparation for a great offensive which General

Ludendorff was mounting against Allied armies on the river Aisne. The pilots were glad to go, because Cappy had too many memories associated with it of the master ace and his scarlet-colored plane.

On arrival at Guise, they were informed that they and several other squadrons on the front were to be re-equipped with an entirely new plane in preparation for the forthcoming offensive. This was the Fokker D-7 biplane, which was to replace the Fokker triplane which they had been flying up till now. The pilots received the news with anything but pleasure, for rumor had preceded the new machine and had it that the biplane was sloppy in performance and lacked the speed of climb and tightness of maneuver which had typified the triplane. They flew it, however, for the next few weeks without any notable disasters, but much was their relief when they heard that yet another new plane would shortly be coming off the production lines, and that this one was a superbly capable warplane. It was the Fokker D-8, a monoplane which the British and Americans later christened the Flying Razor.

On July 3 a number of squadron commanders on the Western Front were summoned to Adlershof to test the new plane, and among them were Hermann Goering and the new Flying Circus commander, Wilhelm Reinhardt. Both men put the plane through its paces and afterward expressed themselves more than well satisfied with its performance. They then retired to the mess to talk and drink with young Anthony Fokker. When they came out again, Goering's eye was caught by a peculiar-looking biplane which was parked to one side of the airfield, and when he asked about it he was told that it was an experimental craft designed by Dr. Claudius Dornier (who was later to build a fleet of famous flying boats) and that it had been constructed by the Zeppelin Company.

Goering said he would like to try it out, and after some hesitation he was given a quick explanation of the controls, the plane was fueled up, and he taxied it out onto the grass and took off. Finding the Dornier extraordinarily mobile and maneuverable, he then proceeded to give a spectacular exhibition of aerobatics. To use an old fighter pilot's term, he "beat up" the airfield at practically nought feet, both right side up and upside down. He looped and spinned and yawed, and finally, after a particularly awe-inspiring flight down the airfield on canted wings, he brought it to a landing and leaped out, laughing with delight at the expressions on the faces of his spectators.

Not to be outdone, Wilhelm Reinhardt declared that he would now show what could be done with the awkward-looking plane. He waited for it to be refueled, and then took off and almost immediately went into a steep climb from which he showed no signs of leveling off even when he had reached more than three thousand feet. Suddenly there was a report like a pistol shot, and the watchers below were horrified to see the plane's portside wing first crumple and then break away. The Dornier went into a spin and crashed headlong into the earth. When they reached the wreckage, they saw that a wing strut had broken under pressure. The commander of J. G. Richthofen No. 1 was dead.

Who would succeed him as commander of what was by now the world's most famous group of combat fliers?

There were two favorites among the pilots of J. G. Richthofen No. 1. One was Ernst Udet and the other Carl Loewenhardt, and they were bitter rivals, not only for Richthofen's command but also in the race to beat the master ace's record of eighty "kills." On July 4 it was announced that Udet was being given temporary control of the supersquadron, but the following day the order was withdrawn. Udet was certain that he had lost the command because of Loewenhardt's intrigues, and there were rumors that he had gone so far as to challenge his rival to a sky duel.

Everyone waited for Loewenhardt's name to be announced as Udet's replacement. But instead, on the morning of July 7, 1918, the J. G. adjutant, Lieutenant Bodenschatz, walked into the mess with a paper in his hand and pompously announced that he was calling an immediate meeting of all pilots and mechanics in the main hangar. There he read them the notice which he had just received from Berlin.

"By direction of the Supreme Commander of the German Armed Forces," he read, "Lieutenant Hermann Wilhelm Goering, Pour le Mérite, Iron Cross First Class, Zähring Lion with Swords, Karl Friedrich Order with

Swords, Hohenzollern Medal with Swords Third Class, presently commanding Jasta 27, is hereby appointed Kommandeur of Jagdgeschwader Freiherr von Richthofen No. 1."

The crowd of pilots and men looked at each other in a heavy silence, and then Ernst Udet said:

"Mein Gott, they've chosen a *Fremde* (an outsider)."

IV. DEBACLE

On the morning of July 14, 1918, the pilots of J. G. Richthofen No. 1 were once more assembled in the hangar of their main airfield at Guise, and there was a tense expectancy in the air of the kind that could usually be felt only when these highly professional fliers were about to be briefed for a major operation. In fact, the ordeal that lay ahead of them was nothing more than their first meeting with their new commander, but in the days between the announcement of his appointment and his arrival on the station antipathy toward him had been growing, and neither Ernst Udet nor Carl Loewenhardt had done anything to damp it down. Though Udet was later on to become one of Hermann Goering's closest friends and collaborators, for the moment he was a thwarted loser with no particular desire to shake hands with the winner.

It was not that the new commander of the Flying Circus was regarded by the pilots he was coming to lead as a poor flier or even an unworthy one. They knew his record, and it was good. They knew him as one of the most fearless men flying on the Western Front. They knew that, of all German awards, the Ordre Pour le Mérite is one that is never lightly given, and that Goering had deserved it.

No, what they chiefly resented in him was that he was an outsider, not a member of their exclusive club. The pilots of Richthofen's Flying Circus were an elite group of brave and skillful men whose exploits were by now as well known to the enemy as to their own people. Their little world was a tight kingdom of its own, from which, they felt, its rulers should always be chosen. They resented the fact that the succession had now gone outside their knightly ranks, and there were plenty of them who loudly lamented the fact that it was poor Reinhardt and not Goering who had been second to fly the doomed Dornier. No

one suggested that it was Goering who had killed their old
commander by fatally weakening the wing-strut, but it
must have been in the thoughts of many.

That morning of July 14, Hermann Goering probably
had only one friend in J. G. Richthofen No. 1, and that
was the adjutant, Lieutenant Karl Bodenschatz. He had
taken to the new commander right from their first meeting,
and it was an admiration that was to last a lifetime. "A
man of personal charm, but underneath, I suspect, he is a
grobe Kunde (a tough customer)," he wrote shortly afterward. "You could see it in the way he moved and the way
he talked."

It was Bodenschatz who succinctly put Goering in the
picture about the feeling among the pilots, and he was
pleased when he saw that Goering was neither angered nor
disturbed by it. "It is understandable," he said. "Let us not
make it worse by keeping them waiting."

In his otherwise authoritative book about World War I
fliers, *The Great Air War*, Aaron Norman says of that first
meeting of the Richthofen Flying Circus and its new commander:

"He then delivered his introductory speech. He told
them—these veterans and victory-rich aces, the flower of
the German flying corps—what they had been doing wrong.
Then he told them how he was going to institute the
necessary reforms. The old order was changing and the
new—as outlined by Goering—was not to the liking of his
audience."

This is far from being a fair or an accurate account of
what happened. Hermann Goering was now twenty-five
years old and no fool. He had just been given command of
the most prestigious group of fliers in the world, and he
knew he could never make a success of the job without
their willing and devoted co-operation. Nothing was more
likely to lose it from the start than to begin the new regime
by berating them. Changes would come later, but, for the
moment, it was necessary to win their confidence.

He walked on to the briefing platform followed by
Bodenschatz and by a junior pilot of the squadron, who,
by tradition, had been chosen to introduce him to his comrades. Lieutenant von Wedel was nervous, and he muffed
his prepared speech, so that a restless murmur passed
through the throng of pilots. Then Bodenschatz stepped

forward and handed over to Goering the *Geschwaderstock*,
the blackthorn unit walking stick which had been made by
a Bavarian craftsman and presented to Von Richthofen.
He had carried it with him in his plane on the day he died,
and it had been dropped over the squadron's headquarters
by the British, and passed on to Reinhardt. Now Goering
took it in his hands and balanced it tenderly, as if the
symbol of majesty had now been passed on to him. He
paused and stared down at the fliers with his piercing blue
eyes, and waited until there was silence, and then he said:

"Gentlemen, let me say at once what a great and special
honor has been done to me by His Imperial Majesty in
making me commander of this illustrious squadron. Great
battles have been fought and great men have died to make
it so. I am only too sensible of the fact that there are no
better fliers in all the world than those I see before me
now. I hope I shall be worthy of your confidence and your
trust. I hope you will continue to be worthy of those of
your comrades who have given their lives for you, for the
Air Force, and for Germany. We will need to give of our
best, all of us, for there are grave times ahead. We will face
them together for the glory of the Fatherland."

It was simple and it was spoken with the utmost gravity,
and the pilots were impressed. "The new commander has
got off to a good start," Bodenschatz noted in his diary.

Three days later he went up with the supersquadron for
the first time and was involved in two separate engage-
ments, one with some British fighters and the other with a
formation of French bombers on their way to attack supply dumps behind the German lines. He came down in a
bad mood, and this time his pilots saw a different side of
him. His own activities had been abortive, for he had attacked the French bombers and used all his ammunition on
them, but had failed to pierce their armor plating.

"The British single-seaters are giving as good an account
of themselves as ever," he wrote in his report on July 17,
"but the French fighters rarely penetrate beyond the front
line and usually avoid serious encounters. On the other
hand, the French twin-seat planes normally show up in
close formation, ruthlessly pushing home their attacks,
usually from low level. They are twin-engined Coudrons
whose armor is proof against our ammunition. I myself
attacked a Coudron on 15.7.18 and wasted almost my

entire ammunition. The Coudron simply flew on completely ignoring me."

He went on to ask why these armored Frenchmen could not be attacked by antiaircraft fire, instead of risking his pilots on missions which could not possibly succeed. He complained that his men were being sent up five times a day, and that neither men nor engines could stand such wear and tear. He demanded more useful tasks and better communications.

But at the same time that he complained to headquarters, he also complained to his men. A few hours after the last squadrons came in on July 15 he called a meeting of wing leaders and soundly rebuked them for the sloppiness of their discipline during the day's operations. There is no doubt that during the brief rule of Wilhelm Reinhardt, that amiable character's habit of handing over leadership to one or other of his subordinates once a dogfight began had had its effects upon the *esprit de corps* of the squadrons. So far as Goering was concerned, too many of them now relied upon the *freie Jagd* (free hunt) or general free-for-all method of going for the enemy, each of them so intent on getting his own "kills" that combined tactics and strategy were being forgotten. In a superunit which contained aces like Udet, Loewenhardt, and Lothar von Richthofen, the dead baron's brother, rivals vying with each other to get their names at the top of the J.G. scoreboard, it was inevitable that membership had begun to divide up into two different categories, the stars and the extras. Both on the ground and in the air the stars had an increasing tendency to behave like prima donnas. Reinhardt had not let it bother him, but Goering was a different character; he was determined that there would be only one prima donna in his outfit, and that would be himself. He would make the decisions, he would decide the tactics to be followed, and he would throw the tantrums if anything went wrong.

To say that the wing leaders took his dressing-down badly is a mild description of their reaction. Goering was well aware that it was perhaps too soon to substitute the stick for the carrot. He had by no means as yet won the unswerving confidence of his men. But he had already decided (as he told Karl Bodenschatz later) that if he was to win them over, he must first provoke a crisis. "The peacocks need to be plucked," he said, "before they fall

over their own feathers." He sent them away stinging from
his rebukes and left them to simmer with their colleagues
in the mess. On the evening of July 17, 1918, he called all
wing and Jasta leaders in once more, sketched out the
operations which the J.G. would adopt on the following
morning, and then dropped his bombshell. Each Jasta
leader, instead of commanding his squadron as usual,
would, on this operation, detach himself and hand over
command to his second. All the Jasta leaders, including
Udet, Loewenhardt, and Lothar von Richthofen, would
come under Goering's personal command and would fly
with him.

They looked at him as if he were joking, and then,
seeing that he was serious, Loewenhardt flushed with
anger, Von Richthofen bit his lip and looked hard at the
ground, but Ernst Udet began to grin. As Goering told
Bodenschatz later, he at once guessed why. Goering may
have been humiliating his squadron leaders by his extraordinary order, but once they were up in the air it was he
who could be humiliated in his turn. He would be flying
with eight of the greatest aces of the air war, and if he was
not to turn the whole thing into a farce, he would have to
lead them according to their standards. Did he have what it
would take?

In the day book of J.G. Richthofen No. 1 for July 18,
1918, there is an entry personally written by Hermann
Goering. It reads:

"At 8.15 A.M. I attacked several [British] Spads. One of
them I forced down and, after some spiraling, shot it
down. It fell into Bandry woods."

But there was more to it than that. From the start to the
finish of the operation, he had behaved as if he were Baron
von Richthofen himself. He had forced his distinguished
satellites to hold back while the seconds-in-command took
over the dogfights and the glory. In the final phase of the
engagement, he had at last signaled that the stars were to
go into action, and had then swooped down at their head
to give a brilliant exhibition of flying and leadership. Time
and again he cut into the British formations and split them
up, so that Udet, Loewenhardt, Von Richthofen and the
rest were able to follow him in and shoot them down. It
was magnificent because each time his proud subordinates
found a target they knew only too well that it was their

commander who had provided it for them. And only in the last few minutes before breakoff did Goering at last point his plane at a British Spad and make it clear that this one was indubitably his. He proceeded almost literally to chase it out of the sky, with a superb exhibition of turns, twists, and finally a series of tightly controlled spirals that took him behind the enemy plane at just the right moment for the kill.

It was the last plane Hermann Goering was to shoot down, his twenty-second. But in a way he didn't need to shoot down any more. He had made his point. It was teamwork that would motivate the Flying Circus from now on.

By early August 1918, Hermann Goering had so won the confidence of the Flying Circus (indeed, he was beginning to be more popular than the Red Knight himself) that he felt able to go off on a short spell of leave. He delegated command of J.G. Richthofen No. 1 to Lothar von Richthofen, and departed for Munich and Mauterndorf. He spent more time with his godfather and Baronin Lilli than he did with his unofficial fianceé. It was obvious to Marianne Mauser's father that the war was coming to a close, and not in Germany's favor; and what sort of a future would a young ex-pilot, no matter how heroic, have inside a defeated Germany? Better to marry off his daughter to another farmer, who could live off his land until times changed, than to a penniless charmer without prospects. It was not until some months later that the break was definitely made,* but its unspoken imminence colored every hour Goering and Marianne spent together.

When he got back to his command, the rot had begun to set in along the Western Front, and World War I had gone into its culminating stages. The Flying Circus was soon running out of pilots, out of replacements, and out of gas. Every day the squadrons went up to meet increasingly strong formations of French, British, and American planes. Bodenschatz reported at the end of September that the strength of J.G. 1 was reduced to 53 officers (including

---

* "What have you now got to offer my daughter?" wrote Herr Mauser to Goering in Munich in January 1919. "Nothing," Goering telegraphed in reply.

admin staff) and 473 NCOs and men. "The strain is beginning to show in Lieutenant Goering's face," he wrote. "He
is lean and hard. We are all growing hard now."

On October 7, 1918, the Swiss Minister to the United
States went to the State Department with a personal message for President Wilson from the German Government.
It asked for an immediate armistice and requested the President "to take steps for the restoration of peace, to notify
all belligerents of this request, and to invite them to delegate plenipotentiaries for the purpose of taking up negotiations." On the Western Front the German armies were
beginning to crumble and retreat in face of the Allied
armies' implacable attacks. Bulgaria had deserted the Central Powers and asked for an armistice. The Austro-
Hungarian Empire was on its deathbed.

No whisper of the German note was allowed to leak out
to the troops, for it would only have increased their panic,
and the German Government at this stage was still hoping
that some sort of peace with honor would be secured, and
was prepared, if it did not get it, to go on fighting. The
actual end of the war was still more than a month away,
and many thousands of men would die while the haggling
went on behind the scenes.

So far as Hermann Goering and the Flying Circus were
concerned, there was no question of giving up. Goering
was angry and appalled when news reached him of unrest
among the troops, of mutinies, of soldiers turning upon
their officers. During the next three weeks operations were
interrupted by bad weather, by the uncertainty of supplies,
and by a breakdown of communication with Army Headquarters. The news from behind the front, in Germany
itself, grew more and more disturbing. There were rumors
that the Allies had demanded the abdication of the Kaiser,
and letters arrived from the relatives of his pilots who lived
in Germany's seaports telling of naval mutinies and the rise
of revolutionary committees. Goering decided that it was
time to call the members of J.G. 1 together, and he addressed them in the hangar at Guise and urged them to go
on fighting, to be loyal to the Fatherland, and, above all, to
ignore "absurd rumors that our beloved Kaiser is preparing
to desert us in our hour of need." He assured them that the
Kaiser would stand by them, and that they must stand by
the Kaiser by continuing to fight and, if necessary, die for

him and for the honor of the nation. He was cheered by every man present.

But a few days later retreating German soldiers came streaming across the airfield, and orders eventually reached J.G. 1 to tell them that the Allies had breached the Meuse and that they must retire to new airfields immediately. Goering set up his new headquarters at Tellancourt on a field ill-adapted for combat operations. It was half flooded by early winter rains and the wheels of the planes clogged in the mud. Clouds were heavy and the drizzle constant, and flying was impossible. Everyone hung around the mess, and listened to the alarming stories from newly arrived replacements of chaos and bloodshed inside Germany. Their fate was being settled in a railway carriage in the forest of Compiègne, where the German armistice delegation was awaiting the decisions of the Allies; and in the meantime a signal had gone out, on November 9, grounding all air operations on the Western Front. Goering's mood was one of frustrated defiance and a refusal to believe that the war was over and Germany defeated, and he told Bodenschatz that he would like to climb aboard his plane, summon his pilots, and fly across to Army Headquarters and strafe its cowardly crew out of existence. But this mood soon passed. In any case the weather was too thick for operations, and it was unlikely that he would have found headquarters, since it too was breaking up and crawling piecemeal back to Germany. But messages were still coming in from some anonymous brass hat, each one contradicting the other, one telling him to surrender to the American forces on the Meuse, another instructing him to take his men and machines back to Darmstadt.

On November 10 news reached the bedraggled and bewildered airmen that the Kaiser had abdicated and that troops carrying the Red banner of a Workers' Republic were marching through Berlin. Now a clear and imperative order reached Goering from Fifth Army Air Headquarters. He was to ground all his planes and surrender himself and his crews to the nearest Allies. This meant the Americans. "I will never surrender to the Yanks!" he said. At an assembled meeting he told his men that at any moment now an armistice would be signed and Germany's defeat acknowledged by her rulers. He told his listeners of the orders he had received.

"They are orders I do not propose to obey!" he cried. "I will allow neither my men nor my machines to fall into the hands of the enemy. We cannot stay here and fight on. But we can make sure that when the end comes, we will be in Germany. The unit will evacuate its records and valuable equipment by road to Darmstadt forthwith. Tents and useless machines will be left behind. As for our planes, we will fly them out—to Darmstadt!"

Bodenschatz was given charge of the convoy and prepared to set off through mud and rain, and roads increasingly clogged with homegoing troops, for the German frontier. The pilots were revving up their planes in preparation for their flight to Darmstadt when a German staff car plowed across the muddy field and slowed to a halt in front of them. Goering climbed down from his plane, his face red with anger, the blackthorn geschwaderstock in his hand, raised as if to strike the staff officer who came rushing up to him.

"How dare you get in our way!" he cried. "Clear that damned car off the field at once."

"I have urgent orders, sir, and you must read them," the staff officer said. He handed over a sealed envelope which Goering impatiently ripped open and read through.

FIFTH ARMY HEADQUARTERS TO KOMMANDEUR J.G. FREIHERR VON RICHTHOFEN NO. 1 [the orders ran] YOU WILL DISARM YOUR PLANES AT ONCE AND FLY THEM TO FRENCH AIR HEADQUARTERS AT STRASBOURG WHERE ARRANGEMENTS HAVE BEEN MADE FOR YOU TO LAND WITHOUT HINDRANCE. ACKNOWLEDGE.

Goering turned to Bodenschatz. "The Frogs want our Fokker D-8s," he said. "They've always wanted to get their hands on them. But they're not going to get them. Get the telephone rigged up, and tell them that, Bodenschatz!"

It was at this point that the staff officer broke in to explain the dire consequences if the order were disobeyed in this fashion. It could convince the French that the Germans were not serious in demanding an armistice, and it could provoke the Allies into starting up their war machine again, before the German forces were ready for it. GHQ and the German delegation were playing for time, the staff officer insisted, and were prepared to resume the battle if the terms were not decent and honorable.† Any defiant action on Goering's part could wreck everything.

The commander of the Flying Circus told his men to cut their engines, and for the next hour strode up and down in the mud, discussing the situation with Bodenschatz, Udet, Loewenhardt and Lothar von Richthofen. Finally, he returned to the staff officer and told him what had been decided. Five pilots (they would be chosen by lot) would fly five planes into Strasbourg, and headquarters would be informed that they were the first flight of the whole unit. But the rest of the planes would fly to Darmstadt instead of into France.

The staff officer protested that this was still disobedience of orders, and that it was his duty to inform his superior officers of the deception that was being planned. Goering smilingly informed him that they had calculated on that, and to relieve him of any sense of responsibility he might feel it had been decided to make him prisoner of the unit.

"Lieutenant Bodenschatz will be your escort from now on," he said. "You will accompany him to Darmstadt." And then, grinning, he added: "In your staff car."

The five planes with their volunteers aboard took off into the mist for their rendezvous with the enemy. Goering did not tell the staff officer that when they reached Strasbourg they had been instructed to wreck their planes on landing, so that they would be useless to the French.‡ By the time they were in the air, the rest of the squadron was revving up for takeoff and the journey back to the homeland.

But the squadron's misadventures were not finished yet. In the appalling weather some of the pilots missed the route and eventually landed at Mannheim instead. When they climbed out of their machines they noticed that a Red flag was flying from the administration building, and that an armed band of soldiers and civilians was approaching them. Mannheim was under the control of a Workers' Revolutionary Council, and they were short of arms for the struggle which they knew was coming for the takeover of Germany. They quickly divested the pilots of their guns, stripped the planes of their weapons, and then reluctantly

† For a time the German people actually believed this.
‡ Which they did.

consented to provide a truck to take the stranded fliers on to Darmstadt. There the discomfited men told their sorry tale to Goering, who was furious.

"They must be taught a lesson!" he shouted.

Quickly, he assembled a small flight of nine planes, placed aboard two of them a couple of the pilots who had landed at Mannheim, and carefully instructed them. Then the flight took off for Mannheim. While the other seven planes circled low over the airfield, beating up the buildings, balefully banking and rolling, the two pilots landed and walked over to the Workers' Council to present them with Goering's ultimatum. Either all arms would be restored at once and a written apology given or the rest of the flight would move in and shoot up everything that moved in the area.

"He will wait four minutes, and no longer," said one of the pilots, pointing up at Goering's plane. He showed his Very pistol. "I am to fire this if you agree to our terms."

"Then fire, fire!" said the workers' leader. "Of course we agree."

The arms were put aboard, the apology written, and the two planes took off to rejoin the flight back to Darmstadt. There Hermann Goering went in to land first. At the end of the runway, he deliberately slewed round his plane and smashed it up beyond repair. The rest of the flight did likewise.

That night he wrote in J.G. 1's daybook:

"11 November. Armistice. Squadron flight in bad weather to Darmstadt. Mist. Since its establishment the Geschwader has shot down 644 enemy planes. Death by enemy action came to 56 officers and non-commissioned pilots, six men. Wounded 52 officers and non-commissioned pilots, seven men. (Signed) *Hermann Goering*, Lieutenant O.C. Geschwader."

It was the end of the Flying Circus as a fighting unit, but not quite the official moment of its demise. It whimpered on for a few days more, before expiring forever.

"After the destruction of our planes," said Karl Boden-schatz, "we were told to report to Aschaffenburg, which was close to Frankfurt, where the remnants of the German General Staff were assembled. Hermann and Ernst Udet stayed in the house of an industrialist on the outskirts of the town, and we set up our headquarters in a paper-making factory. It had a large courtyard suitable for mustering the officers and men, and there was plenty of storage space for luggage. While we awaited the disbandment of the geschwader and our own discharge, I and my clerks had plenty to do, bringing the records up to date. But for the pilots there was nothing to do but wait, and they did most of their waiting in the local restaurant, and they were often very drunk and always very bitter. It was understandable. The Germany we had known and loved and fought for was going to pieces before our eyes, and we were helpless to do anything about it. Officers were being insulted in the streets by their men, the medals they had risked their lives to earn torn from their breasts."

The actual disbandment ceremony took place in the factory courtyard and was short and simple, and no speeches were made. All the men and about half the officers—mostly the younger replacements—collected their luggage and marched away. But Bodenschatz stayed behind to clean up the records, and so did Goering and most of his senior officers, but for less tangible reasons.

"They had homes to go to, but they seemed reluctant to leave, as if they were afraid of what they would find when they got there," said Bodenschatz. "In this new, strange, dreadful and defeated Germany, we all felt like aliens and like aliens we clung together. The restaurant was our ghetto, and most of us left it as little as possible. Hermann's moods, I remember, ranged from the cynical to the savage. One moment he talked of emigrating to South America and washing his hands of Germany forever, but the next he spoke of a great crusade to raise the Fatherland back to the heights from which it had fallen. The last time I saw him for several years was on the night when the geschwader was disbanded, and we gathered in the restaurant to mourn its passing. At one point in the evening Hermann climbed on to the little bandstand with a glass in his hand, and though everyone was shouting and roystering there was something in his manner that made us all suddenly silent. He began to speak. He hardly raised his voice at all, but there was a strange quality to it, an emotional underbeat, that seemed to slip through the chinks in your flesh and reach right into your heart. He spoke of the Richthofen Squadron and what it had done, of how its achievements, the skill and bravery of its pilots, had made it famous the world over. 'Only in Germany today is its name now dragged in the mud, its record forgotten, its officers jeered at.' He began to inveigh against the revolutionary forces that were sweeping through Germany, and of the shame they were bringing upon the armed forces and upon Germany itself. 'But the forces of freedom and right and morality will win through in the end,' he said. 'We will fight against these forces which are seeking to enslave us, and we will win through. Those same qualities which made the Richthofen Squadron great will prevail in peacetime as well as in war. Our time will come again.' Then he raised his glass and said: 'Gentlemen, I give you a toast—to the Fatherland and to the Richthofen Squadron.' He drank and then smashed his glass down at his feet, and we all did likewise. Many of us were weeping, Hermann among them. It was a very emotional occasion."

From Darmstadt, Hermann Goering and Ernst Udet both wished to get back home to Munich, but in the chaotic situation of the time they could only do that by way of Berlin. They arrived there in December 1918, to find that the government had been taken over by a group calling themselves the Majority Socialist Party, under the leadership of an ex-saddlemaker and unsuccessful tavern keeper named Friedrich Ebert. For the moment, Ebert was making a play for the support of the ex-officers of the German armed forces, and he had included in his government as Minister for War an active member of the Army, General Hans-Georg Reinhardt. The two ex-pilots were just in time to attend a great meeting which Reinhardt had organized at the Berlin Philharmonic Hall, at which he planned to urge all officers to support the new government, and also obey its latest edict, which was that all officers should remove their insignia of rank and substitute stripes on their jackets for epaulets. The general himself had done so, and appeared on the platform with simple stripes on his sleeves; he wore no epaulets or medals.

Goering went to the meeting in his ordinary uniform, but when he heard rumors of what the Minister was going to say, he hurried to the apartment where he was staying and changed his clothes. He was back just as General Reinhardt was ending his appeal, and as he sat down Hermann Goering walked onto the platform. He was wearing his full-dress uniform with captain's stars, silver epaulets, his Pour le Mérite, and his other decorations.

"I ask your pardon, Herr General," he said, and turned to the audience. A murmur ran through the massed rows of officers as he was recognized, and he held up his hand for silence. Then, looking once more at the discomfited general, he said:

"I had guessed that you, sir, as Minister for War, would be here today to address us. But I had hoped to see a black band on your sleeve that would symbolize your deep regret for the outrage you are proposing to inflict upon us. Instead of that black band you are wearing blue stripes on your sleeves. Herr General, I think it would have been preferable had you been wearing red stripes."

Waiting for the applause to die down, he went on:

"For four long years we officers did our duty and risked our lives for the Fatherland. Now we come home, and how do they treat us? They spit on us and deprive us of what we gloried in wearing. I will tell you this, that the people are not to blame for such conduct. The people were our comrades, the comrades of each of us, no matter what class they came from, for four long years. No, the ones who are to blame are the ones who have stirred up the people, who stabbed our glorious Army in the back and who thought of nothing but attaining power and fattening themselves at the expense of the people. I ask everyone here tonight to cherish a hatred, deep and abiding hatred, for these swine who have outraged the German people and our traditions. The day is coming when we will drive them out of Germany. Prepare for that day. Arm yourselves for that day. Work for that day."

He was greeted with a great burst of applause and carried from the meeting by enthusiastic officers for a great carousal. But next day the hangover came, and with it the realization that his outburst had made no impact on the situation. He hung around Berlin with Udet for an aimless few days, and then decided to continue his journey to Munich, where his mother was still living. Toward the end of December 1918, he squeezed into the packed third-class carriage of a southbound train. He was dressed in civilian clothes, and no one would have guessed that the subdued, silent young man was one of Germany's greatest fighter aces, a victor in some of the most spectacular battles in the history of air warfare. Like most of the other Germans crammed into the carriage, defeat sat on his shoulders like a shroud.

"That journey home was the most miserable moment of my life," Hermann Goering was to say later. "I have never been in such low spirits."

V. ALIEN WORLD

When Hermann Goering had last stayed in Munich, during his leave in August 1918, the city was still the capital of the Kingdom of Bavaria, with King Ludwig III on its throne. But now, three months later, everything was changed. As early as November 7, four days before the Armistice was officially signed, the people of Bavaria had decided that they had had enough of the war. That afternoon a great crowd of soldiers and civilians had gathered in the Theresienwiese, a huge field where the annual Oktoberfest is usually held, and there, in the warm fall sunshine, had listened to a fiery local journalist named Kurt Eisner provoking them into a rising against their rulers.

"Scatter throughout the city," Eisner had urged his hearers, "occupy the barracks, seize weapons and ammunition, win over the rest of the troops, and make yourselves masters of the government."

They did just that. By nightfall every barracks in the city was flying a Red flag. Eisner himself went on to the Mathäuser Brauhaus, the city's largest beer hall, where a workers' and soldiers' council made him head of the "Bavarian Republic." By November 8, Eisner's "government" controlled the central railway station, all newspaper offices, the Bavarian Army Headquarters and most other main buildings. Even the palace guard at the royal Residenz had joined the revolution, and the king's palace was invaded by sightseers who wandered about, shouting, whistling and hallooing in the corridors, galleries and ballroom to hear the famous echoes.

"King Ludwig III had no stomach for counterrevolutionary attempts," writes Richard M. Watt. "His ministers put it to him that he ought to abdicate. Even the general who was the royal Minister of War was no help. Stunned, he could only mutter apprehensively, 'The revolution—and here I am in my uniform!' Ludwig and his family took an automobile and fled the city, leaving Bavaria in the undisputed control of [Eisner] a Jewish intellectual who had been a drama critic for most of his adult life."

But not for long. The hungry and dissatisfied civilians and dissident soldiers and sailors in Munich had voted Eisner as their leader because they believed he would slip the Prussian yoke from around their necks and introduce a Bavarian socialist republic. But Eisner was a talker rather than a doer. The only socialist measure he took was to order the National Theater in Munich to introduce an egalitarian regime and share the leading roles among everyone, including minor players and members of the chorus. As criticism of his laissez-faire regime increased, and his militant left-wing supporters demanded that he start the revolution forthwith, he replied by inviting all his critics to a "Fete of the Bavarian Revolution" in the Munich Opera House. An orchestra under the direction of Bruno Walter played a program of Beethoven overtures, Handel arias, and a hymn composed specially for the occasion by Eisner himself, entitled "The Song of the People."

Eisner appeared on the platform as the last words, "Oh, world, rejoice!" were being sung, and he was immediately greeted by cries of "rascal, bandit, slacker!" which failed to prevent him from giving a long and utterly irrelevant speech on the subject of "Education and Democracy." Meanwhile, the government of Bavaria was running down and the granaries and treasury were all but empty.

It was into this chaotic and anarchic situation that Hermann Goering and Ernst Udet arrived in December 1918. Goering, who had always been a royalist, whose early education had been fed with kingly romances, winced as he passed soldiers in the streets selling postcard cartoons of Kaiser Wilhelm floating down a Dutch canal in a barge, his crown and scepter floating in the wake. Another cartoon which aroused his ire was one which bore the inscription: "Herr Militarismus, born in Berlin, died in Munich, and buried with all the honors of his rank."

But he was soon sufficiently acquainted with the situation to realize that Eisner's shabby and makeshift administration was on its way out. His chief opponents were members of the majority Socialist Party, which was already in power in Berlin, and now promised to find jobs for the

returning soldiers, houses for their families, and fresh vege-
tables for the market, which, owing to transport break-
downs and hoarding by the farmers, had been nonexistent
for months. The party romped home in a special election
in January 1919, and prepared to take office. Meanwhile,
Eisner was allowed to continue to head a provisional government as a figurehead.

The regime promised by the Majority Socialist Party was
not by any means the type of government which fitted in
with Hermann Goering's royalist, even semi-feudalist ideas
of what was best for Germany, but at least it did not
preach Red revolution, was seeking to curb the excesses of
the Sailors' and Soldiers' Committees (whose members
were avid to see upper-class blood running in the streets),
and its advent would, in Bavaria, give the area a period of
calm after the chaos of the past few weeks. Difficulties
would undoubtedly arise again, especially if the Allies
pressed Germany too hard for reparations and failed to
accord the Germans the just peace for which they were still
hoping. But when that time came, the right wing hoped to
be in a better position to take advantage of the situation.
Goering and Udet had already joined one of the bands of
so-called Free Corps which were springing up all over Germany, consisting of ex-officers, NCOs and professional
soldiers, dedicated to keeping the Army in being and pre-
serving the military tradition until such time as it could
take over again.

But then a fanatic suddenly upset this promising situation. An aristocratic young nobleman named Count Anton
Arco-Valley, who had served during the war in the Bavarian Army, had decided not to join the Free Corps,
whose members he considered too moderate in their aims
for the rehabilitation of Germany. Instead he had applied
for membership of one of the right-wing militant societies
which were springing up at this time. This one was the
Thule Society, which numbered among its members writers
and intellectuals, such as Dietrich Eckart, Rudolf Hess,
and Alfred Rosenberg, and devoted itself chiefly to the
dissemination of anti-Semitic literature and propaganda
against the "Jewish revolutionaries" who, they claimed,
were taking over Germany. The Thule Society used a swastika as its emblem, and members greeted each other with
the cry of "Heil!"

According to one story, Count Arco-Valley was told to commit an act which would prove him worthy of joining the society. According to another, he was rejected for membership on the grounds that his mother was of Jewish descent, and decided out of pique to demonstrate how truly anti-Jewish he really was. At any rate, at 9 A.M. on February 21, 1919, Count Arco-Valley came face to face with Kurt Eisner outside the Foreign Ministry in Munich and fired two shots at him at point-blank range. Eisner died instantly. The ironic thing is that he was, in fact, on his way to hand in his resignation to enable the Majority Socialist Party to take over. But the ex-drama critic's death ended all that.

No one believed that Arco-Valley had acted alone. The revolutionaries in the workers' committees were convinced that it was part of a right-wing plot organized by the Free Corps, the Thule Society, and student groups. The cry went up for revenge. Emotions were heightened after the spot where Eisner had died, ringed round with flowers and designated a "place of martyrdom" by the Red committees, was defiled by the Thule Society, whose members left on the spot bags to flour into which the blood of bitches in heat had been mixed, thus attracting all the dogs in the neighborhood. Two Russian comrades named Levien and Leviné, who undoubtedly would have been dubbed the Terrible Twins by British or American newspapers, arrived from Moscow and turned Munich into a Communist commune. A roundup of all suspected conservatives and Free Corps members was instituted.

Whether Hermann Goering was ever in danger of losing his life at the hands of one of these committees will never be known. It was true that he had joined serveral anti-Eisner associations, but so had most other officers. And it was also a fact that there was one particularly nasty massacre toward the end of the commune's reign, when twenty prominent Munich citizens were murdered and mutilated in the Luitpold Gymnasium, on orders, it seems certain, of Levien and Leviné. Levien was afterward to claim that he had, by these killings, wiped out the leadership of the infamous Thule Society.* But except for this grisly incident,

---

* It wasn't true, of course. Two of the leaders, Rudolf Hess and Alfred Rosenberg, lived to go on to bigger things.

few of those right-wing and Free Corps members who came before the workers' tribunals were sentenced to death. But when a committee arrived at his mother's house during his absence and asked for him, Goering concluded that he figured on one of the Red death lists and decided to go into hiding. By a stroke of good fortune, he knew the exact place to go where the purge committee would be unlikely to find him, or to arrest him even if they did.

It so happened that one of the chief officers on the Allied Armistice Commission in Munich was a certain Captain Frank Beaumont, of the Royal Flying Corps. Goering knew him well. During the war, Beaumont, after shooting down two enemy planes, had crash-landed on German territory and had been taken prisoner by members of Goering's unit. Those were the days when Allied pilots were not being treated particularly gently by German prison-camp jailers, and Goering, who admired Beaumont's qualities as a flier and came to like him as a man, had taken him under his wing. He lived with the unit for several months before finally being sent off to POW camp. Now Beaumont, who spoke excellent German, was in Munich as one of the flying officers attached to the Armistice Commission having been given the task of liquidating the German Air Force. He had food, a car, fuel, diplomatic privileges, and was safely above the battle for survival and political supremacy which was going on all around him.

Goering appealed to him for help in escaping from the clutches of the purge committees, and it was gladly given. Eventually Beaumont enabled Goering to be taken out of the city and turned over to a force of Free Corps troops which had been sent south from Berlin with instructions to liquidate the Munich Commune, and was now encamped around the Munich suburb of Dachau, ready for a general assault on the city. A few days later they had battered down all opposition, gutted the main Red strongholds with artillery and flame throwers, and were goose-stepping down the Ludwigstrasse into the center of the city. Then they began a roundup and a bloodthirsty purge of their own.

Hermann Goering did not wait either for the battle or the right-wing purge. He was in a mood of deep disenchantment with Germany and the German people. He now wished only to get away from the hunger, hopelessness, bloodshed, and fraticidal violence which were now the everyday lot of the defeated Germans.

Where could he go? He had no money, for there were no gratuities for ex-officers or ex-soldiers, and he could not appeal to his godfather, who was out of touch somewhere in Austria. The only profession he knew was soldiering and the only craft that of flying a plane. After the incident at the Berlin Philharmonic Hall there was no place for him in the small army which was all Germany would be allowed in the future, and the Allies had forbidden it an air force.

Curiously enough, however, no Allied prohibition had been promulgated on building airplanes, and a number of firms were still in business, most of them turning out machines for the commercial market abroad. Among them was Anthony Fokker's outfit (which also had a factory near Amsterdam, in Holland), and since Goering had been one of the most successful demonstrators of the excellences of the Dutchman's machines, it is hardly surprising that he was asked to try out a new commercial model when one was produced in the spring of 1919. It was a Fokker F-7 monoplane, and Goering handled it so well that he was asked to fly it at a forthcoming air display in Denmark. There his exhibition of daredevil aerobatics was so spectacular and his spectators so impressed that a delighted Fokker decided to give Goering a permanent loan of the new plane, figuring that wherever he flew it he would attract attention to its potentialities. He began a successful period as a barnstorming pilot in Denmark and Sweden in which he billed himself as the former commander of the Richthofen Flying Circus and allowed it to be thought— though it wasn't true—that the plane which he put through its paces over the heads of the excited crowds was the actual machine in which he had operated over the Western Front against the Allied air forces.

In both Denmark and Sweden he found himself hailed as a dashing hero of the air and all the adulation was poured upon his head which he and his fellow aces had so missed when they came back from the front to defeated Germany. Sweden had been strongly pro-German during World War I, and Goering's exploits and photograph had frequently figured in the newspapers. It was just like Berlin in the heyday of the war, with small boys lining up for his autograph and young women gushing over him. For almost a year he lived, as Bodenschatz afterward put it, "like a world boxing champion. He had more money than he needed and any girl he wanted." On one memorable day in the summer of 1919 in Copenhagen he led a flight of four ex-Richthofen squadron pilots through a series of aerobatics in which the skill and daring of the pilots raised the excitement of the crowd to a fever pitch. After it was over he met an attractive Danish woman and went back with her to her house, where, he later wrote Bodenschatz, "we spent the night in a bath of champagne." Bodenschatz said later: "I never discovered whether he meant it literally, and, of course, I never dared to ask him."

Hermann Goering was now twenty-seven years old, and he was well aware that though the immediate rewards of a barnstorming life were choice enough, there was not much future to it. It was seasonal and it was hazardous. As the crowds grew blasé, he would have to perform stunts that were more and more dangerous in order to hold them. He had already done one which had ripped off his undercarriage. He was more vulnerable than a circus trapezist, for he had no net to catch him if he fell.† He needed a safer and more permanent occupation, and he decided to find it in commercial aviation. It is indicative of his disenchantment with Germany that though a small air transport operation had by this time begun there he made no attempt at this time to get into it, but instead applied for a pilot's job with the Swedish firm, Svensk-Lufttrafik. He was given health and proficiency tests and then told that he would be put on the waiting list, pending a vacancy.

It was during this period that an event occurred which was to have a profound effect upon his life.

One of the ways in which Hermann Goering earned his living when the barnstorming season was over was by operating his plane as an air-taxi. He gave short sightseeing flights to people eager to experience the thrills of flying through the air for the first time; and for more sophisticated customers, chiefly businessmen, he was prepared to fly to any part of Scandinavia at so much per mile. It was in this way, in the winter of 1920, that he encountered

† Though he did, after a time, wear an automatic parachute when stunting, and later became its agent in Scandinavia.

Count Eric von Rosen, who had missed his train and was looking for a quick way home from Stockholm to his castle at Rockelstadt, on the shores of Lake Baven, near Sparreholm, in central Sweden. The weather was bad and it had begun to snow, and few men would have considered making the journey by plane; but Von Rosen was an intrepid and fearless character whose fame was already known far beyond Sweden as an explorer both in Africa and the Far North. He asked Goering if he would fly him to his home, casually adding that three other pilots had already turned him down because of the weather. He offered to pay double the rate if he consented.

It was, in truth, suicidal weather, especially for a flight into the Swedish back country, where likely landing places would be few and far between if things went wrong. But there was the hint of a challenge in Von Rosen's request and Goering accepted at once. It turned out to be an even more hazardous journey than either of them had anticipated, and they lost their way several times among the lakes and mountains until they finally found Lake Baven and skidded to a halt on the surface of its frozen waters just under the tall battlements of Rockelstadt Castle. It was a magnificent medieval stronghold after Goering's heart, and after strapping down the plane, for it was growing dark and he had been invited to stay the night, he stumbled beside his host toward the gates through the buffeting snow with a mounting sense of anticipation.

An account of what happened next has been left behind in a document written by a female relative of Count von Rosen (she was later to become Goering's sister-in-law), and it is worth quoting here because its feverish prose seems to match what must have been the Grimms' fairy-tale quality of the occasion:

"Happily waving, though obviously somewhat worried, the young chatelaine of the castle stood on the steps to greet the men, and then led them into the great hall, where a great blazing fire and hot drinks were soon warming their frozen limbs. What a splendid place this was! On the walls of the great hall, right up to the second floor gallery, hung old weapons and armor, as well as family portraits and rich tapestries decorated with heroic Nordic themes. Everywhere there were hunting trophies to be seen, and mementoes from all parts of the earth of this famous explorer's adventures. At the head of the stairs stood a huge bear, one of the many which the head of the household had, in the old Nordic fashion, killed with a spear."

She goes on: "Hermann Goering stood before the open fire staring into the flames. Two great swastikas of wrought iron hung on either side of the bars on which the logs were burning. The swastika . . . it was as if he had always known it, and had always been here.‡ Symbols should not be explained or talked about. They live in blood and in the soul. Suddenly from the stairs above a woman began to descend, a woman of noble, queenly bearing. It was Carin, sister of the chatelaine of the household. Her deep blue eyes met Hermann Goering's searching glance. This splendid woman . . . a feeling of exultation began to beat in his breast! He stood there, tongue-tied and in awe. It was as if he had always known her. The love that sprang up instantly between them cannot be explained or spoken of. It too lives in blood and in the soul!"

Hermann Goering could not have come into the life of Carin von Kantzow at a more vulnerable moment. Thirty-two years old, a tall brunette with eyes as vividly blue as those of the young German pilot, she was one of five daughters of a Swedish aristocrat named Baron Carl von Fock and his Anglo-Irish wife, Huldine Beamish. Of her four sisters, one had stayed at home, another had married an artist, but the two who were closest to her had also married into the nobility, her sister Mary to Count von Rosen and her eldest sister, Fanny, to Count von Wilamowitz-Moellendorff, a German officer who had been killed in the war. Carin herself had been married for ten years to a professional Swedish soldier named Nils von Kantzow, by whom she had an eight-year-old son, Thomas. But the marriage had been going wrong for some time, not because of any lack of affection on the part of Nils von Kantzow, who loved her deeply and devotedly and would go on doing so to the end of his life. It was chiefly because the lovely Carin, a dreamy person, brought up on romantic Nordic myths, restlessly searching for a hero to quicken her blood, was bored with her respectable husband and the predictable lines of his career and their life together in a succession of Swedish garrison towns.

‡ The swastika has always been an ancient Nordic symbol.

She lay back on the sofa in front of the roaring fire in the great hall of Rockelstadt Castle and listened with growing emotion to the talk between her brother-in-law and the handsome young flier. It was a period in Hermann Goering's life when he had never looked more handsome or seemed so attractive. Encouraged by Eric von Rosen, he talked about his life over the Western Front with the Richthofen Squadron, and then passed on to the terrible things that were happening in Germany and the harsh consequences of the Allied *Diktat* on the defeated German people. He had a deeply sympathetic audience. Despite their mother's English background, all her daughters (as well as Von Rosen himself) had been fervently pro-German during the war and had said prayers for the Fatherland's victory each day in the family chapel. Fired by the wine, the warmth and the evident friendliness of his surroundings, aware of Carin von Kantzow's eyes upon him from her seat in the shadows, Goering was at the top of his form, witty, modest, impassioned in turn. So far as the beautiful brunette was concerned, he was irresistible, the hero she had always longed to meet.

"He is the man I have always dreamed about," she said to her sister Fanny later.

At one point in the evening Eric von Rosen took his glass, "charged with German wine," as Fanny later commented, and toasted the day when "Germany would find the leader who would once more make her people free." He added: "Perhaps we have heard from him tonight." He rose to his feet, grasped the German's hand in his, and then they all solemnly drank to the future of Germany. After which, Von Rosen took his lute and they all launched into a recital of old Nordic and German folk songs about the doughty deeds of their heroic ancestors. Hermann Goering, "touched to the heart by the sympathy of his hosts, joined in with tears in his eyes."

His companions were enchanted. Fanny afterward wrote in a gush of passionate prose:

"Hermann Goering was never able to talk much with Carin about their first memorable evening together. His soul had been too deeply stirred by what had happened. It was as if the lonely stormbird, after flying so long over the empty sea, had at long last come in sight of land."

He did not neglect to ask for Carin's address in Stockholm, and for another meeting.

Captain Nils von Kantzow, his wife Carin, and their son Thomas lived at this time in a small house on the Grev Karlavägen in Stockholm, and it was there early in 1921 that Hermann Goering was summoned to lunch with the family. It must have been a curious experience for Nils von Kantzow, because neither his wife nor Goering were particularly adept at concealing their feelings, and the passion they had conceived for each other at first sight had been nourished by separation. Thomas von Kantzow, although only nine years old at the time, retained vivid memories of this first meeting with Hermann Goering.

"I liked him at first sight," he said. "It was not difficult to do so. He was a jolly fellow. It was obvious that he was not used to children, and he was reserved at first. But he treated me as if I were a grownup just like the others, and he listened very seriously whenever I spoke. He made us all laugh a lot, I remember, especially when he made fun of his flying adventures. I could see that my father was quite taken with him. As for my mother, I noticed that she hardly ever took her eyes off him. I could not have put it into words at the time, but I sensed that she was in love with him."

If the first meeting in the firelight of Rockelstadt Castle had cast a spell on them, this second encounter certainly did nothing to break it. Carin von Kantzow was never one to disobey the dictates of her heart, and not the type to have a clandestine affair. It is typical of her romantic nature that she was quickly comparing herself and Goering with the stricken lovers of her favorite opera. "We are like Tristan and Isolde," she told her sister Fanny. "We have swallowed the love potion and we are helpless, oh, so ecstatically helpless, under its effect."

For a time she took to meeting her beloved at her parents' home on Grev Turegatan in Stockholm, and afterward the two of them would go to a tiny family chapel in the street behind the Von Fock house where they would hold hands and pray together. The chapel was the central meeting place of a religious sisterhood called the Edelweiss Society, which had been started by Carin's Anglo-Irish grandmother and espoused a mixture of pantheism and mysticism. The edelweiss was its emblem, W. B. Yeats and certain Nordic bards its poet laureates. Carin after their first session together in the chapel gave Hermann Goering a sprig of edelweiss, and he wore it in his hat from then on, and later induced many another to do likewise.

The Von Fock family was at first amused by Carin's infatuation, but became alarmed when she announced to them that she had told her husband about her feelings and was proposing to leave his household. Goering had asked her, she said, to marry him, but she did not want a divorce, which she knew Nils von Kantzow would refuse her. He had rightly pointed out that Goering was without a steady job and that Carin was not used to the rigors of living on a budget, or of keeping house. He would wait for the affair to work itself out.

It was at this point that Thomas von Kantzow learned that the handsome guest at the luncheon table was about to wreck his family life. Suddenly he was bundled away without notice to stay at Rockelstadt Castle with his uncle and aunt, Eric and Mary von Rosen.

"There were two towers at Rockelstadt, one called the Tower of Sin and the other the Tower of Virtue," he said. "The Tower of Sin was an exotic place decorated with Eastern statues, pictures of imps and devils, and mysterious hieroglyphics, and the scent of incense hung on the air. In the Tower of Virtue there was a picture of the Virgin, paintings of religious themes and a mosaic of George and the Dragon on the ceiling. One morning my Aunt Mary took me by the hand and led me firmly into the Tower of Virtue, and there she told me that my mother had gone away with a man. She said I must not blame her because she was in love, and that excused everything. I said I would never blame my mother for anything, but I only wished she had taken me with her—and I wished it more than ever when she told me the name of the man. Then I burst into tears."

About this time Carin and Goering moved into an apartment in Stockholm and there lived together openly for several months. Nils von Kantzow continued to make an allowance to his wife, and it was sufficient for them to be able to live in a modicum of comfort, but for Carin von Kantzow, who had been brought up in well-to-do circumstances since childhood, it must have been something of a shock to experience how the semi-poor lived, and it is indicative of the strength of her love for Hermann Goering that she both endured it and never once grumbled about it.

Ironically, it was Goering and not she who was troubled by the scandal which their affair was causing in Swedish social circles. Carin cared nothing for the gossips; for her no love as god-given as the one she felt for Hermann could possibly be sinful. On the other hand, Goering suffered at the thought that the object of his adoration was being dubbed an unfaithful wife, and her refusal to ask for a divorce was the only thing upon which they disagreed. Perhaps there was a guilt complex lurking somewhere in his mind over the adulterous skeleton in his own family closet. Carin repeatedly reminded him that, in the event of a divorce, her husband would undoubtedly ask for custody of her beloved Thomas, and that she would find hard to bear. Already she could only see her son by surreptitious means. He would leave his father's house to go to school and then slip away to see his mother and Goering during his lunch hour. Often he brought them delicacies from the kitchen at home which they could now no longer afford; and when it was very cold and the heating was low, the two lovers and the son would spend the lunch break huddled together, their arms embracing each other tightly for warmth.

"We would feed each other mouthfuls of food," said Thomas, "and we would laugh and joke about how funny it would seem if people could see us huddled together. They were precious moments. I was glad to see the two of them so happy together. But otherwise I missed my mother very much."

It was as much to test the strength of Carin von Kant-zow's feelings for him that Hermann Goering at last decided, in 1921, that it was time he left Sweden. He was getting nowhere there so far as a career was concerned. He was conscious as he talked to Carin, who was well schooled in music, painting, and architecture, of large gaps in his education which he now felt the need to fill. She took him to the art galleries and museums, and aroused in him the enthusiasm for pictures and sculptures which was one day to become the consuming passion of his life. But other things he would have to learn for himself. He had become interested in Germany again and eagerly studied the newspapers from Berlin and Munich to discover how things were going. Finally, thanks to the intervention of his mother, he heard that he had secured a place at the university in Munich to study history and political science. After some hesitation, Carin decided that she would stay behind until her lover was settled. Her real reason, in fact, was that she could not bear to be wrenched away from her son.

But Goering was no sooner gone than she ached to be with him again, and before the month was up she telegraphed that she was on her way to join him. She stayed in Munich with Goering's mother, and Franziszka, who approved of her at once, decided that here indeed was a woman worthy of being the wife to her son. She put the case for a divorce quietly but firmly, pointing out that though marriage ties might be unnecessary in certain circles in Sweden, the same was not true of Germany, no matter how revolutionary the changes which were taking place. If Carin wished to help Hermann in his future career (though what sort of a career it would be, neither woman as yet knew), she would have to make the sacrifice and become an honest woman and marry him.

She returned to Sweden to make the position clear to her husband, and the long-suffering Nils von Kantzow took steps at once. He even agreed to make her an allowance after the divorce was through, and to permit her to have freedom of access to their son whenever she was in Sweden. The case was settled quickly and without fuss, and Carin bade an emotional farewell to Thomas von Kantzow and journeyed back to Munich.

Carin von Kantzow (née Fock) and Hermann Wilhelm Goering were married at the Rathaus in Munich on February 3, 1923. The bride wore a white gown and a garland of white roses in her hair, and she carried a bouquet of deep red carnations around which ribbons with the green-and-white colors of the Von Fock family and the red-and-white colors of the Goerings were wrapped. The bridegroom wore a sprig of edelweiss in his buttonhole. Goering's mother, sisters, and brothers, and Carin's eldest sister, Fanny, together with her daughter, Dagmar von Wilamowitz-Moellendorff, were at the ceremony, and they were afterward joined by friends and well-wishers at a reception

at the Park Hotel. Among them was Major Karl Bodenschatz, now a regular officer in Germany's small Army. A
number of Goering's old flying comrades had sent him a
message to be read out during the speeches:

"That's what we always said: Our Goering will always
do better than anyone!"

They spent their honeymoon in the small hunting lodge
of Hochkreuth near Bayrichszell, in the mountains of Bavaria close to the Austrian frontier. When they came back,
Carin Goering discovered that her husband, now thirty
years old, had found a career at last.

But it was not what Nils von Kantzow would have considered a steady job, nor one with much future, either.

VI. PUTSCH

When Hermann Goering enrolled in the university at Munich in 1922 he found that a temporary (and, in fact, deceptive) calm had returned to the Bavarian state and its capital. The Red rebellion had been crushed and the right-wing reign of terror which had followed it was over. The mercenaries of the Free Corps whose blood-thirsty excesses had so disfigured the defeat of the Red commune had now been disbanded, and the so-called Weimar Republic under the presidency of Friedrich Ebert ruled from Berlin. But, for both external and domestic reasons, the relative peace that reigned in the city was an uneasy one, and the younger elements of the population were growing increasingly disenchanted with the way their government was moving.

Most war veterans and, Goering found, most German students now believed that Germany had lost the war not because of defeat in the field, but because the nation had been stabbed in the back. They believed that the German Government had asked for an armistice too soon and had allowed itself to be tricked by the Allies into accepting impossibly severe terms. The republic was now burdened with intractable economic problems aggravated by the increasing demands which the Allies were making for reparations. There was hunger, unemployment, and despair. Successive governments had failed to deal drastically through currency reforms with the galloping inflation, chiefly because the big industrialists made profits out of it and the government itself found it a convenient way of reducing its national debt. But men, women, and children were dying of starvation as a result of this financial trickery.

War veterans and students alike felt a deep sense of humiliation at the way their country was being treated, and they blamed Germany's plight on two elements—the "bad

Germans" who had got them into the mess in the first place, and the Versailles Treaty which was causing them such misery and shame. The moment he was back in Germany, Hermann Goering felt the same resentments stirring in him against the "traitors" who had lost them the war and the Allies who were being so merciless. But he no longer dreamed of a restoration of the status quo, and his old devotion to Kaiser Wilhelm II, now living in comfortable exile in Holland, had turned sour (though not his affection for royalty).

He discovered that most young men he met, and not just war veterans like himself, now shared the same drive—to restore the prestige of Germany, to liquidate one way or another those "bad Germans" who had "betrayed" the nation, and to get the monstrous terms of the Versailles Treaty off the nation's back. They were all ripe recruits for the so-called Patriotic Societies which were now springing into being all over Germany, particularly in Bavaria. As Professor Harold J. Gordon, Jr., has pointed out, these societies differed in kind and degree, in size and organization, in methods and objectives. But they were all strongly nationalist, anti-Semitic, favored the militant defense of Germany against her foes both domestic and foreign, and all were vaguely allied with one another against the left (of all shades) as traitors and divisive elements in German society.

By the time Hermann Goering had settled in Munich once more, three wings of the Patriotic Movement had developed, and each wing had begun building up its own private army. Their total strength was estimated at the time to number at least 300,000. There was the right or nationalist wing, supported mainly by businessmen, government officials, and the older war veterans, which was anti-left but favored a gradual approach. There was the center element, ostensibly working with the existing government but in reality working behind the scenes to overthrow it. And finally, on the left of patriotic societies, there was a militant force consisting of the Nationalsozialistische Deutsche Arbeiter Partei (the NSDAP, or German Workers' Party) and its allies.

"Here was the highly activist element," writes Professor Gordon, "demanding a violent revolution, a new state and a drastically modified society. These were the so-called

Racist Bands (Voelkische Verbaende), although some members and groups of the Centre also called themselves 'Racist.' These radical groups were of various types, and varying degrees of virulence . . . However, the one organization in the entire left wing of the Patriotic Movement that enjoyed the advantages of both a paramilitary organization and a propaganda organization was the NSDAP. This organization was also the only one that had begun [by the time Goering was back in Munich] the transformation from a more or less amorphous association of likeminded people into a tightly organized political party. It still denounced parliamentarianism and parliamentarians, but it was increasingly prepared to meet them on their own ground, despite its renunciation of participation in parliamentary life. This meant that the NSDAP enjoyed the tactical advantage of being the extreme radical cutting edge of the movement . . . It was the best led, the best organized and the most versatile of all the factions on the left of the movement."

In the winter of 1922, Hermann Goering met the leader of the NSDAP for the first time, and discovered that he spoke the thoughts that were in his own head and advocated the policies that seemed to promise what he now so badly wanted to see—the restoration of Germany's pride and independence.

Life at a university when you are nearly thirty years of age can have its frustrations, and Goering was far from being immune to them. The wave of postwar veteran-students had already passed through the portals of Munich University, and most of the young men with whom he found himself studying were at least nine or ten years his junior in age and a generation different in outlook and experience. It is true that they shared the same bitterness over Germany's plight, the same hatred of the "bad Germans" who, they insisted, had lost them the war, but otherwise they had little in common. The war hero who had been cheered in Scandinavia was just another defeated soldier to these earnest and bookish young Germans. As for Goering, he was discovering that it was too late for him to learn the art of politics from books, when all around him were signs that it was political action that was needed.

So instead of studying he spent more and more time

wandering around Munich, lonely, unhappy, pining for his beloved Carin, and listening with growing impatience to the spoutings of the politicians and rabble-rousers at the political meetings he increasingly attended.

It was November 1922, and this was the time when the Patriotic Movement was whipping itself up into a fervor over the latest indignity which the victorious Allies were trying to inflict upon Germany. Having failed to persuade the Dutch Government to hand over the exiled Wilhelm II for trial as a war criminal,* the Allies were now demanding the extradition from Germany of the leading generals of the old Imperial Army, including Field Marshal Paul von Hindenburg and General Ludendorff. It was a good excuse for the Patriotic Movement to cash in on the general indignation over this insulting demand—for Von Hindenburg in particular was almost universally admired by the German people—and it would provide yet another opportunity for speakers to vituperate against the Allies and the wickedness of the Versailles Treaty.

A Sunday night protest meeting was organized by the combined movement, and Hermann Goering was one of the many thousands who attended it.

It was an unsatisfactory occasion for Goering so far as the speeches were concerned, for most of those who spoke were full of windy rhetoric about Germany's sorrows but conspicuously lacking in any practical suggestions for solving them. But he stayed on because just close to where he was standing was a section where the various party leaders were gathered, waiting their turn to be called to the platform, and among them was one he was curious to hear.

He had seen him before during his wanderings around Schwabing, the artists' quarter of Munich, and he knew that his name was Adolf Hitler and he was leader of the NSDAP. But he had not met him and had never heard him speak, and now the opportunity had come for him to do so.

But when Adolf Hitler's name was called from the platform, Goering noticed that he violently shook his head and refused to move.

"It was pure coincidence that I stood near by and heard

---

* Lloyd George had won a general election in Britain by using "Hang the Kaiser!" as his slogan.

the reasons for his refusal," he said later. "He considered it senseless to launch protests that had no weight behind them. This made a deep impression on me. I was of the same opinion."

But he still had not heard Hitler speak, so a few days later he went to a meeting of the NSDAP in a Munich suburb, and the sentiments that the leader of the party expressed in his speech lived up to his liveliest expectations. He spoke about the protest meeting and his reasons for refusing to address the throng, of his opposition to Versailles and the need to repudiate the treaty. But what was the use of just talking about it? A protest could be successful, a repudiation could make an impact, only if backed by the power to give it weight. As long as Germany had not become strong, Hitler said, this kind of gesture could have no purpose.

"The conviction was spoken word for word as if from my own soul," Goering said later.

He was so impressed that he went home, thought hard about what Hitler had said and of the policies and drives he had expounded, and then decided that he had at last found a man and a cause to which to attach himself. He decided to seek out Adolf Hitler at the NSDAP (or Nazi, as the party was beginning to be called) headquarters in Munich.

"I just wanted to speak to him at first and see if I could assist him in any way," Goering said later. "He received me at once and after I had introduced myself he said it was an extraordinary turn of fate that we should meet."

Even at this early period in the fortunes of the Nazi Party, Adolf Hitler showed unmistakably the qualities of leadership that would soon make his name and those of his followers known far beyond the frontiers of Bavaria. As Goering had discovered on hearing him speak for the first time, Hitler was a spellbinder whose skill with words not only roused to fever heat those who heard him but kept them on the boil long afterward. In the aftermath of World War I he had arrived in Munich (in November 1918) and stayed in the barracks of the List Regiment, where the activities of the revolutionary soldiers' committees became "so repellent to me that I decided at once to leave again as soon as possible." He went to serve as a guard at a prisoner-of-war camp for Russians at Trautstein, near the Austrian border.

He had come back again in March 1919, and was no longer a timid soldier disgusted (and rather frightened) by the Red militants but an ardent nationalist determined to fight the revolutionary forces which, he feared, would soon turn Germany into a Soviet state. Like Goering a few years later, he was looking for a cause to which to attach himself. In September 1919, still in the Army, he passed through an anti-Communist course and, with the title of Bildungs-offizier (or political agent), he was sent out to conduct indoctrination courses among recruits to the new army. He spent his days in the headquarters of the Forty-first Rifle Regiment, lecturing the troops on the dangers of Communism, and his nights wandering round the city's beer halls and coffeehouses, listening in on political conversations. On the night of September 12, 1919, he went to a cheap beer hall in the Herrenstrasse called the Sternecker, which was the meeting place of a small political group calling itself the German Workers' Party. Despite its name, its aims were nationalist and patriotic, indeed militantly anti-government, anti-left, and anti-Jewish.

Hitler arrived to spy and stayed to join. Within a year, by a deft admixture of charm, oratory, patriotic fervor and a series of skillfully organized plots, he had wrested control of the Party from its more lethargic leaders, had changed its name to the NSDAP, and had turned it into the most important, powerful, and dangerous political party in Bavaria. Professor Harold J. Gordon, Jr., has described Adolf Hitler at this time as combining "in his physically insignificant person the talents and characteristics of Demosthenes, Ferdinand of Aragon, and Robert the Bruce; and he added to them the ambition and sweeping aims of Alexander or Napoleon. He was just the man to make the most of the [Nazi] party."

If Hermann Goering did not yet see all these qualities in him, he realized at once that he was in the presence of a man of action. Hitler, in kind, who knew a valuable recruit when he saw one, was well aware of the value to the movement of this young, tough, eager-eyed war hero, and he went out of his way to exercise upon him the magic of his personality and his considerable charm.

"We spoke at once about the things which were close to our hearts—the defeat of our Fatherland, the iniquities of Versailles," Goering said later.

Hitler, in fact, outlined for Goering in a wealth of convincing detail the broad strategy of the Nazi Party's program—"my program," as he continually referred to it. He had three main aims in view, he said. First, he would eliminate from German life the "November criminals" who had given in to the Allies and the "evil" Jews and Marxists who were the real influences behind these traitors. He would then call upon the people to join him and his party in building a new, proud, national Germany. And finally, this new Germany would tear up the Versailles Treaty and fight, if necessary, to reconquer for Germany its proper place in the world.

It was a program after Goering's own heart, and he could not have asked for better. Other patriotic parties raved and ranted against the government and swore to overthrow it, but had nothing to offer in its place. Hitler planned not only to destroy but to rebuild, to make a new Germany.

"I told him," Goering said later, "that I myself to the fullest extent, and all I was and possessed, were completely at his disposal."

A few days later he swore a personal oath of allegiance to Adolf Hitler and was admitted as a full member of the Nazi Party. For Hitler at this pregnant moment in his movement's affairs, Hermann Goering was the most important recruit of them all. He was a great war hero and that would bring prestige to the Party. He had dash and drive. He also had army experience of the greatest possible value to the Nazis—and Hitler already had a position in the organization ready for him.

As for Hermann Goering, he realized that it was a most important (perhaps *the* most important) turning point in his life. He swore his oath of allegiance with such fervor that one of the more cynical members present, Ernst Hanfstaengel, snickered to himself at the emotional overtones in his voice. But Goering had never been more serious. He had already decided that Adolf Hitler was his man.

"When I had more insight into the personality of the Fuehrer," he said later, "I gave him my hand and said: 'I pledge my destiny to you for better or for worse . . . in good and bad times . . . even if it means my life.' "

He had found a hero again, to take the place of Ritter von Epenstein.

In an official report to the State Department at the end of 1922, Captain Truman Smith, an assistant military attaché in the U.S. embassy in Berlin, wrote:

"It is very difficult to gain an impression of the total [Nazi] party strength. Opponents of Hitler estimated it as high as 200,000, other neutral observers as 35,000. It is not easy however to distinguish between actual party members and Hitler sympathizers who as yet take no active part in the movement. These were found in the army, the government, and among the press. It was stated that the larger part of the Munich police was entirely in sympathy with the National Socialists."

By the summer of 1923 an official police report had estimated the party as being 35,000 strong in Munich alone and numbering approximately 150,000 in the whole of Bavaria. And there was also a very strong contingent in neighboring Franconia under the sub-leadership of a notorious Jew-baiter, Julius Streicher. The legend soon spread abroad that it was a right-wing working-class and petit-bourgeois movement, and it is true that it inveighed against the evils of big-boss capitalism. But its members came from nearly all walks of life, and included in the ranks were a quite extraordinary number of university students, as well as hundreds of ex-army officers. More than anything else, it was a movement of young people.

Hitler held in his hand two powerful weapons to make the power of the Nazis felt in the land. He possessed excellent propaganda organs in the shape of the official party newspaper, the *Voelkicher Beobachter*, as well as the sympathy of some of Bavaria's most important newspapers, including the powerful *Nachrichten*. He also had a powerful private army of some 11,000 men which he called the *Stuermabteilungen* or SA, named for the crack commando units of World War I, which included in its ranks many ex-soldiers and veterans of the Free Corps which had fought against the Communists and Socialists in 1919.

But the SA, though it contained some formidable human material, lacked discipline, cohesion, and a dynamic, and it had occurred to Adolf Hitler at once that Hermann Goering, with his army training, his air force record, and his ebullient personality, was just the man to give it the *esprit de corps* that it needed. He told the new recruit immediately after he had taken the oath that he was making him commander of the SA with full responsibility for its reorganization.

Goering asked for two months' respite while he attended to his personal affairs (which included his marriage to Carin) and then he took over. He worked hard and he worked wonders with the odd assortment of ex-soldiers, students, farm laborers, dockers, army officers, and office workers of which the SA consisted. Quickly assimilating the dynamics of the movement, he addressed them at meeting after meeting on the necessity for loyalty, discipline, and patriotism in the cause of building a new Germany. He also drilled them constantly and hard.

Soon the bands of unruly thugs who had previously turned up as guards at Nazi meetings were replaced by smoothly efficient, but no less tough, commandos. Flying squads in motorized transport were organized both to protect Hitler and his cohorts from attacks from Communists and Socialist troublemakers and to disrupt the meetings of these organizations. Squads were also put on parade every weekend in the small towns of Bavaria and Franconia, and their disciplined drill drew applause from the admiring crowds who came to watch them. On parade they wore peaked caps, brown shirts, breeches, and either leggings or jackboots, and they had a band with a swastika on it around their arms. In their clashes with the left they donned steel helmets, and went to work with clubs, knives, and, more rarely, guns.

On April 15, 1923, the newly shaped forces of the SA marched through Munich in a party parade, and drew this comment from a federal government official who had been sent from Berlin to watch it:

"As I was able to ascertain for myself, there were Hitler's 5,000–6,000 man force of SA, National Socialist assault troops, the Blücherbund, Reichsflagge, the Bund Oberland and some smaller organizations. The marchers represented all classes of the population. Besides a large number of workers, former soldiers dominated, partly equipped with steel helmets, though otherwise unarmed.

Also some National Socialist storm troops from the Oberland wore national costume in the parade. *The tight military discipline of the men must be stressed.*"†

But it was more than just discipline which was noted by
other spectators of the parade, and it sent a shiver of apprehension down the spines of all opponents of the Nazis.
Goering had not only welded the SA into a well-drilled
unit, but he had united them emotionally as well, and
imparted to them at last the esprit de corps without which
any fighting force will lack real cohesion in times of
emergency. He had done it by stressing in every lecture he
had given the men that they were comrades in arms, and
with great ceremonial solemnity he had made each of them
retake the oath which all of them had sworn on recruitment but, in many cases, had mumbled purely as a for-
mula. It was an oath which stressed the classless nature of
the force, the equality of every man in it no matter what his
background.

"I promise," each SA man swore, "that I will see in
every member of the Sturmabteilung without thought of
class, occupation, wealth or poverty, only my brother and
true comrade, with whom I feel myself bound in joy and
sorrow."

Adolf Hitler was overjoyed at the transformation of the
units he saw passing before him through the Munich
streets, and when it was over he slapped Hermann Goering
on the back and kissed Carin's hand.

"One day you will be very proud of the beloved one who
is now your second father," she wrote to her son, Thomas,
in Sweden.‡ "Today he paraded his army of true young
Germans before his Fuehrer, and I saw his face light up as
he watched them pass by. The beloved one has worked so
hard with them, has injected so much of his own bravery
and heroism into them, that what was once a rabble, and, I
confess, sometimes a rough and rather terrifying one, has
been veritably transformed into an Army of Light, a band
of eager crusaders ready to march at the Fuehrer's orders
to make this unhappy country free once more . . . After it

† My italics. L.M.
‡ The letter, which Thomas von Kantzow preserved to the end of
his life, was passed on to him by his aunt, Mary von Rosen. Carin
obviously feared that her ex-husband would not have allowed her
son to see it.

was over, the Fuehrer embraced the beloved one and told
me that if he said what he really thought of his achievement, the beloved one would get a swelled head. I said that
my own was swollen with pride already, and he kissed my
hand and said: 'No head so pretty as yours could ever be
swollen.' It was not perhaps the most elegant compliment I
have ever received, but it pleased me . . ."

Hermann Goering had bought a small house in the
Munich suburb of Obermenzing, close to Nymphenburg
Castle, and he had partly furnished it before Carin's arrival. She allowed him to retain in the ground-floor rooms
the heavy gothic furniture, more suitable for castles, for
which he had such a predilection, but upstairs she took
over, bringing down from Sweden the late Victorian furniture which was the fashion of the day, the carpets, Chinese
embroidery, and pictures which had been her own personal
property in the Von Kantzow household, together with a
small white organ on which, when they were alone together, she would accompany Hermann Goering when he
sang folk songs or operatic arias; he fancied himself as a
good light baritone.

But they were not often alone together in these days.
The villa at Obermenzing quickly became a focal point for
the leaders of the NSDAP. Adolf Hitler, who liked pretty
women, was charmed by Carin Goering's blue eyes and
amused by the deceptive quality of her gentle manner. He
knew that she had a temperament that could flare up into
an emotional bonfire when she was provoked. He had seen
the passionate scorn with which she had rounded on someone who once implied that her foreign birth and aristocratic background kept her aloof from the battle in which
the National Socialists were now engaged.

She was, in fact, as much an engaged Nazi as any of
them, and had taken the cause of the party to her bosom
with all the fervor of her temperament. It has been suggested that as the various party chiefs drank and argued in
her house she must have watched them with a jaundiced
eye, appalled by their manners, their language, their coarse
insults against government ministers, the industrialists, and
the Jews. How could a woman of such gentle birth and
refined education share the prejudices of this rough gang of
beer-drinking fanatics?

The answer is partly that, like her husband, she had

fallen under the spell of Adolf Hitler, and these were his prejudices, deeply felt, expressed with an intensity that affected all who listened to him. But it was also true that in much politer circles than those in which Carin Goering was now moving, a skepticism about the government, a suspicion of big business, and a strong current of anti-Semitism was to be found. It was a time when a nation was wallowing in the miseries of defeat and asking themselves why it had come about, and in such times in Europe when have they not made the Jew the scapegoat rather than their own shortcomings?

There is certainly no evidence, in her remarks to her relatives, in her letters to Sweden, that she was ever anything but brimful of enthusiasm at the way her home was now being taken over by the Nazi leaders.

"On the ground floor was a large, attractive smoking room, with an alcove lit from outside by a bull's-eye window," wrote Carin's sister Fanny. "A few steps down from it was a wine-cellar with an open fire, wooden stools and a great sofa. Here there came together all those who had dedicated themselves to Hitler and his freedom movement. Late in the evening Hitler would arrive, and you would see around him the early devotees of the party, Dietrich Eckart, Hermann Esser, Hanfstaengel etc. After the earnest conferring would come the warm, cheerful hours which filled Carin with so much joy. Hitler's sense of humour showed itself in gay stories, observations and witticisms, and Carin's spontaneous and wholehearted reaction to them made her a delightful audience."

Others who joined the late-night discussions were Rudolf Hess, Alfred Rosenberg, and an officer in the German Army, Captain Ernst Roehm, who had a particularly sour tongue when he talked about the Party's opponents. Roehm had reached officer's status through the ranks during World War I, and made it clear that he did not think much of anyone who had come up any other way. Though a homosexual, he could be extremely charming to women, and he went out of his way to pay compliments to Carin and to point out that he excepted her husband from his general contempt of the German officer caste.

There was one other visitor to the Goering villa at this time whose association with the leading Nazis was certainly as invaluable to the prestige of the NSDAP as that of Hermann Goering (though Adolf Hitler was too shrewd ever to put him into the same category so far as his long-term plans were concerned). This was a proud, arrogant, volcanic character named General Erich Ludendorff, one of the few German generals (along with Hindenburg) whose reputation had not been tarnished by the defeats of World War I. He had been dismissed from his post on the General Staff because he had refused to recognize the armistice negotiations and had tried to raise a soldiers' rebellion against those who were prepared to accept defeat. This had made him one of the great heroes of postwar Germany. He had ambitions to become dictator of the nation, convinced that only his strong-arm direction and defiance of the Allies could save his country; and in March 1920, he had been involved in yet another rebellion, against the Weimar Republic this time, which came to be known as the Kapp Putsch.* But though the new German Army under General Seeckt refused to fire on the Free Corps troops involved in the putsch, and though the Weimar administration fled from Berlin, the rebels muffed the second stage of their uprising and the whole thing fizzled out. General Ludendorff was forced to flee to Bavaria, and he went into hiding in the small village of Ludwigshoehe, near Munich, where he lived in a villa behind a high wall, with a day and night bodyguard.

Erich Ludendorff had a weakness for women, as his wife, Margarethe, had found to her cost, and an even greater susceptibility to flattery. In Bavaria, where he had nothing else to do but read the newspapers and simmer over the latest humiliation which Germany was suffering at the hands of the Allies, he was more vulnerable than ever to both. One day, while attending a beerfest in a neighboring village, he met a woman who immediately told him to his face that he was the greatest soldier the world had ever known, and he was bowled over. The name of the woman was Mathilde Kemnitz, and she moved on the fringes of the Nazi Party, and was one of its more perfervid supporters.

Small, attractive, highly cultivated, completely unself-conscious in her hero worship of the general, she had

---

* Because an obscure civil servant named Wolfgang Kapp was to be made puppet-Chancellor of Germany had the rebellion succeeded.

soon won her way so close to him that he became obsessed by her. They shared a bitter shame over the way Germany was being treated, but while Ludendorff had always believed that it was defeatism and inefficiency which had lost his people the war, Mathilde Kemnitz had a much more conspiratorial explanation. Soon, as their association came closer, he began to believe it as fervently as she did.

"Gradually I recognized," he wrote later, "the pernicious forces which had caused the collapse of the people, and in them the real enemies of the freedom of the German race. More and more plainly I became aware of the fission-fungi within the structure of our society . . . in the form of secret supra-national forces—the Jews and Rome, along with their tools, the Freemasons, the Jesuits, occult and satanistic structures."

Mathilde Kemnitz soon convinced him that it was these forces which were systematically destroying the racial inheritance and national characteristics of the German people.

"I adopted it as my own view," he wrote, "that the Christian doctrine and the way of life it had given to the people was the basic cause of the whole evil, and that it served solely as a means for obtaining for the Jew the mastery of the world, which had been granted to him by Jehovah . . . For instance, the Diktat of Versailles was signed on June 28, 1919, the fifth anniversary of the assassination of the archducal pair at Sarajevo. At the time I did not suspect the parallelism of the dates nor have any idea that cabalistic beliefs had determined them. Even less did I realise that the murder of the archducal pair had long been planned by the world brotherhood of the Freemasons, in order to unleash in the Yehova year 1914 the World War which had been decided upon by the Grand-Orient Lodge of France at Paris and furthered by Rome."

He was uplifted by these revelations, for they proved what he had always believed in his heart—that Germany had not lost the war in fair battle but had been defeated by international Jewry, Freemasonry, and the conspiracies of the Church of Rome. But who and where was a force "for good" in Germany capable of fighting back against these black forces of evil, and wrenching the German people from their grasp?

It was at this point that Mathilde Kemnitz introduced

him to Adolf Hitler and persuaded him to join the National Socialist Party.

In Januray 1923, the French Government did something which cast many a German not nearly so mentally unbalanced as General Ludendorff down to the depths of despair. Charging that the German Government had failed to deliver 140,000 telegraph poles (part of the vast reparation payments) on time, President Poincaré ordered French troops to occupy the industrial and economic heart of Germany, the Ruhr. They marched in with enough black colonial troops in their columns to arouse the fears and prejudices of most Germans in the occupied area.

Almost simultaneously Poland demanded changes in the frontiers which had been awarded her at Versailles, although they already encompassed vast tracts of former German territory; and Lithuanian troops marched in and occupied the city-principality of Memel, which had hitherto been a German port on the border of East Prussia.

These moves, especially the occupation of the Ruhr, without whose supplies Germany would shrivel up and die, drove both government and people to the brink of revolt against the Versailles Treaty. General von Seeckt, commander of the new Reichswehr (which had been limited by Versailles to 100,000 men), seriously contemplated armed resistance and told the British ambassador in Berlin, Lord d'Abernon that "the road from Dortmund to Berlin is not very long, but it passes through streams of blood." Reluctantly, however, he eventually decided that his force was not yet ready for such an extreme course and that his only recourse was to take secret measures to build up Germany's strength. He began recruiting for an underground army which was later to be known as the Black Reichswehr.

At the moment when he was thinking of resisting the Ruhr occupation, Von Seeckt actually approached both Adolf Hitler and General Erich Ludendorff to ask if he could count on their help in the event of a clash. Hitler did not bother to reply. He was afterward to say that he did not consider it practical to take armed action against the French at this time, and that his first priority must be that of taking over Germany and making it strong. Ludendorff typically replied that "I will lend my internationally historic name" providing that he would be given supreme command of the German forces in the event of war.

There was no war. A campaign of passive resistance to the French was begun instead. But that some sensational climax was approaching was sensed by most Germans as they endured what was undoubtedly their most miserable spring, summer, and autumn since the end of the war. All Germany's assets and resources were being used up paying reparations to the Allies. Gold stocks were exhausted and there was no backing for the mark. With the taking-over of the Ruhr, the nation's best earner of foreign currency was gone. On the day the French occupied the Ruhr, the mark stood at 10,400 to the dollar (50,000 to the pound sterling). Three weeks later the rate was 50,000 to the dollar and by the end of July, 4,000,000. The big industrialists, farmers and landowners were able to profit from the inflationary situation, but for the middle class it meant the wiping out of their savings, and for the workers it was a time of suffering and starvation as their wages turned into waste paper even as they were slipped into their hands.

This was fertile ground indeed for Adolf Hitler and the Nazis, and not only in Bavaria but everywhere in Germany he could point out the profiteers who went on dining and wining through the suffering and chaos and say: "There are your enemies—the capitalists and the Jews!" The recruits came swarming in.

As the agonizing summer dragged on, Hitler and his colleagues, in conference at the Goering villa or strolling together in the mountains, came to the conclusion that the moment was coming to make a supreme bid for power. But to do so they needed co-operation both from the police and the armed forces in Bavaria. Would it be forthcoming? At one time they had had great hopes of bringing into their camp the commander of the Reichswehr troops in Bavaria, General Otto von Lossow, but he had let them down during an anti-Red demonstration on the previous May Day.†

† Using passes issued to them by Captain Ernst Roehm, two ex-army majors now belonging to the SA had drawn arms from a Reichswehr depot in Munich, intending to issue them to the Nazi storm troops for use against troops of the Communist Party's private army. But Von Lossow, whom they had expected to turn a blind eye to this semi-official arms raid, instead demanded their return and threatened to use troops if his order were not obeyed. Hitler obeyed.

Now they decided to make yet another approach to him. Ludendorff was dispatched to Reichswehr headquarters in Munich and solicited Von Lossow's co-operation in an armed uprising against the Berlin government, offering him the post of Reich Minister of Defense in the new regime once the rebels had taken over. Von Lossow was afterward to say that he rejected the approach with contempt, and said of Hitler and Ludendorff: "I thought they were like children playing 'You be the Emperor and I'll be the Pope.' I said I would have nothing to do with their plots. I was no unemployed *Comitadje*; at that time I occupied a high position in the state."

In fact, however, his reaction was much more cautious and equivocal, and in subsequent days both Hitler and Ludendorff came to the conclusion that, in the event of a rising, Von Lossow and the Reichswehr, even if they did not actively help them, would be willing to look the other way until the appropriate moment came to join them. They got down to the practical task of planning their rebellion, and in the Brown House in Munich, in the house which Adolf Hitler now owned in the mountains near Berchtesgaden, and in Ludendorff's villa at Ludwigshoehe the conspirators worked late, while in the woods around the Bavarian capital the brown-shirted forces of the SA drilled through the night in preparation for The Day.

The Nazi leaders were no longer meeting at the Goering villa in Obermenzing at this time because Carin Goering was ill. At the end of August 1923, Fanny Goering, though only fifty-seven years old, had suddenly collapsed and died. The Von Epensteins did not come to the funeral in the Waldfriedhof, where she was laid to rest beside the remains of Heinrich Goering, but they sent a wreath and their regrets. Carin insisted on accompanying her husband to the funeral, and in the biting chill of one of Munich's notorious foehn winds, she had caught cold. Her lungs had always been weak, and now she was in bed and running a high fever.

It was a difficult time for Hermann Goering. His affection for his mother had always been deep, and it had been strengthened by the bond which had grown up between this brisk and intensely practical countrywoman and the romantic aristocrat to whom he was now married. His intense involvement in Hitler's plans cannot have been helped by his preoccupation with his wife's condition, and he spent most of September 1923 rushing from conferences and secret parades to Carin's bedside.

She did not tell her son Thomas that she was seriously ill but wrote him instead that "I have a slight cold and am writing this in bed, where the beloved one has insisted I should stay until it is better. He is very busy these days and great events are in the offing, but until I am better he insists that I should not concern myself with them. He looks tired and does not get enough sleep, and wears himself out by traveling miles just to see me for a few moments. The Fuehrer has been in to see me too. He brought me some fresh fruit and butter from Berchtesgaden . . ."

Early in September the new government in Berlin, under Dr. Otto Stresemann, announced that it was ordering the end of German passive resistance in the Ruhr to the French occupation. The French had threatened reprisals if it did not cease. Immediately the Nazis and their supporters held a protest rally in Nuremberg which they called "German Day" at which, after villifying the government, they named Adolf Hitler as their "fighting leader" in a campaign against "Marxism, internationalism, pacifism, the Weimar constitution, international capital, and the Jews." More than ever the Nazis now believed they had public sentiment behind them.

But there were others who were trying to snatch it from them.

The Bavarian Government, anti-Berlin itself, also announced its strong opposition to the end of passive resistance and a policy of knuckling under to the French. In order to stress its complete alienation from the policies of Berlin, on September 26, 1923, its members resigned and a state commissioner was appointed in their place with dictatorial powers. His name was Ritter Gustav von Kahr and he was a royalist. He at once announced his intention of seceding Bavaria from the rest of Germany and placing Prince Rupprecht, son of the exiled ex-King Ludwig, on the throne of what would become the Kingdom of South Germany.

The appointment of Kahr could not have come at a more awkward moment for the Nazis. Just as they and their allies had indicated that they were ready for militant action, and just when Adolf Hitler had come forward to lead the fight, this upstart royalist had intervened and was trying to take the wind out of the National Socialist sails. Something had to be done. Already the ordinary members of the SA had been complaining to their battalion chiefs that they were impatient, and desperate for action. As one SA officer, Wilhelm Brueckner, commanding the SA Regiment Muenchen, told Hitler:

"The day is coming when I can no longer hold my people. If nothing happens now the men will sneak away."

He told Hitler that he had very many unemployed men among his troops, men who had expended their last garment, their shoes, their last ten pfennigs on training—"so that we can take action and get out of this mess."

It was necessary to make a move, and quickly. Kahr had to be swept aside or outmaneuvered, otherwise the Nazis at a most pregnant moment would have lost their momentum and their *raison d'être*. Hilter had to act. But when?

In the end, it was Gustav von Kahr who chose the date for him. He announced that his movement for secession had secured the support of none other than General von Lossow, the local Reichswehr commander, and Colonel von Seisser, chief of the Bavarian police. This triumvirate would address a meeting on November 8 in Munich at which they would set forth their plans.

The place of the meeting would be a huge beer hall on the south bank of the river Isar, on the outskirts of Munich, called the Bürgerbräuhaus.

In the afternoon of November 8, 1923, Hermann Goering drove up to the villa in Obermenzing and slipped into the bedroom where Carin Goering was lying half-asleep on a couch by the window. She had been running a high fever all through the previous night and now was in such a languor that she had barely the strength to lift her face to him as he bent down to kiss her.

"I cannot stay long, *Liebling*," Goering said. "We have a great rendezvous in the Bügerbräukeller tonight, and it may go on until quite late. Don't let that worry you."

She looked him directly in the eyes, and replied: "I won't worry. I will be with you there, beside you—even if I do still have to lie here."

Goering hurried away. He had plenty of things to organize before the evening started.

The authorities were well aware of the importance of the beer-hall meeting, and since both the Reichswehr commander and the police chief of Bavaria had associated themselves with its sponsor, they decided to surround Freiherr von Kahr and his supporters with the strongest possible protection, including a company of policemen inside the hall. Colonel von Seisser overruled them, on the grounds that too many visible protectors might give the impression that the sponsors were nervous. Why should they be? Had they not invited everyone from center to right to come to the meeting, including both Hitler and Ludendorff? In the end a troop of forty-five *Landpolizei* was hidden in a building a quarter of a mile from the beer hall, a patrol was put on the surrounding streets, and only a few men posted into the hall itself.

News of the meeting had attracted considerable interest throughout Bavaria, and on the night of November 8 a huge mass of people appeared and tried to gain access to the hall, considerably more than Von Kahr and his aides had anticipated. Only about half of them succeeded in getting inside, and the remainder jostled around in the square and neighboring streets, in frustrated and excited groups.

The doors were closed at 7:15 and a Bavarian band played oompah music while the waitresses humped great armfuls of beer steins to the tables and the ripe fumes of ale and cigar smoke began to rise into the air. There must have been some wrinkling of patrician noses, because among the invited guests was the cream of Bavaria's political, business, and literary world, as well as most of its landed gentry. Prince Rupprecht had sent his representative, Baron Soden, and all the old members of the Bavarian government had turned up, as well as bankers, police chiefs, newspaper editors. About eight o'clock the trombonist played his last glissando and the band slipped away. Onto the stage briskly marched Gustav von Kahr, flanked by General von Lossow and Colonel von Seisser, and followed by a group of associates. The waitresses slammed the last reinforcements of beer on the foam-covered tables, and then a supporter arose to make the keynote speech of the evening.

It was just about this time that Adolf Hitler arrived at the entrance of the beer hall. He expressed unpleasant surprise at seeing so many people milling in the square outside, and he strode over to a policeman, who recognized him, and suggested that it might be best to keep the square and streets clear, in case of trouble. The policeman agreed and began moving the crowd. Hitler was satisfied. He wanted a clear run to the beer hall for his own men, who would soon be arriving.

He went into the anteroom of the beer hall and was greeted by his bodyguard, Ulrich Graf, who fetched him a stein of beer, which he did not touch, and sat him at a table at the back of the hall, where he could see the platform. He had four companions with him, Max Amman, his business manager and a well-known strong-arm man; Josef Gerum and Rudolf Hess, both of whom were no strangers to crowd fights and scuffles; and an unexpected fourth member of the quartet, Ernst (Putzi) Hanfstaengel, a soft-spoken Munich playboy who usually positively cringed from beer-drinking crowds.

Suddenly Ulrich Graf, who had gone out into the streets, returned, slipped across and whispered to Hitler: "They have arrived!"

A truck filled with steel-helmeted Nazi storm troopers jerked to a stop in the square and the men hopped down and began to run across the cobbles toward the beer hall. At their head was Hermann Goering. None of the policemen tried to stop them; they said afterward that the storm troopers' steel helmets persuaded them that these were regular Reichswehr troops. At the same time other trucks, coming in from all directions, arrived in the square and bands of SA men debouched from them and made for the hall.

It was the moment for Adolf Hitler to make his move. He rose to his feet, threw his stein of beer to the floor and drew a Browning pistol from his pocket. His companions did likewise. With Hitler in the lead, the little group moved into the body of the hall. The Nazi leader had intended it to be a dramatic appearance, like the explosion of a demon onto the scene in an old-fashioned pantomime. But the crowds at the tables and on the benches were so thick that it was impossible to make a quick march to the stage. Gustav von Kahr had begun speaking a few moments before, and it was some time before he realized that something was wrong, and allowed his voice to trail away. Eventually, with Ulrich Graf using his formidable shoulders, and the rest waving their pistols, a path was cleared and Hitler reached the stage.

Meanwhile, the murmurs of alarm and annoyance were changing to something like panic as storm troopers and SA men appeared at the exits. Those who tried to leave were roughly pushed back. At one point one of Colonel von Seisser's police aides, Major Hunglinger, lurched toward Hitler, his hand in his pocket.

"I had the feeling he was drawing a pistol," Hitler said later. So he took his own gun, pressed it to Hunglinger's forehead, and snapped: "Take your hand out."

The major did so and his hand was empty.

As the hubbub and the shouts began to rise, Hermann Goering, a steel helmet crammed over his head, a pistol in his hand, climbed onto a table, kicked aside some steins of beer, and shouted: "Silence!" Nobody took any notice of him. Then Hitler lifted his own gun and fired it once toward the roof.

"If silence is not restored," he shouted angrily, "I will order a machine gun placed in the gallery."

A heavy hush fell on the hall.

What then followed, an eyewitness was to write later, "was an oratorical masterpiece, which any actor might envy." Hitler started to speak. Five minutes later he had the audience in his hands.

"He began quietly, without any pathos. The enterprise was not directed against Kahr in any way. Kahr has his full trust and [when the putsch has succeeded] shall be regent of Bavaria. At the same time, however, a new government must be formed: Ludendorff, Lossow, Seisser, and himself. I cannot remember in my entire life such a change in the attitude of the crowd in a few minutes, almost a few seconds. There were certainly many who were not converted yet. But the sense of the majority had fully reversed itself. Hitler had turned them inside out, as one turns a glove inside out, with a few sentences. It had almost something of hocus-pocus, or magic, about it. Loud approval roared forth, no further opposition was to be heard."‡

‡ *Im Wandel eine Zeit*. Karl-Alexander von Müller.

Thereupon Hitler shepherded the apprehensive Von Kahr, together with Von Lossow and Von Seisser, into an anteroom for discussions. As they sat down he did not exactly set them at their ease by gesturing with his Browning and saying:

"There are five rounds left in it—four for the traitors, and, if it fails, one for me."

Nevertheless, after ten minutes of earnest and eloquent argument, he could not persuade the three men to give him the support he needed in the putsch that was now about to begin. After ten minutes, he called in Ulrich Graf (still carrying his machine gun) and Rudolf Hess and told them to keep the triumvirate under guard. He went back into the hall.

"Only now did he say, in deep earnest, with emotion in his voice: 'Outside are Kahr, Lossow and Seisser. They are struggling hard to reach a decision. May I say to them that you will stand behind them?' 'Yes! Yes!' swelled out the roaring answer from all sides. 'In a free Germany,' he shouted passionately out over the crowd, 'there is also room for an autonomous Bavaria! I can say this to you: Either the German revolution begins tonight or we will all be dead by dawn!' "

It was at this moment of high excitement that General Erich Ludendorff arrived, dressed in full uniform of the old Imperial Army, all his medals up, and pouting with temper at having come so late on the scene. But Hitler quickly soothed him down and sent him into the anteroom to use his persuasive powers on the triumvirate. Whether it was the impressive figure and patriotic oratory of the general or the fear of Ulrich Graf's machine gun will never be known, but Von Kahr, Von Lossow, and Von Seisser suddenly gave way. They agreed to co-operate with Hitler and the Nazis.

The party marched back into the hall, where Goering was now trying to calm the restive audience, and Von Kahr immediately announced that he was throwing in his lot with the rebels and had agreed to serve Bavaria as regent for the monarchy. This news was greeted by shattering applause. Hitler came forward and clasped Von Kahr's hand. He then launched into a fervid speech about how he was going to smash the criminals now in command in Berlin. He was followed by the army commander and the police chief, both of whom pledged their support for the putsch and his plans for Germany once it had succeeded.

By this time the crowd was baying with hysterical excitement, shaking hands and patting the backs of the SA men and storm troopers who were still on guard at the doors. The waitresses surged out with foaming steins of beer and trays of hot sausages. The band began to play. Hitler, Von Lossow, Von Kahr, Von Seisser, and Ludendorff stood before the enthusiastic throng, clasping each other's hands.

Hermann Goering was beaming with joy beneath his steel helmet and embracing his SA commanders. He had reason to be pleased. With Von Lossow and the Army and Von Seisser and the police with them, Bavaria was theirs. The opposition could only come from outside the state, and with military and police help they could handle that. The Beer Hall Putsch was a success almost before it had begun.

Or so it seemed at midnight on November 8, 1923. Goering dispatched Putzi Hanfstaengel to the Goering villa to tell Carin the good news, and he came back bringing her sister, Fanny, with him. Carin, she told her brother-in-law, was still running a fever and still very weak, but his message had revived her. The news that the Nazis had won was a tonic in itself.

In fact, however, they had not by any means won yet, and the situation would soon be black with disaster.

For Hitler had made a tactical error.

At the end of the triumphant demonstration on the stage of the Bürgerbräukeller, he had conferred with Goering and Rudolf Hess and, as a precaution, decided to take hostages against any tendency on the part of anyone to have second thoughts during the night. A number of former ministers, bankers, police chiefs and city councilors were rounded up and put under the guard of Rudolf Hess and a squad of storm troopers.

But when it was suggested that Von Kahr, Von Lossow, and Von Seisser should also be included in the group of hostages, Ludendorff bridled at once.

"They have given their soldiers' word that they are with us," he said. "It would be an affront to their honor as officers and gentlemen to doubt them."

Why Adolf Hitler did not, nevertheless, contrive to de-
tain the trio and keep them under surveillance overnight is
one of the mysteries of the whole affair. It can only be that
the euphoric atmosphere of the evening had made him
overconfident.

The three men were allowed to leave the beer hall. The
moment they were out of reach of the Nazis, they went
back on their word. Von Kahr with his aides fled to Re-
gensburg, which he immediately proclaimed the temporary
headquarters of the government of Bavaria. Von Lossow
reached his headquarters and was there handed a message
from Berlin by his deputy, Lieutenant General Jakob Ritter
von Danner. It was from General von Seeckt, Commander-
in-Chief of the Reichswehr, whom Von Danner had kept
informed of the night's events. Von Seeckt crisply informed Von Lossow that if he did not take immediate steps
to put down the putsch, he himself would come down from
Berlin and do it for him.

"You gave your word—but that was just a bluff, was it
not, Herr General?" Von Danner suggested smoothly.

Von Lossow agreed. Yes, it had just been a trick to play
for time. He began to bark out orders, and soon the army
telephone exchange was jammed with calls to outside garri-
sons, ordering troop reinforcements to be rushed into the
Bavarian capital.

It had snowed and sleeted during the night. When dawn
broke over Munich, SA troops and auxiliaries marching
through gray, muddy streets to a rendezvous at the Bürgerbräuhaus were astonished to see posters stuck to the walls,
proclaiming the National Socialists a proscribed party, denouncing any agreement with them, and signed by Von
Kahr. He had ordered the posters printed the moment he
had got away from the beer hall. An emergency edition of
the Muenchener *Post* carried a communiqué from Prince
Rupprecht renouncing any association with General Ludendorff and Adolf Hitler, and an even curter message
from Cardinal Faulhaber, the senior Catholic cleric in Bavaria, condemning the leaders of the putsch.

At the beer hall itself, Hitler, Ludendorff, Goering and
Hess stood amid the dregs of the night before and it was
now not just the stench of stale beer and cigar smoke
which was bringing the sick look to their faces. Things
were suddenly going wrong, and they did not seem able to

decide what to do about it. They had made a rendezvous with General von Lossow at the beer hall at dawn, but he had not come. Repeated messages had been sent to him, but none of the emissaries had come back with an answer. (They could hardly do so. They had been arrested.)

Soon they knew the worst. A radio message from army headquarters to Berlin was intercepted, and the putschists learned not only that the triumvirate had gone back on their word, but that warrants were out for the arrest of Hitler, Ludendorff, and other putschist leaders. This was followed by messages brought in from outlying parts of the city and from the railway station reporting the arrival of Reichswehr reinforcements. But the arriving troops did not have a pleasant reception from spectators now beginning to gather in the streets, most of whom seemed quickly aware of the anti-putschist nature of their mission, and very much on the side of the National Socialists.* They shook their fists and howled with rage at the troops and one Reichswehr officer afterward wrote of the crowd:

"As we marched through the Maximilianstrasse we were showered with names: 'Pfuie! Jew defenders! Betrayers of the Fatherland. Bloodhounds! Heil Hitler—down with Kahr!' etc. As we crossed the Odeonsplatz, the passers by roared, whistled, howled and threatened with their fists . . ."

What were the rebels to do now? Both Hitler and Ludendorff knew that once they had lost the support of the Reichswehr their enterprise was in danger. Though they had a certain number of arms and had received a certain amount of training, they were in no position to fight regular troops, who could bring up field guns and armored cars against them. Suddenly the self-confident Adolf Hitler seemed to be grasping for a decision. He tentatively suggested that the Nazi forces should be grouped together and a retreat begun toward Rosenheim, to the south, and that emissaries meanwhile be sent to Prince Rupprecht, asking him to mediate with Von Kahr and Von Lossow.

Ludendorff shook his head. "We will march on the city," he said.

---

* Von Lossow had attempted to ban any newspapers carrying accounts of the previous night's meeting in the Bürgerbräuhaus, especially those describing his own part in the proceedings and the enthusiastic reaction of the audience, but a number had found their way to the streets.

Someone at once interjected that if they did that their passage through would be blocked by troops, who would open fire.

A look of scorn passed over Ludendorff's face. "The heavens will fall before the Bavarian Reichswehr turns against me," he said.

Not only did Ludendorff believe it, Hitler believed it too. That any soldier or policeman of the Reich would dare to turn his gun against a national hero of Ludendorff's stature was unthinkable. The thought of his invulnerability comforted the Nazi leaders in this chilly morning of doubt and disillusion, and suddenly they began to be optimistic again.

Yes, Ludendorff had the right idea. They would march. They would assemble the SA men and all the followers of the Party, and they would move in a solid phalanx across the bridge over the Isar into the city. And they would defy the Reichswehr or the police to hold them back.

Hitler was so sure that they could restore the situation by this demonstration—and so sure of the magic of Ludendorff's mystique to protect them—that he told Goering to assemble the SA men and the storm troopers in the beer hall, and there, with the bemedaled general standing at his side, he made the men swear a solemn oath of allegiance to Ludendorff. It was a shrewd psychological move and it restored a sense of unity, of commonness of purpose, to a force that was beginning to be permeated with defeatism.

Now they moved out of the Bürgerbräuhaus into the square and the surrounding streets, and formed themselves into a column. The signal was given and they began to march. At their head was an SA man carrying a huge party flag flying the swastika emblem of the Nazis. Behind marched SA men and storm troopers with their rifles slung over their shoulders. And in the front rank were the leaders: Ludendorff in the center, Adolf Hitler on his right and Hermann Goering on his left, then Ulrich Graf, Max von Scheubner-Richter (a Nazi district leader), and Ludendorff's aide-de-camp, Major Hans Streck.

The first crisis for the marchers came when the great column reached the Ludwigsbrücke, the bridge over the river Isar. A force of Bavarian police was waiting there with orders to stop them from crossing, their guns raised. Hermann Goering had anticipated this. More skeptical than his leader about Ludendorff's invulnerability, he was marching with none of the confidence the others felt over the attitude the Reichswehr would adopt toward the Nazis when the confrontation came. He was afterward to say that he always knew what would happen. And Goering knew how to deal with the policemen guarding the bridge.

While the column halted, he went forward to talk with Lieutenant Georg Höfler, the commander of the guard, and gesturing to a little group of bent and rather frightened-looking men a few yards down the column, he explained that these were the hostages of the putschists, the ministers and police chiefs whom they had taken into custody the night before. If the police opened fire, he explained, he had given orders for the hostages to be shot.

"There are some of my men who have promised to beat them to death," he added. "Of course, I do not want this to happen. They are decent, family men."

The police fell back and the column marched across the bridge into the city.† And now it was a triumphal progress all the way. Munich had turned out in force to greet the marchers, and there was no doubt about the way they felt about them. To the sound of cheers and shouts of "Heil Hitler!" they reached the Marienplatz and proceeded up the Residenzstrasse, the swastika flag waving and the men behind singing. Ludendorff had a smile of satisfaction on his face. Adolf Hitler was lifting his hand in a shoulder salute to acknowledge the plaudits of the crowd.

The Residenzstrasse is narrow, and the column was crammed together, pressed shoulder to shoulder, as it made its way toward the wide-open space of the Odeonsplatz at the end. But at the end a cordon of police was waiting, blocking the way.

Hitler made a signal to Ulrich Graf, who rushed forward ahead of the others and shouted to the captain of the guard: "Don't shoot! General Ludendorff and Adolf Hitler are coming!"

But the commander, Michael Freiherr von Godin, had received the strictest orders from his chief, Colonel von

---

† This appears to be the first time Hitler realized that the hostages were with them. Not wishing to have martyrs on his hands—non-Nazi martyrs, that is—he ordered their immediate return to the beer hall. They remained there until released by the Reichswehr.

Seisser, that at all costs the Nazi column was not to be allowed through. Had it passed, anyway, Reichswehr troops were waiting for it at the Feldherrnhall. But they were not necessary. As the brown-shirted phalanx of SA men moved nearer, Von Godin raised his voice and shouted: "Fire!" When his men hesitated, he seized a gun and leveled it at the column, shouting "Fire!" once more. This time there was a volley of shots.

Scheubner-Richter, marching beside Hitler, took a bullet through his head and fell at his Fuehrer's feet, and Hitler stumbled and went down with him. Hermann Goering ducked but felt the thud and the sharp, burning pain of a bullet in the thigh, and then he too was down on the cobbles. There came another volley and a short reply from the Nazis, and then the rest turned and fled for cover.

Only General Ludendorff and his aide, Major Streck, continued to march, heads held high, as if nothing going on around them was their concern. General Ludendorff had refused to believe that anyone would dare to fire at him, and now that they were doing so, he ignored them.

He marched into the arms of the police, who took him into custody. A small car rushed up and snatched Hitler from the spot where he was crouching beside his dead associate, Scheubner-Richter. His shoulder had been wrenched as he fell to the ground, and since there was a warrant out for his arrest, he was taken to a hiding place in a country cottage owned by Putzi Hanfstaengel. There the police arrested him a few days later.

Hermann Goering, bleeding badly from bullets which had gone in at the groin and the hip, was carried by some of his SA men into the house of a furniture dealer, whose wife, Frau Ilse Ballin, and her sister had fortunately had some wartime training in nursing. They removed his breeches and cleaned up the wounds as best they could, and then stanched the flow of blood with towels. The Ballins were Jewish and they knew who Goering was and what his party stood for, and they were also aware that he was a wanted man; but these facts neither diminished the quality of the care they gave him nor tempted them to call in the police. They kept him with them until night had fallen, in the meantime making contact, at Goering's urgent request, with a Nazi sympathizer, Professor Alwin Ritter von Ach, who operated a clinic in the city. He was carried there, his wound cleansed but still bleeding, in the early hours of November 10.‡

Out in the Odeonsplatz the bodies were being cleared away. Three members of the police had died, and sixteen members of the National Socialist Party. The sixteen Nazis were all young and they came from all walks of life. They were good material for martyrdom—and martyrs are what the Nazis would make them in the days ahead.

But meanwhile, the Beer Hall Putsch had failed, its leaders were on the run, and everywhere men were writing off National Socialism as a force for the future in Germany.

So far as Hermann Goering was concerned, the future could not have looked blacker.

‡ Goering never forgot the ministrations of the Ballins, and he tried to repay his debt to them later.

VII. HOOKED

Fanny von Wilamowitz-Moellendorff, Goering's sister-in-law, had been in the Odeonsplatz when the firing began, and she had seen the National Socialists scattering for their lives as their leaders fell beneath the volley of police bullets. She could not get near enough to Goering to find out what had happened to him, and since a roundup began immediately of Nazis and spectators alike, she decided to go back to Obermenzing.

Once there she was unable to tell Carin for certain whether her husband was alive or dead, only that the putsch had failed and its supporters were on the run. Carin Goering, though still running a high fever, got up at once and began to dress. She seemed to have no doubt that Hermann Goering was still alive, and she sat patiently with her sister, waiting for news.

It reached them in the early hours of the morning when an SA man arrived to tell them that Goering was safe in Professor von Ach's clinic. Despite doctor's orders that she was in no circumstances to venture out into the raw winter night, Carin called immediately for a car and was with her husband half an hour later. The relief at seeing her was such that Goering, who had been in considerable pain, fell asleep almost at once, his hand in hers. Her sister Fanny was astounded at the change which had come over Carin, for only a few hours before she had been a semi-helpless invalid with high fever and an occlusion of the lungs.

"Now Carin is quite calm," Fanny wrote, "full mistress of the situation and of herself. She sits quite still in the sickroom, her hand in his, her eyes never leaving his face for a single moment, and all the time she is thinking hard. For every moment that passes is crucial to his destiny."

Fanny kept popping in with news from outside. The whole population was with them, she said; but unfortunately power was now in Von Kahr's hands, and the chase was on for Hitler and his followers. General von Lossow had personally signed the order for the capture of Hermann Goering, dead or alive. Fanny wrote:

"Every second is costly, Carin knows. Plans must be made quickly, friends alerted. Hermann Goering must be got out of the city before daybreak, even at the risk of his life, even if the bleeding starts again and the pain is unbearable. Carin gives not a single thought to herself, to the fact that she is just out of a sick bed, feverish, her heart palpitating, her lungs choked! Now *his* heart has felt the dagger's stab, and will never be the same again. She must save him."

With the help of the remnants of Goering's own body-guard of SA men, he was smuggled into a car and taken out of Munich to friends of Carin's who lived at Garmisch Partenkirchen, some sixty miles south of the capital. He was put to bed in the friends' villa and stayed there for two days, but soon news spread through the town that the famous Hermann Goering was there, and crowds began to gather outside, cheering and demonstrating in favor of the Nazis.

"We found it best to leave and get across the frontier into Austria," Carin wrote to her mother on November 13, 1923. "We got as far as the frontier in a car but there were arrested, and armed police took us back to Garmisch. On every side there were great crowds who cried out 'Heil Goering!' but had nothing but mockery and whistles for the police, who were on the verge of being lynched by the indignant crowd. Sick though he was, Hermann had to quiet them and point out that the police were only doing their duty. During the whole journey in the car, and you can guess how hard it was for him to endure, his only thought was that I should not be alarmed or frightened, and he was marvelous in the way he bore the mental and physical pain he was feeling."

Back at Garmisch the police took possession of his pass-port and conveyed him to the local hospital, which was then ringed around with police and other guards. Goering had given his word of honor that he would not escape, but Carin with hard female logic pointed out that the authorities to whom Goering had given his word (Gustav von Kahr et al) had already broken their word to Hitler and to him, and he must therefore have no compunction about going back on his pledge. In the meantime, with the help of friendly policemen and disguised SA men, a false passport was procured for him and an escape plan worked out.

"It was like a miracle," she wrote to her mother. "Hermann was carried (he cannot walk a step) to a car and then, clad only in his nightshirt under a fur coat and rugs, was driven off and within two hours his false passport had taken him across the frontier. I don't dare to tell you how it was arranged, that will have to wait until I see you. Our flight from Munich was so precipitate that I had only time to pack a tiny handbag, every moment was so precious. Dear Mama, you can understand how it has all been!!! This has been a time when we have learned how God can still help, and how many people have we learned to love! So many have helped us, with great sacrifice and danger, and that we will always remember, I think."

She went on: "Mama, you must not think that Hitler's cause is lost, that they have given up, no, just the opposite, the drive is stronger than ever before. And he will win, I feel it, I know it, we have not seen the end yet. I dare not write and tell you everything, but you will see that we too, in our prosaic times, will live to see miracles. And that this first misfortune will make the final victory deeper, richer and more serious."

She added a postscript counseling her mother to write to her at Innsbruck in double envelopes, the outside one to be addressed to their doctor, since letters addressed to Goering were being opened.

On November 21, 1923, she wrote again from Innsbruck to say that his wound was improving and his temperature had dropped, but that he was still weak from loss of blood and was finding it hard to sleep.

"Here in the hospital," she went on, "a stream of people come in from morning until evening, bringing gifts and invitations to go and stay with them and thanking him for what he has done for Germany . . . Hitler's sister (Paula) was here the day before yesterday, a fascinating, volatile creature with great soulful eyes in a white face, all a-tremble with love for her brother . . . The work goes on and new members are joining as never before, and thousands of workers are writing in, condemning Kahr's treachery and his broken word. The weapons have been safely hidden, the combined efforts are warm and intensive, and despite the difficulties the different [SA] regiment commanders report to and political conferences take place with Hermann personally or by courier. . . . Thirty of the leaders have been arrested [by the Kahr government] and all have been offered amnesty if they will give their word to stop working for us, but they have all refused . . ."

In the weeks that followed the failure of the putsch, the National Socialists established a regular underground service between Munich and Austria, where several other leaders, including Rudolf Hess and Putzi Hanfstaengel, had also found refuge. Couriers brought messages from Hitler and instructions for liaison with the Austrian Nazi Party, and others, who were smugglers by profession, emptied the Goering house at Obermenzing of its clothes and ornaments and brought them through the snow-covered passes to the Goerings. But the Kahr government had blocked the Goering bank account and seized most of their valuables. All over Germany now there was a large poster to be seen with Goering's photograph on it and the offer of a reward for information leading to his capture. In December 1923, Carin Goering's name was added to the list of those whose arrest was being sought for implication in the beer-hall plot.

There had been a temporary improvement in the condition of Goering's wound, but by the beginning of December there was a relapse in his condition. One of the bullets had stopped just short of an artery and, in ricocheting off the cobblestones, had carried a good deal of dirt and stone-splinters into the flesh. The hard work of Frau Ballin and her sister had failed to cleanse the wound properly, and it had healed over with a good deal of dirt left inside.

"Hermann goes badly," wrote Carin on November 30 to her mother. "His leg hurts so much he can hardly hold on. Four days ago the wounds that had healed broke out again. A strong formation of pus in the leg itself. He was X-rayed and several pieces of bullet and bits of stone from the street were found deep inside the muscles of his thigh. They operated on him under chloroform, and for the past three days he has been running a high fever, his mind wandering into fantasy, weeping, dreaming of street fighting, and suffering indescribable pain. The whole leg is covered with rubber tubes to draw out the pus. He is so sweet, so patient, so good, but in his heart he is deeply unhappy. . . . I have been living by his side for three days, here in the hospital. The most skillful professor in the land is looking after him, and I pray to God that He can help us through this bad time and the difficult days that we will have to bear. We have no future plans—we can't make any."

The pain which Hermann Goering was enduring at this time will figure several times more in this chapter, because it has an important bearing on his development in the years to come. Doctors who have been consulted on the wound from which Goering was suffering at this time all agree that the pain in the groin which it can produce is often well-nigh unbearable. There is no particular evidence that Goering was extrasensitive to pain, and he is known to have endured the wounds he received during the air battles of World War I with considerable fortitude. It is even likely that at this stage in his life he was in a better position to bear pain, and more determined to do so without complaining, than most men.

Nevertheless, every letter from Carin Goering from now on mentions the terrible nature of the pain which he was now experiencing. True, she played it down in her letters to her mother, but in writing to her sister Lily on December 8, 1923, she poured her heart out.

"I am sitting here in the sickroom," she wrote, "by my beloved Hermann, and I have to watch how much he is suffering in body and in soul. And there is hardly anything I can do to help him. You know how that can feel. The wound is nothing but pus, over the whole of the thigh. It hurts so much that he lies there and bites the pillow, and all I can hear are inarticulate groans. You can understand how this cuts into my soul. Today it is just a month since they shot at him, and though they are giving him morphine every day now it does nothing to diminish the pain. It is two weeks since I left the hotel to be here in the hospital, and I feel so much easier being here with him all the time."

She added: "Our villa in Munich is now being watched. Our letters are being opened, our bank account blocked, our automobile seized. Everything will no doubt work out in the end. It is just that Hermann is so desperately ill and

I can do so little to straighten things out with my poor German."

Gradually the wound began to respond to treatment but the pain stayed, and the morphine injections were increased to twice daily. On Christmas Eve 1923, Goering was at last allowed to leave the hospital though he had to use crutches and, in Carin's words, looked "sick, lost and white as snow. I hardly know him, he has changed so much, and he says scarcely a word—he is so cast down by this reverse, in a way that I never imagined would happen. But I hope that his spiritual balance and his old energy will return once he finds his strength again."

They moved into the Tiroler Hof in Innsbruck and found, when they reached their hotel bedroom, that well-wishers had sent them a Christmas tree decorated with red, white, and black ribbons. Carin had bought him no Christmas present because "it would only have reminded him that he could not buy one for me," so she sat beside him on the bed until he fell into a restless sleep. Then, unable to bear looking at him any longer and pitying him in his painful and miserable exile, she went outside for a breath of air. She took little notice of the fact that a full-scale snowstorm was blowing and walked aimlessly around until, from one of the houses, she heard a harmonium and a violin playing "Stille Nacht, heilige Nacht."

"So wonderful and strange was it," she wrote her father, "that suddenly everything in me was at peace. Naturally I wept but at the same time I was full of confidence again. I hurried back to Hermann, was able to summon up the courage to wake him, and then helped him to find the incentive to go on—and two hours later we both of us were sleeping the sleep of tranquillity."

But next morning she discovered that standing too long in the snowstorm had taken its toll, and she was running a high fever. Now both of them were confined to bed.

The Von Kahr government was by this time preparing for the trials of Adolf Hitler, Ludendorff, and others implicated in the Beer Hall Putsch, and Hitler's lawyer came to Innsbruck several times to talk to Goering to get his help in building up the defense. Suddenly Rudolf Hess, unable to bear being separated from his beloved Fuehrer any longer, slipped across the border and gave himself up to the authorities, so that he too could stand beside Hitler when the trial began.

Hermann Goering was sorely tempted to do likewise, and no doubt visions passed through his mind of himself hobbling on crutches into the dock, the wounded hero defiantly facing his accusers; but when he wrote to Hitler (in a letter smuggled into jail) and suggested that he should return, he was speedily told to banish the idea from his mind. It may well be that Hitler had visions of martyrdom himself and had no intention of being upstaged by his second-in-command, but he simply pointed out that there was work to be done for the Party outside, and that Goering's arrest would benefit no one but the hated Gustav von Kahr.

So far as the people of Bavaria were concerned, Von Kahr's actions against the Nazis were not forgiven and, after his arrest of Hitler and Ludendorff, his hold on the populace loosened rapidly. Early in 1924 he resigned. Von Lossow, who was also unpopular, was replaced as commander of the Reichswehr in Bavaria, and in the elections in Bavaria, Franconia, Thuringen, and North Germany the National Socialist candidates badly beat the Communists and in several places were second only to the Social Democrats. For the first time they were entitled to seats in the Reichstag in Berlin. Goering fretted with frustration at the fact that he was not among them, but repeated applications for an amnesty had been turned down and he was forced, for the time being, to stay on in exile. But the news of the rising power of the Nazis ("half a million more members in Bavaria than before the putsch!" exulted Carin) seemed to help him both in body and in spirit. He had not lost the pain and was still being given morphine injections against it, but he could get around with a stick now and something of his old energy had returned. He moved a great deal between Innsbruck, Salzburg and Vienna, where he was in contact with National Socialist cells and visiting officials from the Party in Germany.

His main worries during this period were about Carin and money. Carin had not improved since her experience in the snowstorm, and her heart was giving her trouble. She stayed in bed for long stretches at a time, and to keep her occupied the local Nazis bought her a typewriter on which she typed their bulletins and memoranda. Those who saw her at this time say that she had never looked lovelier, for the fever brought color to her cheeks and a fire to her magnificent eyes, and Hermann Goering was perhaps even more madly in love with her than ever.

But money was lacking, both for themselves and for the Party. With their bank account still frozen in Munich, they had to rely upon the charity of friends and associates for their day-to-day needs. Not that they lacked for all the food and comfort they needed. Far from it.

"We are living well here in Innsbruck in this hotel, the best in the town," Carin wrote to her mother on February 20, 1924. "The owner is a Hitler man and lets us live here at cost price. We have a large bedroom with bath and a splendid living room. The food is very good, we eat à la carte, and we get 30 percent off everything we order! The waiters are all storm troopers and adore Hermann . . . There was a time when we couldn't pay for anything, and they told us not to think about it . . . Whatever Hermann could pay they would give to the Hitler movement anyway. Don't you think that is magnificent??!!"

The money so given would come in useful, for the Party was badly in need of funds to take care of the expenses of the coming trial of Hitler, Ludendorff, and the others. All the advocates announced that they were giving their services free, but leaflets were being printed, propaganda made, and the exchequer was empty after the elections. One of Goering's tasks was to approach wealthy Austrians, especially those with interests in Germany, and wheedle out of them sums for the National Socialist coffers.

It was these activities as much as politics which attracted the attention and the distaste of the Austrian Government, anxious not to see precious currency being drained out of the country in favor of a foreign movement. One of Goering's chief agents and collectors, a lieutenant named Rosbach, who had been an SA commander in Bavaria and marched during the putsch, was arrested in Vienna and charged with carrying a false passport. Shortly afterward detectives visited Goering in Innsbruck and politely suggested that it was perhaps time for his "convalescence" to come to an end. They gave him no ultimatum or time limit, but hinted that it would be best perhaps not to tarry too long.

Carin Goering had been longing for some time to visit

her mother in Sweden, for Baroness von Fock had recently been taken to a sanitarium,* and only her own illness had kept her from making the journey. She was homesick, too, for a sight of her son, Thomas, and now that an amnesty had been refused and they had been asked to leave Austria, perhaps she and Hermann would be able to go together.

"So long as the trial lasts I want to stay here," wrote Goering to Baroness von Fock on February 22, 1924, "but if thereafter there is no prospect [of returning home] we would like to take a ship to Sweden via Italy, Italy being so much cheaper and more beautiful than Austria. I have already thought that it might be better eventually to sell our villa [in Munich] and ship our furniture to Sweden, where we could then rent a place to live . . . Perhaps I will be able to find work in Sweden until it is possible to return to Germany. I only want to go back to a national Germany, and not to this Jew republic they have now. I love Sweden above everything, and there I will be in the front line of Germanism where every house has the clean feel of our common heritage. Also I dearly wish to go with Carin and be with you all, who have been so sympathetic and good to us. It has been Carin's wish for some time to be with her family and her friends, after all the excitement and self-denial of the past month . . . Once more accept my deepest thanks and the assurance of how happy I am to be allowed to call you Mother."

The trial of Adolf Hitler and his fellow putschists began in Munich on February 26, 1924, and ran for over a month. At the end of it Adolf Hitler was sentenced to five years in Landsberg Jail and so was Rudolf Hess. General Erich Ludendorff was acquitted, the jury commenting that he had obviously been so overwrought at the time that he could not have known what he was doing. He stormed out of court, his medals jingling (he had worn uniform throughout) and announced: "I consider my acquittal a disgrace to the uniform and the medals I wear."

Hitler was cheered by a great throng of Nazis and sympathizers as he and the faithful Hess were driven off to begin their sentence. So far as the Fuehrer was concerned, the trial had gone well, because (unlike Ludendorff, who

* None of the Von Fock family was exactly a pillar of health and strength.

had fished for lame excuses) he had boasted of his part in the putsch and impressed the audience and newspaper readers by his bearing. It was already strongly hinted that he would not have to serve the whole of his sentence, and he was received by his jailers as if he were an honored guest.†

Hermann Goering had gone on hoping so long as the trial was in progress that its outcome would lead to his own amnesty, but the jail sentence to Hitler put an end to that hope. He was suddenly plunged into the old depths of depression, and his leg wound began giving him trouble again. It was stiff and painful and he was finding it difficult to get around.

Carin wrote to her father that she was "dying of home-sickness" for Sweden, but that she must first make the journey to Munich in order to try to raise some money there for their stay in Italy and their voyage home. Leaving Goering in the hospital, where his wound was to be examined, she arrived in the Bavarian capital in mid-April and went immediately to the villa in Obermenzing. It had now been desequestered as had Hermann's car, and this latter she sold to the Party in order to add to the savings she was now able to draw out of their bank account.

She was back in a few days and pleased to find Goering had recovered his mobility and was not in such pain, "but he never stops being nervous." At the end of the month they set forth for Italy, and, Carin hoped, an end of the long nightmare through which they had been living since the day of the Beer Hall Putsch.

And, for a time, it did indeed seem that Italy would provide them with the therapy they needed. They arrived in Venice on May 4, 1924, and stayed at the Hotel Britannia, on the Grand Canal and only half a minute away from the Piazza San Marco. The director was a German and an admirer of Hermann Goering, so that once more they were able to live and eat well at cut-rate prices. "The food is marvelous," Carin wrote to her mother, "lobster, soup, omelet, chicken with salad, lamb cutlets with spaghetti and fruit for lunch yesterday!"

† He served, in fact, nine months (just long enough for him to finish *Mein Kampf*) and was released in December 1924.

It was the first time either of them had been to Italy and they were ravished by the sun and warmth, the colors and the sounds.

"The lilac is already in bloom and the fruit trees too," she wrote on May 5, 1924. "But everything else blooms so magnificently here. Never in my life have I seen such colors as there are here. One day we bathed in the sea off the Lido. It is just like a dream . . . Yesterday ended with an absolutely heavenly evening, we went out at about 10 o'clock in a gondola, from which dangled a green lamp. The Grand Canal swarmed with gondolas, each with a different colored lamp. And everyone sang. Beguiling and so natural—O God, how romantic it was! In many of the gondolas they had castanets and nearly everyone had a guitar. It is such a different atmosphere here in the South, so much warmer, smoother, more seductive. Bohème, Bajazzo, Toselli's Serenade and others like them all evening, so that one can't sleep, one's heart is so full."

They wandered through the Venetian lanes beside the canals, they visited the islands, the churches, and the shops, and Goering showed off his schoolboy Italian. For Carin it was like a honeymoon and both of them forgot the precarious state they were in and the uncertainty of their future. Though there were reminders.

"Enticing shops, trinkets and jewelry that one must pass by with one's head in the air, lest one weep over one's own poverty!!! And coral!!! And shells and color everywhere, and glassware and genuine and ungenuine antiques. Oh, dear mother, if we had a million it would not be too much!!! But we don't even have a lira!!!"

They managed to raise the fare to go on to Rome by way of Florence and Siena, but in the Italian capital they could find no Nazi sympathizer or Goering fan to offer them luxury hotel accommodation at cheap hotel rates, and they were forced to take lodgings in a small pension. Hermann Goering began the approaches necessary to set up a meeting with the new Italian dictator, Benito Mussolini, whose victorious march on Rome with his Fascist supporters Adolf Hitler had so dearly hoped to imitate with a march on Berlin, had his Beer Hall Putsch succeeded. It took some time, but when the two men did come face to face they liked each other at once. Goering had dosed himself with the painkillers with which the doctors were now providing him, and he was as boisterous and exuberant as his host. But he was too proud to mention the straitened circumstances in which he was now living, and the Duce's information from Germany may have indicated that Goering was now a spent force. At any rate, the Duce made no attempt to arrange another meeting, and Goering returned to his pension and Carin in a state of the deepest gloom.

By this time it would have been hard to recognize in him the gay, brisk, purposeful young man of a year before. There is little doubt that he was undergoing a change in personality and appearance which may have been caused by some glandular disturbance resulting from his wound, and his condition was certainly not being helped by the regular painkilling drugs he was now taking and his staple diet of cheap but fattening pasta. He had begun to look pale, flaccid, and increasingly plump. He was morose and given to flaring outbursts of temper, and it was to spare his beloved Carin from his irritation and restlessness that he went off for long hours at a time, walking the streets of Rome, marching with dogged determination through museums, galleries, and churches, and trying to appease his despair by a crash course in art appreciation.

"I remember once standing before the Trevi fountain at three o'clock in the morning," he told his stepson, Thomas von Kantzow, later, "and wondering what everyone would say if they found me lying at the bottom of it instead of those coins that people throw in for luck. Then I decided that the water was too shallow to drown in, and I did not throw myself in."

This must have been the time when Carin Goering was not with him in Rome, because he would certainly never have contemplated taking his life while she was holed up in their tiny pension. Carin Goering's physical condition was now such that she spent increasingly long hours in bed, and sickness, worry about money, worry about Hermann, and a desperate longing to be back in Sweden had disenchanted her with Italy. The romance had gone out of the place, the colors now seemed garish, the people noisy and brash.

If they were ever to leave, they must somehow get together sufficient money for their fares to the North, and since they had already been living for too long on the

charity of Carin's parents, it was decided that this could
only come from Germany. Suddenly, however, their line of
communication with the Party in Bavaria had been cut,
and it was only by a roundabout means that they learned
why. While Adolf Hitler had been serving his sentence in
Landsberg Jail the Party rolls had been taken over by the
malevolent Nazi philosopher, Alfred Rosenberg, whose in-
coherent writings on race and politics had more than once
been the butt of Goering's contempt. Now Rosenberg re-
venged himself during the Fuehrer's absence by putting
Hermann Goering's name first on the "inactive" list, and
then by expunging it altogether. It was still expunged at the
time Hitler was released, but no one seems to have drawn
his attention to it.

Goering could not go back to Germany himself, and
repeated letters which he wrote received no answers. So it
was decided that Carin, weak and sick though she was,
must make the journey back to Munich to discover what
had been happening and, at the same time, raise money
enough for them to get out of Italy. She left by train at the
beginning of April 1925, but arrived in Munich only to
discover that Adolf Hitler was not in the city. This was a
shock because she knew he had been released from prison.
She did not feel up to a confrontation with Alfred Rosenberg at Party headquarters and drove instead to see General Erich Ludendorff, who was now living in Cölln. He
too was a changed man. He was now in process of being
divorced by his wife and was living with Mathilde Kemnitz,‡ and he was now more than ever under the baleful
influence of that formidable female. Both of them had
become disenchanted with the Nazis and were now obses-
sionally engaged in turning out pamphlets blaming the ills
of the world on the Jews and the dark plots of the elders of
Zion. Like the rest of her family, Carin Goering considered
the Jews an unhealthy element, but the malevolent fanta-
sies of Ludendorff and his mistress were too strong even
for her, and she left Cölln without asking their help in
getting Goering restored to the Party.

Hitler finally returned to Munich and agreed to see
Carin on April 15, and, as always in the presence of a
pretty woman, he was charming and attentive and listened

‡ They later married.

with the appearance of deep sympathy to her story of
Hermann's misadventures since the failure of the Beer Hall
Putsch. He professed to be completely amazed at Rosenberg's action in removing Goering's name from the membership list and said it would be restored at once (it was),
and in response to her sorry story of the state of their
finances he went to a cupboard in his office and pulled out
a pile of notes, in lire, marks, and Austrian schillings, and
thrust them into her hands. But Carin was later to say that
she had the feeling that Hitler had forgotten about her and
Hermann Goering's troubles the moment she left his office.
This was probably the case, for there had been a good deal
of plotting and intriguing by members of the Party during
his imprisonment, and he was preoccupied with the need to
restore the situation and reassert his supremacy.

Carin came back with funds and with a signed photograph of the Fuehrer inscribed "to the respected wife of
my SA Commander." It showed a raincoated Hitler staring
emotionally into the future, and Carin henceforth carried it
wih her wherever she went, putting a sprig of edelweiss
beneath it whenever she propped it on her dressing table or
mantelpiece.

Within a month of her return they were on their way to
Sweden, via Austria, Czechoslovakia, Danzig, and Poland.
For Carin Goering it was a joy to be home, to embrace her
family, to be reunited with her beloved son Thomas. But
for Hermann Goering it was the beginning of purgatory.
He stood pale and flabby in the revealing Scandinavian
sunshine, a hero badly frayed around the edges as he tried
to summon up for his in-laws some of his old bounce and
charm. He could see that it did not deceive them and that
they were shocked by his physical deterioration.

They would have been even more shocked had they
known that he was at the moment under the influence of a
morphine injection he had given himself a short time before, and that he would look much worse when the effect
of it had worn off. For he was now a morphine addict.

VIII. CURE

Thomas von Kantzow was thirteen years old when his mother and her new husband arrived back in Sweden. He was a lonely child and he had suffered badly during the separation from Carin, for his love for her amounted to an obsession, a fixation; now that she was back, his only thought was to stay together with her and never be parted again. It did not seem to have occurred to Carin (and it certainly did not occur to Thomas at the time) that this must have been extremely hurtful to her ex-husband, Nils von Kantzow, and that even had the situation in the Goering household been normal he would have resented the fact that Thomas now wanted to spend every moment of his time with Carin and the man who had taken her away from him.

But the situation was far from normal, and the condition of the Goerings was soon going from bad to worse.

Carin Goering's physical state worsened considerably shortly after her return to Sweden. Considering how many things were wrong with her now—weak lungs, bad heart, low blood pressure—it is amazing how little, unlike her husband, she showed of her condition. She was if anything more beautiful than ever before, illness and languor imparting an ethereal air to her that affected everyone who saw her. For the first weeks of her return she appeared at many parties and dinner tables with her husband, but she was soon showing signs of an epileptic condition, a sort of *petit mal*, which manifested itself by sudden faints or periods of unconsciousness of which she was completely unaware when she came to. She was advised by her doctors to spend even more time in bed.

Hermann Goering started off well by cutting his morphine injections to two a day, one when he awoke and one when he went to bed. The stiffness in his leg made walking difficult and the pain in his groin was considerable, but he did a great deal of tramping around Stockholm in those early days in search of some sort of position. It is surprising that the Von Focks and the Von Rosens, both of whom were rich and influential, could do nothing to help him to find a job, and his sister-in-law, Fanny, simply says:

"This was a really bad time for Hermann Goering. In Sweden there was a great deal of unemployment; from the Baltic states and from Russia too a great number of refugees had come flooding in. All of them hoped for work, or at the worst charity, from the socialist government. For this capable officer, known to have been involved in a revolt, things were much more difficult. Civil jobs, particularly in aviation, were few and far between, and there were far too many applicants when one came along. Goering did his best, and you can't ask of a man more than that."

The Goerings had taken the lease of a small apartment in the old part of the city, and they had brought over most of their furniture from Munich. They had money in the bank from the sale of the villa at Obermenzing, and with Carin's small income from her ex-husband and considerable economy they had enough to live on. But Goering's enforced idleness became daily more difficult for him to endure, and he was soon eating his heart out with frustration over his exile and homesickness for Germany. The Party seemed to have forgotten about him entirely, and all he knew about their doings was from what he could read in the newspapers, most of them hostile to the Nazis.

His abject spirits were soon affecting him physically, and he went back to injecting himself four, five, and six times a day. He had brought a considerable stock of morphine with him from Austria and Italy, and the Swedish doctor whom he consulted gave him a prescription for further supplies against the recurrent pain from his old wound. The pain was genuine enough, but soon it was a moot question whether it came because Goering needed to take morphine or vice versa.

Morphine addiction is not exactly a pleasurable experience, even when the drug has taken effect. It gives its victim no moments of euphoria or ecstasy, and its after-effects are deeply depressing. In the case of Hermann Goering, there is some evidence that he was allergic to it and should never have been given it in the first place, for only the heaviest doses put him out of pain. Lesser amounts induced sleeplessness, nervous crises, and ungovernable spasms of rage, during which he shouted and raved and threw articles about the room. Carin Goering became increasingly appalled at his behavior, and it is a measure of his deep affection for her that when she looked at him reproachfully during one of his outbursts he never once laid a violent hand on her; she was luckier than she knew.

It was against this background of sickness, pain, and torment that young Thomas von Kantzow began to haunt the Goering apartment in the Odengatan. He too never became the victim of Goering's increasingly violent outbursts, and he was to say later:

"He must have made an enormous effort to be normal whenever I was there, for he was just the same jolly fellow I had known as a young child. He made jokes for my benefit and didn't mind when I laughed at his Swedish, and whenever I said something he listened gravely and replied very seriously to everything I said."

But Thomas preferred to be alone with his mother and the bond between them was such that he would often play truant from school in order to spend the day with her. It was this habit which alerted Nils von Kantzow to the fact that his son was, in his opinion, seeing too much of Carin, and he sent her a note mildly suggesting that she space out his visits in order not to interfere with his schooling. In the meantime, he or a servant from now on escorted Thomas to and from school to make sure that he was not slipping away to his mother.

Carin Goering reacted to this in a fashion which was both thoughtless and stupid. Nils von Kantzow was trying to be fair. In many ways, he was almost too good to be true. He had behaved like an officer and a gentleman by giving Carin her divorce the moment she asked for it, and had gone on making her a monthly allowance. He had allowed her unlimited access to her son so long as she was in Sweden. If he had felt any jealousy or resentment toward Goering for taking away his wife, he had always been meticulous in concealing it.

But now Carin called in the family lawyers and instructed them to apply to the courts on her behalf for custody of her son, making the point that she was now permanently in Sweden (she was determined not to leave again if Thomas was given to her) and that Thomas was badly in need of the motherly care which he was not getting in Nils von Kantzow's bachelor establishment.

It is just possible that Von Kantzow would have made the final sacrifice and meekly handed over his son had he not been genuinely concerned by rumors of what was going on in his ex-wife's home. He knew that the Goering apartment was an extremely modest one, that Carin was unwell and Hermann out of a job. But now he hired a firm of private detectives to confirm other things he had heard, and he was so shocked by their report that he immediately informed the courts that he would fight his wife's custody action with all the resources at his disposal.

He pointed out in his affidavit that his ex-wife, whose state of health had been delicate for some time, had now developed epileptic tendencies and was subject to an increasing number of fits and faints. Her unemployed husband was a man of ungovernable temper and apt to be violent when thwarted, probably owing to an addiction to dangerous drugs. Neither of them was a fit parent or surrogate parent for a sensitive child in the most formative period of his life.

This riposte could not have come at a worse moment, from Carin Goering's point of view. The family records of the Von Fock family do not go into any details of what was happening, and all her sister Fanny writes about it is this:

"Carin's mother . . . tried to help in every possible way, holding out her hands and opening her heart. But she could not prevent grief, misery, sickness and unrest from taking over the Goering home. Carin did her utmost to cheer up the atmosphere and dissipate the gloom. Bit by bit the furniture had to be sold. Sickness and poverty were daily guests in the house. There comes a time in the life of the strongest man when the black waves break over him from every side, when the violence of the storm threatens to carry everything with it . . . Firm and true stood Carin by the side of her beloved husband. Always her thoughts

were on his future and the future of his people. If her heart
condition was bad, so that she must lie prone for hours, or
her fainting fits overcame her and the pain and the misery
were almost too much to bear, she never spoke of it. She
concentrated her thoughts on other things and above all on
him."

What this touching passage conceals is the fact that
Carin's parents and relatives, the Von Focks, had had a
family council just about this time as a result of a report
from the family doctor. Carin Goering's condition was
being daily aggravated by her unhappiness and concern
over her husband, who was by this time showing signs of
acute morphine addiction. The doctor announced that he
could not answer for the consequences if the burden of
trying to cope with her husband was not taken from
Carin's shoulders. The man, he said, was violent, dangerous, so unbalanced that any moment he might kill himself
or someone else.

It was decided that the family should pay for Goering's
medical attention, and a private room was booked for him
at the Aspudden Hospital, where his condition would be
studied. He went willingly enough, for he was quite well
aware of the gravity of his case and, at least for certain
periods at a time, determined to recover. Unfortunately,
none of the doctors at the hospital seems to have realized
how much morphine Goering really needed before he
could numb the anguish and pain he was feeling, nor has
understanding and sympathetic nursing ever been a particular feature of the Swedish hospital system. The plan
was to begin a tapering-off regime that would gradually
wean him from his addiction, but the amount of morphine
they now allowed him was so small in comparison with his
intake that it was tantamount to a cold-turkey treatment,
and Goering reacted accordingly. He asked for drugs and
was told that he must wait until morning for his next
injection; the thought of having to pass a night in hell
moiling in the toils of deprivation made him whimper and
plead. When this did not work and he was bluntly told to
act like a man instead of a sniveling coward, he burst into
an ungovernable rage and leaped at the nurse. He was mad
enough to kill her, but she was rescued in time.

But the police were called, Goering was put into a strait
jacket, examined by two doctors, and formally certified to

be insane.* He was taken to Langbro Asylum for the Insane on September 1, 1925, and spent the next few days
racked by the horrors of deprivation in a padded cell.

Those were the days when a good many medical men
believed that the best and shortest method of curing a drug
addict was by the so-called "cold turkey" treatment,
whereby the patient is taken off the drug completely and
left to sweat it out. It needs a strong body and an even
stronger mind to weather the shock this cruel and drastic
treatment gives to the constitution, and there are plenty of
addicts whose bodies or sanity have failed to survive it.

Hermann Goering survived. The psychiatrist who dealt
with his case at Langbro Asylum was afterward to classify
his patient as "a sentimentalist lacking in basic moral courage." He wrote this after Goering, having endured three
months without drugs, was released and sent home to the
apartment in Odengatan, into a situation where Carin was
in a weaker condition than ever, money was short, and
there was still no job. He went back on drugs and had to
be taken back to Langbro. But at the end of another two
months of complete deprivation, he was cured. He never
took morphine again.† To a solid Swedish psychiatrist this
may not have been impressive, but considering the harsh
grip which morphine addiction had on him together with
the fact that the pain from his old wound was still with him
(and always would be), it would be giving an inadequate
picture of Hermann Goering not to recognize his cure as
an achievement.

He had put on considerable weight during his period of
addiction, and there is little doubt that in some way morphine or the wound in his groin, or both, had unstabilized
his glandular functions. From the summer of 1926 onward
Hermann Goering, now thirty-three years old, can no
longer be thought of as a slim, handsome, young ex-war
hero. He became fat in a way that Thomas von Kantzow,
no matter how strong his affection for him, would hardly
describe as "jolly."

* The certification papers are no longer available in Stockholm,
and are believed to have been handed over to Goering when he
was in Sweden in 1934. But other documentation describes the
nature of his incarceration.
† What he did indulge in later will emerge in this story.

But he was ready to face the world again, and more than ever eager to get back to Germany.

Politics was changing in Germany, and more and more were the parties polarizing toward the left and the right. Ostensibly the nation had a centrally oriented government under the chancellorship of Wilhelm Marx, but it was continually running into difficulties, and the mood was set by the noisy conflicts in the Reichstag between the Communists on the one hand and the Nationalists and Nazis on the other. Field Marshal Paul von Hindenburg had been elected President of Germany in 1925, and he was now eighty years of age and simmering with suppressed rage over the iniquities of the Versailles Treaty and the accusation by the Allies that Germany alone had been responsible for World War I.

In the autumn of 1927 he went to Tannenberg, where one of the great battles of the war had been fought, to take part in the greatest demonstration of patriotic fervor which had been seen in Germany since the war. The occasion was the dedication of the Tannenberg Memorial, a vast arena suitable for military demonstrations, and both Hindenburg and the right-wing parties used it as an excuse for a great propaganda operation.

The aging field marshal traveled to East Prussia, where Tannenberg lies, in the cruiser *Berlin*, which took him from Swinemünde to Königsberg and thus enabled him to travel from Germany proper without setting foot on the hated Polish Corridor, which lay in between. From start to finish, the militaristic, royalistic, and reactionary nature of the demonstration was made clear. Certain veterans' organizations had been invited to take part, including the Nazis, but the Jewish ex-servicemen's association was expressly forbidden to appear. However, all the German generals were there, and they rumbled their approval as Hindenburg cried:

"The accusation that Germany was responsible for this greatest of all wars we hereby repudiate. Germans in every walk of life unanimously reject it. It was in no spirit of envy, hatred or lust of conquest that we unsheathed the sword . . . With clean hearts we marched out to defend our Fatherland and with clean hands did we wield the sword."

He ended by calling on God to bless the German people

and the German royal family and to rid both of them of the injustices with which they had been saddled.

It was a speech broadcast by radio to all parts of Germany, and it aroused intense patriotic feelings wherever it was heard. Hermann Goering read it in the Swedish newspapers and happily told Carin that sanity was returning to Germany, and that the hour of his release must be at hand.

Indeed it was. Shortly afterward a petition was presented in the Reichstag for the freeing of all political prisoners and the amnesty of all political exiles. Since the Communists had several of their number still serving in jail or in hiding abroad, they joined with the right wing to vote the measure through, against the wishes of the Marx government.

His exile was over at last. Hermann Goering was free to return.

He sent a joyful telegram to Adolf Hitler and began preparations for his return. There was no question as to whether or not Carin would go with him, because she was now far too weak to make the journey. But she would not hear of his waiting until she was well enough to travel, and even forced herself to get out of bed and helped him to pack in order to convince him that, though sick, she was mending and would soon be better.

In October 1927, they bade each other a tearful farewell during which Carin Goering was only just able to conceal from her husband the fact that she was on the verge of a complete collapse. The moment his train had disappeared out of the station, she fell back into the arms of her sister, Fanny, and was rushed off to the hospital. For the next few weeks she was gravely ill, but at her insistence the news of her condition was kept from him.

"He has so much to do—so much to catch up," she kept telling her sister. "Worrying about me would make it too much for him to bear."

She was right. It was not exactly as a returning hero that Hermann Goering was greeted when he arrived back in Germany. It was four years that he had been away, and the Party had changed and so had its Fuehrer. In 1923 Hermann Goering had brought to the Party the assets of his glamorous war record, his shining patriotism, and his eagerness to serve, and he had lent prestige to a body of men upon whom the mass of the German public still looked down their noses.

But this was 1927. The National Socialist Party had established itself to such an extent that its name was known the length and breadth of Germany. People were voting for it in elections and there were Nazi members of the Reichstag and the provincial assemblies. Adolf Hitler had earned enormous political dividends from his term in Landsberg Jail and from being a martyr so long as he was incarcerated had emerged a celebrity. His political treatise, *Mein Kampf*, was attracting much attention.

What need did he have of a pale, fat, limping ex-captain without a pfennig to his name in whom the old crusading fire seemed to have been damped down? There were other men scrambling for the high positions in the Party. His old job as commander of the brown-shirted SA had been filled by someone else. Goering's worst enemy in the Party, Alfred Rosenberg, had his hands on much of the political machine and did not fancy having a rival to work with, and both he and Putzi Hanfstaengel, who was an inveterate gossip, saw to it that Hitler was told about the occasions in exile when Goering had criticized Hitler's leadership or joked about his mannerisms. They were well aware that the Fuehrer was ultrasensitive to criticism, and did not easily forgive anyone who ridiculed him or made derogatory remarks.

So what had been envisioned as a triumphant homecoming turned out to be a deflating anticlimax. The upshot of Goering's two interviews with Hitler in Munich was that he should "keep in touch," but that he should concentrate for the time being on finding himself a job in the commercial world that would earn him some money and enable him to re-establish himself.

"And then," said Hitler, "we will see."

Early in November 1927, Goering left for Berlin carrying with him a commission to act as representative there for the Bavarian Motor Works (BMW), which had recently been taken over by an Italian named Camillo Castiglioni, and was trying to re-establish itself as a manufacturer of aircraft engines. The fact that Castiglioni was a Jew did not seem to trouble Hermann Goering, and though the Italian once complained that "Hermann wastes too much time kissing ladies' hands and not enough getting their husbands' signatures on contracts" their association, so long as it lasted, was friendly if not thumpingly successful. Once in Berlin he made contact with a number of wartime colleagues, including his flying comrade, Bruno Loerzer, who had an association with the Heinkel aircraft company and with the fledgling air-transport firm, Lufthansa.

He lived in a small room in a hotel behind the Kurfürstendamm but returned to it only for a few hours every night. But though this scratching around for a position in life took up practically every hour of the day, he never ceased being desperately lonely for Carin, and they poured out their hearts to each other in a series of daily letters. Carin used to read Goering's long screeds to her son, Thomas, and he carried for the rest of his days a clear memory of the romantic passion with which every sentence was laced.

There was no doubt that his love for his frail Swedish bride was as fervid as ever, and that Christmas he could bear the separation no longer and journeyed to Stockholm in order to be with her. But she was still in hospital and it was not until the spring of 1928 that she was at last able to summon up enough strength to join him in the small furnished apartment he had rented at 16, Berchtesgadnerstrasse, Berlin.

Her presence brought him good luck. Prospects began to look brighter again, for Adolf Hitler suddenly showed himself willing to welcome his erstwhile associate back into the inner circle.

IX. THREEPENNY OPERA

There was a cartoon by Karl Arnold published in the Berlin *Tageblatt* the spring of 1928 which sharply summed up life in contemporary Germany. It showed a slim, almost bosomless girl with the latest fashion in short-cropped hair, short skirts, and high heels, facing a very fat man with a large cigar between his lips. Inside the fat man was a skeleton-thin child clinging to the skirts of a ravaged woman with a baby in her arms. The caption said: "Some are fat by choice, some are thin by choice, and others are thin of necessity."

The hit musical of the year was Bertholt Brecht and Kurt Weill's *Dreigroschenoper* (*The Threepenny Opera*), their biting, modernized version of Gay's *Beggar's Opera*. It portrayed Berlin as one vast thieves' kitchen, its hero was a crook, its heroines whores, and honest folk were dolts to be laughed at and ridiculed. Its parallels with what was happening in Germany were too close for it to be regarded as more than slightly farfetched, and the philosophy expressed in the opera's key song, "Mack the Knife," was not entirely foreign to many of those who packed the theater every night.

Berlin was full of foreigners living it up on the pocketsful of marks their dollars, pounds, francs and guilders could buy at the exchanges. There was plenty of entertainment on which to spend it, for all kinds of taste: Elisabeth Bergner and Franz Lederer playing Max Reinhardt's version of *Romeo and Juliet*, Marlene Dietrich in films from the UFA Film Studios, Richard Tauber singing operetta, plays by Gerhardt Hauptmann and Leon Feuchtwanger, new works by Richard Strauss, concerts by Furtwängler and the Berlin Philharmonic, Josephine Baker's brown young body dancing naked at feverish after-dinner parties, and night clubs of every exotic and erotic kind.

But behind this façade of culture and entertainment the Weimar Republic, in which democrats had placed such hopes, was sick of a terminal illness. In the back streets of the working-class quarters of Berlin every weekend, the Communists and the Nazis fought each other with blood-thirsty ferocity, and what the newspapers on Monday would describe as "factional political squabbles" were, in fact, the early rounds of a fight to the death for the take-over of Germany. You did not have to have a sensitive nose to smell the bomb fuse burning, nor a sensitive ear to catch the opening bars of Nero's fiddle.

Like plenty of others of his class, Hermann Goering thrived in this febrile environment. It was an environment in which a smooth talker who had contacts and could put on a show could hardly fail to make a good living. It was a salesman's world and there were buyers everywhere. Galvanized by a desperate eagerness to have money, a position, to win back Hitler's respect, Goering went after every influential connection he had ever made during the war, and shamelessly used them to further his ends.

Soon after arriving in Berlin he ran into an ex-officer whom he had met casually during the war. Paul (Pilli) Koerner was another one of those looking for a place in the flashy world of Berlin. His only assets were a very small allowance from his family and a Mercedes Benz motorcar. They were sufficient for Goering to propose a partnership, so that henceforth he could ride about Berlin to his various appointments in an impressive car with his own private chauffeur, who was, in fact, Pilli. Bruno Loerzer had meanwhile married a rich wife and she was persuaded to give opulent lunches and dinner parties for potential customers of Goering's BMW engines, Swedish parachutes, and other gadgets for which he held the agencies. Soon he felt secure enough to call up his other wartime friend, Prince Philip of Hesse, now married to a daughter of the King of Italy, and use him as an unwitting bait at parties for potential customers.

The success which he began to enjoy brought Hermann Goering's health and good spirits back with a rush, and it was soon hard to credit that less than a year before he had been a whimpering wreck in a Swedish lunatic asylum. Carin thrived too in the glow of her husband's revival, and plainly loved the life they were now leading. Describing

typical days to her mother in a letter dated May 18, 1928,
she wrote:

"Three of Hermann's best friends arrived and carted us
off to one of his lunches. Then we made a three-hour car
journey to a racecourse for cars where we went round the
track at 115 kilometers an hour!!!* Then back to Berlin in
the sunshine and to a lake in the city's suburbs where we
drank tea. Then back home for a half hour's rest, and
afterward to dinner, together with a friend and his wife,
and back at ten to sleep like a log . . . We eat breakfast
here and then out to lunch. This time we had lunch in a
Chinese restaurant where we ate swallows' nests!! And
strawberries on sticks!! Everything tasted marvelous, the
waiter was Chinese!!!"

On one of his trips to Berlin, Adolf Hitler called Hermann Goering to see him at the small hotel, the Sans Souci,
where he always stayed on his visits to the capital. Goering
went with a good deal of eagerness, because new elections
for the Reichstag were in the offing, and he knew that the
Fuehrer was drawing up the lists of Nazi candidates. He
was determined that his name would figure on them, and
not simply because a Reichstag member received a good
regular income, a free first-class railway pass, and a number of other useful perks. His period on the sidelines of the
Nazi Party was the only thing which had marred this period of renewal, and he was determined to force himself
back into the forefront of the Party. His patriotism was
still strong, and despite the merry life he was leading he
was well aware of the shoddy nature of German existence
and of the time bomb ticking in the background. On one
occasion, while lunching at Horcher's, Berlin's best-known
restaurant, he gestured across the room at the well-fed
faces surrounding him, and was heard to say:

"One day we will sweep this all away, and bring justice
back to Germany. It is time we cleared out these blood-
suckers and fed the German people instead."

It did not stop his coming back to Horcher's the next
day, but it did remind his hearers that he still considered
himself to be a Nazi, and one who shared Hitler's recently
published program for a more equitable distribution of
Germany's resources.

* 70 m.p.h.

Now he was eager to jump back on the Hitler band-wagon, and the meeting in the Sans Souci Hotel was of crucial importance to his future plans. Some reports of the meeting between the two men suggest that Adolf Hitler had no intention of offering Goering a candidacy in the forth-coming election, and that it was not he but Goering who had initated the meeting. On the other hand, in a letter which Carin wrote to her son, she told Thomas that "the Fuehrer asked to see his old comrade and welcomed him with open arms, happy to see how well and how prosper-ous (!!) he looked. He asked him to take up the flag again on behalf of the Party, and to fight for Germany's redemp-tion at the elections in May."

Hermann Goering came back from the meeting jubilant at having received an official invitation, and to celebrate he carried off Carin and Paul Koerner for a celebration dinner —at Horcher's, it goes without saying.

"All Berlin has election fever," Carin wrote home on May 18, "and it will be settled on Sunday. They have already begun to shoot each other dead. Each day Com-munists with red flags and hammer-and-sickles on them drag their way through the city, and always there are clashes with Hitler-men carrying their red banners with swastikas on them, so that there is strife, killings and woundings. We have to wait to see how the election goes on Sunday. But it must, it must go well for Hermann, and then we will have a long period of peace. Darling Mama, let your thoughts be with us!"

The campaign Hermann Goering waged in Berlin was short, rowdy, and effective. He was a good speaker, and, when the occasion warranted it, a quietly convincing one. But the Nazis in 1928 were not aiming at quiet or moder-ate voters but determined to stir up emotions and get them-selves elected through the fears and hatreds of the mass public—fear of the Communists, fear of inflation, fear of unemployment and starvation, hatred of the Allies, the French, and the Poles, hatred of the capitalists and the Jews. Goering discovered the knack of rabble-rousing, hav-ing modeled himself closely on Adolf Hitler's technique, and he obviously enjoyed exchanging insults, obscenities and challenges with the Red hecklers who followed him around from meeting to meeting. Considering his family and educational background, he had a surprisingly good

ear for vulgar slang and dialectical humor, and it was when
his mood was at its most sarcastic and jokey that he
seemed to carry his audience along best.

It was a rough election, and when voting closed on the
night of May 20, 1928, the mortuaries in Berlin and Munich were doing extra business and the hospitals were full
of broken heads. Even those Nazis who had not gone down
under Communist riot sticks were holding their heads
when it was all over, because the left-wing combination of
Communists and Socialists had mopped up 40 per cent of
the seats, the Center, the Republicans and the Nationalists
had heavily lost ground, and the National Socialists had
polled only 800,000 votes and garnered a mere twelve seats
in the Reichstag.

But Hermann Goering won one of them, and to Carin
that was all that mattered. She cabled at once to her
mother: HERMANN ELECTED YESTERDAY. MOTHER, YOU
UNDERSTAND. YOUR CARIN.

Among Party members elected with him were Adolf
Hitler himself, Dr. Paul Josef Goebbels, the Nazi district
leader in Berlin, Gregor Strasser, at that time one of the
Fuehrer's closest associates, Wilhelm Frick and General
Ritter von Epp, a regular army officer who had resigned his
commission to fight with the Nazis. In a way, Goering was
pleased at the result of the poll, for no matter how disap-
pointing it might be to the Fuehrer, it at least made the
eleven who had been elected with him the cream of the
leadership of the Party. He began calling himself and the
other Nazi members the Eleven Disciples, and looked forward to taking his seat in the Reichstag as the final confirmation of his reconstitution.

The new Reichstag met on Wednesday, June 13, 1928,
and Carin Goering, radiantly proud, was in the gallery to
see her beloved Hermann seated.

"Hermann had an excellent place reserved for him, next
to General von Epp from Bavaria," she wrote to her
mother next day. "They sat all alone at a table, well forward . . . But [across from them] it was really dismal
having to see so many Red Guards, they have made
unheard-of progress and take up a colossal number of seats
in the Reichstag. They were in their uniforms, wearing
Jewish stars of David, Red stars, it's all the same, and red
armbands etc. Young types, most of them, a pugnacious

lot, perfect criminal types. Aside from Hitler's party, so many of the new members are Jews!"

On the night of the Reichstag opening, Goering was the chief speaker at a "victory" meeting of the National Socialist Party in Berlin, and five thousand turned up to listen to him. Compared with his campaign speeches, his remarks were a reasoned exposition of the Nazi program for ending poverty in Germany and restoring Germany's place in the world, and he was given a roof-lifting ovation when he sat down. He immediately rose again and said:

"If you are so eagerly behind us now, why were you not there at the polls? Next time, make everyone you know vote for us, your wives, your parents, your sisters, your sons and daughters, your girl friends, your illegitimate children, if they're old enough!"

He was given another rousing reception, and drove home with Carin, well pleased with himself. There he found a letter awaiting him from the ex-Kaiser's eldest son, Crown Prince Wilhelm, congratulating him on his election. "Your extraordinary talent, your skill with words and your bodily strength are just what are needed for your new profession of people's representative," he wrote.

What did he mean by that? Carin asked her husband.

Goering grinned and replied that Wilhelm was thinking of all those muscle-bound young Communists who were now crowding the Reichstag, and of the fights that would be coming once they started mixing it with the Nazis.

"Hermann is now so terribly busy," wrote Carin that June, "that I now only see him when he pops in and out. But he gives me all his free time, and at least we can eat together. But I don't think there is a single meal we have had alone, there are always people there, and never less than three. But I love it here in Berlin. I like the people and I love the country so much more than any other, aside from Sweden."

She went on to tell her mother that Goering had relinquished none of his other activities now that he was a member of the Reichstag. He was still working as an agent for several aircraft firms. He was still representing a Swedish parachute manufacturer and "on Sunday or Monday we fly for a few days to Zurich and Bern in Switzerland. Hermann has been asked to give a couple of lectures, and he is also to give a demonstration of the Tornblad parachute. There have been a lot of accidents (with other parachutes) and Hermann is going to show them what the Tornblad can do."

A few days later she was hosting a lunch in Berlin for a group of Swiss generals, majors, and lieutenants who had come down for further conversations, and regretting that it had to be given in a restaurant, so much more expensive than eating at home. For though the financial future now looked considerably brighter, there were debts to be paid from the past, and they were draining all their resources.

"How marvelous it will be when we have our own home!" she wrote. "It's hard that we always have to go out and sell things at such ridiculously low prices. Here in Berlin it is terribly expensive. In restaurants you have to pay considerably extra just for bread, and what you buy in the shops is very much dearer than Sweden."

But fortunes were changing, and soon Carin Goering would no longer have any reason to complain about shortage of money. For one thing, Adolf Hitler had once more recognized her husband as one of the most considerable assets of the Party and decided to use his talents as a speaker to the utmost. He was put on the payroll with a salary of eight hundred marks a month and expenses and sent on speechmaking tours to all parts of Germany where recruits were needed or spirits were flagging. In addition to this, Goering had met and come to a firm arrangement with an ex-army officer named Erhard Milch, who was now head of the German civil airline, Lufthansa, to lobby for the company in the Reichstag. Milch had no doubt whatsoever that he had brought off a considerable coup in persuading Goering to work for his organization.

"His record as a hero of the air war was well known," he said later, "and his postwar experience, in flying planes, in selling engines, in acting as an agent, had given him a shrewd understanding of aircraft and air transport problems. We knew him to be enthusiastically behind our aims as well."

Milch and his wife soon became regular visitors in the Goering household. "In the beginning," said Milch, "we had Frau Carin Goering as our hostess, and she had obviously a great influence on her husband of the best possible kind. In intimate circles Goering was quiet and sympathetic, even when, from time to time, harsh words were said, and I saw through him when he started to brag. I had already come up against his great vanity and egotism, and knew that anyone who wounded his pride would live to regret it."

Henceforward Goering's considerable oratorical talents were used in the Reichstag on behalf of Lufthansa, in return for a retainer of a thousand marks a month. This, added to his Reichstag salary of eight hundred marks a month, plus his Nazi Party subsidy of the same sum, enabled the Goerings to acquire at last the home that Carin had dreamed about. They took a house in the Badenschestrasse, and Carin was so busy choosing the furnishings, traveling with Hermann to his meetings, hosting luncheon and dinner parties for the businessmen, princelings, politicians and bankers whom they were now meeting that she did not even have time to write home to her mother.

At last, after a lapse of several weeks, on February 21, 1929, she got around to writing:

"Recently there has been so dreadfully much to think about, arrange and control . . . Even today Hermann gives his first big speech in the Reichstag, so that I don't have much time for letters, because naturally I shall be there to hear him. Tonight he speaks at Berlin University before students from all the different parties. Since more than half of them are already National Socialists, I hope that he will win over the rest of them! Tomorrow he speaks in Nuremberg and then he goes off on a ten-day trip to East Prussia to make twelve different speeches in twelve different places. The whole house is filled with politicians, and it would be terribly unsettling if it were not all so exciting."

It was Hermann Goering's task by this time to superintend the new policy of the Party, which was to make the Nazis seem respectable, "civilised," bourgeois enough to attract the attention and the sympathy of the influential elements in German life, such as the big industrialists, the bankers, the princelings and aristocrats whose snob value had been by no means diminished by the fall of the monarchy. One of the first to succumb to Goering's blandishments was Prince August Wilhelm, second son of the ex-Kaiser. Goering was soon calling the prince by his nickname, Auwi, but Carin stuck to the more formal approach. Her closest friends in Berlin were now the Prince and

Princess Victor zu Wied, both of whom were taken with
Carin's beauty and charm, amused by the energy and enthusiasm of her husband, and sympathetic with the aims of
the National Socialists. Through both these contacts, the
social world of the Goerings widened, and soon the names
of those who sat around the dinner table at the Badenschestrasse could be found either in the Almanac de Gotha or
Who's Who in Germany.

That did not stop Hermann Goering from making his
new home an open house for any member of the Party, no
matter how rough or humble his origins, who happened to
be in Berlin and looking for shelter, a drink or a meal. The
fact that a princess was apt to find herself with a Bavarian
farm laborer as a dinner partner was soon the talk of
Berlin. It did no harm at all to Goering among the rank
and file of the Party, and it emphasized among his guests
and their friends the democratic make-up of the National
Socialist organization.

"Today I can tell you things in more detail, because
there is more time," wrote Carin to her mother on February 28, 1930. "The [Prince and Princess zu] Wieds are in
the Tyrol to rest for a few weeks. They come back in the
early days of March and I'm certainly happy about that.
They were and are so quietly helpful and true, and I am so
fond of both of them. The Wieds have brought us in touch
with many pleasant families. In the last few weeks so much
has been happening that we have seldom been at home for
a meal, and then only when we have had guests. And that
eats into our strength, Hermann's as well as mine, because
we want to do our utmost. Ordinary living is no longer
possible for us, and we know that, if we are asked, we will
give whatever we can, because that is how we wish it."

So, apparently, did their new friends.

"The Wieds want everyone they know to become interested in the Hitler movement, and Hermann is bombarded
with questions—they are the same old ones, only from
different people. It is an attempt to find chinks in Hitler's
armor, criticisms of his program, etc. And so Hermann
must explain, answer, elaborate to an exhausting degree. . . .
But I can see that it is all for the best, and that the circle
around is constantly growing and that we have already
won many for Hitler and his cause. [Prince] August Wilhelm now follows us, as do the Wieds, together with a

large group of interesting people. Yesterday we had breakfast with Prince Henckel-Donnersmarck, he is forty years
old and is confined to a wheelchair, paralyzed, it is so sad.
He goes to every meeting where Hermann is speaking. We
like him very much and he is so good and intelligent. . . . A
few days ago Baron Koskull was here for lunch, he is at
the Swedish Legation here, and at the same time there were
the von Bahrs, August Wilhelm and two National Socialist
workers, who had come up from Munich and were staying
with us. Later Count Coms arrived with his wife and the
Duchess von K. with daughter. You can imagine what big
eyes the Swedes made of this mixture!!!"

Hermann Goering was drum-beating for the Party all
over Germany now, and recruits were flowing in, from
among the growing army of unemployed workers, from the
bankrupt and disillusioned middle class, and, largely
thanks to the Goerings, from the aristocracy. He was quite
fat now and no longer looked like a Wagnerian hero, but
he had not been so fit since the war, and he thrived on the
challenge that his new activities provided. Carin tried to
keep up, and in the cold of a particularly inclement February she drove one afternoon with Goering to Magdeburg
for an eight o'clock meeting, drove back at midnight and
was not home until six-thirty in the morning. True, while
he went straight to work, she stayed in bed to recover, but
not even love and enthusiasm could bolster her enough to
keep up this pace for long.

The newspapers, particularly the National Socialist
organ, the *Voelkischer Beobachter*, were carrying stories of
the death of a Nazi company leader named Horst Wessel
in one of the bloody clashes with the Communists which
were now a nightly feature of life in the big German cities.
Hitler's chief representative in Berlin, Dr. Josef Goebbels,
had freshened up Horst Wessel's somewhat tainted persona
(he had a murky criminal background) and presented him
as a Nazi martyr, victim of brutish Communist hooligan-
ism. It certainly had its effect on Carin's princely friends.

"Yesterday we had the Wieds for lunch together with
Doctor Goebbels, the leaders of the movement in Berlin,"
she wrote to her mother on March 22, 1930. "The princess
had made a wonderful drawing of a Hitler company on the
march, with swastikas held high, and between the soldiers
one could see the shining shapes of those who had been

murdered by the Communists. The whole effect was so beautiful, so inspiring. I will bring it with me when I come to see you."

But the excitement of the lunch party was such that she was too frail next morning to leave with Goering on a new speaking tour he was making in East Prussia and the Rhineland, this time with Prince August Wilhelm as his companion, who was now "a real and true Hitlermann . . . so modest, helpful, obedient and hardworking."

She stayed in bed with a high temperature and confessed to her mother:

"It is so empty when Hermann is away, and I have a constant yearning for him. I am so alone here, and unlike other women I can't talk about my state of health to my friends and acquaintances. It is only when I think of how I can help him, or the Hitler movement, in some way or other, that strength seems to come to me from above."

That summer she managed to summon up enough strength to attend the Day of the Party congress at Nuremberg, and heard Hitler address the greatest gathering of National Socialists that Germany had seen so far. But she was too weak to join in the festivities and was hurried away the next day with heart trouble to a sanitarium at Kreuth, in Bavaria.

There were new elections coming up once more, and Hermann Goering was on a speaking tour. Carin was writing home from the sanitarium in a tone that sounds as if she were desperately trying to keep her courage up.

"Everyone is so good to me, and it suits me well just to lie here," she wrote. "I wander around or play patience—otherwise I really do nothing. If the sun is shining, I lie out on the balcony. I look out over the mountains, at the sky, at the clouds, it is absolutely still—oh—it gives me such quietness and peace, and I thank God that I have come here."

Desperate over her condition, but unable to break his program at this crucial moment of the election campaign, Goering wrote to her every day. But he did more. He swallowed his pride and wrote to Nils von Kantzow in Stockholm to explain how ill Carin was, and asked him to allow her son Thomas to visit her. He arrived in July 1930, and stayed for ten days with his mother, and he wheeled her through the lanes in a bath chair or motored with her in the mountains. He was eighteen years old now, but his fixation for her had been strengthened by separation, and they were like reunited lovers, rarely out of each other's touch.

"I was very emotional when I left her after ten days," Thomas von Kantzow said later. "I loved my mother very much. But oh, what a mix-up she had made of my life."

By the beginning of September, Carin reported that she was able to read newspapers and magazines, but that books were too heavy for her.

"How strange life is," she wrote to her mother. "It has worked out so differently from what I expected. Life is so much deeper, gives one so much more anguish. There is almost nothing left of the me that used to be, dreamy, remote, hypersensitive. I have become so hard, my skin has thickened, I don't think I could have stood things otherwise . . . I am so happy over my son, he is so good, so chivalrous and mature, because he has suffered so much and learned so much. Mother, how I yearn for you. Do you not feel the wave of longing coming to you from dear, beloved Germany?"

This letter was written on September 9, 1930, the eve of the Reichstag elections. The next day millions of Germans went to the polls and demonstrated that their mood had changed, and their political inclinations with it. When the results were counted, 108 National Socialists had been elected. From a gadfly group, the followers of Adolf Hitler had become overnight the second-largest party in the Reichstag, with a vote of six and a half million behind them.

Carin's room at the sanitarium filled with flowers, and telegrams of felicitation arrived all through the day. Finally, Hermann Goering appeared, glowing with triumph, not only because of the Party's enormous gains but because he had his own personal advancement to announce to her. Hitler, he told her, had appointed him the chief political director and spokesman for the Party.

For Adolf Hitler and his immediate collaborators, 1930 had been a difficult year and there were several moments when his leadership had been threatened and the Party faced by a potential takeover. The conspirators against him were two brothers, Otto and Gregor Strasser, who favored

accession to power by revolutionary means and a program
of militant socialism far to the left of anything proposed
even by the official German Socialist Party. The Strassers
had gained considerable support in the ranks and among
the company commanders of the Brownshirt SA, the
Party's private army, and were becoming dangerously critical of any attempts to make the Nazis seem respectable.
Goering was soon complaining to Hitler that each time he
was on the point of bringing another banker or princeling
into the Party's fold, Otto Strasser sent them scurrying for
cover by a tendentious speech or a sabotage raid on a big
store or factory. Goebbels backed him up with complaints
that his own line of propaganda was being continually
thwarted by Otto Strasser's "red rag" tactics.

Adolf Hitler decided on a showdown with the Strassers,
and at a heated meeting in May 1930, he ordered the
brothers to toe the Party line, and was promptly called a
lackey and a bootlicker by Otto Strasser, who vehemently
refused to back down. There was only one thing to do, and
Hitler did it. Otto Strasser was expelled from the Party,
and went off to form (with a number of dissident SA men)
a splinter group called the Black Front. His brother Gregor
decided to stay with Hitler, a decision he would come to
regret.

No sooner had the Strasser question been solved than
another cropped up, this one involving a large section of
the Brownshirt SA and its leader, Captain Walter Stennes,
who commanded all SA forces in Prussia and East Prussia.
Captain Stennes, an ex-army officer and ex-policeman, had
stayed in the Party after Otto Strasser's departure, but he
too favored an activist line and was convinced that a gun
in the hand was vastly more effective than a vote in the
ballot box. Nevertheless, he and his men had worked hard
during the election campaign, not only at the routine jobs
of guarding their own speakers and sabotaging those of
their rivals, and not only in the street fights with the Communists which once more disfigured the campaign, but at
an activity which he and they considered much more de-
meaning: door to door canvassing on behalf of the Party.

For all this activity, Stennes considered that his troops
deserved some reward. Most of them were poor workers
whose low wages (even with Party subsidies added) bought
them barely enough for their families to eat in the infla-

tionary conditions of Germany at the time. Meantime, rumors spread among them of the life of velveted ease in which some of the Party leaders were living. For some reason, Hermann Goering was not the target of their wrath, but Josef Goebbels certainly was, their resentment of him fanned by stories in the opposition press, not all of them exaggerated, of his amorous philanderings and expensive parties. When Nazi headquarters in Munich refused Stennes' request for an immediate grant to his men and for a considerable augmentation of their weekly subsidy, he called his troops together and marched them into Berlin, where they descended on the newly built Nazi headquarters (where Goebbels presided) and proceeded to sack it. Meanwhile SA men walked the streets, handing out leaflets denouncing Goebbels as a profligate and an embezzler of Party funds.

Since this took place in the last days of the election campaign, nothing could have been more embarrassing for the Nazis. Adolf Hitler was forced to interrupt his speech-making tour and rush to Berlin. The opposition parties were making the most of this internecine squabble, mocking and ridiculing Hitler for the indiscipline inside his Party. For the next few days after his arrival in the capital he neither ate nor slept, but traveled incessantly from one SA headquarters to another, talking to the men, pleading for unity, warning them of the dangers of a schism. He was at his most fervent and eloquent, and he convinced them. Even Walter Stennes was won over and promised to toe the line in future, and since, for the moment, he was too powerful to be sacked, Hitler left him in his command.

But a scapegoat had to be found somewhere, and the over-all commander of the SA, Captain Franz Pfeffer von Salomon, was chosen as the man to put his head beneath the ax. He was not dismissed from the Party but dispatched to Munich, where Hitler could keep an eye on him.

Who would now take over the Brownshirts of the SA? It was a job Hermann Goering had once held and vastly enjoyed. He coveted it again now. In a National Socialist Party now marching toward supreme power, it was a truly powerful position, the key to the domination of the Party. He waited for the Fuehrer to confer it upon him.

He waited in vain. For Adolf Hitler that was far too

simple, and far too dangerous, a solution. His Byzantine mind had already worked out a different approach to the problem. First he announced that he would take over the command of the SA himself for the time being, believing, rightly as it turned out, that the magic quality of his leadership would quell the restiveness of the rank and file for the moment. Then he wrote off a letter to Bolivia to Captain Ernst Roehm, asking him to return to Germany at once.

Ernst Roehm was the regular army officer who had joined the National Socialists during the Munich putsch in 1923. He was a highly capable and fearless soldier, a fierce patriot but an implacable enemy of the Old Guard and the officer class, who, he believed, had lost Germany World War I. Dismissed from the army after the Beer Hall Putsch, imprisoned for a time and then placed on parole, he had become disenchanted with the conditions in Germany and, in 1928, had gone to South America with a contract as an instructor with the Bolivian Army.

Roehm, as Hitler, Goering and Goebbels well knew, was a homosexual. Once he had "discovered" his sexual predilections at the age of twenty-four, he had never, in fact, made any particular secret of them. But to Adolf Hitler's fury, the moment Roehm replied to his letter, saying that he was leaving for Germany at once, a campaign against this "pervert" and "sodomite" began appearing in the German opposition press. Private letters which he had sent from Bolivia to his friends, complaining of his loneliness, of the locals' ignorance of "my kind of love," were printed.

There is no doubt that someone had learned that Hitler intended to appoint Ernst Roehm the new commander of the SA, and had leaked his letters to the press. It could only have been someone inside the Party. There was only one person who was seriously interested in sabotaging his chances and embarrassing Hitler by bringing his homosexual tendencies to the notice of the public, and that was Hermann Goering, who wanted the SA job himself.

But Hitler refused to be embarrassed, or swayed in his judgment. He lashed out at the "vile traducers" of "this honorable fighter for justice" and promised that one day he would obtain expiation for this "filthy and disgusting slander." Meanwhile, Roehm would remain "my trusted chief of staff, now and after the elections."

Hermann Goering swallowed his disappointment with good grace and accepted, instead, the position of *politischer Bevollmächtigter des Fuehrers* (the political representative of the leader). He welcomed Ernst Roehm when he arrived to take over the command of the SA, but still envied him the job. As it turned out, he need not have.

Everything was now going well for the National Socialists. True, the ruling party was still the Social Democrats (with 143 seats compared with the Nazis' 108), but its leader, Chancellor Heinrich Bruening, knew that time was definitely not on his side. A world-wide depression was chilling the hearts of the Western democracies, and each plea he made for some relaxation of their grip on the German economy was contemptuously rejected. The draconian measures which he was forced to introduce would have been made palatable for the German people only if he had been able to secure some sort of triumph abroad, some sort of recognition by the Allies of Germany's place in the world, some appeasement of Germany's hurt pride and sense of inferiority. But the rest of the world was too busy with its own problems to worry about Germany, and all Bruening got for his overtures was a slap in the face. He was soon the head of the most unpopular government in German postwar history, and malcontents were flocking to join the National Socialists.

A few days after the 1930 elections the Bruening government made a maladroit move. In an attempt to discredit the Nazis, they brought forward the trial in Leipzig of three young German officers accused of having spread Nazi propaganda among their troops. Adolf Hitler was called as a witness, and the prosecution relished the prospect of turning the witness box into a spit on which to roast him. They had not reckoned with his skill.

Evading all attempts to make him sound like the rabble-rousing leader of a militant and rebellious force, he used every opportunity to emphasize that his Party was seeking power not through violence but through the ballot box, and that the "enemies of Germany will be crushed by us legally," as would "the iniquities of the Treaty of Versailles." Then he added:

"Another two or three elections, and we will have the majority in the Reichstag. Then power will be ours and a people's tribunal will judge the November criminals.† And I frankly predict that then you will see heads rolling in the sand."

It was an impressive performance and it secured world-wide attention for the Nazi leader. No one was now in any doubt that the National Socialists were on their way to power.

In the circumstances, Christmas 1930 was a happy one in the Goering household, despite the continuing weakness of Carin Goering. Carin's son Thomas had come down for the holidays and helped his mother, who was running a temperature of 100 degrees, to decorate the tree on Christmas Eve and pack the presents.

"At eight o'clock Goebbels arrived to spend Christmas Eve with us," Carin wrote to her mother. "He came loaded with presents for us all. For supper we had just cold meats and fruit. Then Goebbels played the harmonium, which I had brought into the living room for the holiday, and we all sang the old Christmas songs, 'Stille Nacht, heilige Nacht,' 'O, du fröhliche, O, du selige' etc. Thomas and I sang in Swedish, Goebbels and Cilly‡ sang in German, and we harmonized. The fir tree was lighted and the presents were handed round. Then I got a shivering fit and it was so violent that I fell back on the sofa and had to be carried off to bed, and I had fever and a bad headache. Today it is somewhat better."

On Christmas day their friends the Prince and Princess zu Wied, arrived with their two daughters ("the elder is a beauty"), Prince August Wilhelm with his son, Goebbels, Pilli Koerner and a host of other guests. Thomas, the young prince, and the Wied daughters ate together in an anteroom.

"In the dining room sat fourteen guests!!! I had 99 degrees and happily dozed. The doctor came to see me twice, while Hermann and Cilly took over all the arrangements, and I slept, much relieved to be free to do so. August Wilhelm arrived bringing some lovely gifts, a great bucket of white lilies and a huge camelhair rug, light as a feather, for me, as well as many other little things, a silk shawl, a

† By November criminals he meant the Socialists and Communists whose revolt in 1918 hastened Germany's capitulation.
‡ Cilly Wachowiak, a young peasant girl they had now hired as maid.

Dürer madonna, writing blocks, etc. I had stitched or painted things for everyone, and I think they were pleased with them, and Hermann had gathered together his own presents for the guests."

On January 4, 1931, the names of two men crept into her letters whose presence there signalized that Goering's frenetic socializing had succeeded, and that the Nazi Party was now indeed respectable. One was the multimillionaire Fritz Thyssen, the great Ruhr industrialist who was later to say:

"Hermann Goering I came to know in the following manner. One day the son of one of the directors of my coal mining companies, a certain Herr Tengelmann, came to me. 'Listen to me,' he said, 'there exists in Berlin a Herr Goering. He is trying very hard to do some good for the German people, but he is finding little encouragement on the part of German industrialists. Wouldn't you like to make his acquaintance?' I consequently met Goering in due course. He lived in a very small apartment in those days, and he was anxious to enlarge it in order to cut a better figure. I paid the cost of this improvement. At that time Goering seemed a most agreeable person. In political matters he was very sensible. I also came to know his first wife, Carin, who was a Swedish countess by birth. She was an exceedingly charming woman and showed no signs of the mental derangement which clouded her life before she died. Goering idolized her, and she was the only woman who was able to guide him—as though he were a young man."*

The other important guest at the Goering table (and mentioned in Carin's correspondence) was Dr. Hjalmar Schacht, and his adherence to the Nazis was a coup indeed. A financier of great brilliance and a shrewd judge of political horses, he had been President of the Reichsbank until the Allied powers imposed the so-called Young Plan upon Germany, a panacea that only made the financial situation worse. Schacht had resigned his position in disgust and looked around for a party capable of uniting the German people against further humiliation at the hands of

* This statement was made sixteen years after the event, and contains several mistakes. For instance, Thyssen's subvention was not a small sum to Goering but a large sum to the Party, and Carin Goering never became mentally deranged, etc.

the Allies. Hermann Goering had persuaded him that the National Socialists were the ones most capable of utilizing his considerable talents.

Now he had agreed to come to the Goerings' New Year's Day party not only to meet the Wieds, Goebbels, Thyssen, and other German industrialists, but also Adolf Hitler. The Fuehrer was in a jovial mood and spent some time entertaining Carin, but later he, Goering, Thyssen, and Schacht retired to another room for a long discussion. Carin was up and about again, and "Cilly helped me to serve pea soup, pork, and Swedish apple tart with vanilla ice cream. I could tell from Hermann's positively beatific smile that it was a most successful party."

The Nazis were now beginning to sound like the men who could solve a dire and humiliating situation, and they were attracting men and women of all classes. A hint of just how desperate the situation in Germany had become appears in a letter Carin wrote home on January 4, 1931:

"Yesterday we had a small tea party here, and while we were sitting there a certain Count X arrived with his wife for a visit, quite unannounced. She is Swedish by birth. He is a young man, really pleasant, two children, he without employment, the whole family living dispersed among relatives, and he looking for work and here to ask Hermann's help. All poor Hermann could do was show him a list of applicants with over a hundred names on it. On Christmas Eve twenty-eight people shot themselves because of want and hunger and despair. Among them was a young officer, a flier, well known during the war. On Christmas morning Hermann received a letter which began by saying: 'My true comrade and friend, by the time this letter is in your hands I shall be no more.' He went on to write about his fight to keep himself, his son and the small estate where his family had lived for over 600 years. Now he was completely penniless, and the only way for his wife and son to save the house was for him to shoot himself and allow them to collect on his small life insurance. Hermann telegraphed at once by express telegram: 'Don't be too hasty, I'm hoping to help you,' but his wife telegraphed back that he was already dead."

Carin grieved for those who killed themselves, but there were millions in Germany now who went on living in conditions of hopelessness and despair, with no work, not enough to eat, and all the maladies of malnutrition blighting the growth of their children. It was this countless army of unhappy Germans, with not even pride of race to buoy them up (for did not the Allies continually point out how beneath contempt they really were?), who were now turning to the National Socialists in search of some salvation. In the midst of their misery, the speeches of Adolf Hitler and Hermann Goering filled them with hope. They reached out through the darkening gloom and, drowning, grasped the rope the Nazis were throwing them.

X. THE DEATH OF CARIN

Berlin was now a city of heartrending contrasts. At the Deutsche Staat Theater one of the wonders of the decade was on view, Max Reinhardt's new production of *A Midsummer Night's Dream*, in which a team of young players moved as if on air through the enchanting world of Shakespeare's imagination. But the smug complacency of the well-fed audience moved even that aristocratic socialist Count Harry Kessler, otherwise a doughty anti-Nazi, to a whiff of anti-Semitism.

"In the first row of the stalls," he wrote in his diary, "sat the former Crown Prince and his wife. He had gone quite gray, almost white; the Crown princess is a fat, elderly woman. Nevertheless, he has retained all his junior officer mannerisms, standing among the audience in the intervals with a cigarette hanging from his mouth, or prancing up and down and fawningly holding open doors for fat old Jews to pass in or out . . . The hereditary Hohenzollern lack of taste reaches in him almost monumental proportions."

But outside the Nazis were on the march, and the spectacle moved Kessler to comment: "The vomit rises at so much pigheaded stupidity and spite."

The Nazis on that particular day had surged down the Leipzigerstrasse smashing the windows of the department stores, swarming into the Potsdamer Platz and shouting their slogans: "Germany Awake!" "Death of Judah!" and "Heil Hitler!"

"In the main the Nazis consisted of adolescent riff-raff which made off yelling as soon as the police began to use rubber truncheons," Kessler commented. "I have never witnessed so much rabble in these parts . . . These disorders reminded me of the days just before the revolution, with the same mass meetings and the same Catilinian fig-

ures lounging about and demonstrating. If the government
does not take matters firmly in hand, we shall slide into
civil war. In any case today's rioting will, I estimate, cost
us between five hundred million and a milliard marks in
stock exchange losses and the withdrawal of foreign assets."

These events happened just before Ernst Roehm took
over the command of the SA, and as Walter Stennes'
Brownshirts were, at his incitement, having their last fling.
Stennes suspected, quite rightly, that he would not last long
under the new regime and was making a last bid for control of the SA. He had addressed his troops before the
march in a passable imitation of Hitlerian demagoguery,
exalting the power of the machine gun over the ballot box,
and sneering at the homosexual "in frilly underwear" who
was about to take over. Did they want a sissy to lead them?
he asked. And when they loudly cried that they did not, he
shouted:

"Then let us go out and show this sodomite what men
can do!"

It was a challenge not only to Roehm but to Hitler too,
for Roehm was his chosen man, and action had to be taken
quickly. The Fuehrer gave Roehm full powers, and the
new SA commander moved fast and ruthlessly. Forty-eight
hours after the Leipzigerstrasse march, every one of
Stennes' sub-commanders had either disappeared, was on
the run, or was in the hospital with a broken head or limb.
Roehm had recruited some of his old comrades from the
days of the Munich putsch, many of them sharing his
sexual predilections. They proved to the rank and file of
the SA Brownshirts that homosexuals they might be, but
sissies they were not. As for Walter Stennes, he left the
Nazi Party and joined Otto Strasser's Black Front, leaving
the field clear for Roehm to mold the Brownshirt Army
exactly to his liking.

Nineteen thirty-one was a painful year for most of the
world, but most of all for Germany. In other countries the
depression was producing breadlines, but in Germany there
was no bread to line up for. Even the Allies recognized at
last that the defeated enemy just could not go on paying
out the gigantic amounts with which they had been burdened by Versailles, and the Americans proposed and persuaded the others to accept a temporary halt in the repara-

tions, a move which was named after the U.S. President of the day and called the Hoover Moratorium. But its effect would take time to ameliorate Germany's economic situation, and meanwhile the Nazis thrived on the widespread misery. Though Bruening was still Chancellor and the Socialist Democrats still formed the government, the Nazis were by now the largest party in the land. They signalized their triumph by heaping continuous demands on the Reichstag for measures which they knew were beyond the scope or power of the Bruening administration; and when they were turned down, they marched out in a body in February 1931, and refused to return to the Reichstag until the following October.

For Hermann Goering this was a curious period, because every new advancement of the Party and of his own position in it was accompanied by a deterioration in the condition of Carin. During the spring of 1931 she had grown sicker than ever before, her heart so weak that she often lay for hours at a time, her pulse barely detectable, apparently in a deep coma. It was during one of these periods that the doctor, in answer to an anguished question from Goering, expressed the opinion that there was now no hope and that she would shortly die.

Carin gave no sign, but she had, in fact, heard the doctor's words. She did not tell her husband about it, but she confided in her sister Fanny.

"I now know what it is to die," she told her, during one of her conscious moments. "I have heard all about it from the doctor. He has told Hermann he can't do any more for me, it is quite hopeless. When I heard it I felt nothing, and I could do nothing, say nothing, not even open my eyelids. And then suddenly I saw before me a high door, so high and so fine, and glowing with color and light. My soul felt free, and I had left earthly life behind and was in a great new, absolutely undescribable world. I knew that when I went through that door, I could never come back. Then I suddenly felt Hermann's presence—and I knew at once that I must not allow myself to leave him yet."

At the end of June she had strengthened enough for Goering to take her to a sanitarium at Bad Altheide, in Silesia, and she wrote her mother that she was "getting better, so that I can fulfill all the duties that will be awaiting me once the summer is over." Carin's mother herself had taken a turn for the worse, and the two invalids spent their time writing comfort to each other in their afflictions.

If Carin Goering had needed proof of her husband's devotion, she was given it now. These were vital days not only for the future of the National Socialist Party but for Hermann Goering's position in its hierarchy. In the early summer he had been asked to go to Rome by Adolf Hitler on a mission that was part window dressing by the Party strategists. They wished to assure Roman Catholic voters in South Germany that the Nazis were not anathema to the Vatican, even if not approved by the Holy See. It was also partly, Goering afterward suspected, to get rid of him while other members of the Fuehrer's entourage jockeyed for position. The intrigues which were going on among the political parties of the right in Germany at this time are too complicated to go into here. Arrangements that were being made behind the scenes were as serpentine as the couplings of a basket of asps, and as cold-blooded as a Renaissance marriage contract. Once established as the undisputed master of the Brownshirt SA, Ernst Roehm had begun using the strength of his formidable private army as a bargaining counter with those enemies of Chancellor Bruening and the Social Democrats who had the ear of Von Hindenburg. The President was now eighty-four, unhappy with Bruening, and obsessed with the idea of bringing Kaiser Wilhelm back to the throne of Germany before he died.

An influential Reichswehr general named Kurt von Schleicher was in process of persuading the stubborn old warhorse that it could be arranged, providing some sort of fusion could be brought about between Adolf Hitler's National Socialists and the pro-royalist forces of the Nationalist leader, Alfred Hugenberg. Between the two forces, he suggested, a coalition could be forged that would be strong enough to force through the Restoration. In fact, there was no likelihood that Adolf Hitler would ever allow a monarchy to be re-established in Germany, but for his own purposes he needed the ear of President Hindenburg, and he encouraged Ernst Roehm to dicker with General von Schleicher in order to bring about a meeting. The intrigues went on behind Goering's back while he was away in Rome, and he was considerably discomfited when he returned and found out about them.

To appease him, Adolf Hitler made a shrewd and effective gesture. He knew that Goering had a weakness for motorcars, and that he still grieved over the car which he had had to relinquish after the failure of the Munich putsch. Now that the Party was growing rich, with mounting subventions from Thyssen, Bechstein, Krupp von Bohlen, and other Ruhr magnates, there was enough money in the kitty to buy the Party *Bevollmächtigter* a new automobile. Hitler presented him with the latest open-topped-model Mercedes Benz for his exclusive use, and the mollified Goering climbed behind the wheel at once and drove at high speed (he was a regular Mr. Toad in a motorcar) to show it off to Carin at the sanitarium in Silesia.

She was so fortified by his quite evident pleasure in his new acquisition that she insisted on accompanying him for a ride to a neighboring beauty spot. The presence of Hermann Goering at her side was always a remarkable tonic for Carin, and to the astonishment of her doctors she rallied when he told her that he had been given fourteen days' holiday from his political affairs, and exclaimed at once:

"We will go for a motoring holiday!"

They did indeed. A tiny motoring cap coquettishly perched on her nut-brown hair, a dust-colored cloak over her shoulders, her eyes flashing with joy, Carin sat beside her husband with her sister Fanny and Pilli Koerner in the seats behind, and they set forth first for Dresden. Goering did not tell her until they were almost there that Adolf Hitler had agreed to snatch a few days of rest at the same time, and that they would have a rendezvous in Dresden at the Palast Hotel.

"When the news spread through the town that Hitler was among them," Fanny wrote later, "masses of people gathered in front of the Palast Hotel to wave and cheer. The crowds were such that police trucks had to come in and force a way through the crowd so that we could move about. Carin was blissfully happy. 'When the whole of Germany realizes what we have in Hitler,' she told her sister, 'a new era will dawn in Germany.' "

For fourteen days they drove through the small towns of Bavaria and then slipped across the frontier into Austria, where Goering took her to Mauterndorf to meet his old childhood mentor and godfather, Ritter von Epenstein. The arrogant old man was now eighty-two years old, sick, weak and a shell of the proud feudal lord who had once ruled these mountains, but he ordered Baronin Lilli to lay on a banquet for the guests and summoned up the strength to come to the table, drink a toast, and listen to the minstrels playing in the gallery as of old. When they left, Baronin Lilli patted Carin's hand and said, gesturing to the mountains:

"Isn't it beautiful? Did Hermann tell you? One day this will all be yours."

They returned to Munich to attend the christening of a daughter who had just been born to Hermann Goering's sister, Frau Paula Huber. His other sister, Frau Olga Rigele, Goering's favorite, was also there, and most other members of the family, and they were all afuss because one of Hermann's grand friends, the Duchess of Coburg, had come specially to be present. But the one guest whom they were all hoping to see, Adolf Hitler himself, did not turn up. He had gone into seclusion at a house on the Tegernsee, in the Bavarian lake district, in a state of shock at the news which had just reached him of the death of his niece, Geli Raubal. "We all knew how close the Fuehrer had always been to his niece," Olga Rigele said later, "and the news that she had shot herself put quite a blight on the christening ceremony. Hermann was deeply troubled by the news and went off several times to telephone to Bad Wiessee, where the Fuehrer was staying. I gathered that he had offered to go to Geli's funeral in Vienna, but was told to return to Berlin."*

Political negotiations in the capital were moving toward a climax, and Hitler wanted Goering on hand to be ready for action when the moment came. Rumors were rife that President Hindenburg was at long last willing to discuss Germany's situation with Adolf Hitler.

On September 25, 1931, Carin's mother, Baroness Huldine von Fock, who had been seriously ill for some time, finally closed her eyes and died. The strenuous events of the summer had exhausted Carin Goering, but she begged to be allowed to travel to Stockholm for the funeral. The doctor warned that the journey would kill her, but Carin

---

* Geli Raubal shot herself in Munich, but her body was sent to Austria for burial. Ernst Roehm and Heinrich Himmler represented Hitler at the funeral.

pleaded with such anguishing persistence that Goering finally could not bear to refuse her. But days had passed and
the funeral was over by the time the two of them finally
reached Stockholm.

Thomas von Kantzow was on the station platform when
their train drew in.

"My mother had always looked most beautiful when she
was most seriously ill," Thomas said later, "and she had
never looked lovelier than she did when I first saw them.
Hermann had a long overcoat draped over his shoulders
like a cloak, and when he reached out to lift her down to
the platform the two loose sleeves went around her neck,
so that it was as if four of his arms were grasping her. She
put her own arms around him and tucked her head into the
hollow of his shoulder, and it looked just as if a chubby
bear were fondling its cub. The picture of them clinging
together stayed in my mind for always, and it would come
back to me in the years to come whenever anyone said
anything bad about Hermann."

They went back to the Von Fock house on Grev Turegatan where the baron and his four other daughters were
waiting. It was to be the last time all his five children were
in the house together. The house was sad and silent and
everyone spoke in whispers.

That night Carin collapsed and had to be carried to bed,
and when the doctor had finished examining her he called
Hermann Goering aside and expressed the gravest doubts
about his wife's chances of lasting out the night. Carin
Goering did not overhear what the doctor was saying this
time, but did not need to. In a momentary period of consciousness, she opened her blue eyes and said out loud:

"I did so hope I was going to join Mama."

For the next four days Hermann Goering stayed at his
wife's side.

"He would only steal away to shave or bathe or snatch a
bite to eat," said Thomas later, "when he was absolutely
sure that my mother was unconscious. Otherwise he spent
all his time on his knees at the bedside, holding her hand,
stroking her hair, wiping the perspiration from her face or
the moisture from her lips. I would sit in a corner of the
room and watch him, and sometimes he would suddenly
turn and look at me, and he would be weeping silently. We

were both weeping. We both loved her very much, and our hearts were breaking."

On October 4, 1931, a telegram arrived at 68, Grev Turegatan for Hermann Goering. It was from Adolf Hitler.

After six months of boycotting the proceedings in the Reichstag, the Fuehrer had decided to order the Nazis back, this time with the definite plan of harrassing the Bruening administration into defeat. Meanwhile, General von Schleicher had at long last persuaded President von Hindenburg that Adolf Hitler was the coming man in Germany and that it would be wise for him to receive him in audience. Schleicher, as a close friend of Ernst Roehm, had suggested both to Hindenburg and Hitler that Roehm should accompany him to the interview. That was all right with the Fuehrer, but President von Hindenburg angrily refused to allow his rooms to be "defiled by that pervert." Roehm was out. Who would now accompany Hitler to this vital meeting, whose presence and background would appease this irascible old soldier's ire?

RETURN AT ONCE, the cable to Goering said. YOU ARE NEEDED HERE.

In the sickroom where Hermann Goering and Thomas von Kantzow were keeping their vigil, Carin's life was draining away. But exhausted though she was, she did not die. One morning, when she seemed in a deep trance and Goering had stolen out of the room, her eyes opened and she called out to her son. Thomas came across and knelt beside the bed.

"I am so tired," she whispered, "so terribly tired. I want to follow Mama. She keeps calling for me. But I cannot go. So long as Hermann is here, I cannot go. I cannot bear to leave him."

Thomas told her of the telegram Goering had received recalling him to Berlin, but said that he had ignored it and had no intention of going back so long as she was ill. Tears began to stream from Carin's eyes, and when her husband returned she reached out and forced his head close to her face.

"I could not hear all that she was whispering," Thomas said later, "but I knew that she was begging, pleading, even ordering him to obey Hitler's call. After a time, he began to sob and she took his head and laid it on her breast, as if he too were her son and it was he who was in need of comfort. A strange change seemed to come over her. At that moment, probably because she had heard the sound of Hermann's sobs, my Aunt Fanny came into the room, and my mother looked across at her. She was very calm and controlled. 'Hermann has been called back to Berlin. The Fuehrer urgently needs him,' she said. 'You must help him to pack his things.' She lifted Hermann's head up and suddenly smiled. 'Thomas will look after me,' she said."

Goering climbed to his feet. "Until I come back," he said.

"Yes," said Carin, "until you come back."

He left for Berlin next morning. And at 4 A.M. on October 17, 1931, Carin Goering, free at last of the overwhelming presence of her husband, relaxed and died.

She lay in her coffin in the Edelweiss Chapel behind the Von Fock house until Hermann Goering arrived from Germany to see her for the last time. She was buried on her birthday, October 21, in the family tomb at Lovö near Drottningholm. Pilli Koerner and Goering's brother Karl had come with him from Berlin, and representatives of most of Sweden's titled families were among the mourners. It was an occasion for many tears and sighs of regret, for Carin had been liked by most poeple who had met her. She was a naïve romantic who hero-worshiped too easily, and she had many of the thoughtless prejudices and *idées fixes* of her class and generation, but at heart she was good and kind-hearted and would never have hurt a fly—or a Social Democrat, a Communist, or a Jew.

As her body was carried into the family tomb, two men drew apart from the rest of the mourners and stood together in silent grief. And that was right. For these two, for Hermann Goering and Thomas von Kantzow, it was more than just the death of a woman they had loved. A force had gone out of their lives, and they would never be the same again.

There are no official records of what took place at the meeting on November 10, 1931, of President von Hindenburg, Adolf Hitler, and Hermann Goering. The mood of the two Nazi leaders was not exactly propitious. Hitler was still deeply affected by the suicide of his favorite niece, and

Goering's spirit was still in Stockholm at his beloved Carin's bedside. The only thing that could have dissipated the morosity of the first and the profound anguish of the second was some gesture from the old President that indicated his recognition of their importance to Germany's destiny.

But whatever motive had persuaded him to agree to meet Hitler in the first place was forgotten by the time the Fuehrer was shown into the presidential study. Hitler had expected to be greeted not only as the man who could save Germany but as the only political force able to preserve Hindenburg himself and all he stood for. When he discovered that this was not so, that the old man was distant, patronizing, even contemptuous of him, his temper became mean and (Goering was to indicate later) he launched into a long diatribe which induced in Hindenburg a severe bout of the fidgets. When the Fuehrer was at last finished, the President simply sat on, drumming his gnarled fingers or fingering the ends of his flowing mustaches. There was nothing else for Hitler to do but say a perfunctory good-by and march out.

"Make that man my Chancellor?" Hindenburg was later to say of Hitler. "I'll make him a postmaster, and he can lick stamps with my head on them!"

The time would come when Adolf Hitler would be in a position to revenge himself on the haughty marshal for that loftily contemptuous reception, but by that time Hindenburg's mind would be too encrusted with the limpets of age for the humiliating barbs to get through. For the moment, Hindenburg still held the keys to power in Germany and was determined not to hand them over to a nondescript man who ranted at him and had never risen in the Army higher than the rank of corporal.

So it had been a wasted meeting for Adolf Hitler and a needless journey from Stockholm for Hermann Goering, and it must have been a moment when both of them were tempted by Ernst Roehm to put the Brownshirt SA on the streets and take over the government by force. Roehm had been in close consultation with General von Schleicher and had been assured that the Army would be on the Nazis' side in the event of a rising; this time, Roehm swore to Hitler, there would be no betrayal and debacle, as had happened during the Beer Hall Putsch. But it was not because of any fear of failure that Hitler refused to order

the SA into the streets. Both he and Goering had been
elated by the results of the last election, and confident that
at the next one a majority of votes would put most of the
nation behind the National Socialists. Why spill blood un-
necessarily—and why frighten the big industrialists who
were now so strongly behind them—when it could all be
done quite legally? All they needed was a new general
election.

On July 31, 1932, they got one. It was preceded by the
bloodiest and noisiest street scenes in Germany since the
last days of World War I. If Ernst Roehm was not to be
allowed to commit his troops to a takeover, at least he
could use them for battering the forces of the opposition.
Both the Communists and the Socialists had their own well-
trained private armies, but the Brownshirt SA was now
400,000 strong and, through Roehm's army connections,
had found weapons with which to back up the pikes, iron
bars, and truncheons with which they, like their opponents,
usually fought. In Prussia alone in the first twenty days of
June 1932 there were 461 pitched battles in the street
which cost 82 lives and seriously wounded 400 men. In
July, 38 Nazis and 30 Communists were listed among the
86 people killed in street riots. The worst day was Sunday,
July 17, when the Nazis marched through Altona, the
working-class district of Hamburg, under police escort, and
were attacked by the Communists. Nineteen people were
shot dead and 285 wounded in the brutish confrontation
which followed.

The interim Chancellor of the day was an adroit German diplomat named Franz von Papen, and he immediately made the Altona incidents the excuse for banning all
further political parades until after the elections, and for
proclaiming martial law in Berlin. But meetings went on,
and there was no doubt from the attendance at them which
way the tide was running. Hermann Goering seldom had
fewer than 40,000 people to hear him speak. Adolf Hitler
did even better. At his final meeting in Berlin on July 27,
120,000 people crammed the Grunewald Stadium to listen
to him, and 100,000 gathered outside to hear his speech
relayed on loud-speakers.

The vote was a resounding victory for the Nazis. When
the returns were in, the Party was by far the largest in the
new Reichstag, with 230 seats. Next came the Social Dem-

ocrats with 133. The Communists had won 89, the Catholic Center 73. 13,574,000 Germans had voted for the National Socialists, and though this was 38 per cent of the total vote, it outnumbered that of the Communists and Social Democrats combined, and had come from all classes of German life, from Ruhr workers and Ruhr magnates, from farmers and farm laborers, from the petite bourgeoisie, and from the rank and file and the officer ranks of the armed forces.

Hermann Goering flew down to Munich for a conference with the Party leaders on the Tegernsee and planned the tactics to be adopted now that victory had been secured. He shared Hitler's conviction that the moment had arrived, and that President Hindenburg would now be forced to call in the Fuehrer and ask him to form a government. With whom must they make an alliance in order to secure an overwhelming majority in the Reichstag?

In the days that followed, while the meetings went on, and political pacts were made and broken, the Nazis waited for the summons. On August 13, 1932, a telegram arrived at last for Adolf Hitler summoning him to Berlin for an interview with the President.

"It could mean but one thing," wrote Hindenburg's biographer. "Schleicher [with whom the Nazis were negotiating] had carried out his plans, Papen was about to resign, and he, Adolf Hitler, former corporal and house-painter, would become Chancellor of the German Reich. The united command of the hundred thousand Reichswehr and of his own half million brown legionaries would be his; the control of Germany was within his grasp."

Unfortunately, it was not. Faced with the prospect of handing over power to Hitler, Von Hindenburg balked. During the days of his interim administration, Franz von Papen had successfully ingratiated himself with the old soldier, who was charmed with his smooth manner and his elegant ability to skirt around a situation without having to say a blunt yes or no. Hindenburg had decided that he would like to keep Von Papen in power. He was told to go to Hitler and offer him the job of Vice-Chancellor to himself, plus that of Prussian Minister of the Interior to Hermann Goering.

Hitler and Goering stared at Von Papen with astonishment as, in urbane tones, he broke this news to them.

"What?" said Goering. "Adolf Hitler as Vice-Chancellor? The Fuehrer has never been *vice* to anyone."

Hitler was even more angry and began a furious diatribe that made his diplomat host wince with embarrassment. Hitler blustered, threatened, reminded Von Papen of the Brownshirt Army waiting for an order to go out on the streets, and finally refused any offer except that of the chancellorship. Von Papen, he said, must go back and tell Hindenburg that this was his ultimatum. Von Papen shook his head. *He* was certainly not going to tell the President anything like that. Hitler would have to convey his feelings to the old soldier himself.

Hermann Goering now lived in a small apartment on the Reichskanzlerplatz. [He had never gone back to the apartment he had shared with Carin, but he had transported to his new abode many mementoes of his wife, including her white harmonium, her ornaments and pictures.] It was here that he now went with Josef Goebbels and Hitler, and they were served lunch by Cilly Wachowiak, Carin's peasant maid, beneath a large portrait of Carin. They picked at the pheasant in aspic and drank Moselle while Hitler disdained the vegetarian dish set before him and inveighed against the tricksters and the traps with which the road to power was beset. At three o'clock the telephone rang and it was Erwin Planck, secretary of state at the Reichschancellery, to inform him that Hindenburg would see him in an hour's time.

Some sudden surge of optimism seems to have persuaded them all that perhaps Hindenburg had heard of Hitler's wrath and had decided to appease him with an offer of power. Only Goebbels was still skeptical, and he asked Planck:

"Has a decision already been reached? If so, there is no point in the Fuehrer's coming."

Planck was vague. "Nothing has been decided. The President wishes to see Herr Hitler first."

When Adolf Hitler arrived at the presidential palace, he did not realize that he was walking into a trap. Von Papen, ever the skillful diplomatic manipulator, had managed to suggest to the short-tempered old field marshal that what the Nazi leader was after was not just the chancellorship of the government but dictatorial control over the nation. This had put Hindenburg in a mood of barely suppressed anger, and his attitude by no means calmed down when Hitler came into his presence, for, as if in a gesture of defiance, he had brought the "loathsome" Ernst Roehm with him.

Leaning on his cane in a corner of the room (so that he would not have to ask Hitler and his hated companion to sit down), the old President gave no sign that he was eighty-five years old and had suffered a stroke not long before. His eyes never wavered from Hitler's as he listened to the Fuehrer make his demand for the chancellorship and powers to put the nation's affairs in order.

Then, in icy and contemptuous tones, the old man replied that because of the tense situation prevailing in the country he could not in good conscience risk transferring the power of government to a new party such as the National Socialists, which did not command an over-all majority and whose members were "intolerant, noisy and undisciplined."

Otto Meissner, chief of the Presidential Chancellery, who was present at the interview, said afterward that Hindenburg's somewhat quavery voice hardened and became extremely harsh from this point onward, and he did not bother to disguise his antipathy toward the truculent Nazi leader and his epicene companion. Meissner wrote later:

"[He] referred to several recent occurrences—clashes between the Nazis and the police, acts of violence committed by Hitler's followers against those who were of a different opinion, excesses against the Jews and other illegal acts. All these incidents had strengthened him in his conviction that there were numerous wild elements in the Party beyond control . . . He should give up the one-sided idea that he must have complete power [and] in cooperating with other parties, Hindenburg declared, he would be able to show what he could achieve and improve upon . . ."

It was the riposte of an outraged patrician father to a suitor of humble origin who has dared to ask for the hand of his daughter. With bare civility, Adolf Hitler was dismissed.

Not only that. He had barely returned to Josef Goebbels' apartment, where the Party hierarchy was awaiting him, than Berlin newspapers were on the streets with a communiqué from the President's office. Under headlines like HITLER DEMANDS SUPREME POWER, HITLER'S SHOCKING

BREACH OF FAITH AND HITLER REPRIMANDED BY THE REICH
PRESIDENT, it gave Hindenburg's version of the meeting
and "regretted that Herr Hitler did not see himself in a
position to support a national government appointed with
the confidence of the Reich President, as he had promised
to do before the Reichstag elections." It suggested that
Hitler had demanded dictatorial powers, which had been
sternly refused by the President, and it went on to say:

"The President gravely exhorted Herr Hitler to conduct
the opposition on the part of the N. S. Party in a chivalrous manner, and to bear in mind his responsibility to the
Fatherland and to the German people."

The Party propaganda machine had been caught by surprise and was in no position to counter Hindenburg's
charges, and by the time Hitler got around to pointing out
that he had never asked for "dictatorial powers" but only
for his constitutional right to form a government, it was
too late. The damage was done.

That night Hitler called in his advisers and conferred
over what was to be done. Most important was what orders
should be given to the Brownshirt SA, whose troops were
assembled all over Germany, waiting for the signal to celebrate Adolf Hitler's victory. Ernst Roehm was all for sending them into action at once. He pointed out that he had a
million eager Nazis itching for action, that there were also
70,000 SS men, or storm troopers, and a highly trained
automobile corps on call. Moreover, Nazi governments in
the states of Brunswick, Hessen, Anhalt, Thuringia, Meck-
lenburg, and Oldenburg had the police directly under their
orders, and the movement was strong in Berlin, East and
West Prussia, Silesia, Saxony, and Brandenburg. Berlin
could be surrounded overnight and starved into capitulation.

"How can we tell our followers that victory has been
snatched out of our hands?" asked Roehm. "We can only
satisfy them with action."

But Goering and Goebbels were against a military coup,
and it was Goering, arguing with particular eloquence, who
finally convinced the Fuehrer that they must swallow their
disappointment and hold their hand. The order was given
to the crestfallen Roehm, and he was sent away to order
the Brownshirts to stand down. Amid rumors that he might
be arrested at any moment, Adolf Hitler departed for

Berchtesgaden, to nurse his chagrin and work out what should be done next. Josef Goebbels left for a holiday on the Baltic, and wrote in his diary: "Great hopelessness reigns among the party comrades."

As for Hermann Goering, he climbed into his Mercedes and drove away to Weimar, where he hoped that a date with an actress would assuage his fallen spirits.

XI. POWER PLAY

Hermann Goering in 1932 was thirty-nine years old and in better physical condition than at any time in the last nine years. True, he had two weaknesses which he found it difficult to control: he suffered from an insatiable appetite which he tried to keep within bounds through a strict diet, but at regular intervals he succumbed and gorged himself on good food and wine; and he also suffered from insomnia and rarely slept more than two hours at a time. Diet pills helped to keep his weight down, and sleeping pills sometimes gave him a full night's rest, but after his experience with morphine in Sweden he was scared of getting addicted to drugs again, and he tried to ration his intake of both. The result was that, already plump, he began to get fatter, and whenever he felt the flesh beginning to press him out of his clothes, he went in for continuous bouts of horse-riding and sauna baths.

What he possessed in abundance that most people envied was enormous energy and great brightness and ebullience of spirit. These were the days when he was never cast down for long by political setbacks, was always on hand to comfort and encourage the more morose and rancorous Hitler, and was so openly and sincerely optimistic about the future of the Party that comrades and noncomrades alike found it difficult to withstand his blandishments. He was a master of intrigue because he sounded so open and idealistic. And he was tireless. Back and forth he went, between the leaders of one party and another, seeking allies, making deals, and taking the Nazis step by step toward the legal attainment of power which was now the main object of his existence.

Yet when he relaxed, there was no easier nor more attractive companion. For a time after Carin's death he had brooded in a suite at the Kaiserhof Hotel and only reluc-

tantly been persuaded by Pilli Koerner to take the apartment in the Kaiserdamm. One of its rooms he filled with
Carin's portraits, her shells and pebbles, her harmonium,
her Viking statues and trolls and eskimo boots, and ever-
green wreaths from her tomb. As many a visitor said, it
was like a museum.

So far as human relationships were concerned, Hermann
Goering had become something of a museum piece himself. As a young man he had always entered with great zest
into his relationships with girls, and if, during World War
I, his engagement to Marianne Mauser had never been
consummated, he had more than compensated for his frustration during his furloughs in Berlin and Munich. Nor is
there any reason to believe that his life with Carin Goering
was anything but a normal relationship (except of course
for the period after the Beer Hall Putsch), and it is wrong
to suggest that it was not so because no child was produced
of the marriage. Thomas von Kantzow has pointed out*
that his was a premature birth and that his mother had
been told by the doctors afterward that she could never
have any more children. Her last words to Thomas before
she died were:

"Hermann has promised that he will always regard you
as his son. But you must tell him that I hope one day he
will find someone who will give him the child I could not
give him."

But this disability aside, Carin Goering seems to have
been a normal and uninhibited Swede in her attitude toward her physical relationship with her beloved husband,
and there are several indications in her letters (particularly
those to her sister Lily) of her pleasure in this aspect of
her married life. It is a common mistake to assume that
invalids do not have, or do not enjoy, sexual relations, and
Thomas von Kantzow (who never showed any jealousy
whatsoever toward Goering) mentioned that his mother
and his stepfather shared a marital bed almost until the
last.

What, however, is possible and desired by a serious invalid cannot always be reciprocated with the same uncar-
ing rapture by the object of her desires, and for Hermann
Goering the last stages of his wife's illness must have pro-

* In a conversation with the author.

duced intense psychological stresses. The knowledge that each time he responded to Carin there would follow an emotional and physical encounter which could easily kill her, weakhearted as she was, was an inhibiting, not to say unsexing, thought. One of Hermann Goering's intimates was later to say he confided to her that shortly before and for some time after Carin's death he was all but unmanned.

But time and a pretty woman can work wonders, as Goering was now discovering. At this point in his life, a third great female influence enters his story, and she was as different from his mother, Fanny, and his first wife, Carin, as could possibly be imagined.

Her name was Emmy Sonnemann and she was an actress. A natural blonde, thirty-nine years of age (the same as Goering), she had all the qualities that blondes are said to possess but seldom do: she was cheerful, uninhibited, generous-hearted as well as being sexually attractive. She had been married once before, to a Stuttgart actor, but they had drifted apart and mutually arranged for an amicable divorce. In 1932 Emmy Sonnemann had been a member of the repertory company of the Weimar National Theater for eight years, and specialized in parts for romantic heroines (which she did well) and sophisticated society women (less successfully).

In many ways she was a typical actress much more than a typical German, and you could have found her counterpart in any group of professional players anywhere in the Western world. She was completely absorbed in her craft to the extent that when she opened her morning newspaper it was to the entertainment pages, and she rarely glanced at the news on other pages. She had absolutely no interest in politics and who became the new Chancellor of the Reich was of much less importance to her than who was playing Margarete in the next production of *Faust*. The team of players at the Weimar Theater included a number of Jews or half-Jews, but the idea that they should cease therefore to be her intimate friends was too ridiculous to contemplate. As she was to say, in a phrase that was to cause a wince to pass across Goering's features when he heard it:

"We are all gypsies here!"

Emmy Sonnemann first met Hermann Goering early in

1931, when Carin was still alive, but it was so casual that, so far as he was concerned, it had no impact. The Weimar company, which spent a good deal of time playing in small towns and villages in Hesse, had on this occasion been asked to perform a play written by the Baroness von Stein on the baron's estate near Kochberg.

"Late that evening Hermann was introduced to me after the show," Emmy wrote later. "I can not say that on that evening he made any profound impression on me. But his wife fascinated me. Sitting on a bench in the park during the interval she looked ill, but there emanated from her a charm which I could not resist. I would like to have chatted with her but I did not have time because we had to repeat the performance for a second time since the theater held only forty people at a sitting. So I had to go back to the stage."

The following year, during the election campaign, Adolf Hitler came to Weimar and the performance that evening was canceled so that he could use the theater for his meeting. The crowd was so great that Emmy had to stand in the wings "from where" she said later, "I could hear only scraps of the speakers' phrases, and could not form any real impression." But shortly afterward she was introduced to Hitler, and he assured her gravely that when the National Socialists came to power he would see to it that there was "a real artistic rebirth" in the German theater. Emmy could not understand what he was getting at, since she considered that the German theater was "extremely well developed" at that time.

A few days later, Hermann Goering came into her life. Each day after rehearsals, Emmy and an actress friend, Herma, were in the habit of lunching in a local restaurant and then going on to the Kaiser Cafe for cakes and coffee. Goering and Pilli Koerner came in, and Emmy, having forgotten exactly who he was, whispered to her friend:

"Herma, is that Goebbels or Goering?"

Herma giggled. "Goering, of course. You met him at Kochberg."

It was at this moment that Goering came over and asked permission for him and his friend to join them. When the two women got up and said they were going for a walk, Goering said:

"May we come with you?"

For the next two hours they strolled through the Weimar woods.

"For the first time in my life," wrote Emmy later, "I forgot the theater, my parts and everything else. I listened to Hermann Goering with a pleasure which I could not dissimulate. He spoke of his wife, who had recently died, with so much love and genuine sadness that my esteem for him grew with every word."

They said good-by at the theater, and she heard no more from Goering for a long time—"or so it seemed to me." But at last she got a telegram.

"He was still thinking of me, would soon be in Weimar again and wanted to meet me." They met a few evenings later, after Goering had addressed a political meeting. Typically, Emmy did not go to hear him, lest his image as a man be destroyed by Goering the politician.

"After his meeting I joined him at the Goldene Adler, the restaurant where I usually lunched. He came accompanied by Paul Koerner [and] Herma came with me. It was a thrilling evening. I felt that my life was about to be transformed; I only felt sorry for my friend. I felt as though I was behaving like a young girl—which I certainly no longer was. I changed my dress three times. The first one seemed to me too dressy, the second one too simple, and I finally decided on a skirt with a blouse. I found out only later on that this was the one thing Hermann detested. But he can hardly have noticed it because he was just as affected himself, as he told me himself later. He walked back alone with me to my door and left me. The walk was not long—but it decided the rest of my future life."

Emmy Sonnemann lived in three furnished rooms in a theatrical pension in Weimar. Her landlady was a strict disciplinarian and forbade any male visitors, though, until Goering's advent, "that did not worry me very much. I was far more worried by my landlady's prohibition on my taking a bath every day; she claimed that it wore out the bath." But now that he had come into her life, the need for them to be alone together became more and more exigent, and that was impossible in a small town like Weimar without everyone's knowing about it. Soon everyone knew that the golden-haired actress from the National Theater had taken a lover and that he was one of the bigwigs of the Nazi Party. On the night after Hitler's disastrous interview with Von Hindenburg, Hermann Goering arrived at the theater just as Emmy Sonnemann, who was playing Clärchen in *Egmont*, had reached the big scene in which her mother questions her about her lover. As Goering slipped into a seat in the box which he had reserved, she cried:

"Ah! I ask myself only if he loves me—and is there any question that he loves me?"

Half the faces in the house turned toward Goering's box, and titters ran through the audience. Goering beamed broadly. He looked supremely happy.

Since his election to the Reichstag, Hermann Goering had been appointed leader of the National Socialist group of members, and now that he headed the largest party in the house he was also elected President of the Assembly. One of his first actions upon taking possession of his office was to scrawl across a sheet of his personal presidential notepaper a message to Emmy: "*Ich liebe Dich. H.*" (I love you. H.) which he sent off with a bouquet of flowers by messenger to Weimar.

As it is in most parliaments of the world, the role of President (or speaker) in the Reichstag has always been a vital factor in the smooth running of the assembly's affairs. Goering took his job seriously, and there was a convincing ring in his voice as he said in his opening address:

"I promise that I shall fulfill the duties of my office impartially, justly, and in accordance with the existing rules of the House. I shall show due regard for the regulations and for the dignity of this House. But I must make it perfectly plain that I shall be equally vigilant in watching that the honor and dignity of the German people are not assailed in this House. The glorious record of the German people will always find a ready champion in me. I proclaim to the whole German people that this session has clearly proved that the new Reichstag has a large working majority, and is capable of conducting the affairs of State without recourse to emergency measures. The fact that we have a national Cabinet inspires in me the hope that I shall be able to discharge my duty as President of the Reichstag, and that the honor of the people, the safety of the nation, and the freedom of the Fatherland will be the chief guiding stars of all my actions."

The reference in his speech to the fact that the House was capable of conducting the affairs of State "without recourse to emergency measures" was a direct reference to the Chancellor, Franz von Papen, whom President von Hindenburg had once more instructed to form a government. Von Papen, well aware of the fact that he lacked a working majority, and that both the right and left were against him (and most of the center too) was seeking ways and means of getting rid of his opponents or of emasculating them as political forces. To this end he sent the Prussian police on a raid of Communist headquarters in Berlin, and then, on the grounds that treasonable material had been discovered, he drafted a decree ordering the dissolution of the Red Banner, the Communists' private army. But the decree before becoming legal had to be signed by the President of the Reichstag, and when it reached Hermann Goering he sent for Ernst Torgler, the Communist leader. He gestured at the sheet of paper on the desk before him and is said to have remarked:

"I have the means here to wipe out your forces, my friend. This is an order for the dissolution of the Red Banner."

Torgler said bitterly: "Von Papen is as dangerous as a viper. It will be the Brownshirts' turn next."

"I know," said Goering. "That is why I am not going to sign it."

Like Adolf Hitler, Hermann Goering had nothing but contempt for the smooth-talking but completely unreliable Von Papen, who was now mouthing platitudes about democracy on the floor of the Reichstag but working behind the scenes to inaugurate his own form of dictatorship. On the other hand, he did not share Hitler's hatred of President von Hindenburg, the man whose nominee Von Papen was. Goering had known the field marshal during World War I and admired his military qualities, his stubbornness, his great love of tradition and country. Despite everything, he had continued to maintain contact with the old man, visiting him at his country home at Neudeck, hoping to soften his antipathy toward Hitler and the National Socialists.

Now as President of the Reichstag he had additional reasons for seeing Von Hindenburg, and he did not waste

his opportunities. Hitler had already made him his chief
political negotiator, with liberty to deal with all parties
from the Communists to the extreme right in order to act
jointly in the Reichstag. In addition, his had been the task
of bringing various influential elements in the nation into
or behind the Nazi Party, the industrialists and the Church
among them. Now as President of the Reichstag his task
was eased, for he had legal authorization behind him to
participate in all political events.

"If, for instance," he said later, "a government resigned
in the Reichstag or was brought to a fall by a vote of no
confidence, it was my duty . . . to suggest to the Reich
President [Von Hindenburg], after having negotiated with
the parties, what the possibilities were in my opinion for a
new coalition government. Thus the Reich President was
always bound to receive me in this capacity with regard to
these matters. Therefore I could bring about a rather close
connection between the Reich President and myself. But I
should like to emphasize that this connection had already
existed before. It was a matter of course that Field Marshal
von Hindenburg, if I requested it, would always receive
me, because he had known me in the First World War."

He worked on the old man to persuade him of Adolf
Hitler's integrity, the genuineness of the National Socialist
Party's patriotism, and their attachment to legality, respectability, and German tradition. At the same time, he
learned the tricks of his office and watched Chancellor von
Papen like a hawk to make sure that that serpentine diplomat did not sabotage him and the Nazis.

On September 12, 1932, Von Papen tried. By this time
strongly aware that all sides of the House were against
him, and that his government was a head without a body,
he persuaded President von Hindenburg that the only way
to avoid chaos was to give him a decree allowing him to
dissolve the Reichstag whenever conditions became impossible. He intended to invoke this on September 12, because
he knew on that day the Communists proposed to ask for a
vote of censure against his government. His plan was to let
the Communists make their proposal, wait until the other
parties refused to allow the vote to be taken (as he had
been told they would do), and then rise to his feet. First he
would make a fighting speech, blaming the Communists

and their allies for the chaos in the Reichstag, and immediately afterward introduce his decree to prorogue the House.

But Goering had heard about his plan, and hastened to inform Hitler. The Party leaders put their heads together and decided that here was a chance to get Von Papen before he got them. Instead of voting against the Communist censure, the Nazis announced that they would support it. As the vote was being taken, Von Papen hurried away to get his decree of dissolution and present it to the Reichstag President in time. He came back with the dispatch box containing the decree and hurried to Goering's desk. But Goering deliberately turned his head away and loudly asked the deputies to register their vote on the motion of censure.

"The House became a scene of complete disorder," Von Papen wrote later. "The session resolved itself into a shouting match, and amidst the tumult Goering refused to recognize my right to speak . . . There was no other solution but for me to march over to the presidential platform, slap the dissolution order on Goering's desk, and walk out of the Reichstag with the members of the Cabinet, to the accompaniment of a positive howl of derision."

But still Goering took no notice. He registered the vote first: 513 for the motion of censure, 32 votes for Von Papen. Only then did he take up the decree, read it to the deputies, and then announce, to laughter and cheers, that the dissolution was invalid because it bore the signature of a Chancellor who had just been voted out of office.

In the new elections which took place on December 6, 1932, the National Socialists lost some ground and a number of seats in the Reichstag, but Hermann Goering was once more elected President. He had no doubt in his mind by now that this was the crucial period for the National Socialist Party, and that if they failed to attain power in the new session of the House, the last opportunity would have been lost and there would be no other way to take over the nation than by revolution. That he was still determined should not happen, and the fear of it acted as a goad in all he did in the following weeks. He intrigued, manipulated, made deals, pleaded with President Hindenburg, plotted with the old man's son, all in the cause of getting Adolf Hitler made Chancellor of the German Reich.

The story of the Byzantine ploys which eventually brought the National Socialist Government into being are too complicated to summarize here. Let it simply be said that to no one more than Hermann Goering did the credit for Adolf Hitler's victory belong. On January 29, 1933, he arrived at a Party conference in the Kaiserhof Hotel in Berlin with the announcement that it had all been arranged. Von Hindenburg's corrupt son (until now anti-Hitler) had been squared with bribes and promises. The Army had been fixed, in spite of desperate plots on the part of General von Schleicher, who wanted power for himself. The President had finally succumbed to pressure and blandishments and consented.

Hermann Goering rushed around to Goebbels' apartment where his advisers had gone to wait with Hitler, and proudly announced that the President would be appointing Hitler as Chancellor of Germany on the morrow.

Josef Goebbels later wrote in his diary:

"This was certainly the finest hour in Goering's life. For years he had been smoothing the diplomatic and political path for the Fuehrer by exhausting negotiations. His prudence, his strong nerves, and above all his force of character and his loyalty to Hitler were sincere, strong and admirable."

Now, wrote Goebbels, "this upright soldier with the heart of a child" had brought Hitler "the greatest piece of news of his life."

The meeting adjourned and the members of the Nazi hierarchy, practically hugging themselves with jubilation, went off to prepare for momentous events on the morrow. After they were gone, Hermann Goering relaxed for the first time for weeks. He needed sleep, and he believed that for once it would not escape him. But before he climbed into bed, he telephoned to Weimar and caught Emmy Sonnemann in her dressing room just after the curtain fell.

"It's all fixed," he said. "Adolf Hitler will be Chancellor tomorrow. You absolutely must come to Berlin. I'll send a car for you."

To those who saw him on the afternoon of January 30, 1933, Hermann Goering had never looked calmer nor more content. He had called domestic and foreign correspondents into the reception room of the Reichstag President's palace to announce the composition of Adolf Hitler's Cabinet.

"It was a humble, sweetly reasonable Goering, obviously overwhelmed by the stroke of luck to which he owed his success," wrote Willi Frischauer, one of the correspondents. "In this mood Goering was charming, captivating, far removed from the turmoil of the streets which were already filling with Nazi supporters."

In fact, despite appearances, Goering was not as relaxed as he seemed. He was well aware that though the Nazis had won a battle they were a long way from having won the war. Power had certainly been put into Adolf Hitler's hands, but it was restricted power. President von Hindenburg was eighty-five years old but wily enough to have seen to that. He had appointed Hitler as Chancellor of the German Reich at ten-thirty that morning and shaken his hand for the first time. But he had, he hoped, surrounded him with men who would be watching his every move and would restrict and confine him.

Goering himself had been given a key post in the Cabinet as Minister without Portfolio and also made Prussian Minister of the Interior. Another National Socialist, Wilhelm Frick, would be Reich Minister of the Interior. But the rest of the important jobs had all gone to non-Nazis. Foreign Affairs was in the hands of Baron Constantin von Neurath, General von Blomberg of the Reichswehr was Minister of Defense, Alfred Hugenberg of the Nationalists was Minister of both Economy and Agriculture, and other ministries had gone to men who, until now, had been convinced anti-Nazis. Above all, the President had forced Hitler to accept Franz von Papen as his Vice-Chancellor and stipulated that whenever the Chancellor wanted an audience with the President, he must bring his Vice-Chancellor with him.

So here was a Cabinet in which the Nazis were outnumbered by eight to three; and the eight non-Nazis and President Hindenburg were convinced that they were strong enough to put a brake on any tendency on Hitler's part to ram through the radical ideas in his program.

So while he smiled for the correspondents and accepted the congratulations of his friends, Hermann Goering was preoccupied with the problem of the next step to be taken. How were the President and the Cabinet to be circumvented, and the Nazis given full powers to rule over the German people?

If he did not show his concerns to the outside world, he dropped the mask a little when he was alone with Emmy Sonnemann. There was to be a great torchlight parade of the Brownshirt Army through the main streets of Berlin that night, and he had reserved a room at the Kaiserhof Hotel for Emmy so that she could have a good view of the marchers.

"However, he did not seem very sure of the sentiments of the crowd," she remarked, later. "He handed me a revolver with the remark: 'Here, take this in case anything happens.' "

Emmy, who was terrified of guns, passed it covertly over to Cilly, Goering's maid, who accompanied her to the Kaiserhof.

Hermann Goering, wearing SA uniform ("It doesn't suit him—brown is not his color," Emmy said later), went off to the Reichschancellery as darkness fell. In the Tiergarten, the torches were lighted and soon the great parade began, and the watching crowd, no doubt to Goering's relief, began to roar its admiration and enthusiasm as the river of lights flowed down the Wilhelmstrasse. They passed President von Hindenburg's window where the old warrior, ramrod-straight, gazed down at the precisely marching men and was said to have remarked:

"If I'd known he could train troops like this, I'd have sent for the fellow before."

At a window of the Reichschancellery stood Adolf Hitler, flapping his hand in the Nazi salute, calmly surveying the scene and accepting the plaudits of the crowd. Behind him, Hermann Goering was broadcasting to the German people.

"My German comrades," he cried, "as I stand here at the microphone, hundreds of thousands of our people are massed outside the Reichschancellery. They are in a mood which can only be compared with the enthusiasm of August 1914, when the nation stood up to defend Fatherland, honor and freedom. January 30, 1933, will enter Germany's history as the day on which the nation, after fourteen years of anguish, pain, and shame, is restored to its former glory . . . See the great field marshal who has united himself now with the young generation. He stands beside the young new Fuehrer who will lead the nation to a new and better future. May the German people herald this day as it is acclaimed by the hundreds of thousands in front of these windows, inspired by the new faith [that] the future will bring us what we have fought for in spite of reverses and disappointments: Bread and work for the German people, freedom and honor for the nation."

The parade ended, and the Brownshirts and the great crowd stayed up to cram the cafes and carouse in the beer gardens. In the Reichschancellery there was a reception, but soon Hitler, Goering, and most of the other prominent Nazis slipped away to the house of Prince August Wilhelm, for Auwi's birthday began at midnight and he had organized a double celebration. Toasts were drunk to the royal family, to Hitler, to the National Socialists and to the Fatherland.

It was nearly 3 A.M. when Goering returned home, where Emmy Sonnemann was waiting for him. But when he suggested that they retire to bed as a fitting place to consummate a triumphant day, Emmy shook her head. She had to go back to Weimar at once, she said.

"Go back to Weimar on a day like this?" said Goering, in astonishment.

Yes, said Emmy. There was a rehearsal of *Faust* at the National Theater that morning, and it was vital that she should be there for it, because she was playing the principal role of Margarete.

Hermann Goering had not taken on the job of Prussian Minister of the Interior just for the title. He knew that when he was handed the keys to his new office in the Justice building he held in his hands the keys to power. For the Prussian Minister of the Interior controlled the police, and with the police at his orders there was little he could not do.

For the next three weeks it was just as well that Emmy Sonnemann was busy playing Margarete, for she saw little of her lover during that time.† He moved into the Ministry of Justice and called for the dossiers of all senior officials, and studied them with an official named Rudolf Diels, who seemed to be a walking encyclopedia of the political activities of his colleagues. Goering was determined to weed out of the Police and Justice departments anyone faintly suspected of being anti-Nazi. Diels had always been a virulent anti-Communist, but he now considerably broadened his scope to bring within the range of his antipathies anyone mildly left of center, and added their names to the blacklist for Goering's attention. He also provided his new boss with some entertainment in the shape of dossiers from the department of the political police in which the private lives of some of his National Socialist colleagues were set out in embarrassing detail. There was, for instance, a detailed account of a lawsuit which had somehow escaped the press in which a certain German baroness recounted how she had formally adopted Joachim Ribbentrop, now a prominent member of the Party, so that he could add an aristocratic "von" to his name; she was now suing for the sum of money which he had promised to pay her the moment he contracted a "satisfactory" marriage. Payment had become due, the baroness maintained, when Von Ribbentrop had made the daughter of the Henkell champagne millions his bride. There was a long report on Ernst Roehm's taste in boy friends, of Alfred Rosenberg's friendship with a Jewish girl (particularly cited because he was the chief apostle of anti-Semitism), of Adolf Hitler's suspected perjury when applying for German citizenship (he was an Austrian by birth), and of Gauleiter Gottfried Feder's involvement with Jewish money-lenders, Feder being one of the Party's experts on economics.

Goering read these through with audible sounds of delight, and later repeated them to Emmy Sonnemann. But what he did not tell her was about his own dossier, in which full details of his morphine addiction and his sojourn in a Swedish lunatic asylum were given; he swallowed these unhappy revelations with good grace, but roared with angry indignation when the dossier concluded

† Though Emmy says he did make "some dangerous night journeys" by car from Berlin to Weimar, and she sometimes came up by the last train to Berlin and went back first thing next morning.

with the words: "He exhibits many of the signs of a suppressed homosexual, and is given to flamboyance in dress and the use of cosmetics. There is however no evidence that his close friendship with Paul [Pilli] Koerner is anything but normal." The implication that he shared the sexual inclinations of an Ernst Roehm—whose predilections he tolerated but did not approve—annoyed him so much that he tore the dossier to shreds and flung it across the room.

By February 17, 1933, he had already absorbed enough information to begin the great purge of the Berlin and Prussian Police and Justice departments, and suddenly scores of departmental heads and district superintendents received curt notes telling them that their employment was at an end. To those due for pensions there was a note appended telling them to fill in details on an attached form and await a tribunal which would hear their case. The more important officials were dismissed personally by Hermann Goering, and among them was a young man named Dr. Robert Kempner. Kempner, a lawyer of great brilliance, headed the state prosecutor's department and had been responsible for several successful cases against SA and SS men involved in political demonstrations. In Kempner's dossier Goering discovered a proposal the young lawyer had made for the arrest of Adolf Hitler for treason against the state, on the grounds that at one period he had connived with Ernst Roehm for an armed rising of the Brownshirt SA.

Goering gave Kempner a fierce tongue-lashing for his temerity in daring to have considered touching the Fuehrer, and told him he was being sacked out of hand.

"You are lucky I am not having you flung into jail,"‡ Goering shouted. "Get out of my sight, I never want to see you again."

But he did, as will become apparent in this narrative.

With the Augean stables cleaned out (as Goebbels put it when writing of the purge), Goering was able to introduce his own men into key departments. His friend Pilli Koerner was made a secretary of state in the Justice Department, Rudolf Diels was promoted to chief of the political police,

‡ He was to be arrested later.

Count Wolf Helldorff, a Nazi group leader and soldier of fortune, was made a departmental chief. For his own staff Goering chose Dr. Erich Gritzbach, who later wrote his biography, as his right-hand man, Martin Sommerfield, who also wrote his biography, as his press chief, and a brisk and efficient woman named Frau Greta von Kornatzki as his secretary.

To those members of the police and the civil service who had escaped the purge (and it should perhaps be emphasized that the great majority of the Justice Department were eager and willing to serve their new chief) he issued a manifesto. In this he bluntly told the police that in future they must avoid anything suggesting a hostile attitude toward "national associations and parties" and counseling them to treat these organizations with "understanding." But he then made it clear that he was referring to the Nazi and Nationalist bodies and not to anything further to the left.

"On the other hand," he went on, "the activities of organizations hostile to the State are to be checked by the strongest possible measures. With Communist terrorism and raids there must be no trifling, and when necessary revolvers must be used without regard to consequences. Policemen who fire their revolvers in the execution of their duties will be protected by me without regard to the consequences of having used these weapons. But officials who fail, out of mistaken regard for the consequences, must expect disciplinary action to be taken against them. The protection of the people demands the strictest application of the legal regulations governing prohibited demonstrations, prohibited meetings, smashings, incitement to high treason, mass strikes, revolts, newspaper offenses, and all other punishable offenses of the disturbers of law and order. No officer should lose sight of the fact that failure to adopt a measure is more heinous than the making of mistakes in its application. I hope and expect that all officers will feel at one with me in our common purpose of saving our Fatherland from threatened calamity by the strengthening and consolidation of our national forces."

On February 22, he took a further step toward turning the police into an instrument completely under his control by drafting SA and SS men into the force as auxiliaries.

They wore their Party uniforms with a white armband signifying their auxiliary status, and soon, if not yet, they would be a power in the land.

Hermann Goering had proved during his command of the Richthofen Squadron that he could be a first-rate administrator, but he had also shown that he liked to remind everyone under him continually who was boss. In his new job he quickly demonstrated that he had lost neither the managerial know-how nor the dictatorial inclinations.

"In the future," he said, in a speech at Dortmund, "there will be only one man who will wield power and responsibility in Prussia and that is myself. Whoever does his duty in the service of the State, who obeys my orders and ruthlessly makes use of his revolver when attacked, is assured of my protection. Whoever, on the other hand, plays the coward will have to reckon on being thrown out by me pronto. A bullet fired from the barrel of a police gun is my bullet. If you say that is murder then I am the murderer."

He paused and then said:

"I know two sorts of men only—those who are with us and those who are against us."

One condition which Adolf Hitler had meekly accepted from President von Hindenburg when he had been appointed Chancellor was that the moment there was dissension in the Cabinet, he would call an election. At the time it had seemed to some of his advisers a dangerous restriction of the Nazi leader's freedom of movement, and they had urged him to reject it. Now they understood why Goering, on the other hand, far from balking at the proviso, had welcomed it. Now he was able to demonstrate why. With a police force and their Brownshirt auxiliaries ready to move at the crack of his whip, he was master of the streets and no Communist force would dare (as some of the Nazis feared) attempt a rising. The future would be decided at the polling booths. And who would be in charge of the polling booths? Why, the police, of course.

So Adolf Hitler did not wait for a cabinet crisis in order to decide on new elections. He deliberately provoked one, and then announced that Germany would go to the polls once more on March 5, 1933. Even Goebbels, who had been skeptical about turning to the country so soon, was now delighted, because Hitler had appointed him Reich

Minister of Propaganda and, as Goering had done with the police, he was gathering the instruments of press, radio, and "public enlightenment" under his control.

"Now it will be easy to carry on the fight," he wrote in his diary, "for we can call on all the resources of the State. Radio and Press are at our disposal. We shall stage a masterpiece of propaganda. And this time, naturally, there is no lack of money."

This was a reference to the fact that once Adolf Hitler had become Chancellor, all the big-business men of Germany, who had gone under cover during the setbacks of 1932, had come forward enthusiastically with their purses open. Hermann Goering gave a party in his presidential palace for a group of industrialists on February 20, among whom were Krupp von Bohlen, Bosch of the magneto enterprise, Schnitzler of I. G. Farben and Voegler of United Steel. Dr. Hjalmar Schacht acted as host. Hitler made a short speech in which he promised, when he had won all-out power at the polls, to eliminate the Marxists from the streets and the factories, and to restore the power of the Army (which would mean big new armament contracts for the industrialists of the Ruhr). Hermann Goering asked the guests to make "financial sacrifices," pointing out that this was a now-or-never election demanding a now-or-never contribution. If the Nazis won, he pointed out, there needn't be another election for ten, maybe even a hundred years.

As Dr. Schacht later put it, he then "took around the hat" and collected three million marks.

With the election campaign in full swing, Goering gave his first big political command to his reconstituted police. He ordered them on February 24 to raid the Karl Liebknecht Haus, headquarters of the Communist Party in Berlin. He announced the same night that incriminating documents had been discovered "proving" that the Communists were about to launch a revolution, but did not for the moment give out any details to the public. To the Cabinet, however, some of whose members were skeptical, he circulated a memorandum giving details of the Red plans which had been uncovered, and these were later summarized in an official statement from the Prussian government.

"Government buildings, museums, mansions and essential plants were to be burned down," the statement said. "Women and children were to be sent in front of terrorist groups . . . The burning of the Reichstag was to be the signal for a bloody insurrection . . . [There were to be] many terrorist acts against individual persons, against private property, and against the life and limb of the peaceful population, and also the beginning of a general civil war."

It is not unlikely that incriminating papers were, indeed, found in the Karl Liebknecht Haus by Goering's raiders, for most political bodies in Germany at the time not only had their private armies but had drawn up contingency plans for using them in an emergency. In that, the Communists were no different from the Socialists or the Nazis. What is doubtful is that the documents "proved" that the Communists were on the verge of a rising. They realized that the situation in Germany was rapidly polarizing into a Them or Us condition, and that they might soon have to fight for their existence. But first they needed the propaganda value of a good showing at the elections on March 5.

Almost certainly, Hermann Goering did not consider the crisis so imminently threatening as he made out. Otherwise he would have at once initiated a campaign of preventive arrests, instructed Ernst Roehm to put his Brownshirts on a state of alert, and flung guards around all Berlin's most important buildings. He did none of these things. He was later to say that he was keeping details of the Red plots secret from the public until after the Nazis had won the election—as they were now certain of doing—when he could use them as a justification for the actions against the Communists which the Nazi leaders were now planning.

So he obviously did not really believe that Red riot and bloodshed were going to break out in Berlin at any moment. According to the Prussian government statement issued later, the signal for "bloody insurrection and civil war" was to be the "burning of the Reichstag."

Why was it not, then, immediately cordoned off and closely guarded night and day from the moment the Red "plot" against it was discovered? On the night of February 27, six days before the election, there were only a night porter, a postman, and a lamplighter inside the Reichstag and only a police sergeant on duty outside it. And that was the night that someone set fire to it and burned it down.

XII. AVIATION MINISTER

One of the perks of being President of the Reichstag was a residential palace adjoining the assembly building, and it was there that he was expected to live. But Goering disliked its gloomy air and heavy furniture, and he used it only for official receptions and press conferences. He preferred his apartment in the Kaiserdamm, which, as Emmy Sonnemann remarked the first time she saw it, "was furnished in very good taste in a style which reflected his personality, though it was rather above his financial situation."

For his duties as Police Chief of Prussia he had an office in the Prussian Ministry on the Unter den Linden, but normally he preferred working in his office in the Reichstag building. This he had decorated with some family pictures, good furniture and a couple of valuable tapestries, which had been left to him by his father and were, Goering believed, Gobelins. He was particularly fond of them.

As domestic help in his Kaiserdamm apartment he still had Cilly, who had now learned to cook, plus a kitchen maid, and the parties he gave were soon popular in Berlin for their good food and wine, and for the gaiety of the company.

One of his female friends, a certain Baroness Holdorff, pointed out to him (it would never have occurred to Emmy Sonnemann) that no man in his position should be without a valet, and volunteered to procure one for him. It so happened that she made the offer at one of Goering's official receptions, and she was overheard by an SA Gruppenfuehrer named Karl Ernst, who, since he controlled the Brownshirts who had been drafted into the police force as auxiliaries, had also been given the title of Police President.

Karl Ernst was one of the few men whom Goering

hated, loathed, and feared. He showed good taste in this. Ernst was not only a homosexual, which Goering was at least prepared to tolerate, but he was a pervert of a particularly vicious kind, as well as a sadist and a troublemaker. He had a taste for small boys, the more unwilling the better. He encouraged his men to beat and torture the prisoners they took into custody, particularly political opponents. And he was vocally critical of the National Socialist policy of winning power through the ballot box, loudly proclaiming that the only good Reds and good Jews were dead ones.

It was Ernst who had insisted on providing his Minister with a bodyguard whose members, Goering soon decided, were more interested in spying on his activities than protecting his life. They were a particularly thuggish group of Brownshirts and Goering had complained several times to Ernst about their behavior, particularly the way they roughed up anyone who got in his way or Emmy's when they were out in public together. In answer to his protest, Ernst pointed out that since the "gnädige Frau" was not married to the Minister, people might not understand her importance to him and they had to be shown that her progress was not to be impeded.

Insolences of this kind had to be swallowed because if he needed the Brownshirt auxiliaries, which he certainly did, he knew he would have to take Karl Ernst, who was a close friend, in more ways than one, of Ernst Roehm, the Brownshirt commander-in-chief. But what he did not have to swallow was Ernst's offer of one of his own bodyguard to act as his valet. The thought of one of these perverted thugs inside his house, his wardrobes, and his bedroom, was a thought too awful to be contemplated. He snubbed the Brownshirt police president and quickly accepted Baroness Holdorff's offer.

As a result, a small advertisement was inserted by her in the *Kreuz Zeitung*, a favorite paper among veterans of the armed forces. From the candidates who came forward she picked an ex-navy man named Robert Kropp as the most suitable applicant for the job, and sent him to the Kaiserdamm to see Goering. He kept him waiting for several hours but when he was at last shown into Goering's study, he saw that his testimonials and his war record were lying on the desk in front of him.

"You seem just the man," Goering said. "What wages do you want?"

Kropp, who had worked for a number of wealthy Ruhr industrialists, asked for the going rate of 140 marks a month.

"I'll give you 80 to start with, and if you are satisfactory you will get a rise," Goering said. "If not—out!"

Three months later, he doubled Kropp's salary and made the increase retroactive, and an association began between man and manservant which was to last almost to the end of Goering's life.

On the night of February 27, 1933, Robert Kropp was making himself a cup of mint tea in the kitchen of the apartment in the Kaiserdamm when the telephone rang, and when he answered it Aderman, the night porter at the presidential palace, was on the other end. He was excited and shouted:

"You must tell the Minister at once! The Reichstag is on fire!"

Hermann Goering was working that night in the Prussian Ministry offices in the Unter den Linden, and it was there that Kropp telephoned. Goering had just heard the news from the police, and was on his way out of his office. He seemed to be completely astonished and made no mention whatsoever of sabotage. Kropp too assumed that the fire was accidental.

But later he began to wonder. He knew the presidential palace well, because he was almost always there when Goering's presence demanded it. He knew that there was a tunnel connecting the palace with the Reichstag itself, for he frequently used it to take messages from his master to his staff in his Reichstag office. And, since he shared Goering's antipathy for Police President Karl Ernst, he had also noticed that he had been around the presidential palace surprisingly frequently, and for no obvious reason, in the preceding days, usually accompanied by two of his more unpleasant-looking cohorts.

This occurred to him later. In the meantime, Kropp alerted Cilly to stand by the telephone and slipped on his coat and went out and across to the Reichstag, from the dome of which he could now, as he approached, see flames licking. Goering's official car had already arrived and he had gone inside the building; Kropp followed. He realized at once where his master must have gone and made for the corridor in which the presidential office was situated. He was just in time to see Goering staggering back from a gout of flame and a gust of smoke. He saw Kropp and shouted:

"We must save my Gobelins!"

But it was too late for that. His office had by this time been burned to a cinder and all the paintings, furniture, and tapestries with it. The session chamber itself had been burned out. The fire brigades were working hard to bring the flames under control, but whatever they achieved, the Reichstag would be only a shell from now on.

When Goering eventually came out into the forecourt again, it was to find that Adolf Hitler had arrived. He struggled across the tangle of fire hoses to greet the Fuehrer, and as his faithful valet followed he was astonished to see the look of triumph, almost of pleasure, on Hitler's face.

"This is a beacon from heaven!" Hitler shouted, above the crackle of the flames.

Goering's face was black and he appeared to be crying, whether from smoke or from the loss of his Gobelins, Kropp could not tell.

Hundreds of books and reports have been written about the Reichstag fire, but none of them has been able to pin the blame on anyone except the man who was eventually executed for it, Marinus van der Lubbe. Perhaps the most complete study of all the evidence available was made by the Institut für Zeitgeschichte in Munich, but years of poring over all the documents and examining all the statements have failed to incriminate anyone except this pyromaniac who was found on the scene of the crime.

While the fire was still going on, the twenty-four-year-old Dutchman named Van der Lubbe was arrested in the rear rooms of the Reichstag, and he was caught practically with the match in his hand. He had stripped to the waist because of the heat, leaving the rest of his clothes (the charred remains of which were found) in the session chamber. He readily confessed to having set the place on fire. A check of his record revealed that he belonged to a Communist group, though it was a Trotskyist rather than a Stalinist faction; that he was an avid publicity hound and had once tried to swim the English Channel without any preliminary training; that he had a psychiatric record and pyromaniac tendencies; and that he was inclined to claim credit for crimes, strikes, and sabotage, even when he was innocent.

No one had any doubt, however, that Van der Lubbe was telling the truth when he said he had started the Reichstag fire. The only question was, had he done it all by himself?

In these days it is not, perhaps, so difficult as it used to be to believe that one man alone can commit a crime of enormous political magnitude. We have learned to live with the fact that it was almost certainly one man who killed President John F. Kennedy, beyond doubt that one man killed Robert Kennedy, and equally certain that one man killed Martin Luther King. There may have been conspirators with them in spirit, but they did their evil deeds alone.

But in the climate of Berlin in 1933, everyone automatically assumed that there was a conspiratorial basis to the fire. The question was, which side had done it—the Communists or the Nazis?

Since there was considerable political advantage to be gained from pinning the blame on the Communists, the National Socialists did not wait for an official inquiry before blaming them. Within a few moments of his remark that the fire was "a beacon from heaven," Hitler had named the Communists as the culprits, and ordered Goering to start arresting them. Goering already had the lists prepared.

"The lists were there. The fire did not have to start for that," he said later. "They would have been arrested anyway. I already had some valid reasons for action to be taken against the Communists, in the form of assassinations they had committed and so on."

But neither he nor Hitler could accept the fact that Van der Lubbe might have acted alone, and since Goering swore he knew nothing of any Nazi involvement, and was convinced that Hitler was equally ignorant, why not pin it on the Reds?

On the other hand, most opponents of the Nazis automatically assumed that the Reichstag had been fired by the Hitlerites with the deliberate intention of blaming it on the

Communists and then taking reprisals against them. As early as February 20, 1933, four days before the raid on Communist headquarters, in other words, four days before any "documentary proof" of Red revolutionary plots had been unearthed, Count Harry Kessler was writing in his diary:

"Wieland Herzfelde asked to see me on a matter of great urgency. He had absolutely reliable information, he said, that the Nazis plan a fake attempt on Hitler's life which is to be the signal for a general massacre. The sources of his information are the SA in Dortmund and a tapped telephone conversation between Hitler and Roehm."

And on February 27, the day of the fire, he wrote:

"A historic day of prime importance. The planned assault has taken place, though not on Hitler but the Reichstag building . . . Goering has immediately declared the Communist Party guilty of the crime."

Kessler was not the only one in Germany or abroad who voiced the suspicion that Goering himself had been the mastermind behind the fire. Foreign correspondents were soon pointing out that Goering lived in the presidential palace, which was connected by a tunnel to the Reichstag, and followed this by fanciful accounts of how he had superintended the passage of conspirators with incendiary materials into the building by way of the tunnel. The arsonists had then come back the same way, leaving Van der Lubbe literally holding the torch.

Goering's reaction to these charges varied from the cynical to the indignant.

"I knew people would say that," he remarked, when the stories in foreign newspapers reached him. "I suppose they think that, dressed in a red toga and holding a lyre in my hand, I looked on at the fire and played while the Reichstag was burning."

But in another mood he exploded:

"If I am accused of having myself set fire to the Reichstag in order to get the Communists into my hands, I can only say that the idea is ridiculous and grotesque. I did not need any special event to enable me to proceed against the Communists."

He added: "I can really tell you frankly that the Reichstag fire was very inopportune for us. To the Fuehrer as well as to me as President of the Reichstag. If we had wanted to burn a building [and blame the Communists] there were others which could have been used which were not as essential. The Castle of Berlin, for instance, or some other building. But look what happened after the fire. I had to use the Kroll Opera House for the use of the meetings of the Reichstag. And you know what a great interest I had in the State Theater, which came under my control. It was very hard on me, because the Kroll building was one of the only two places in Berlin where small opera performances could be given."

For the rest of his life he went on denying that he had anything to do with the fire. Like Robert Kropp, he suspected that the hated Karl Ernst might have had something to do with it "because he wanted to create difficulties for us," but it is doubtful if he ever knew for sure. But he was adamant about his own innocence. Being Goering, however, he couldn't help adding:

"Even if I had started the fire, I wouldn't brag about it. And if I had started the fire, I wouldn't have done it to get the Communists but for a completely different reason."

"For what reason?" he was asked.

"Because the session hall of the Reichstag was so ugly," he replied. "My dear fellow, it had *plaster* walls!"

As for Emmy Sonnemann, she never had any doubt about his innocence. On the night of the fire he telephoned her at Weimar. He was very excited but she found it difficult to understand the significance of the event.

"Is it very serious?" she asked. "What do you think?"

"I'm thinking about my personal belongings and my family pictures," he said. "Why did I put into that office of all places all the things I valued most?"

This convinced her beyond all doubt. "Against [the] rumors I had only one argument," she wrote later. "I knew Hermann and I knew how greatly he valued the furniture which was destroyed in the fire, the last things he would have wanted to sacrifice. To be sure, that is a woman's argument which carried little weight either for or against a predetermined theory. But for me it is a certitude which, however, I cannot of course compel anyone to share."

In the rush to blame the Communists for the fire, and at Hitler's urgent behest, Goering ordered the political police to come up with some culprits, and Rudolf Diels produced four men. Three were Bulgarian Communists working with their comrades in Berlin: Georg Dimitrov, Blagoi Popov, and Wassil Tanev, and they were at once arrested. The fourth was Ernst Torgler, the German Communist Party leader, who gave himself up when he heard he was wanted.

Their trial was set for the following September, and Goering planned to use it as a platform for destroying completely the reputation of the Communist Party in Germany.

It was to be one of the most serious miscalculations of his political career.

There is no doubt, however, that immediately after the Reichstag fire the National Socialists made good propaganda use of it. On the day after it had happened, while the ruins still smoldered, Adolf Hitler prevailed upon President Hindenburg to sign a decree suspending the seven sections of the constitution guaranteeing individual and civil liberties. It was directed against "Communist acts of violence endangering the State" and it ordained:

Restrictions on personal liberty and on the right of free expression of opinion, including freedom of the Press;

Curtailment of rights of assembly and association;

Censorship of mail, telegraphic messages, and telephone conversations;

An abrogation of the legal limits on house arrests, requisitions, and searches.

It was now that the auxiliary SA and SS members of the police came into their own. Though Goering signed an order for the arrests of Communists only, liberal and left-wing elements now began to be brought into police headquarters as well, and were harassed and beaten. Meetings were banned and any attempts at assembly were raided and brutally broken up, and many leading Communists and Socialists fled for safety over the Austrian and Czechoslovak frontiers.

The violation of his orders would soon bring Hermann Goering into direct confrontation with his *bête noire*, Police President Karl Ernst, but for the moment he was too closely engaged in exploiting the Communists' discomfiture and winning the election.

With every loud-speaker in Germany blaring out Nazi propaganda and accusations against the Reds, the people of Germany went to the polls on March 5, 1933. Under the circumstances, the National Socialists did not do as well as they had expected or their opponents feared. True, they polled 17,277,180 votes, an increase of five and a half million over the previous election. But it was still only 44 per cent of the total votes, meaning that more Germans voted against than for them.

The Center Party actually increased its over-all vote from 4,230,600 to 4,424,900. The Socialists lost only 70,000 votes in polling 7,181,629. And considering all that had been said and done against them over the past two weeks—including the arrest of one of their leaders, Ernst Torgler—the Communists emerged with the most surprising result of all, polling 4,848,058 votes, a loss of only a million on their previous poll.

The Nazis could console themselves with the fact that the Nationalists, led by Franz von Papen and Alfred Hugenberg, had polled 3,136,760 votes, which, if added to the Nazi vote, meant that a majority of Germans had voted for the right. With the Nationalists' 52 seats added to the Nazis' own 288, Hitler would have a majority of 16 seats in the new Reichstag. But neither he nor Goering found that satisfactory.

What they now had in mind was not a small parliamentary majority, but control of the nation, and that could only be brought about by placing the Reichstag's total power in abeyance. They wanted to do it legally and there was a legal way to do it. What they could do was bring an enabling bill before the House which, if voted through, would allow them to adjourn the assembly *sine die*. But an enabling bill needed a two-thirds majority to be passed, and all they had was sixteen votes more than the rest combined.

What was the answer to that one? Hermann Goering did not hesitate to produce it.

He pointed out that the decree which President Hindenburg had signed for Adolf Hitler on the morning after the Reichstag fire gave Goering's police forces full powers of arrest not only of ordinary members of the general public, but of Reichstag deputies, whose immunity was automatically waived.

"The answer is simple," said Goering. "We will arrest all the Communist deputies and enough Social Democrats to frighten the rest, and then we will put the enabling bill to the vote."

This they did on March 23, 1933. Meeting in the Kroll

Opera House where, a few weeks before, enthusiastic audiences had gathered to applaud Richard Tauber singing the gay tunes from the long-running musical, *The Land of Smiles*, the cowed deputies from both Center and Social Democrats joined the Nazis in voting the enabling bill through with a majority of 441 to 84. Democracy was dead in Germany. Adolf Hitler and the National Socialists had been legally accorded the powers to rule Germany from now on.

Hermann Goering rushed home to telephone Emmy Sonnemann with the news. Then he read a message which was lying on his desk from his friend Pilli Koerner, now a secretary of state in the Police Department, and knew that the clash which he had long been trying to avoid was coming with the egregious Brownshirt police president, Karl Ernst.

It was all very well to wield dictatorial police powers and send out your minions to smash political parties, breach parlimentary immunity, and carry out wholesale arrests. But when you have apprehended political prisoners in droves, what do you do with them?

The answer was the establishment of concentration camps, which Goering was ever afterward to claim were modeled on the lines of those used by the British to hold Afrikaners captured or arrested during the Boer War. But Goering offered one improvement.

"I instructed the controllers of the camps," he said, "that they should be used not just to deprive men and women of their liberty, but to re-educate and rehabilitate them."

As the purges continued all through March 1933, hundreds of Communists, Socialists, and Social Democrats were herded into these camps, and control of them was handed over to the civil servant who was now chief of the political police, Rudolf Diels. Information about them was passed on to Goering through Pilli Koerner.

It was Koerner who started sending memoranda to Goering pointing out that the political prisoners who were now being arrested by the SA not only included thousands of Communists and Socialists but many members of the Center and Catholic parties, civil servants, and anyone against whom the SA chiefs or their local representatives seemed to have grudges. Moreover, alarming rumors were begin-

ning to circulate that the SA had begun setting up camps
of their own, in addition to those which Goering had authorized, and that in these secret places acts of great brutality were being committed against the occupants.
Koerner pointed out that one of them was under the personal control of Police President Karl Ernst himself, and
that he ran the place like a circus, terrorizing the inmates
by striding around cracking a bull-whip. There were prisoners here of all ages—"and you know what that means,"
noted Koerner. "Small boys!" Goering explained to Emmy.

Emmy herself was coming up against the hard facts of
life in the new Germany, and realizing that terrible things
were happening on the other side of the footlights in
Weimar. Soon she knew enough about concentration
camps to ring up Hermann Goering on behalf of relatives
of prisoners, who knew she had the Minister's ear. A ministerial director named Hermann, who worked in the Justice Department in Kassel, had been carted off to camp one
night after being overheard criticizing the Nazis in a *Wein-
stube*. She beseeched Goering to find him and get him
released. He did so, but was embarrassed to discover that
the man in the meantime had suffered a broken arm and a
broken jaw.

Soon she began to be bombarded with telephone calls
and letters from families asking her to intercede. She had a
kind heart and no one asked in vain.

One day Pilli Koerner sent Goering a note informing
him that Ernst Thaelmann, the Communist leader, who
had been in a camp for some time, was being brutally
tortured by the Brownshirts, with the express approval of
Karl Ernst. Goering ordered Thaelmann to be brought to
his office, and he was hastily cleaned up and transported to
the Ministry.

Goering had always been careful to keep on good personal terms with his political opponents in the Reichstag,
and he shook Thaelmann by the hand and immediately
apologized for the treatment to which he had been subjected. But he added:

"My dear Thaelmann, I know that if you had come to
power I would not have been beaten up, but you would
have chopped off my head pronto."

He promised to have anyone punished who dared to ill-
treat him in the future, but if Thaelmann had hoped to be

released he was disappointed, because Goering had him taken back to the camp where he was being held. Cases of brutality, unnecessary brutality, as he would have termed it, distressed him, but as he was to say later, "When you use a plane on a piece of wood, you can't help making splinters."

What annoyed him, because they constituted a threat to his authority, were the illegal camps which the SA were setting up. He blamed Karl Ernst for these, because the most notorious ones, in addition to Ernst's own, were run by two of his closest homosexual friends, Gauleiter Karpfenstein of Pomerania, who had a camp near Stettin, and Obergruppenfuehrer Heines, who conducted a particularly sadistic regime in a camp outside Breslau.

He called Ernst into his office for a showdown. That Koerner was later able to testify. But what happened between the two men will never be known, except that Ernst presently emerged in triumph, to be followed shortly afterward by Goering, who seemed strangely subdued and kept muttering:

"One day I will have that monster's head!"

It seems that Ernst had defied him. But Goering eventually went over his head to Ernst Roehm himself, and the camps were closed. However, when he ordered his minions to shut down a fourth camp, which had been established near Osnabrück without his permission, he ran into opposition not from Ernst and the SA but from Heinrich Himmler and the SS. The SS guards not only barred entry to the camp for Goering's police but opened fire on them when they tried to insist, forcing them to beat a hasty retreat with one of their number shot in the stomach. The situation was grave enough for Goering to go direct to Hitler this time with his complaints, and the result was that the Osnabrück camp was broken up* and both Himmler and Roehm were told to avoid "unnecessary brutalities" to the inmates of the official camps in future. Himmler did not remind Hitler or Goering that he was already running another camp at Dachau to which no outsider (except the unfortunate prisoners) was admitted. He and Roehm agreed on Goering's urging to use "re-education" and "re-

* It was reopened later.

habilitation" on the inmates with the idea of bringing them back as "good Germans" into the mainstream of life in the new Germany, but neither man bothered to mention that they had very different ideas of re-education and re-habilitation from those of Hermann Goering.

Himmler was more successful than Roehm in concealing his contempt for Goering over what both the SS and the SA leaders called his "squeamishness." Roehm openly sneered at Goering's concern for the proper treatment of prisoners, at the shock and anger he displayed when evidence of torture was produced for his examination. Himmler was equally disdainful of his "weakness" but, for his own reasons, concealed it.

There is little doubt that Goering hated having the responsibility for the infliction of so much terror, pain and suffering. He was once to say to Emmy that he never minded shooting a man or an animal.

"I am a hunter by nature," he said. "I do not get bad dreams about killing. But I will never cause a man pain for the sake of inflicting pain. When I shot down a man in the war, I honored him as a defeated foe if he was unhurt and I looked after him if he was wounded. I prevented him from fighting against me again, but otherwise I treated him well. I would always wish to do the same for a political opponent. Why should I make him suffer? What pleasure can it give these monsters? Shoot him, if you must. But to torture him is as bad as wounding an animal and failing to finish him off."

The corridors of the Ministry of Justice were beginning to smell of terror and echo with the sounds of pain. But it took him some time before he did anything about it.

When Adolf Hitler formed his first coalition government, one of the jobs which had been handed to Hermann Goering was that of Commissioner for Aviation, and he continued to hold it when the Nazis had full power. No one outside Germany at first took the post very seriously, because they knew that under the terms of the Versailles Treaty an air force was strictly forbidden the Reich. It was a courtesy title, a sop to an old fighter pilot's pride, the Allies decided, and forecast that Goering would spend little time superintending the activities of the Lufthansa passenger and postal service and the small aero and gliding clubs, which was all the "air force" Germany was permitted under the treaty.

But Hermann Goering had never, in fact, forgotten the black day in 1918 when he had ordered his squadron to crash their planes on the airfield at Aschaffenburg, and one of his principal ambitions had been to see the memory of that humiliation wiped out by a resurgence of the Luftwaffe. He had pleaded in the Reichstag since 1929 for funds to help the Lufthansa build up its service, because he knew that the commercial firm would employ and train pilots who would one day fly fighters and bombers. And he had fought to keep aircraft firms going which would one day be able to switch to warplanes.

As Minister of Aviation, he was determined that just as the German Army had built up its strength by training a Black Reichswehr, over and above its permitted regular force of 100,000 men, so would he construct a Black Luftwaffe that would take to the German skies once the Treaty of Versailles was broken. So the moment the Nazis were in power, he had taken the necessary steps to get the secret air force on the wing.

While the coalition government was still in power, he called the old adjutant of the Richthofen Squadron, Karl Bodenschatz, back into service. Bodenschatz had transferred to the Army after the end of World War I and was now a full colonel in the Reichswehr. Goering summoned him to the Kaiserdamm apartment, and proudly pointed to a picture of his old squadron, Jasta 27, which had just been painted and presented to him by Claus Bergen. He was then taken on a tour of the apartment to see Goering's collection of art treasures, and it was not until he had admired his three Lucas Cranachs (the gift of the city of Dresden), his Madonna statue (a gift from Mussolini), and his huge portrait of Carin, that Goering got to the point of the meeting.

"Bodenschatz, what we have discussed so often in the past is now becoming a reality," he said. "I am Commissioner of Aviation but in reality the first German Air Minister since the end of the War. What I have promised when we parted in Aschaffenburg in 1918 I shall carry out—we shall have a German Air Force again. Not a military affair as yet . . . you understand! The Treaty of Versailles is still in force. But as soon as the Fuehrer has completed the political preparations to do away with the treaty, I want to be ready. I need a reliable friend to work with me—will you be my adjutant again?"†

Karl Bodenschatz hardly hesitated. He had never really got over his infatuation with Hermann Goering, and for the rest of his life, no matter how the shape or sound or personality of the man changed, he would always see beyond the plump man in the gaudy uniform to the dashing young blue-eyed hero of World War I.

"It took me barely a moment to say yes, and I renewed my association with him with gladness in my heart," he said later.

Getting Erhard Milch to join Goering's staff was rather more difficult. An army officer in World War I, and a particularly bellicose and arrogant one, Milch had taken over the civil air firm of Lufthansa in the early twenties, and by prodigious efforts and lobbying among government officials had built the firm into one of the most modern and forward-looking in the world. It was his personal baby and he was proud of it. Moreover, until now Hermann Goering had never been particularly close to him. Their paths had never crossed during World War I and Milch was not particularly dazzled by Goering's achievements as a pilot. To him he was just another politician to whom he had paid a subsidy in order to argue Lufthansa's case in the Reichstag. Once you have had a man on your payroll, it is difficult to go to work for him.

On January 28, 1933, Hermann Goering went to see Milch at his home and offered him a tempting job. He would be the secretary of state at the Air Ministry, and he would have control over all the day-to-day plans and activities of the Black Luftwaffe. Yet he played hard to get. It was not until Goering took him to Adolf Hitler himself that Milch finally gave way and accepted. Hitler said to him:

"Now look, I don't know you very well, but you are a man who knows his job, and we have few enough people in the Party who know as much about the air as you do. That is why the choice has fallen on you. You have *got* to take the job. It is not a question of the Party, as you seem to

† Quoted from *Goering* by Willi Frischauer.

think. It is a question of Germany—and Germany needs you for this task."

It was because of that speech, Milch was to say later, that he finally accepted.

Can one of the reasons for his hesitation have been that the National Socialist Party was anti-Jewish, and Erhard Milch was half-Jewish himself? Hermann Goering had known about it for some time. When the question of Milch's appointment had first come up, it was the wily civil servant-turned-political policeman, Rudolf Diels, who had slipped into the Minister's office one morning with Milch's dossier, and pointed a disdainful finger at the relevant paragraph. Erhard Milch's mother was pure Aryan but his father, a pharmacist in Breslau, was Jewish. That made his son Jewish in Nazi eyes and therefore proscribed. If the tenets of the Party were followed, not only could Milch never be Goering's secretary of state, he could no longer remain head of the national airline. He was beyond the pale.

Not, however, as far as Hermann Goering was concerned. One of the ifs of history is to wonder what might have happened if Goering, who was held in great esteem by Hitler at this time, whose advice he listened to and frequently took, had stood up to the Fuehrer and said:

"What is this nonsense about Jews, mein Fuehrer? I have been under the influence of Jews all my life, but here I am a loyal supporter at your side. The godfather whom I admired more than any other man until I met you is a Jew. The poets I liked most as a child were Jewish. I like Jewish music, Jewish playwrights, Jewish painters, even Jewish comedians! They like making money—but no more than I like money myself. And now here is poor Milch. You yourself have said that Germany needs him. You yourself have praised him for the way he has built up our national airline. He has not stinted himself, and it has not been for personal gain. But he is a Jew. Does that change everything?"

Goering had not the courage to say those things, and probably feared that Hitler would have replied:

"Yes, it changes everything—including your own position in the Party." So Hermann Goering did not speak out. More's the pity. Instead, he embarked on an elaborate ploy.

Erhard Milch's mother was called to Berlin and there persuaded to besmirch herself and humiliate her husband in the cause of her son. At all costs, she was told, it must not be revealed that Erhard was half-Jewish, and the only way to do that was to "prove" that he was, in fact, a pure Aryan. Frau Milch finally consented to make a sworn statement before a notary that during her marriage she had had a clandestine affair with a certain Baron Hermann von Bier and had born a son as a result. "If we're going to take his real father away from him, let us at least give him an aristocrat as a substitute!" Goering said.

The original birth certificate was withdrawn and a new one drawn up in its place giving Von Bier as the father, and Erhard Milch was safe. Thereafter there was no one in Germany more vocally contemptuous of the Jews or more enthusiastic over the anti-Jewish program.

So Goering had a first-class secretary of state, if hardly a first-class human being, to take care of his secret air force, and soon a number of his wartime comrades were brought in to strengthen the growing organization. His first flying friend, Bruno Loerzer, was made head of the "Air Sports Club," a euphemism for an underground training group for German pilots. Ernst Udet, who had flown under him in the Richthofen Squadron, and, like him, had barnstormed for a living after the war, was enrolled as an adviser in the Air Ministry.

On January 30, 1933, Hermann Goering joined a great gathering of fliers and aircraft manufacturers who had come to celebrate the twenty-fifth anniversary of the German Aero Club in Berlin. He introduced to them the new members of his staff and then told them that Adolf Hitler had authorized him to bring them good news. Below him in the audience he could see most of the better-known aircraft manufacturers, their skeptical expressions reflecting the disappointments they had so far experienced. With the advent of the Nazis, they had expected a renaissance of the industry.

"I agree with you," Goering had told them on arrival. "The position is shocking. But don't worry. Changes are coming."

Now he informed them that the government had arranged for substantial credits to be made available to the industry, and the go-ahead would be given for the increased production of the Junkers 52, the Heinkel 70, the Focke-Wulf FW-200 and the Dornier flying boat.

"You will need workers," Goering said, "but you can take your pick from six million unemployed. We shall put them to work building new airdromes, factories, aircraft, and engines. We shall pay men to take up flying and we shall bring in experienced NCOs from the Reichswehr to discipline them. Even if they are not allowed to wear the uniform of airmen, they must be trained like real soldiers."

The audience below him burst into wild cheers of approval, and then someone began to chant and everyone joined in:

"*Heil der Dicke! Heil der Dicke!* [Hail to the Fat One, Hail to the Fat One]!"

Hermann Goering blushed and grinned with delight as a group of burly pilots surged forward and hoisted his huge frame on their shoulders and danced with him round the room.

"Look, Hermann is flying again!" Bruno Loerzer cried.

XIII. ORDEAL BY TRIAL

Emmy Sonnemann was a happy-go-lucky character and not the type to complain, but there must have been moments in her association with Hermann Goering when her patience was severely strained. For instance, in the spring of 1933 she received a telephone call from Ernst Joost, director of the State Theater in Berlin, asking her if she would leave Weimar and come to the capital to play the lead in a new play called *Schlageter*. He sent her a copy of the script, and though she did not think it was any great shakes as a play, she recognized that the female role was a good dramatic one.

She had never played in Berlin and the prospect of doing so at last thrilled her, the fulfillment of a German actress's dream. She was convinced that the offer had come to her purely on merit, for she knew that Josef Goebbels controlled the theater now in Germany, and his relations with Hermann Goering had lately been strained. He had no reason to do Goering's mistress any favors.

To make sure that Joost knew exactly what he was doing, she learned the first act of the play and then pleaded with him to come down to Weimar and hear her do a run-through. He did so and said at once that her performance convinced him that she was the right actress for the part. Only then did she break her contract with Weimar and telephone Hermann Goering with the news. He shared her joy and laughed when she said:

"I don't know which pleases me most, to be playing in Berlin or to be able to see you every day from now on."

It was only when she arrived at the State Theater that she discovered that this establishment and the opera were the two places of entertainment in Berlin which were not under Goebbels' control but that of Hermann Goering, and that everyone in the company already cordially resented her because they believed she had got the part by favoritism and had been planted in the theater as one of her lover's spies.

She had always had her own room in Goering's apartment in the Kaiserdamm and she expected that she would be using it from now on, but he gently asked her, "for the time being" to find herself a small apartment of her own. She came to the rueful conclusion that she had been a fool in throwing up her job in Weimar. All Hermann was doing was bringing the affair to an end, and paying her off with a job at the State Theater.

She soon discovered that that wasn't the situation at all. Goering seemed if anything more devoted to her than ever. He was a constant and overnight visitor at her small apartment, and was with her whenever he had time to spare. She came to the conclusion that perhaps the presence in the Kaiserdamm apartment of his new valet, Robert Kropp, had been the inhibiting factor—Hermann might not have wanted to shock him. It was not until later that she discovered that Thomas von Kantzow, Carin's son, had been on a visit to Berlin, and for some reason Goering did not want the young man to know there was another woman in his life.

For the first time in their association, Emmy Sonnemann began to be concerned about Goering's state of health. Despite the ebullience of his manner at the annual meeting of the Aero Club, Goering was an overworked and worried man. He had worked without rest to bring Hitler and the Nazis to power, and now that it was accomplished, the reaction set in. He was suddenly tired and full of doubts—doubts about the way the Party was going, doubts about his private life.

When Hermann Goering was worried, he ate. And when he ate he got fat. Sometimes, even when he had been to a state banquet at which he had eaten and drunk heavily, Robert Kropp would find him in the kitchen in the middle of the night helping himself to a leg of chicken or a plate of wurst, and drinking a glass of beer. He blushed and looked sheepish at first when he was discovered at these midnight feasts, but as relations with his manservant became easier he had no compunctions about rousing him in the middle of the night and telling him:

"Kropp, bring cheese, sausages, cakes, and plenty of beer! And some *Schlagsahne* (whipped cream)! I haven't had a thing all evening."

Then, his huge body bursting out of his frilly nightshirt, he would settle down to stuffing himself with all the zest of a schoolboy enjoying a clandestine dormitory feast.

The result was that his weight quickly reached 280 pounds, his buttons began to burst, his collars were too tight, and he sweated profusely. All this only increased his worry. Tailors were called in to alter his growing horde of uniforms and suits and vests of many colors. He was a fastidious man and his tendency to perspire heavily filled him with self-disgust; it explains why he disappeared so many times in one day to appear in a new uniform or a new suit. Their brightness of color would have provoked only minor interest in modern times, but in Berlin in the 1930s he stood out like a peacock in a henrun, and everyone noticed when he changed his shirt yet again.

When he reached what he regarded as his peak of 280 pounds, Goering embarked on a frantic regime of saunas, walking and riding, and slimming pills, and by prodigious efforts could sometimes take ten pounds off his weight over a weekend. But it weakened him considerably, and when he visited Emmy during these periods he would often flop into a chair and fall asleep, looking, as she described it, "like an exhausted bear," but probably more like a stranded whale.

In April 1933, toward the end of one of these frantic weight-losing regimes, Adolf Hitler asked him to lead his first diplomatic mission abroad. He and the Vice-Chancellor, Franz von Papen, were to confer with the Vatican and persuade the Pope's advisers that the National Socialist regime was not as anti-Catholic as some of the cardinals inside Germany had been indicating. It was not a mission to which Goering looked forward with any enthusiasm, especially in view of his physical condition; he had no particular antipathy toward the Roman Catholic Church, but neither did he consider it worth appeasing. He allowed Von Papen to do most of the negotiating with the Holy See and declined a suggestion that he might care to have an audience with the Pope. Instead, he and Erhard Milch, who had accompanied him, spent most of their time in

Rome in the company of the head of the Italian Air Force, Marshal Balbo, an ex-fighter pilot like himself, and Mussolini. The nights were long and gay and enjoyable, and when the time came to leave Goering was exhausted.

He was determined to be back in Germany in time for Adolf Hitler's birthday, on April 20, and while Von Papen and the rest of the delegation took the train home, Goering and Milch boarded a tri-motored Junkers 52 for the flight to Munich via Milan. By the time they had refueled and taken off from Milan, the weather had begun to close in and the crew found it necessary to climb to 20,000 feet to get over the massed banks of dangerous thunderclouds. Soon the plane began to yaw badly, and when Milch went into the pilot's cabin he found Goering lying flat on his back, frothing at the mouth and his eyes staring.

There was no oxygen left ("No wonder," Milch remarked later, "he had been taking it since we reached 1,500 feet") and the crew had forgotten to put any extra supplies aboard for emergencies. They opened Goering's collar and splashed water on him, but he stayed blue in the face and semi-conscious. Meanwhile, the crew had also begun to be affected by the altitude and had lost their way. Milch instructed the radio operator to call Milan for aid, but was told that Milan had gone off the air after receiving a message from the plane thanking Balbo and Mussolini for their hospitality and beginning: "As we leave Italian territory."

It was not until four hours later that they were able to get a bearing and eventually touch down at Munich. By that time Hermann Goering had recovered and made light of it when Milch mentioned his "collapse" to the Fuehrer at the birthday party.

But as a result of his physical collapse, he had a sudden recurrence of the pain in his old wound and began to limp badly. Emmy Sonnemann gave him some pills which she was taking for her sciatica, and from these he got some relief. The ache gradually passed away, but it was an ominous reminder that it was still around, and that when it plagued him it was bad enough for him to need painkillers to keep it at bay.

At the trial of the five men accused of starting the

Reichstag fire, which opened in Leipzig in September 1933, Hermann Goering made a fool of himself and knew it. He accepted the invitation to be chief witness for the prosecution, and confessed afterward to Emmy that it was a colossal error on his part. The trouble was, he had been deeply wounded, in spite of his outward nonchalance, by the accusations of his culpability which had been made by the press outside Germany, and he looked forward to the trial as an opportunity for demonstrating his complete innocence. That might have been easy enough to do if the unfortunate Marinus van der Lubbe had been the only one in the dock. There would be no trouble proving him guilty, because even non-Nazis accepted the fact that he had been found *in flagrante delicto*, and had readily confessed to setting the fire.

But the case against the other four men accused—Ernst Torgler and the three Bulgarians, Dimitrov, Tanev, and Popov, was much flimsier, and Goering knew it. To get a conviction against them a biased court of Nazi judges was needed, and this happened not to be that kind of court. The laws of cross-examination would prevail, and that meant that anything that Goering said was subject to questioning by the defense lawyers or the defendants themselves. One of the defendants, Georg Dimitrov, was a formidable character with great powers as a courtroom lawyer and as a political spokesman for his party, and he seized the opportunity thus given him to cross swords with the second most important man in the Nazi Reich.

There now seems little doubt that Georg Dimitrov was never in danger of execution or imprisonment at the hands of the National Socialists, even if he had been found guilty of plotting the firing of the Reichstag. He probably knew it, too, for the lawyers visiting him in prison during the preparations of his case must have told him that the Soviet Government was working hard on his behalf.* He was a member of the Comintern and not just any foreign Red, and he had been in Berlin on Moscow's orders when he was arrested. The National Socialist Government, despite the fulminations of its leaders against German Commu-

---

* They had already offered to exchange him for two captured German spies.

nism, had no thought of breaking off relations with Moscow and there were many in the Party in favor of closer relations with the Soviet Union. At this point in his government's career, Adolf Hitler was by no means eager to provoke a clash with Moscow over one of their favored plenipotentiaries, especially since he and Goering knew that he was innocent of the crime of which he was accused.

So Georg Dimitrov must have felt reasonably confident as he listened to Hermann Goering take the oath and begin his evidence. It seemed straightforward enough and was delivered with considerable conviction. He explained how the raid on the Karl Liebknecht Haus had produced "undeniable" proof that the Communist Party was plotting a revolution in Germany, and that all the dispositions had been made. Why then, he was asked, had he not pounced on the Reds immediately? Why had he waited until after the Reichstag fire, and then acted so precipitously?

"I was like a commander in the field," he replied, "who is about to put into operation a considered plan of campaign, and by an impulsive action of the enemy is suddenly forced to change his whole tactics."

He described in some detail his own personal actions on the night of the fire, scornfully rebutting any suggestion that he could have been involved in the catastrophe, and then went on to explain how he and Adolf Hitler had both come to the conclusion that the Communists were responsible, and that measures should be taken immediately against them.

"I intended to hang Van der Lubbe at once," he said, glancing contemptuously across the court at the Dutchman lolling, torpid, in his seat, apart in more senses than one from the other accused. "I only refrained because I thought—we have one of them but there must have been many. Anyway, perhaps we shall need him as a witness."

And then suddenly, as if aware of the weakness of the case against those "others" he said defiantly:

"I knew by intuition that the Communists fired the Reichstag. Let the trial end as it will, I will find the guilty and lead them to their punishment."

Dimitrov was conducting his own case, though his German was halting and ungrammatical. Now he rose to cross-examine and the eighty foreign journalists in the press box leaned forward for the high point of the trial.

It began quietly enough, with the Bulgarian taking the Reichminister step by step over the events leading to the arrest of himself and his colleagues. He scored a small coup when he forced Goering to admit that he had been wrong when he said Van der Lubbe had a Communist Party membership card in his pocket, when the police themselves had admitted he had not. Then suddenly he said:

"Is it not a fact that because you, in your position, have accused the Communist Party of Germany and foreign Communists this has prevented you from following up certain investigations and blocked the search for the real incendiarist?"

"No!" cried Goering, and was going on when Dimitrov interrupted:

"What has the Minister done to get the police to check Van der Lubbe's movements, his stay at Henigsdorf, his acquaintance with two people there—what have your police done?"†

Goering replied that he had obviously not followed every trail himself, but had left the day-to-day investigations to the police. He added:

"For me this was a political crime and I was convinced that the criminals are to be found in your party." And then, in a sudden access of rage, he shook his fist and went on: "Your party is a party of criminals and must be destroyed!"

It was more than the defendants could have hoped for, this violent outburst of passion, and Dimitrov was quick to press home the prod that would stir up the fire.

"Is the Minister not aware," he said, "that this party rules a sixth of the earth, the Soviet Union, with which Germany maintains diplomatic, political and economic relations, from which hundreds of thousands of German workers benefit—"

† This was a reference to rumors in Berlin that Van der Lubbe had met and been taken in hand by two Nazis at Henigsdorf after boasting that he would like to fire the Reichstag. They are said to have taken him away with them.

The president of the court leaned forward and said, sharply: "I forbid you to make Communist propaganda here."

Dimitrov turned to the president. "But Herr Goering makes National Socialist propaganda. Is it not a fact that Communism has millions of supporters in Germany—?"

Goering (shouting now): "It is a fact that you are behaving insolently! It is a fact that you came here to burn the Reichstag—. In my opinion you are a criminal who should be sent to the gallows!"

Even the judges looked embarrassed at this outburst, and the president leaned toward Dimitrov and said:

"Dimitrov, I had told you not to make Communist propaganda. You must not be surprised if the witness gets excited."

The Bulgarian smiled. He said: "I am satisfied, very satisfied with the Minister's reply."

The very mildness of the tone of voice seems to have stirred Goering into a raging fury, and now he was purple in the face and waving his fist.

"Out with you, you scoundrel!" he cried.

The president signaled for Dimitrov to be taken away, but just before he left the dock he could not resist a final thrust.

"Are you afraid of my questions, Herr Minister-präsident?" he asked.

Both Goering's hands were above his head and he was shouting so loudly now that it seemed that his round face would burst.

"You wait until we get you outside this court, you scoundrel!" he screamed.

It was a disgraceful exhibition, and it was a crestfallen and sheepish Hermann Goering who left for Berlin that night. He had allowed himself to be trapped into losing his temper, and he had thus ruined the propaganda effect of the trial. He was ashamed of himself. He lost all further interest in the trial and showed little reaction when Van der Lubbe was convicted—and executed—but the others were all acquitted.

Ernst Torgler was returned to protective custody in a concentration camp, from which he never emerged again.

The three Bulgarians were expelled from Germany.‡ So far as Goering was concerned, he never wanted to hear about any of them again.

On the surface, he appeared to take the whole affair with his usual nonchalance, but Robert Kropp knew otherwise. There were many midnight feasts after the trial was over, and his suits and uniforms had to be let out again.

It was only in Hitler's presence that Goering made it clear how bitter he was over the outcome of the trial. He urged the Fuehrer to let him begin at once a "reform" of the German judicial system which would make sure that an important government official would in future he treated with respect by the judges and that prisoners would never again be allowed such latitude in court.

Hitler bade him be patient until such time as President Hindenburg was removed from the scene, when work could begin on the creation of a truly National Socialist system of law.

In the meantime, one of the tasks which preoccupied Hermann Goering was to consolidate his position as the Fuehrer's right-hand man. Not only had his foolish behavior at the Reichstag Fire Trial lost him prestige abroad and with the German people; it had also enabled his strongest rival in the Party, Ernst Roehm, to make inroads on his influence with Hitler himself. On September 15, 1933, six days before the trial began, Goering had demonstrated his position and prestige in the new Nazi Reich by having 100,000 goose-stepping Brownshirts and SS men march before him in Berlin.

True, Ernst Roehm and Heinrich Himmler were on the reviewing platform with him, but it was for him, Prime Minister of Prussia, that the men were marching, and it was he who made the fighting speech that followed at which he hailed the arrival in Germany of the new force of National Socialism. Never before had such a march-past taken place for any Nazi except the Fuehrer himself.

But then followed his lamentable performance at the trial. The damage to his prestige was such that though Hitler professed to hold him in as much esteem as ever,

‡ Dimitrov subsequently became Prime Minister of Bulgaria, but fell during one of the Stalinist purges.

Goering sensed the vulnerability of his position when he learned, on December 1, 1933, that Roehm had been made a member of the Nazi inner cabinet. Not only that. On New Year's Day 1934, a letter from Hitler to his Brownshirt commander was issued to the press. It ended with the words:

"At the close of the year of the National Socialist Revolution, therefore, I feel compelled to thank you, my dear Ernst Roehm, for the imperishable services which you have rendered to the National Socialist movement and the German people, and to assure you how very grateful I am to fate that I am able to call such men as you my friends and fellow combatants. In true friendship and grateful regard, Your Adolf Hitler."

It only served to emphasize the closeness between Roehm and Hitler that the Fuehrer had employed the familiar "du" in addressing the Brownshirt leader, a form he would never have used to Goering.

Alarmed by his rival's rising fortunes, Goering now began, amid all his other tasks, to make efforts to restore his waning prestige. It was a period of intense activity. He held almost daily conferences with Erhard Milch and Karl Bodenschatz, drawing up new plans for the expansion and development of the growing forces of the Black Luftwaffe. He sensed that Adolf Hitler, now that he was in power, was anxious to stress the respectable side of his regime, and wished to put an end to the continuous series of stories which were appearing abroad of the anti-Semitic and anti-democratic persecutions which were taking place in Germany, and in particular, rumors of the sinister happenings inside the concentration camps.

The camps were Goering's responsibility, but he knew he was losing his control of them to bullies like Ernst and ruthless bureaucrats like Himmler. He decided that he would let them have them, for they were only tarnishing his reputation abroad and affecting his "respectability" vis-à-vis Hitler. As a preliminary to passing police, camps, and Gestapo to the control of Heinrich Himmler, he endeavored to smother the effect of the Fuehrer's letter to Roehm by publicly announcing the release from the camps "as a New Year's present" in 1934 of 5,000 detainees. At the same time, he allowed the newspapers to reveal details of the amount of financial help he and his department had meanwhile been making to relatives of prisoners in the camps.

The police, the camps, and the Gestapo were finally passed over to Himmler in the spring of 1934. Thereafter Goering quietly began organizing his own personal police and espionage service, which he named the Landespolizeigruppe. Its purpose was to give him private information and personal protection, in anticipation of the struggle for power under Hitler which he now sensed was coming.

XIV. BLOODLETTING

Hermann Goering had discovered one sure way of securing relaxation from the tensions of his position and worry about his weight, and that was to get away, any moment that Hitler would let him free, to the forests that stretched away from Berlin into Prussia and eastward to the Polish frontier. Here he would spend his weekends hunting and also planning a project which was now dear to his heart.

Goering had been a hunter since he was a small boy, ever since Ritter von Epenstein had given him his first gun at Veldenstein and taught him how to take game on the wing and rabbits on the run. Since those days, he had progressed to bigger animals, and was apt to turn his gun up at anything smaller than a roe deer. But he was a quick and accurate shot, he never overhunted, and he always made sure that his quarry died a clean, quick, and painless death.

One of the other positions to which he had been appointed when the Nazis took over, and one which gave him great pleasure, was that of Master of the German Hunt, and to this was added in 1934 that of Master of the German Forests. They were no mere sinecures and he took their duties seriously.

Were Goering to be judged today simply for what he did for Germany's flora and fauna, he would probably have been hailed as a conservationist of great imagination and achievement. In his position as Master of the Hunt he restocked the forests of Schorfheide and Rominten Heath with the birds and animals which had been overhunted or poached to the point of disappearing. He imported elk and bison from Sweden and Canada, wild ducks, swans and game from Poland and Spain. He tightened up the German hunting laws in 1934, making it mandatory for all would-be hunters to pass a test in handling a gun. Permits were strictly limited, and all hunters had to be accompanied by a trained dog to make sure wounded animals were found and killed. He also imposed heavy penalties on anyone shooting beyond their allotted quota; forbade hunting on horseback or from cars, using wire or steel traps, poison, lights for night-hunting; and increased the penalties for poaching.* In the next few years the forests and lakes of the German Reich became a model of wise and controlled conservation. As Master of the Forests, Goering inaugurated planting schemes which provided green belts around all the great cities, as playgrounds and lungs for the working population, but also as sanctuaries for wildlife.

He hung in his office a sign saying: *"Wer Tiere quält, verletz das deutsche Volksempfinden"* (He who tortures animals wounds the feelings of the German people), and it was ironic that at a moment when he must have known his fellow ministers in the Nazi government were perpetrating unimaginable horrors and persecutions upon the German people, Goering was laboring hard to make life safe and decent for the animals who lived among them.

One of the perks of being Prime Minister of Prussia was that he could prevail upon the Prussian government to grant him, in his other role as Master of the Forests, terrain upon which he could build himself a headquarters inside his domains. He chose the area around Schorfheide, a great rolling expanse of forest, lakes, and moorland some two hours drive northeast of Berlin; and here he persuaded the government to decree one hundred thousand acres as a zone in which no other building would be allowed, with a further area inside it where he would build his official residence, surrounded by a game reserve in which only he, local villagers, and his invited guests would be allowed to hunt.

From its inception, the house was to be a memorial to his dead wife, Carin, and Goering put more into its creation than any other project in his lifetime.

The site stood on the shores of a small lake called the Wuckersee, surrounded by old oaks, junipers, and gorse. It seemed so far from civilization that it might have been at the end of the world. With the aid of two architects, Tuch and Hetzelt, the house was built in ten months, and his

* He also included a clause in the law banning vivisection.

official biographer, Erich Gritzbach, maintains that its conception from start to finish was that of Hermann Goering.

"It is the fulfillment of a dream he has worked all his life to make come true," he wrote. "Only because he had carried the details of it around in his head through all the long and difficult years could it be completed in ten short months . . . He planned everything, the building, the surrounding garden, the furniture, the fabrics, the carpets, the lamp fittings and hangings, even the door handles, and places for his pictures and works of art. In short, it was his house in every sense of the word."

He added: "The setting is perfect, the placing of the house without fault. That is the most marvelous part of the achievement. Wherever you look and from whatever window you gaze there is always a glimpse of the lake or the forest, and inside too you look up to the clean pine roofs and oaken beams. The house might have been planted there. Hermann Goering knows Schorfheide. He knows the spring, the summer, the autumn and the winter, he knows in the forest every one of nature's changes. Here on his beloved silent heath, he can think and work away from the confinement and noise of the great city."

Gritzbach then goes on to describe Carin Hall in all its grandiose detail, a forest stronghold worthy of a feudal monarch, with its great courtyard, surrounded by thatched buildings, its elaborate garden beds and lily pond and its equestrian statue with a nude hunter sighting his bow from the horse's back. But that was written in 1937, and in 1934 it was a simpler and humbler dwelling. The additions would come later as Goering grew richer.

For the moment the bulk of his expenditure was going on a project on the other side of the lake. There he was building a mausoleum for Carin. He had been to Stockholm in the summer of 1933 to attend the wedding of one of Count von Rosen's daughters, and while there he had placed a wreath on Carin's grave. The wreath had a swastika attached to it, and Swedish anti-Nazis had taken it away, leaving behind a note accusing him of using his wife's grave to make propaganda. Distressed at what he called "this desecration," he had gone to a firm in Stockholm and ordered a huge pewter coffin to be made, big enough to contain his own body as well as the remains of his wife. He obtained the Von Fock family's permission, and had made arrangements to bring Carin to Germany. She would lie in the mausoleum across the lake, within sight of his windows, until the time came for him to join her.

On June 10, 1934, Goering gave his first reception at Carin Hall and invited members of the diplomatic corps to join him there. Among those who accepted was the new British ambassador, Sir Eric Phipps, the U.S. ambassador, Thomas Dodd, and the Italian ambassador and his wife, Signor and Signorina Enrico Cerutti. Sir Eric Phipps, who was much less frightened of the Nazis at this time than he would be later, had decided that Hermann Goering was the clown of the German revolution, and devoted his first long dispatch to the Foreign Office to a sardonic description of his arrival to meet his guests. They had gathered in a clearing in the forest and Goering came late to greet them, skidding to a halt in a large racing car and climbing out clad in "aviator's garments of indiarubber, with top boots and a large hunting-knife stuck in his belt." You can almost see Sir Eric's patrician lip curling as he goes on to describe Goering, with microphone in his hand, lecturing his guests on the flora and fauna of Germany, and exactly what steps he was taking to encourage it to flourish. Examples were shown of the various animals he had imported from abroad to restock the forests, and eventually he led them to a stockade where one of the bison from the Canadian prairies was to be seen mating with the cows which had been assembled for this purpose. At least that was the idea.

"The unfortunate animal emerged from his box with the utmost reluctance," Sir Eric observed acidly, "and, after eyeing the cows somewhat sadly, tried to return to it."

Their host then disappeared again in his racing car, leaving the guests to be taken by road through the forests to Carin Hall, where he was waiting for them at the entrance, now clad in white drill trousers and white tennis shoes, white flannel shirt and green leather jacket, with the hunting knife still stuck in his belt.

It was the first time Goering had had the chance of showing off his new home to foreign guests, and he was the proud house owner of a type that should hardly have been unfamiliar to an American. After all, many a Hollywood film had been devoted to the same subject, and *Mr. Bland-ings Builds His Dream House* was a bestseller in the United States. Like Mr. Blandings, Hermann Goering had built the place himself and might have been forgiven a little boasting as he showed his guests from room to room. But Ambassador Dodd was not beguiled and thought his host vulgar in "displaying his vanity at every turn." He could not understand why Goering, while conducting the tour, carried a "curious harpoon-like instrument" in his hand.†

In the great hall of the new house the guests eventually assembled for a reception, at which they were introduced to Emmy Sonnemann for the first time. Hermann Goering constantly referred to her as his secretary, but did not bother to conceal that she was of a very special kind, for he frequently put his arm around her waist and hugged her. Emmy then acted as hostess at the meal which fol-lowed, after which the guests were taken across the lake to Carin's mausoleum, which Goering displayed with equal pride, drawing their attention to the thickness of the walls and the vault in which his dead wife would shortly lie, and, "when the time comes, I will lie beside her."

Signorina Cerutti was thrilled by the whole thing and when Goering was out of hearing she confessed to her fellow guests that she thought him a charming and magnifi-cent anachronism. "In his conception of a princely exist-ence he reminds me of the Borgias," she said, not perhaps the best comparison she could have chosen. Dodd replied gruffly that it seemed strange that his host could be allowed to fulfill such an elaborate and costly project in a Germany whose economic situation was so dire. Sir Eric Phipps ended his dispatch by saying that "weary of this curious display," he stole away, and so did Ambassador Dodd.

On June 19, 1934, a few days after Hermann Goering had shown the mausoleum to his disdainful guests, the body of Carin Goering was taken out of its tomb in the churchyard of Lovö, near Drottningholm, in Sweden. Thomas von Kantzow, the Von Focks and the Von Rosens, Prince and Princess Victor zu Wied, General Wecke of the Reichswehr, Colonel Karl Bodenschatz, a guard of

† It was, in fact, a Scandinavian hunting spear, a gift from Count von Rosen, and Goering was looking for a place to put it in preparation for Von Rosen's arrival the following day.

honor from a German torpedo-boat flotilla and two Swedish Nazis with swastika flags watched as the coffin was
placed aboard a railway car and taken to the ferry at
Sassnitz for transport to Germany. The bells of Drottningholm Church tolled as it passed by; and in Germany itself
all the villages of northern Prussia through which the train
passed were draped with mourning. A special holiday had
been declared so that women and children could gather to
watch as the railway car, bedecked with wreaths and
greenery, went by.

Carin's sister Fanny was of course there to record the
moment when the train pulled into Eberswalde station and
the coffin was lowered into an open cart for transport to
Carin Hall.

"On all sides were black obelisks with flaming torches,
and a band played," she wrote. "Bolt upright and rigid
were the riders astride their horses, old mothers offered
flowers, and schoolchildren watched with widened,
wounded eyes as Hermann Goering came forward, at last
able to bring his dead wife back home. Slowly the wagon
moved through a lane of men on its road to the Schorfheide. In every village the church bells tolled, and strong
was the warmth and sympathy of all it passed by, who
would never forget this journey to the resting place."

All the Swedish relatives, including Thomas von Kantzow, had arrived for the ceremony, and Adolf Hitler had
also come, together with most of the leaders of the Nazi
party.‡ The Fuehrer made his appearance promptly at
twelve, and the ceremony began. Perhaps only Fanny's
rich prose can do justice to the way it went.

"Lovely as in a fairy story is this peaceful spot in the
German forest, and one felt that spirits from ancient times
were watching from above," she wrote. "Stone steps led
down to the vault, and the light from a small deep-blue
colored window fell upon the tiled walls. Through the window there was a glimpse of edelweiss growing by the lake.
Above in the earth lay the same gravestone which had once
been at Lovö and Swedish soil surrounded it; beyond were
the loveliest flowers. When Carin's sarcophagus was

‡ Heinrich Himmler arrived later, excitedly exclaiming that someone had tried to shoot him en route through the forest. Bullet holes
were found in his car, but the mystery of who had done it was
never cleared up.

brought into the open place muffled drums sounded a tattoo, and then came the sounds of the funeral march from
'Götterdämmerung.' The Fuehrer's great wreath was then
brought in as a last tribute to the woman who had been so
stout and true to the Third Reich, in whose cause she had
died. Then came the service . . . Hardly was it over than
from the far side of the lake came the sounds of the hunting horns of the foresters sending forth their last tribute."

Fanny ended her account with these words:

"When the guests were gone, and Carin's coffin had been
brought into the vault, Hermann Goering himself put in
order every wreath, every spray of flowers which had been
brought for his wife. The sky was dark blue and still, with
no clouds, and the stars gleamed overhead. The lonely man
had brought his sacred one back home at last."

It had indeed been an emotional day for Hermann Goering, but it would be untrue to say that he was without
human comfort when it was all over. Not only was Emmy
Sonnemann with him, but Thomas von Kantzow stayed on
too to share with his stepfather the memories of a moving
if melancholy day.

Emmy Sonnemann, practical woman that she was, never
became jealous of the passion which her lover continued to
hold for his dead wife, and it was her evident sympathy
and understanding which did much to reconcile Thomas to
the fact that another woman had come into his stepfather's
life. The weekend which the three of them spent together—
and the warm friendship which rapidly ripened between
Emmy and the lonely Thomas von Kantzow—seems to
have made up Goering's mind about his future plans for
his private life.

Until now, there had always been those in the Party who
swore that Emmy would never be anything more than
Goering's mistress. But Thomas von Kantzow's manifest
admiration of his choice, and Emmy's maternal reaction to
the unhappy young man banished any doubts Goering
might have had of a permanent liaison with the softhearted
actress. From then on, he not only continued to be seen in
public with Emmy Sonnemann, he also began bringing her
into Adolf Hitler's presence as well. It was one of the high
points of his life when the Fuehrer indicated that he heartily approved of her.

By the summer of 1934, Emmy Sonnemann had let all

her theatrical friends know that she was madly in love with Hermann Goering. She adored his flamboyance, she found his huge girth cuddlesome (and, of course, she was not exactly a wraith herself), she relished his wit, she shared his taste in music and the arts, and she liked the way he spoke his mind.

But she was disconcerted when she discovered that, no matter how forthright he was with others, he became a yes-man in the presence of Adolf Hitler, seeming to lose all sense of individuality or criticism, and slavishly agreeing with the Fuehrer's every whim.

"It was so obvious that even my niece, aged eighteen, noticed it," Emmy wrote later. "Since she was with me most of the time, she met not only Hermann but also Adolf Hitler at private gatherings. She was very fond of her 'Uncle' Hermann and could not bear always hearing him echo 'yes' to Adolf Hitler, whom she did not like at all. 'He agrees,' she said to me, 'even when his opinion is completely the opposite. Yet Uncle Hermann has a stronger personality. Why does he take everything which Hitler says as gospel?' "

It was not an unusual trait among members of Hitler's entourage. In the memoirs which he wrote later, Albert Speer, Hitler's chief architect, was much more contemptuous than Emmy over Goering's servile attitude to the Fuehrer. Yet Speer himself never said "no" to the Fuehrer in those days, knowing that doing so would have lost him the patronage (and the architectural opportunities) which he was now savoring.

Speer resented the fact that Goering, just about this time, had all but ordered him to drop all his other work (except that for Adolf Hitler, of course) in order to remodel his new official residence.

The place he had chosen was a building which had been built for the Prussian Minister of Commerce before 1914, and it was situated on one of the gardens behind the Leipziger Platz.

The residence had been extensively redone according to Goering's instructions only a few months before, but Hitler had come to see it and commented:

"Dark! How can anyone live in such darkness? Compare this with my professor's work. Everything bright, clear and simple!"

Speer was dragged to see the palace after a dinner party with Hitler, and found the place a romantically tangled warren of small rooms with stained-glass windows and heavy velvet hangings, cluttered with massive Renaissance furniture.

"There was the feel that something terribly solemn and tragic would always be going on in this place," Speer wrote later. "It was characteristic of the system—and probably of all authoritarian forms of society—that Hitler's criticism and example produced an instant change in Goering. For he immediately repudiated the decorative scheme which he had just completed, although he probably felt fairly comfortable in it, since it rather corresponded to his disposition. 'Don't look at this,' he said to me. 'I can't stand it myself. Do it any way you like. I'm giving you a free hand; only it must turn out like the Fuehrer's place.'"

Speer was told that money, "as always in the case of Goering," was no object, so he ripped out whole walls to turn the ground floor into four large rooms. The biggest was Goering's study, and an annex was added, mostly of glass framed in bronze. Bronze was practically a precious metal in Germany at that time, and there were penalties for using it for nonessential purposes. But Speer says this fact did not bother Goering in the least (nor does it seem to have bothered Speer at the time). "He was rapturous every time he made an inspection," Speer wrote later. "He beamed like a child on its birthday, rubbed his hands and laughed."

Most of the discussions about the alterations took place between Goering, Speer, and the Superintendent of Works, and they met in the presidential palace, just opposite the Leipziger Platz. The room where they talked was decorated in a Wilhelmine rococo style, adorned from top to bottom with roses in bas-relief, and it was one of the reasons why Goering had never lived in the place. "Quintessential atrociousness" was Speer's description of the decor.

But one day Goering wagered Speer that he would make the Superintendent of Works, who probably thought it as ghastly as they did, admire it. He thereupon gestured to the roses on the wall and said how much he admired the decor, and didn't the Superintendent think likewise. Artistic conscience battled with expediency until the sweat stood out on the Superintendent's brow, but eventually he gave way and agreed with Goering that the decor was beautiful.

"They're all like that!" said Goering afterward, contemptuously.

With equal contempt, Speer agreed. "It was true enough," he wrote later. "They were all like that, Goering included. For at meals he never tired of telling Hitler how bright and expansive his home was now, 'just like yours, mein Fuehrer.' If Hitler had had roses climbing the walls of his room, Goering would have insisted on roses."

Once the work on the palace was completed, Goering sat in his huge new study (it was almost as vast as Hitler's own) behind a giant Renaissance desk on a high-backed chair which looked as if it had once been a royal throne. On the desk were two silver candelabra with enormous parchment shades, the light from one of which fell upon an oversized photograph of Hitler. On the wall opposite hung Rubens' "Diana at the Stag Hunt," which Goering had "borrowed" from the Kaiser Friedrich Museum; it could be hoisted to the ceiling at the touch of a button to reveal a cinema projector.

Each morning Goering's first exercise of the day was to read his "intercepts." One of the last services Rudolf Diels did for him before the Gestapo was passed over to Himmler (and Diels went on to become police chief of Cologne) was to bring Goering a new electronic gadget which had come into his hands from abroad. It was a machine by which telephone calls could be monitored, and Diels wished his chief to be aware of its existence, for his own security, before he passed it on to the central intelligence bureau. But far from allowing it to be passed on, Goering decided to keep control of the monitoring device, and prevailed upon Hitler to agree. He passed it over to his Landespolizeigruppe and told them to turn it into the main tool of Goering's own intelligence service. The service was organized under the innocuous-sounding title of Forschungsamt [Directorate of Scientific Research], and would one day have 3,000 employees listening in on all types of telecommunications, breaking codes, and generally monitoring sources of information, including foreign embassies, newspapermen and Party officials.

To begin with, Goering instructed the Research Office staff to start monitoring the telephones of a list which he had compiled with the aid of his secretary of state, Pilli Koerner. They included all members of the Fuehrer's Cabinet, with the exception of Hitler himself (Goering would never have dared to bug his hero), key members of the Brownshirt SA, particularly Roehm, certain generals in the Army, and certain ambassadors and embassies. He gave instructions that a summary of all conversations should be available to him each morning, and that any conversations in which there were references to himself were to be sent to him in full.

The result was a daily treasure trove of information and entertainment. He followed with mischievous delight the daily telephone calls to Josef Goebbels from his latest starlet, for the road to stardom in Germany nowadays ran through Goebbels' bedroom. He read all the latest jokes about himself which were bandied about by army officers and Party members. (His favorite: "Why were all the motorists on the Unter den Linden dazzled last night? Because Hermann failed to dip his medals when he walked along to his office.") He had even had a tap put on Emmy Sonnemann's apartment, and was irritated to discover that his mistress was keeping contact with several old Jewish actor and actress friends who had long since been dismissed from Weimar and the State Theater.

But the most intriguing phone taps were those of General Werner von Blomberg, Minister of Defense and Head of the Reichswehr, and conversations between Ernst Roehm, commander of the Brownshirts, and Gruppenfuehrer Karl Ernst, his chief representative in Berlin. Von Blomberg's talks with various members of the Reichswehr reflected his growing concern over the increasing belligerence of the Brownshirts and the apprehension he felt over the ambitions of "that pervert" Roehm, whom he suspected of wanting to combine the Brownshirts and the Army into one force and make himself commander-in-chief of it. Roehm and Ernst confirmed in their frequent telephone consultations that this indeed was one of the plans which they were turning over in their minds; but what made Goering prick up his ears was the hostility which both men displayed in their references to himself. When they referred to him by name it was usually "that pig Goering" (when

Emmy was mentioned she was called "Goering's sow"),
but even more often they called him Herr Reaktion (Mr.
Reaction) and talked enthusiastically of "the day" when
this friend of the big bosses would be swept out of the way
and the true aims of the National Socialist revolution
would be fulfilled. He ruefully chuckled over the record of
one conversation in which Karl Ernst regretted that Goering had dispensed with the SA bodyguard with which
Ernst had provided him* because "they would have made
it easy to blow the pig's brains out when the time came."

Goering consulted with Heinrich Himmler over these
revelations (though he did not tell him how they had come
to him) after deciding, quite rightly, that the head of the
SS was as much an enemy of Roehm's as he was himself.
Himmler's spinsterish face and quiet, prim manner concealed a ravenous ambition, and Goering knew that it
could not possibly be fulfilled so long as Roehm and his
Brownshirts stood in the way. So long as Roehm kept them
armed, drilled, and prepared for action, they would always
constitute a force superior to the SS, and a menace to
anyone who did not agree with Roehm's plans for Germany.

The question was, how could Goering and Himmler
convey to Adolf Hitler that he was as much in danger as
any of them from Roehm's growing strength and belligerence. It was necessary to compile a convincing dossier, and
this, with the aid of the Gestapo, Himmler promised to do.
But it would not be easy to persuade Hitler. Roehm had
always been one of the Fuehrer's favorite "old fighters"
and one of the few men in the Party permitted to use the
familiar German "du" (thou) form of addressing him. Hitler had been known to grin and bear it when Roehm threw
his arms around him and gave him a hug—he who was so
undemonstrative in public that he never even touched Eva
Braun or made any affectionate gesture toward her. And
though he knew that Roehm and many of his closest associates were unabashed homosexuals, Hitler, whose opinions
on sex were apt to be prudish, tolerated the predilections of
the Brownshirt leader.

As they soon discovered, it was not difficult to procure
evidence that Roehm was a danger to the stability of the

---

* He had substituted a bodyguard of his own.

Third Reich, for the Brownshirt leader was too confident
that things were going the way he wanted them to conceal
his thoughts or plans. In February 1934, he was foolish
enough to propose at a cabinet meeting that the SA, SS,
and the Reichswehr should be made into a combined force
with himself as Minister of Defense. The "suggestion" was
turned down, but when word reached the Army, they bombarded General von Blomberg with protests. The prospect
that their ranks might be swamped by Roehm's hooligans
and perverts thoroughly alarmed them, and General von
Blomberg, aware that Roehm wished to sack him as well,
marched across from the War Ministry to see Hitler.

Hitler was perturbed for the first time. At all costs, he
did not wish to quarrel with the Army at this moment. The
old President, Von Hindenburg, was at last showing signs
of shuffling off this mortal coil, and Hitler was anxious to
take over as his successor when he died. To promote the
national unity behind his image that would be necessary
for him to be accepted as President, Hitler needed the
support of the Army. They could just as easily back the
idea of a regency after Hindenburg's death, which was
believed to be what the old President was going to suggest
in the last testament he was now writing. And that might
mean military support for some sort of royal restoration,
with Prince August Wilhelm representing his absent father,
Wilhelm II. The Fuehrer was prepered to promise the
Army anything to buy them off this possibility. As a result,
he told Von Blomberg that not only would he never allow
Roehm and his Brownshirts to infiltrate the Army, he
would also curb their exuberance and severely curtail their
military power.

This was a good moment for Goering and Himmler to
present Hitler with the dossier they had been compiling
about Roehm and his cohorts. The Gestapo had done well,
and brought in some reports about the goings-on at the
Brownshirts' newly opened headquarters in Berlin that
made Hitler's nose wrinkle with disgust. They had details
and photographs of the extravagant orgies which were taking place, and a file of letters of complaint from irate
parents complaining that their sons had been "defiled" by
the degenerate leaders under whom they found themselves
in the Brownshirts.

There was also a transcript of a conversation General

von Schleicher, ex-Chancellor and close friend of Roehm, had had with the French ambassador in Berlin, André François-Poncet (Goering did not explain how it was obtained; it was, of course, one of his "intercepts"). The Frenchman made several references to a meeting which had apparently taken place recently among himself, Schleicher, Gregor Strasser, and Ernst Roehm, as a result of which he was informing Paris that they should delay any negotiations with Berlin "pending a change of regime."

It was this particular item which affected Hitler most, and his emotion was a sour mixture of rage and fear. He summoned Roehm to see him immediately, and there was a confrontation between the two men which lasted from the afternoon until midnight. The Fuehrer raged at the Brown-shirt leader over the laxity of his morals and ordered him to dismiss his harem, curb the sexual excesses of his staff, and change the nature of his leadership. He also told him that the arms arsenal which the Brownshirts were now building up must be surrendered to the Army, and that Roehm must henceforward make it clear to the Reichswehr that he had no intention either of supplanting them or taking them over. Finally, he made a plea for Roehm's co-operation, as an old comrade, and pointed out that with Hindenburg's death imminent, any rash move on the part of the Brownshirts could ruin everything for him.

Roehm's reply was both defiant and unyielding. He is said to have bitterly accused Hitler of "betraying the revolution" by giving in to reactionaries like Goering, who wanted only to feather his own nest and keep in with the bosses. He urged Hitler to defy the Reichswehr and achieve supreme power by overthrowing their influence with the aid of the Brownshirt SA.

It was from this moment onward that Hitler was completely on Goering's side, and realized that if he wished to become supreme chief of the Third Reich there was only one way of achieving it, and that was by "trampling them [the Brownshirts] to dust."

On June 7 Roehm, who was a sick man, left Berlin for a summer furlough at the Hanslbauer Sanitarium at Wiessee, a lake in Upper Bavaria. His sleazy friend, Edmund Heines, a Brownshirt Obergruppenfuehrer, went with him. On arrival there, Roehm sent out a message to the Brownshirts telling them to take a month's furlough from July 1, but added a clause threatening that "those enemies of the SA" who circulated rumors that the Brownshirts were breaking up for good "would be given a suitable answer in due time and in whatever form is necessary." He ended his message with the words: "The SA is and remains Germany's destiny," and did not add the customary Heil Hitler.

Herman Goering had no doubt of whom he was thinking when he referred to "enemies of the SA" because his intercepts soon brought in new conversations between Roehm and Karl Ernst in which both men speculated with relish over the way they would dispatch "the pig Goering" when the "due time" arrived.

"I will personally slice slabs of flesh off his fat body," said Ernst, "until he is half his size, and only then will I stick my knife in his throat."

"Do that," said Roehm. "But don't eat any of the cuts. Forbidden meat!"

Unlike Hitler, who was frankly apprehensive about the way things were going, Hermann Goering looked forward to Roehm's challenge with a zest which was by no means soured by the knowledge that his own life was now in danger. If anything, that factor heightened his enjoyment of it, and sharpened his wits. In reading over the transcript of the Roehm-Ernst conversations, he was struck by the frequency with which Ernst jocularly remarked that his "furlough" was not going to be as enjoyable as Roehm's. He had the records played over for him, and came to the conclusion that Ernst was not planning to take a furlough at all. He asked Himmler to make inquiries, and the answer came back: Sure enough, Ernst had gone so far as to postpone his honeymoon,† and he had instructed the officers of the 280,000 Brownshirts in the Berlin area that Roehm's instructions did not apply to them and that they were to keep their men on stand-by.

Goering passed the word to Hitler, Von Blomberg, and Himmler. Blomberg quietly put the Reichswehr on a state of alert from June 25 onward, and Himmler made a similar order to his SS troops. The following day, Hitler made a last gesture to Roehm in the hope of securing some sort of rapprochement. He put up his friend Rudolf Hess to

† Ernst had been married a few days before. Goering had been his best man and Hitler was also present at the ceremony.

make a speech in Cologne in which he called upon "certain elements in the Party" to renounce their desire for "a second revolution." Such revolutions, Hess said, belonged not to Germany but were modeled on "the annual little revolutions in small exotic republics," an obvious reference to Roehm's service in South America. But Hess promised that all could be forgiven and forgotten.

"An old National Socialist," he said, "must be generous toward human peculiarities and weaknesses in National Socialist leaders if these go hand in hand with great achievements. And because of great achievements he will forgive the little weaknesses."

To Hermann Goering it seemed obvious that no good could come from such overtures, which would only strengthen Roehm's belief that he was irremovable, and he must have been glad when the Brownshirt leader's reply was absolute silence. Instead, he sent out a telegram instructing all Brownshirt leaders to come to Wiessee on Saturday, June 30, for a "leaders' conference."

Hitler meanwhile seems to have worked himself up into a dither of indecision. He spent the last week of June speeding from one end of the Reich to another, first to South Germany to open a new alpine road, then to the Northwest to address a meeting, and finally to Bad Godesberg to stay at the hotel of an old Party comrade. He sat on a terrace overlooking the Rhine, and while a company of the Labor Corps performed a torchlight tattoo for his benefit, he was lost in thought and nervous in the extreme.

Hermann Goering had by this time decided that there would be no rapprochement with the Brownshirt leader, and that the hour of reckoning was bound to come, no matter how hesitant the Fuehrer still remained. He was now convinced that this was the most serious challenge to Hitler's leadership since the aftermath of the Munich putsch, and that a war could break out in which people were going to get killed. He was determined not to be one of them, and began drawing up a list of the Brownshirts most to be feared.

On June 28, on Goering's advice, all preparations were made for civil war. Police reinforcements were called up, commandos organized, SS troops stood to in a "state of alarm." The next morning, when he read his intercepts he found a conversation between one of the police inspectors

and Karl Ernst, informing the Brownshirt of the preparations being made. He added the inspector's name to his
list.

Shortly afterward Karl Ernst himself was on the line to
the Reichsminister. What was all this he was hearing about
"mobilizations"? Was Goering in trouble? Did he need any
help? He had only to ask and the Brownshirts were ready.

"My dear Karl," Goering replied, "I know I can rely
upon you. Was I not best man at your wedding? The
Fuehrer knows too that you are our most stouthearted
supporter. No, there are some police exercises in progress,
but no special mobilizations. It's holiday time, my dear
fellow. Go away and enjoy your honeymoon."

Later in the day he had a report of Ernst's latest telephone call to Roehm. Herr Reaktion, he said, was up to
something, and he was keeping his Brownshirts on a state
of alert. But he was reassured enough to say that he was
leaving on a delayed honeymoon. Neither he nor Roehm
seemed to realize that Hitler was also "up to something."
They were not even alarmed when the Fuehrer wired
Roehm that evening and told the Brownshirt leader that he
was on his way to see him and to take part in the "leaders'
conference." Roehm was so sure of Hitler's friendship that,
in preparation for his arrival, he had a local artist make a
bookplate dedicated to the Fuehrer for inclusion in the
next edition of *Mein Kampf*.

But in fact Hitler had made up his mind. In the early
hours of June 30, 1934, he landed at Munich with an
entourage of cold Nazi killers and set out by car for the
Hanslbauer Sanitarium. A few hours later, the killings
began. Heines and his boy lover were found in bed together, and were dragged out and shot in a car. A young
aristocratic member of the Brownshirts, and also a homosexual, Count Spreti, made a gesture which Hitler inter-
preted as reaching for his revolver, and he beat him sav-
agely about the head and face until his features were a
bleeding pulp and he collapsed on the floor. Next he
hammered on Roehm's door and when the Brownshirt
leader sleepily appeared, he upbraided him as a traitor and
then handed him over to the killers. Roehm was offered the
chance to commit suicide and, having refused, was shot.

The plane which had brought Hitler to Munich was now

used as a courier plane to keep Hermann Goering in touch
with what was happening. The moment he knew that Hitler had struck he set his own plan of action in motion.
Special police commandos under Major Wecke moved out
of their camp at Lichterfelde on motorcycles and in trucks,
and they made for Berlin by a circuitous route. When they
reached the city center they threw a cordon around Brownshirt headquarters and penetrated the building without resistance. When Goering arrived, he found the Gruppenfuehrer in command (a certain Wilhelm Schmidt) standing
with his back to the wall of his office, his hands in the air,
under the rifles of the commandos.

Goering was brisk and efficient. He had a long list in his
hand, for he had long since worked out just who among
the Brownshirts were the most dangerous to the regime or
who were the most degenerate. He jogged at a trot from
room to room, where the Brownshirts had been assembled,
and with a stubby finger he would point among them,
saying: "Arrest him . . . arrest him . . . no, not him, that
character skulking behind . . . and him . . . and him. . . ."
The arrested men were taken down to the trucks and
driven away to Lichterfelde.

Meanwhile, Gruppenfuehrer Karl Ernst was being
sought. It was known that he had left on a honeymoon trip
with his bride, and small planes were sent up to spot his
Mercedes on the road to Bremen. He was eventually intercepted, hustled aboard a plane, and brought first to Berlin
and then to Lichterfelde. He simply could not believe it
was happening to him, and was convinced that this was an
anti-Hitler rebellion led by Herr Reaktion and his friends.
The Fuehrer, he was sure, would shortly rally the Brownshirts and rescue him. Toward the end, he even came to
the conclusion that Goering had succeeded in capturing
and imprisoning Hitler as well, and when he was lined up
against the wall to face the execution squad he raised some
wry smiles among his SS firing squad when he cried out:
"Heil Hitler!" just before he died.

Now mass executions began in earnest. And all would
take place on June 30. The Brownshirts were led out in
groups from the cellars into which they had been crammed.
An SS man opened their shirts, made a charcoal circle
around their left nipples, and lined them up against the

wall just seven yards from a squad of eight SS men. The
latter were all marksmen but they had been brought close
to make absolutely sure that they did not miss and that
their target would need no *coup de grâce*. But since the
nearness of the guns tore a large hole in the victims, the
wall behind soon became festooned with bleeding flesh
which no one thought to hose away between executions.

In the meantime, Hermann Goering was back home at
his palace in the Leipziger Platz keeping in contact with
Hitler and conferring with Himmler and Goebbels. Every
so often Brownshirts who had been picked up on the
streets or arrested in their homes would be brought in for
his inspection, and, after consulting his list, he would decide their fate. At one point Franz von Papen, the Vice-
Chancellor, was escorted in. Goering knew that both
Himmler and Goebbels wanted to have him assassinated,
and that was something he was determined to avoid. He
had conceived a sort of contemptuous affection for the
wily diplomat, and he was also aware that Von Papen was
a close friend of the old President and a well-known figure
abroad. His death would cause an international scandal. So
Goering kept Von Papen with him until Himmler and
Goebbels left the Leipziger Platz, and then ordered him to
be sent back to his own home and put under house arrest
and under the guard of his own men.

"Goering saved my life," Von Papen was afterward to
say.

He did nothing, however, to save General von Schleicher,
whose presence alive in Germany he considered a danger
to the regime, and he was not cast down when he heard
that two SS guards had killed Von Schleicher and his wife
"while they were trying to escape." But as the news began
to reach him of the continued killings at Lichterfelde, he
began to realize that Himmler and his chief assistant, Reinhardt Heydrich, were using the occasion as an excuse for
settling old scores.

Not only Brownshirts were falling beneath their bullets,
but right-wing and center politicians against whom they had
grudges. One of them was Gustav von Kahr, who had
reneged on Hitler just before the Munich putsch in 1923;
now an old man of seventy-three, his body was found,
hacked to death, in a swamp near Dachau. Gregor Strasser

Hermann Goering in the cockpit of his plane on the Western Front in 1917. He had shot down fifteen planes and had just been recommended for Germany's highest award, the Pour le Mérite.

Goering's white Fokker G7 over the Western Front. The picture was taken by an Allied bomber pilot.

Hermann Goering as Commander of the Richthofen Squadron. The stick is one he inherited from the original Commander, Baron von Richthofen, the famed "Red Baron."

(*above left*) A painting of Carin von Kantzow—one of the belles of Swedish society—shortly before she met Goering.

(*above right*) Goering with his friend and aide Paul Koerner when the two wheeled and dealed in the inflationary conditions of Berlin in the twenties.

(*below*) Adolf Hitler and Nazi followers lining up in Munich during the Beer Hall Putsch of 1923. The man in civilian clothes is a local councillor being held as hostage.

(*above left*) This picture, which Hitler gave to Carin Goering, was taken shortly after his release from prison.

(*above right*) Carin Goering shortly before her death in 1931.

(*below*) The main entrance to Carin Hall in the forests north-east of Berlin, which Goering built as a memorial to his first wife. He buried her remains on the grounds.

Goering poses for a sculptor at Carin Hall in 1933.

Emmy Sonnemann, the blond German actress who became Goering's second wife, seen here in costume for Queen Luise in *Prince of Prussia*.

Goering and Hitler in conference in the Reichschancellery in 1937. Goering was controller of the Nazi Four Year Plan at the time.

British Prime Minister Neville Chamberlain shakes hands with the Italian dictator Benito Mussolini at the time of the Munich Pact of 1938. Count Ciano, the Italian Foreign Minister, is next to Mussolini, Hitler is behind him and Goering is on the far left.

Hitler and Goering on the former's arrival at the Nuremberg Congress. Ribbentrop is on the right.

(*above left*) Goering conferring with Production Minister Albert Speer as Goering's control over the Luftwaffe building program loosened and Speer began to take over.

(*above right*) While Germans were going without meat and butter so Hitler could have guns and planes, Goering, as Marshal of the Reich, kept an animal collection that consumed enough meat to feed the population of a good-sized village.

(*below*) On July 20, 1944, a clique of German officers tried to assassinate Hitler but bungled the job. Here Martin Bormann, Goering, Hitler and Heinrich Himmler are seen together on the day of the attack.

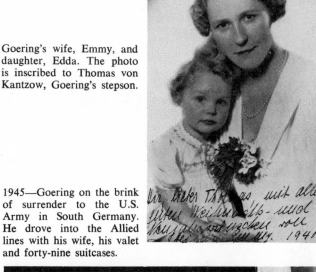

Goering's wife, Emmy, and daughter, Edda. The photo is inscribed to Thomas von Kantzow, Goering's stepson.

1945—Goering on the brink of surrender to the U.S. Army in South Germany. He drove into the Allied lines with his wife, his valet and forty-nine suitcases.

Goering confers with his lawyer in Nuremberg Jail during his trial for war crimes.

The major war criminals in the box during the Nuremberg Trial. Goering is the first man in the front row, seated next to Rudolf Hess.

was shot to death in a cellar. But the killing which Goering found most personally distressing, and unnecessary, was the murder of a former Catholic ministerial director named Erich Klausener. He was one of those on whose behalf Emmy Sonnemann had intervened during the first Nazi purge in 1933. Klausener was an honest man with an unfortunate habit of saying what he thought, and he had too clearly indicated his opinion of some SS members of his department.

Goering, responding to Emmy's plea, had succeeded in getting him released from the Party headquarters to which he had been taken before he was too badly roughed up, and for his own safety he had had him transferred from his own department to the traffic ministry. But old grudges die hard, and now he heard that Klausener had been arrested by the SS and done to death.

It was news of Klausener's death (and the thought that he would have to appease an irate Emmy because of it) which as much as anything persuaded Hermann Goering that the killings had now gone far enough. The Brownshirts had been broken. Any potential which they might have had for revolt had now been crushed once and for all. On Sunday morning, July 1, he intervened personally with Hitler and asked him to call off the killers.

It had all happened in the course of one day. Goering himself had drawn up a list of thirty-two Brownshirts to be executed, and Hitler himself had seen to the dispatch of another forty in the south. It was this total figure of seventy-two which Goering later announced in the Reichstag as the number of killed or executed. In fact, because of Himmler's and Heydrich's grudge lists, there were at least a hundred more, but no one was told about them, and only slowly did the news come out that they were dead.

Hitler, who had been in a state of semi-hysteria all through June 30, had begun to simmer down by July 1, and his spirits rose when he went to see President von Hindenburg. Instead of reproaching him for the bloodshed, as he had feared, the old man was full of doddery congratulation.

"When circumstances require it," he said, "one must not shrink from the most extreme action. One must be able to spill blood also."

To Hermann Goering he sent a telegram:

MINISTER PRESIDENT GENERAL GOERING BERLIN.
088/TELEG.4012
ACCEPT MY APPROVAL AND GRATITUDE FOR YOUR SUC-
CESSFUL ACTION IN SUPPRESSING THE HIGH TREASON.
WITH COMRADELY THANKS AND GREETINGS. (SIGNED)
                                    HINDENBURG

There was a similar one for Hitler, and when they were
published the German public was suitably impressed. As
Albert Speer wrote later:

"The fieldmarshal of the First World War was held in
reverence by people of middle-class origins . . . For as long
as I could remember he had been for me the symbol of
authority. That Hitler's action was approved by this supreme judge was highly reassuring."

It was, in fact, Hermann Goering who was now hailed
as the hero of the hour, the man who had guided the
Fuehrer and by his masterly handling of the revolt had
saved the nation from a bloody civil war. When he walked
in the street now or drove past in his open car, he was
cheered by the populace.

"It was no accident," wrote Speer, "that after the Roehm
putsch the Right, represented by the President, the Minister
of Justice, and the generals, lined up behind Hitler. These
men were free of radical anti-Semitism of the sort Hitler
advocated. They in fact despised that eruption of plebeian
hatreds. Their open display of sympathy for Hitler's intervention sprang from quite different causes: in the Blood
Purge of June 30, 1934, the strong left wing of the party,
represented chiefly by the SA, was eliminated."

On August 2, 1934, just twenty years after the declara-
tion of the World War which had made him famous, Field
Marshal Paul von Hindenburg died in the castle of Neudeck. He was eighty-seven years old.

Within an hour of the old president's death it was announced that the office of President would in future be
merged with that of the Chancellor, and that Adolf Hitler
would become Head of the State and Supreme Commander
of the armed forces of the Reich. There was no opposition
to the change. The right wing and the middle class had
been satisfied by the Blood Purge and convinced that they

had been saved from revolution. The left wing, if such a term could be given to the Brownshirts, had been broken up and the SA turned into a "sports association." The Reichswehr was appeased and immediately swore an oath of allegiance to the new Head of State.

Hermann Goering could not resist extracting the utmost drama out of the situation. He was, in fact, deeply moved by the death of the old soldier, and when he gathered the officers of the Luftwaffe together at the Air Ministry to tell them the news his voice was on the point of breaking with emotion. But the occasion was not to mourn the death of an old President but to swear allegiance to the new.

He was in his dress uniform and he now drew forth his sword. Erhard Milch stepped forward and put his hand on it. Karl Bodenschatz began to read the oath of allegiance. And solemnly, the officers of the Luftwaffe (like the Reichswehr before them) swore an oath of allegiance not to the state but to Adolf Hitler personally.

After which Hermann Goering raised the sword high above his head and cried:

"Heil Hitler!"

There were German air-force officers who were later to claim that they never used the Hitler salute, but on that day they did.

There was another death to touch Goering's heart in 1934, and that was Ritter von Epenstein's. He was eighty-four and had been in ill health for some time, and he died in his bed at Mauterndorf Castle. It was just as well that he went when he did, before Austria was annexed by the Nazis. In Von Epenstein's case, Goering could hardly have had a birth certificate forged to prove he was of non-Jewish origin, and there would undoubtedly have been considerable difficulty ahead for both godfather and godson. But he had gone while he was safe.

Goering sent a huge wreath to the funeral and a long letter to Baronin Lilli asking her to come and see him the moment she felt up to the journey. She came to stay at Carin Hall and as Hermann Goering showed her over the house and the estate he sighed and said:

"What a pity that the old man did not live to see this. How I would have loved to show him Carin Hall."

Now Goering had only one hero left alive.

XV. WEDDING

One morning in February 1935, Hermann Goering was in his bath when he called out to Emmy through the half-opened door leading into the bedroom:

"I've got something very important to say to you."

Emmy was just finishing dressing and preparing to leave for a rehearsal at the State Theater, and she looked up warily. When Hermann used the words "serious" and "important" to her it was usually because he had some reproof for her, about her friendships with Jewish actresses or her persistence in patronizing Jewish shops. It nearly always happened when he came back from a visit to Hitler, and he had returned from Berchtesgaden the previous night.

"Is it something unpleasant?" she asked, and made ready to slip out through the door.

But Goering had evidently changed his mind about speaking to her, and instead she heard the splash of water as he climbed out of the bath. Presently, he came to the door, a towel wrapped around his huge waist, and handed her a slip of paper, which he told her to read on her way to the theater.

Convinced that the note would merely re-echo one of Hitler's complaints about her unorthodox behavior,* she did not bother to read it until she was in the car. Robert Kropp heard her say, as he was about to drive her to the theater:

"My God, at last!"

Then she was out of the car and dashing back into the house. The note said:

"Will you marry me at Easter? The Fuehrer will be our witness."

* He had recently complained of her habit of traveling around in the underground railway, and talking to strangers with Stars of David on their shoulders.

She left Hermann Goering in no doubt of her willingness, and then hurried away to the theater to tell Herr
Lundgrens, her director, that she would not be playing the
lead in the play *Agnes Bernauer* that season.

The official announcement of the engagement was made
in mid-March 1935, and on the twenty-second of that
month Hermann Goering invited the diplomatic corps to
meet his bride-to-be. Among those present at the dinner
were all the ambassadors and their wives, the latter all
eager for a glimpse of the mistress about whom they had
heard so many tales. Among the guests was, it almost goes
without saying, the British envoy, Sir Eric Phipps, who
cabled his comments to the Foreign Office the following
day.

"General Goering thus resumed," he reported, "the series of sumptuous repasts inaugurated by the late Captain
Roehm in February 1934, interrupted by the 'blood bath'
of June 30 and contemptuously described by the Fuehrer
in the Reichstag in July as 'so-called diplomatic banquets.'
This occasion was more auspicious, however, for it served
to introduce to the world Frau Emmy Sonnemann, no
longer as the 'private secretary' but as the fiancée of our
host."

It was a sumptuous affair, even by Sir Eric's standards.

"The dinner was served in the white marble dining hall
hung with Gobelins tapestries of great value and brilliantly
illuminated. An invisible string band played to us during
dinner. Our host informed us that he was about to build a
swimming bath some 50 metres long (this had also been
Captain Roehm's intention, though it was frustrated, with
others less innocuous, on 30th June). He explained almost
apologetically to my wife that he was only marrying Frau
Sonnemann at the behest of the Fuehrer, who felt that
there were too many bachelors in high places in the Nazi
party. Meanwhile, Frau Sonnemann next to whom I had
the privilege of sitting and who did the honours for her
fiancé with simplicity and charm, imparted to the occasion
a delicate tinge of regret by informing us of her approaching retirement from the stage. The public will bear this
news with fortitude for I am assured that Frau Sonnemann
lacks any trace of histrionic talent."

He ended his dispatch in similar vein:

"After dinner General Goering led the French ambassa-

dor and myself round his vast residence and showed us a
series of magnificent pictures by old masters which, he told
us with pride, he had requisitioned from the Kaiser Friedrich Museum . . . A concert by some of the best singers
from the State opera was followed by two films of stag life
on the Schorfheide; in these our host attired in his familiar
leather suit reminiscent of the advertisement for Michelin
motor tyres was 'discovered' seated in the Wotan living
room of Carin Hall, with harpoon close at hand. We then
experienced the strange and two-fold pleasure of hearing at
one and the same time his talking and his 'talky' voice ex-
patiating again on the beauties of primeval forest life. . . ."

It had been intended that the wedding should take place
on April 7, but this turned out to be the anniversary of the
death of the former Empress of Germany, and that would
have meant that her son, Prince August Wilhelm, who had
been invited, would not have been able to come. So it was
postponed until April 10. The night before a great reception was given in the foyer of the Opera House, after
which Goering and his guests filed in to hear a performance of Richard Strauss's *Die Ägyptsche Helena.* The
streets outside were ablaze with lights and filled with cheering spectators.

For Emmy it was the biggest production of her lifetime.
"On the evening of the ceremony," she wrote later, "we
were able to judge the importance of the reaction which it
caused; the presents we had already received filled two
enormous rooms. They had come from all sides and all
countries. The King of Bulgaria, for instance, sent to Hermann his country's highest decoration and to me a splendid
sapphire bracelet. Hamburg had presented me with a sail-
ing boat with silver sails which I had always admired on
school visits to the City Hall. This gave me very special
pleasure. The firm of I. G. Farben sent two splendid speci-
mens of their synthetic precious stones. And innumerable
simple folk sent me scarves which they had knitted themselves and a veritable mountain of handicraft gifts."

She also had a picture from the Fuehrer of Bismarck by
his favorite painter, Lenbach. And Goering himself presented her with a tiara of amethysts and diamonds.

It had been raining the night before during the reception
at the opera, and Emmy had been apprehensive about the
morrow, for Hermann insisted that he drive her to the civil

ceremony at the city hall in an open car. But the sun came out, and as they drove on to the cathedral for the religious ceremony the sun blazed down, and overhead a squadron of the latest German warplanes flew over in salute.

Once more Goering's unfriendly Boswell, Sir Eric Phipps, was on hand to report on these momentous events, and his dispatch to the Foreign Office on April 17, 1935, read as follows:

"On the next day the wedding itself took place, and a visitor to Berlin might well have thought that the monarchy had been restored and that he had stumbled upon the preparations for a royal wedding. The streets were decorated; all traffic in the interior of the city was suspended; over thirty thousand members of the para-military formations lined the streets, whilst two hundred military aircraft circled in the sky, and at a given moment escorted the happy couple from the Brandenburger Tor to the Cathedral."

Contrary to the reports of most observers, who thought the crowd was dense, cheerful, and enthusiastic, Sir Eric thought that it was none of these things, but, he added, "the weather was fine and all crowds enjoy a wedding."

Adolf Hitler's car headed the great procession to the cathedral, while "the bridal pair brought up the rear in a car decorated as though for a battle of flowers." In the Protestant cathedral, where the pro-Nazi Bishop Ludwig Müller conducted the ceremony, the diplomats were seated in a gallery facing the altar.

"Below," reported Sir Eric, "were gathered all that is prominent in the Nazi world, with many of the old regime as well, such as the Duke of Saxe-Coburg, Prince August Wilhelm of Hohenzollern, Field Marshal Mackensen and many others. The German ladies wore evening dresses and diamonds, the men wore uniform or dress clothes with decorations . . . The Chancellor sat in an armchair at the foot of the altar steps. When the bridal pair entered he rose and kissed the bride's hand, and shook hands with General Goering—this he did again after the conclusion of the service. Four little girls in pink satin preceded the bride; two boys of the Hitler Jugend held her train; numerous bridesmaids in various discordant shades of blue followed her."

He did not add that among Goering's groomsmen was

Thomas von Kantzow, the only foreigner and the only man not in uniform. Rather to Goering's surprise, Thomas had taken the news of his stepfather's plans to marry with genuine pleasure, and by the time the wedding took place he had already formed a lasting friendship with Emmy.

"The Opera, which is under Goering's orders," the British ambassador went on, "supplied some of the best singers and a great part of its orchestra to swell the volume of sound in the Cathedral and to render tribute to its master. Reichsbishop Müller who performed the ceremony, delivered a curious address in which God, Herr Hitler and the National Socialist movement were inextricably mixed. I caught the words 'Faith, Hope and Love, and the greatest of these is Love.' A reception and banquet at the Kaiserhof Hotel, at which speeches were made by Herr Hitler and others, concluded the day's proceedings which had lasted since noon and had caused traffic to be held up for seven hours."

He ended his dispatch with these words:

"General Goering would thus seem to have reached the apogee of his vainglorious career. I see for him and his meglomania no higher goal, apart from the throne, unless indeed it be . . . the scaffold."

Unaware of the thoughts which were curdling in the mind of at least one of them, Emmy Goering moved among her guests, making herself as pleasant and gracious as she knew how, well aware that she was now, as Hitler had just told her, the First Lady of the Third Reich. Finally, the bridal pair and a small group of friends slipped away to Carin Hall, where Hermann Goering immediately went across the lake and stayed for an hour beside Carin's tomb in the mausoleum.

Next day they left for a quiet honeymoon in Wiesbaden, and then traveled to Yugoslavia to stay in a villa at Ragusa, on the Adriatic. Bride and bridegroom were both forty-two years old, but they behaved toward each other as if they were half that age.

It was not even an open secret any longer that Germany, despite the Versailles Treaty, now had an air force. The disguise had been dropped in March 1935, and a month before that Hermann Goering had visited pilots at a station at Schleissheim to inform them that they would soon be "going public." Most of them had done their training secretly, either in Russia or in Italy, and were highly skilled fliers lacking only modern machines to bring them up to battle standard.

One of them, Adolf Galland, who was later to become Germany's most celebrated fighter pilot, listened to Goering that evening in their mess in the Castle of Mittenheim.

"He gave us a convincing resume of the development of German aviation during the last two years," he wrote later. "Something stupendous had been achieved in that period. Out of nothing had arisen the elaborately planned foundations of the German Luftwaffe, although they were still under cover, and upon these an imposing edifice would soon stand."

Goering, who considered himself a connoisseur, had brought along a sample of the uniform the pilots were to wear once they emerged from their anonymity, and it was modeled for the fliers by a sergeant-major from the old Richthofen Squadron. The Reichminister had chosen the design himself as being sufficiently eye-catching to identify at once the *corps d'élite* of pilots which he intended the Luftwaffe to become. The pilots were suitably impressed. The big innovation was that, for the first time in the history of German uniforms, collars and ties were going to be worn with it.

"This caused a sensation," Galland wrote, "and the army nicknamed us 'mufti soldiers.' "

But if, as Goering said, the Luftwaffe had made great strides, it was by no means as powerful as foreign governments claimed or feared, and when the British Government in a White Paper put the front-line strength of the German Air Force as two thousand five hundred planes they were wildly over the mark. Two thousand planes were for the moment about all Germany could put into the air as a whole, and many of them were biplanes.

What Goering needed was money with which to subsidize the aircraft firms, money to pay for raw materials, money to expand Luftwaffe personnel. He had been warned by Hitler that 1936 would be the year in which Germany would finally show what it thought of Versailles, principally by reoccupying the demilitarized Rhineland. The prospect alarmed Goering, who thought it was too soon for such gestures of defiance.

"The British and the French will come in and squash us like flies," he said.

"Not if we buzz loudly enough," the Fuehrer replied.

He was told to go away and build up the Luftwaffe so that its buzz would be loud enough to be heard, and loud enough to scare off, both the Quai d'Orsay and Whitehall.

General von Blomberg, the Minister of Defense, also counseled a policy of gradualness, and was given the same advice the Fuehrer had given Goering.

But where was the money to come from to pay for the air-force expansion? Goering went to Dr. Hjalmar Schacht, who was in charge of the Reich's economic affairs, and asked that bossy and self-confident character for increased subventions. He was told that the German lemon was just about squeezed dry.

"I have taken from the German people just about all they can tolerate giving," Schacht said, in effect. "I have forbidden them to take money abroad. I have repudiated all foreign loans. I have cut down imports almost to vanishing point. I have put them on austerity rations. All in the cause of providing huge sums for our rearmament. But one can only go so far, and then the people will cry halt. They are being starved of oil to cook with, butter for their bread, meat even for a Sunday dinner. Soon there will be a black market, and then we will have to start shooting people. I simply cannot spare you any more money."

Not even, Goering asked, if he demonstrated to Schacht that the German people were ready for even further sacrifices than they were already making?

"Not even you can perform miracles," replied Schacht sourly.

For the next three weeks Hermann Goering worked with Pilli Koerner on a big speech which he intended to make at a mass meeting, and when he was satisfied with it, he arranged for it to be delivered before a vast concourse of the Party faithful in Hamburg, where some of the most vocal grumbles about food restrictions had lately been heard.

He had just finished his latest slimming cure, and he was much paler than usual, with hollows under his eyes and a fold of slack skin under his chin. He dressed in air-force uniform and for the first part of his speech he reported on the progress of Germany and the improvement in her pres-

tige since the advent of Hitler; but then he began to remind
his audience of the restrictions which still confined her
freedom as a result of Versailles. Germany had not yet
won her rightful place in the sun, but she must. And the
only way it could be done was by being strong, bold,
capable of standing up to her enemies, and that meant
being rearmed.

"But rearmament is only the first step toward the goal of
making the German people content," he said. "Rearming
for me is not an aim in itself. I do not want to rearm for
militaristic reasons or to oppress other people, but solely
for the cause of Germany's freedom. Party comarades,
friends, I believe in international understanding. That is the
reason why we are rearming. Weak—we are at the mercy
of the world. What is the use of being in the concert of
nations if German is only allowed to play the kazooh?"

He paused to let the cheers die down, then went on with
the words that were to make headlines all over the world:

"I must speak clearly. Some people in international life
are very hard of hearing. They can only be made to listen
if they hear guns go off. We are getting those guns. We
have no butter, comrades, but I ask you: would you rather
have butter or guns? Shall we bring in lard or iron ores? I
tell you, preparedness makes us powerful." He brought a
chubby hand slapping down on his belly. "Butter only
makes us fat!"

The mass meeting rose to its feet and acclaimed him.
Hitler sent him a telegram of congratulation. Schacht reluctantly agreed to find him some money for the Air Force.

Among the planes on which Goering spent it was one
which, for a time, was to revolutionize methods of warfare
almost as radically as tanks had done in World War I, and
its acceptance by the Luftwaffe meant the apotheosis of
one of Goering's more remarkable associates. Ernst Udet
had never been one of Goering's close friends, even though
they had served as fighter pilots together in the last war.
Udet had been Germany's champion fighter pilot, with
more "kills" than any other flier, and when the time had
come for someone to be chosen to replace the dead Richthofen as commander of his squadron, Udet had expected
the job to fall to him. He had never really got over the fact
that it had gone to an outsider, Goering, instead.

After the war he had bummed and barnstormed his way

around Europe, and finally ended up with a small aircraft-manufacturing operation, making light commercial planes. But he had ideas about a new kind of plane that would be almost a flying bomb. It would carry bombs under its fuselage, and when it reached its objective it would go into a dive and make head-on for the target, releasing the bomb load and pulling out at the last moment. He believed it would prove both an accurate and a terrifying weapon.

Someone pointed out to him that the Americans had already developed a similar plane, a Hell Diver, and with his last resources Udet had bought a couple of models and experimented with them. He was soon sure he could improve upon them, and by the time he joined Goering's Aviation Ministry in 1934, he had drawn up detailed plans and was ready to make a prototype.

But at first no one would listen to him, neither Goering nor Milch, nor any of the manufacturers. It was only after a weary round of all the companies, pleading and arguing, that he at last persuaded the Junkers company to make a prototype at its factory in Sweden, and finally two models were delivered to him in 1935.

Udet was a handsome, swashbuckling type who, in other days, would have captained a ship on the Spanish Main. He spent a large portion of his life whoring and drinking, and it was rare when there was no blonde in his bed or glass in his hand. On the day he was due to test the first dive-bomber he still had the scent in his hair and the liquor on his breath from a heavy night's carousal. He took up one of the two planes to three thousand feet, put it into a vertical dive, and tried to pull out at five hundred feet. He had miscalculated his height and the speed of his dive, and he failed to do so. Miraculously enough, he stepped out of the wreck not only unharmed but looking more alert, and certainly less drunk, than when he had taken off.

He persuaded his audience, which included General Erhard Milch, to allow him to take up the second machine, and this time he gave a dazzling display of skillful flying, screaming down upon the field and accurately peppering it with dummy bombs before pulling out just in time.

Milch agreed that it was an effective and a psychologically frightening weapon, and so reported to Goering, who asked for a personal demonstration. He too was impressed by the plane's potential and afterward said what a pity it was that the dive-bomber did not make an even more terrifying noise when it roared down toward its target.

"That's easy," said Udet. "We'll fix a wind whistle to it, and it'll scream like a demon out of hell when it dives down."

Such a device was used later, with devastating effects on the troops who heard it. Meanwhile, Goering endorsed the new plane as a vital attack weapon in the Luftwaffe arsenal, and ordered it into production. He was immensely pleased with Ernst Udet, and demonstrated his pleasure by appointing him, on January 1, 1936, Inspector of Stuka Fighter Pilots.† This was a wise appointment, because the new plane demanded a difficult and dangerous new method of flying which only an old barnstormer like Udet could get across to the young generation of fliers coming up.

But then Goering overstepped himself. In his enthusiasm for Udet, he also appointed him as Director of the Technical Department of the Air Ministry, responsible for the structural and forward planning. Although, like Goering himself, Udet was bold, brave, and a firstclass flier, he was unfortunately no planner. It was a mistake on Goering's part that was to mortally handicap the Luftwaffe and cost Ernst Udet his life.

In the spring of 1936 a young captain in the French Air Force named Paul Stehlin arrived in Berlin to join the French embassy as assistant air attaché. The French ambassador, André François-Poncet, knew that he was also a member of that branch of the intelligence service known as the Deuxième Bureau, and that he was admirably qualified for co-ordinating certain information and intelligence services inside the Third Reich.

Stehlin was a first-class pilot, and a brand-new small plane had accompanied him in order that he could move speedily around Germany. He had been born in Alsace-Lorraine while it was still under German occupation, and had been educated in German-controlled schools, so that his grasp of the language was faultless. He was good-looking, charming, and a good listener, and just the type to make his mark with Hermann Goering.

† Stuka was short for *Sturzkampfflugzeug*—"dive-attack plane."

He had his first appointment with the Reichminister a few days after his arrival, at the new Air Ministry building which had recently been completed, and was shown into his vast study.

"I saw him from a great distance as I came through the door," Stehlin wrote later, "rather as if I was seeing from the back of the stalls of a theater a single actor on the stage. His welcome was courteous, cordial even, very different from what I had expected of a high-ranking general toward a lowly captain, especially since he was the second most important person in the National Socialist regime."

Stehlin knew all about Goering's war record, and on seeing him for the first time was immediately struck by the way his body had changed from his early pictures; but his face, he thought, still remained as handsomely sculptured as ever. What particularly impressed him was the eyes, clear and full of good will, but somehow also hard, disquieting, without pity. He had a feeling at once of being in the presence of a man of remarkable intelligence.

Nothing particularly happened during that first meeting between the two men. Goering bade Stehlin sit on a large fauteuil while he went back to his working table. The Frenchman noticed that there was not a letter or paper on the table, and remembered that Goering had the reputation, like Hitler, of giving out his orders verbally, of striding up and down his study as he dictated memoranda or listened to the reports of his subordinates, and of writing or reading as few documents as possible.

They talked of St. Cyr, where Stehlin had been trained, of Alsace-Lorraine, of the war in the air during 1914–18, and Goering went out of his way to praise the French aviators of the day. Then they shook hands and parted, and they did not meet again for a whole year except at official events, receptions, or air shows, when Goering would come over for a brief word of greeting. But Stehlin had a feeling as he walked back in the spring sunshine to his embassy that an association had begun, and that it would be fruitful. As indeed it proved to be.

Nineteen thirty-six was a crucial year both for Germany and for Goering. On March 7, despite the nervousness of his associates, Adolf Hitler gave the order for German troops to march into the demilitarized Rhineland, and everyone waited for the inevitable retaliation by the Allies.

But France afterward said that her armies would have reacted had Britain mobilized her fleet, and Britain said she would have mobilized her fleet if the French armies had reacted, and neither did anything. Some said that Hitler would have called back his troops if the French had shown any belligerent intentions, and certainly not even the Fuehrer believed that his small army and inadequate air force were capable of withstanding what was still thought of as the most powerful armed force in Europe.

But he had no need to worry. The Allies meekly accepted Germany's move and the German public acclaimed Hitler's triumph a few weeks later by overwhelmingly approving him in a national referendum. It was the first big test of Allied solidarity, and it had crumbled at the challenge. The Germans were on their way.

With that obstacle overcome, there was not much doubt about the answer when, later in the year, General Franco and his fellow officers appealed to Hitler for help in their rebellion against the Spanish Government. At a conference between the Fuehrer, Goering, and General von Blomberg, it was agreed that Germany should provide the Spanish junta with aid in arms, men, and planes, particularly planes. Goering was delighted that the opportunity had arisen to try out his fledgling pilots in real combat.

A few months later, German fighters and bombers were in action, bombing Spanish troops, towns, and villages, fighting Spanish and Russian pilots in the skies over Madrid.

But there was no hint of war threats or any other kind of strife in Berlin that summer, for Josef Goebbels had had every anti-Jewish poster removed from the streets and urged the citizens to be full of sweetness and light, because the outside world was flooding in for the Olympic Games.

Thomas von Kantzow came south from Sweden to spend his holidays with Hermann Goering and Emmy that summer, and his stepfather got him a ticket for the Games in the box reserved for Adolf Hitler and other Nazi bigwigs. "Hitler was in his Brownshirt uniform and looked rather drab," said Thomas later, "and so did Josef Goebbels in his off-white suit. The two men who stood out among the Nazi leaders were General von Mackensen, who wore the uniform and the busby hat of the Death's Head Hussars, and

Hermann, who was in his sky-blue air-force uniform. I found the opening ceremony very moving, and so did my stepfather. Richard Strauss conducted a huge orchestra and a chorus of thousands in the 'Deutschland Über Alles,' the 'Horst Wessel Lied' and a new Olympic hymn which Strauss had composed for the occasion, and when it was all over Emmy was crying with emotion and Hermann was surreptitiously holding her hand."

So far as the American team was concerned, the Olympics had already been soured by a series of contretemps, beginning even before the members left America. Aware of Hitler's views on race, and his anti-Semitic persecutions inside Germany, Negro and Jewish organizations in the U.S. had campaigned for members of both races to boycott the Games. Fortunately, since their subsequent triumphs were to do inestimable good for their prestige and that of the U.S., the campaign failed and there were both blacks and Jews on the team which arrived in Berlin. Only one member had disappeared from the line-up on the way, and that was the beautiful and headstrong swimmer, Eleanor Holm. The lissome Miss Holm, who contended that the good life did not in any way affect her prowess as a swimmer, and proceeded to prove it by winning each race she entered, was irked by the conditions which had been imposed on the U.S. team by its arrogant, stern, and unbending Head of Delegation, Avery Brundage. On the voyage across the Atlantic aboard the S.S. *Manhattan* she took to slipping out of her poky third-class cabin to live it up and drink champagne with the reporters in first-class, particularly the late Charles MacArthur. She was reported, warned, reported a second time, and this time sacked from the team by the implacable Mr. Brundage. Sympathetic reporters got her a job covering the Games for a news agency, so she sat in the stands for the events—and thus met the Goerings.

At one of the receptions for the working press, Miss Holm was introduced to Emmy Goering, and Thomas.

"My poor lamb!" said Emmy, folding her in her arms. "Just for a glass of champagne! My dear, you are so lovely they should be drinking it out of your slipper. You must come to Carin Hall, and we will help you to forget those terrible prudes!"

The American team got itself involved in controversy again over the inaugural march on opening day. It so happens that the ancient Greek salute by which the competitors have always greeted the reviewing stand is a hand held straight up, palm downward, and therefore not very much different from that of the National Socialist salute. To demonstrate that they were obeying Greek tradition and not acknowledging the politics of their hosts, most delegations put their arms out sideways from their bodies, to demonstrate the difference.

This was the fashion in which the British, the Swedes, and their fellow Scandinavians gave the salute. On the other hand, the Italians, the Bulgarians, certain members of the Belgian team, and the Japanese all gave plain Nazi salutes. So, to the amazement of their friends, did the French, as a result of which their team received one of the greatest ovations of the Games from the largely German crowd.

On the other hand, the Americans were determined to demonstrate beyond all doubt that they were showing allegiance to no one. With the proud defender of *amour-propre* and amateurism, Avery Brundage, at their head, they marched into the stadium and as they passed the reviewing stand took off their hats and deliberately crooked their arms and hats across their breasts to avoid any resemblance to a Hitler salute. They did more than that. The other delegations had all dipped their national flags as they passed the reviewing stand. The Americans kept their flag flying high.

The crowd began to boo and jeer.

"Adolf Hitler half-turned to Hermann," said Thomas von Kantzow, "and without letting the smile go off his face, he hissed : 'Not only do they put Negroes and Jews in their team, but they insult us too.' Hermann whispered back: 'It's an American tradition, mein Fuehrer. They never dip their flag to anyone.'‡ But Hitler, very red in the face although he was still smiling, slowly shook his head. I

---

‡ The non-dipping routine dated back to the 1908 Games, when a standard bearer passed King Edward VII on the reviewing stand in London and held it high, saying, "This flag dips for no earthly king."

think at that moment he would have liked to shoot every member of the American team."

To celebrate the Games, several of the Nazi leaders had decided to give parties, and Goering was determined that his should be the most elaborate and successful.

"We spent long hours at Carin Hall discussing just what kind of a party it should be," said Thomas von Kantzow. "He already had his spies out and learned that his two principal rivals were Joachim von Ribbentrop and Josef Goebbels. He didn't seem to be worried about Ribbentrop, whom he despised. 'He's going to roast an ox and serve champagne,' he said. 'It will be burned to a frazzle and the champagne will be that well-known piss.'* But Goebbels was a different matter."

The little Minister was already converting a small islet on a lake near Potsdam and building a pontoon bridge to it, and invitations had gone out to 2,000 guests, including the entire diplomatic corps and all the delegations to the Games. It was to prove a highly successful party, with good food and lavish drinks, and plenty of Goebbels' favorite starlets to titilate the guests.

But Goering went one better. Reluctantly, he had decided that Carin Hall was too far away for the guests to make it in between the Olympic events, but his palace on the Leipziger Platz was a more than adequate substitute. Albert Speer had made it an impressive abode quite worthy of the Borgia prince whom Goering so much resembled, and it was now hung with some of Goering's most precious art treasures. The grounds were spacious, and down below were a sauna, a gymnasium, and a heated swimming pool.

In one part of the huge garden Goering set his minions to work. They transformed it into a sort of Munich Oktoberfest beer garden, with a fairground in the middle, *helle* and *dunkel* beer on tap (as well as champagne and liquors), sausages, roast game, corn on the cob, and mounds of potatoes and sauerkraut.

For entertainment Goering had engaged the principal dancers and corps de ballet of the Berlin Opera, and

---

* A reference to the fact that Ribbentrop was married to a member of the Henkel (German) champagne family, for whom he had once been a salesman.

shortly after the guests assembled on the lawns Ernst Udet came over in a biplane and gave a fantastic display of aerobatics.

"As it happened," said Thomas von Kantzow, "it was not the ideal night for an outdoor party. The weather was cool. Like many of his guests, Hermann had dressed in Bavarian leather pants, a frilly shirt and a hat with a sprig of edelweiss in it, and at times his knees looked quite blue. But everyone was determined to have fun and they were very cheerful and happy, winning big prizes at the shooting galleries, riding on the roundabouts, the giant wheel and a crazy airplane."

The party went on until four or five in the morning until, eventually, there were only a few couples left waltzing to a Bavarian band, or, inside the great house, necking or sleeping it off.

"Just about dawn," said Thomas von Kantzow, "I went downstairs to the swimming pool. The underwater lights were on and there was a single girl slowly swimming up and down, occasionally pausing to fill a glass with champagne from a magnum on the side. She was naked. She was very lovely and I recognized her as the American swimmer, Eleanor Holm. Then I noticed that I was not alone. In the shadows at the side of the pool, Hermann and Emmy were sitting together, his arm around her shoulder, watching the beautiful American sliding through the blue and gold water."

The National Socialists were well satisfied with the results of the 1936 Olympics. The only "incident" was caused by Adolf Hitler, who left the stand rather than shake hands with the black American runner, Jesse Owens, the hero of the Games.†

But despite the superb athletic prowess of black U.S. athletes, the U.S. was well beaten by Germany at the Games. With 33 gold, 26 silver and 30 bronze medals, Germany scored 181 points against America's 124 points (24 gold, 20 silver, 12 bronze).‡ In addition, it had been a

---

† America was "unfair" to use Negro athletes, he ranted, and called them "animals."
‡ Behind them came Italy, Finland, France, Hungary, and Sweden. Britain was tenth.

considerable propaganda triumph. Of the scores of thousands of visitors who came to Germany that summer, few would have realized that there was a menacing cloud over the land. Second-class citizens stayed home, unharried for the moment, hopeful that the tide of hatred and prejudice had passed over them. Of course, it had not.

XVI. PAINKILLERS

Goering's weight was more of a problem during 1937–38 than at any time previously, and there were occasions when it rose well above the 280 pounds which he considered to be the limit. He was by now, without any doubt, the busiest man in the Reich. He was not only Reichminister for Air, but Hitler had now given him charge of the so-called Four Year Plan through which money would be found to finance the growing demands of rearmament. Dr. Hjalmar Schacht had flatly refused to serve under him and had washed his hands of the whole economic mess, and neither Goering nor his assistant, Pilli Koerner, were Schacht's equal in squeezing blood out of stones. He still took his responsibilities seriously as Master of the Forests and the Hunt, he was an inveterate visitor to museums and antique shops in search of objets d'art, and he insisted on having at least an hour a day with Emmy.

There was something about this frenetic activity, his travels abroad, his constant consultations with Hitler, whether in Berlin, Munich, or Berchtesgaden, which gave him a morbid appetite which he tried in vain to curb. He was always nibbling. He would descend from his own house, which he had built above Hitler's at Berchtesgaden, and glumly sit in at one of the "appalling meals," as he termed them, which the Fuehrer gave each day for his hangers-on. Hitler ate salads and carrot juice and did not notice that the ordinary food was execrable, the beer stale and warm, the wine extremely *ordinaire*, and Goering could not stomach it. He would then join Hitler at the head of the procession he led on a hike across the mountains, discussing matters of high policy—how to appease Mussolini over the takeover of Austria, how to frighten the French and woo the British, how to persuade Poland to give up the Corridor between Prussia and East Prussia without having to go to war.

At the end of it, he would return home with his huge stomach rolling and rumbling with starvation symptoms, and he would gorge down great spoonfuls of eggs Benedict, or rusks piled with pâté de foie gras, and sometimes Emmy would personally cook for him a favorite dish of blinis with caviar tucked inside and a smother of whipped cream. All washed down with champagne or good vintage claret or Moselle.

When he was positively bursting, he would whimper off to Carin Hall and there descend to the sauna bath which he had built in the basement and try to sweat away the surplus pounds, or be rubbed and pummeled by his masseur, or goaded into a swimming race by Emmy or Robert Kropp.

The pounds would drop away until the next crisis of overwork and the next bout of overindulgence.

It was during one of these slimming regimes in 1937 that he hauled his sweating body out of the sauna and was summoned to a telephone call with Hitler, who wanted his advice on the strategy to be used toward Austria. The talk lasted nearly two hours, during which time Goering sat in a drafty corner of the gymnasium with no covering other than a towel around his waist. It was always forbidden to come near him when he was talking to Hitler, so no one looked in to see whether he was getting cold. By the time the talk was finished, he was shivering and that night it had turned into a fever.

The next day, when he reached Berlin, the fever had gone down but what had taken its place was a violent and continuous jaw-ache and toothache. He put in a call for his dentist, Professor Hugo Blaschke, to come at once.

Hugo Blaschke was an interesting character. He had trained as a dentist in the United States and set up practice in Berlin in the nineteen twenties. Goering had been introduced to him by Prince Victor zu Wied in 1930, when he wanted some bridgework done, and through this connection he had subsequently become dentist to Adolf Hitler, Eva Braun, Heinrich Himmler, Joachim von Ribbentrop, Robert Ley, and Martin Bormann.

Blaschke was apt to think of men and women in terms of their teeth, and when he saw Himmler he would think to himself "good teeth" or, in the case of Goering, "poor teeth, difficult gums." On the whole he didn't much admire any of his National Socialist patients with the exception of Eva Braun ("very firm teeth, she'll die with them; and a charming person, too") and Emmy Goering ("weakish molars, but an honest, forthright, attractive person").

He had little sympathy for anyone who showed signs of fear when they sat in his dentist's chair, and on this occasion Hermann Goering's eyes rolled in apprehension "and he seemed prepared to scream the place down even before I touched him." The Reichminister was in a highly nervous state, and sweat was pouring out of him to such an extent that Blaschke suggested that he take his shirt off, which he did.

An examination quickly showed that the aching teeth and jaw owed more to nerves and exposure than to any individual dental fault, and Professor Blaschke decided to give his patient a sedative. A German medical firm had just recently developed a paracodeine pill which contained a mild morphine derivative, and some samples of it had come into the dentist's hands. He gave a small bottle of them to Hermann Goering, and told him to take two every two hours until the pain stopped.

Five days later, Goering was on the telephone to the professor to tell him that he now felt fine, but where could he obtain some more of the pills? Blaschke warned the Reichminister that it would be unwise to continue taking paracodeine after the need for it had passed, and was vague about how the tablets had come into his hands.

But Goering found out. By the end of 1937 he was taking about ten of the pills a day. The amount of morphine in them was mild, and never enough to provide more than a slight sedative; but they were hard to stop, especially for a nervous man, once their consumption had started. Soon Hermann Goering was "on the pill."

He was, however, well aware of the dangers of overindulgence (for the moment, anyway) and he was determined that never again would he fall victim to the addiction which had brought him low in Sweden. For Hermann Goering, it was a time of great opportunity for advancement in the Party and in Germany, and he was conscious of it every moment of the day and night. His most dangerous rivals had been swept aside. Roehm was dead The

Brownshirt army he had led was no longer a threatening
force. Himmler and his cohorts in the SS were lying low.
With the Luftwaffe and the Four Year Plan both under his
control, Hermann Goering was, next to Hitler, the most
powerful man in the Reich.

But his ambitions did not stop at that. There was one
more position which would make him even more powerful,
perhaps even master of the Reich—and certainly the un-
doubted heir to the Fuehrer himself, secure from any bids
for succession from his rivals. As commander-in-chief of
the Luftwaffe, he could terrify Germany's enemies. But as
commander-in-chief of the German armed forces, he could
control Germany and Germany's destiny.

His discussions with Adolf Hitler during this period had
made him acutely conscious of the fact that the Fuehrer
was dissatisfied with the situation in the armed forces.
Practically every other branch of German life had, by
1937, been effectively National Socialized. But the Oberkommando of the Wehrmacht was in the secure hands of
General Werner von Blomberg, who was also Minister of
Defense, and the commander-in-chief of the Army was
General Baron von Fritsch. Both were non-Nazis. Both
made it a matter of policy to keep the German Army non-
political, and its officers corps in large measure stayed
aloof from the Party.

It was a dangerous situation, and Hitler knew it as well
as Hermann Goering. If, for instance, the Fuehrer had
decided in 1934 to back Ernst Roehm and the Brownshirts
in their radical policies instead of cutting them down, he
was aware that Von Blomberg and the German Army
would have opposed him at once. One of Roehm's plans
had been to incorporate the Brownshirts in the armed
forces and take over the command, and the corps of regular officers had been resolved to prevent that by armed
action if necessary.

Roehm was gone, but other situations might come up in
which the Nazis had one policy and the Army another.
What then? Hitler would be forced to back down. He did
not possess the resources to triumph.

The situation would remain dangerous for the Nazis so
long as the Army remained apolitical and its commander-
in-chief non-Nazi. But how could Von Blomberg be removed? He could not be sacked. The Army and the officers

corps would never allow it. And he would certainly not resign voluntarily. So how to get rid of him?

It was with this problem that Hermann Goering was now personally and continuously involved. Its solution promised not only the Nazification of the armed forces, but great rewards for himself.

Goering had always been an ardent and romantic royalist, and though his enthusiasm for the Hohenzollerns had considerably cooled since the nineteen twenties, he still retained an inordinate admiration for the British royal family. His great ambition in 1937 was to go to London as the official German representative at the coronation of King George VI. But a Labour Member of Parliament, Ellen Wilkinson, got wind of the plan to invite him and promised trouble for him if he dared to set foot on British soil. Joachim von Ribbentrop, who was now German ambassador in London, sent a copy of the speech and newspaper comment to Hitler, who told Goering to stand down. It was a pity in many ways, and a good example of how righteous public indignation can sometimes thwart useful diplomatic contacts. Goering was by far the most reasonable of the Nazi leaders and, presuming he was coming to London, an arrangement had been made for him to talk to Winston Churchill. From this and other contacts he might have carried back information about British feelings and intentions that could have cured Adolf Hitler of some considerable misunderstanding about how the British saw Germany and her ambitions. Goering was cast down by the cancellation of his visit, and the egregious Von Ribbentrop and General von Blomberg took his place.*

Goering was convinced that the Duke of Windsor, whom King George VI had replaced, had lost his throne because he was willing to discuss an Anglo-German rapprochement and did not share his government's antipathy to National Socialism. In this opinion the unsuitable liaison

---

* It has been stated by some historians that Goering decided to fly to London anyway, but on arrival was persuaded by Von Ribbentrop not to show himself; he stayed one night and then flew home, with only the Foreign Office and the special branch at Scotland Yard aware that he had been in Britain. I have checked this story carefully and can find no proof whatsoever of it. Goering himself said it never happened.

and marriage he had made with Mrs. Simpson was only a pretext for getting rid of him.

Nevertheless, the unsuitable marriage had certainly enabled the British Government to dethrone an embarrassingly "political" monarch, and that fact must have stayed in Goering's mind when General von Blomberg came to see him on his return from London. He wanted the Reichminister's advice. Though now nearly sixty years of age, he informed Goering that he was planning to marry again. The difficulty was, he explained, that the girl he had chosen as his bride was thirty years his junior and not quite in the same social class as himself. Did Goering think that anyone—the snobbish members of the officers corps, for example—would be likely to object?

Now it so happened that Von Blomberg was completely unaware of certain facts about his bride-to-be, beside her youth and her social status. He was unaware that she was a registered prostitute in several German cities, well known to the police, and that she had served a prison sentence for dealing in pornographic pictures and literature.

Did Hermann Goering know these juicy facts? Had his private intelligence service already informed him of the gaudy past of Von Blomberg's fiancée? No one can be quite certain.

What is certain is that the Reichminister immediately assured General von Blomberg that he need have no doubts about proceeding with the nuptials. Was not the National Socialist Reich one in which all men (except Jews and Communists, of course) were equal? To make Von Blomberg doubly confident, he went into another room and spoke on the telephone to Adolf Hitler, and then came back with the Fuehrer's felicitations and the news that both of them would be guests at the general's wedding.

They were indeed. But then the ax fell on Von Blomberg's neck, and if Hermann Goering did not wield it, the execution could not have been more convenient for him and the Nazi Party. For almost immediately after the happy pair departed for their honeymoon, both he and Adolf Hitler were to their "utter shock and horror" informed of the sleazy nature of the young Frau von Blomberg's background.

The humiliated general returned to Berlin to be told by an emotional Hermann Goering that he must forget his wife's past, and ignore the scandal it was causing. But he must have been only too well aware that the officers corps of the German Army would never accept a commander-in-chief whose wife was an ex-prostitute. Certainly, Von Blomberg was quickly made aware of their contempt and indignation.

There was nothing else to do. He handed in his resignation as commander-in-chief and retired to private life.

Who would take his place? The generals immediately began agitating to have General Werner von Fritsch, the army commander, promoted to the position of over-all commander of the armed forces.

But Von Fritsch was almost at once involved in a scandal himself. Heinrich Himmler produced a dossier which he showed to Goering and Hitler which seemed to prove that the proud, upright, and rather puritanical general had been involved some years back in a sordid homosexual affair with a notorious pervert. A confrontation was arranged during which the two men were brought in contact, and Fritsch was positively identified by the pervert as the other man in the squalid affair.

In fact, General von Fritsch was completely innocent (a colonel named Frisch was the man actually involved). But racked by scandal as it was, the Army insisted on a court-martial and Von Fritsch resigned as commander-in-chief before appearing before it. Hermann Goering presided at the court-martial and by himself cross-examining the accusing homosexual, swiftly proved that the man had perjured himself. General von Fritsch was at once acquitted and the first to congratulate him was Hermann Goering.

But, of course, Von Fritsch's name had now been tarnished with scandal even if he had been proved innocent, and no one was willing to suggest that he withdraw his resignation.

Thus yet another non-Nazi was removed from the second key position in the armed forces. Which good Party man would now take over as commander-in-chief of the Oberkommando of the Wehrmacht, and thus have the combined might of the German armed forces in his hands?

Hermann Goering sat back to await his reward, and heady visions of the power that was coming must have passed through his head as he waited. But it was not to be.

On February 4, 1938, Adolf Hitler named himself as commander-in-chief of the German armed forces and abolished the post of Minister of Defense. At the same time he dismissed six army generals known to be anti-Nazi in their sympathies.

As a sop to Goering, the Fuehrer promoted him to be field marshal, but, of course, it wasn't the same.

In a speech to the Reichstag on February 20, 1938, the Fuehrer made clear the significance of the changes.

"There now exists," he cried, "not a single institution of this State which is not National Socialist . . . The Party during the past five years has not only created a National Socialist State, but it has arranged for itself a perfect organization which will maintain forever its independence. The greatest guarantee of the National Socialist revolution is the control we now have of all the institutions of the Reich, at home and abroad. The nation is protected, so far as the rest of the world is concerned, by our National Socialist armed forces from now on."

Hermann Goering took what comfort he could from that, and donned his new field marshal's uniform.

A month later the armed forces, now firmly in Nazi hands, marched into Austria and occupied the state in a bloodless campaign largely organized and stage-managed by Hermann Goering. He was afterward to boast that he had brought about Austria's capitulation mainly through a series of strategically arranged and tactically worded telephone calls, and to a certain extent this was true. It was war by long-distance telephone, and by the time the Wehrmacht crossed the Austrian border, Goering's words had talked the Austrians into accepting defeat without firing a shot.

When he was sure that there was going to be no serious opposition inside Austria to the Anschluss with Germany, he took Emmy on her first visit across the border to the Castle at Mauterndorf where he had spent some of the most rewarding hours of his childhood and adolescence. Baronin Lilli welcomed them as if they were the two remaining civilized people in a world of barbarians, and was obviously on the edge of a nervous breakdown as a result of the German occupation.

It turned out that her immediate anxiety was about Her-

mann's younger brother, Albert, the one who bore such a
striking resemblance to the late Baron von Epenstein.
Some years previously, disenchanted with the Nazis, he
had gone to Austria and lived for a time on a subvention
from his godfather. Now he was working in a film studio in
Vienna, and Baronin Lilli feared that he might be in trouble, for he had often spoken out boldly against Adolf Hitler. Goering promised that he would keep him out of the
hands of the Gestapo.

She blessed him for his kindness. Once more she said to
Emmy, as they stood on the battlements of Mauterndorf:
"Don't forget, this will be yours some day." Then she
sighed and murmured: "If only I could get away from all
this strife and trouble. There won't be a war, will there? I
don't think I could bear it."

Hermann Goering assured her that there would be no
war.

In Vienna, the streets were daubed with anti-Jewish
signs and glass from the smashed windows of Jewish shops
piled up in the gutters. It was rumored that 7,000 Jews had
committed suicide since the Nazis had arrived, and the
Gestapo persecutions had begun. Goering played his part
in stirring up feeling against Jews, for he at once agreed
when a delegation of Austrian Nazis visited him and asked
him to "work up" the populace about the "Jewish danger."

He had a curiously ambivalent attitude toward the Jews.
He was one of those who could have said: "Some of my
best friends are Jews," because it was literally true. His
godfather, Ritter von Epenstein, his second-in-command,
Erhard Milch, several of Emmy's actress friends, had all
been or were still close to him. He liked Jewish composers
(Mendelssohn particularly) and painters (Rubens). But he
also believed that the Jews, by profiteering and scheming
behind the scenes, had helped to bring about Germany's
defeat in World War I and he was convinced that they had
battened and profited from Germany's sufferings in the
terrible years immediately afterward.

In the privacy of his bedroom, he agreed with Emmy
that the Jews were just like any other people ("but a bit
smarter," he would add, grinning), and that they had their
good and bad, like every other race. As for himself, he had
long since decided that if he liked someone, then the best

thing to do was to decide that he or she was not Jewish, racial background notwithstanding.

"I'll decide who is and who is not a Jew!" he once said to a subordinate who made a reference to some visitors to his household.

He would, if given the choice, have chosen any Jew in the world to the companionship of a creature like Julius Streicher, the Party Jew-baiter. He became uneasy and made excuses to leave them when he heard congenital anti-Semites like Goebbels or Himmler calmly discussing the liquidation of the Jews. A rasping, rancorous anti-Jewish peroration from Adolf Hitler made him glum for hours afterward, and he risked the Fuehrer's wrath by helping Emmy time after time to get Jews out of the clutches of Himmler's Gestapo.

But he did not possess the courage to stand up and argue with Hitler about it (or about anything else, for that matter). The Party line was anti-Semitism, and so he went along with it. And afterward he was to say:

"I had no desire to see the Jews liquidated. I just wanted them to get out of Germany. But what could I do once the process had begun? Why, the monsters eventually wiped out one of Emmy's closest friends—and I had fought very hard to save her, at great risk."

It was true, though it made him no less guilty than the rest of them.

On March 23, 1938, shortly after the occupation of Austria, Goering made a speech in Vienna in which he said:

"I must direct a serious word to the city of Vienna. Today Vienna cannot rightly claim to be a German city. How can one speak of a German city in which 300,000 Jews are living? This city has an important German mission in the field of culture as well as in economics. For neither of these can we make use of Jews."

The speech was printed under flaring headlines in the next day's newspapers, and, as the U.S. Embassy in Vienna reported in a dispatch to the State Department, one sentence which Goering used was significantly cut out by the Nazi censors.

"The Jew must clearly understand one thing at once," he had declared. "He must get out."

The next day there were 3,000 applications for visas at

the U.S. embassy. At Goering's insistence, and much to the irritation of the local Gestapo, the frontiers were left open to all Jews who wished to leave Austria, until November 1938. They left their belongings behind, their houses, their pictures, their jewelry, and most of the Nazi leaders were soon boasting of the bargains they had been able to buy up cheap from the departing Jews. Hermann Goering was satisfied with a number of art treasures which his experts were able to pick up for him, but otherwise showed little interest in the scramble for bargains. He knew he had a castle coming his way, anyway.

Then something happened in Paris, and in November 1938, the iron curtain clamped down on Jews trying to get out of Austria.

XVII. "THE JEWS, THE JEWS!"

Hermann Goering had never had much time for the other leading members of the National Socialist Party. With the exception of Adolf Hitler himself, for whom he had an admiration almost amounting to worship, he thought them a rough lot or a dull lot, greedy and undiscriminating, and with few tastes for the good things of life. For a time during Carin's lifetime he had been on visiting terms with the Goebbels ménage, principally because he was very fond of Magda Goebbels, and Carin and the volatile Josef had built up a feverish kind of rapport. But after Carin's death they had drifted apart, and met only on Party occasions. Goering made it quite apparent that he objected to the way Goebbels' constant philandering humiliated his long-suffering wife, and the Minister of Propaganda got his own back by spreading any malicious gossip about Goering that came within his ken. They were not quite enemies, but they were certainly no longer friends.

By 1938, Goering had residences at Berchtesgaden and on Rominten Heath (a small hunting lodge) as well as his palace in Berlin and his feudal grange at Schorfheide, and he liked to keep them all filled with interesting and happy people who would not bore him with Party intrigue. Ernst Udet came often with one or other of his more respectable girl friends; Pilli Koerner with his wife; Burno Loerzer; Karl Bodenschatz, the Zu Wieds, the Thyssens, the Krupp von Bohlens, art experts from Munich, Amsterdam, and Brussels, and Emmy's old theater friends (so long as they weren't Jewish). He also kept up with Carin's relatives, and her younger sister, Lily, was a frequent visitor. Her older sister, Fanny von Wilamowitz-Moellendorff, would have liked to come as often, but was gently dissuaded, since both Emmy and Goering found her a little too

Gothic and too starry-eyed about National Socialism for their liking.

He also kept up a close relationship with his own brothers and sisters, and was particularly happy when his sister-in-law Ilse Goering was around. She was a tall, slim, elegantly glowing blonde who said little but didn't really need to.

There was also his favorite of them all, his sister Olga. Toward the end of 1937, he let it be known to his family circle that Emmy was pregnant. Enormously excited at the prospect of being a father, and desperately anxious that all should go well, he sent Emmy off to cosset herself at Carin Hall.* In the months that followed, Olga took Emmy's place as hostess at Goering's dinner parties, and it was to her house that he would frequently come when he was at a loose end and in search of diversion. Olga Rigele was married to a quiet and complaisant Austrian who was a member of the Party but frequently away from Berlin, and she went her own way. She was uncannily like her brother Hermann in appearance. She was plump ("It runs in the family," she said), jolly, a good talker with a ready wit, and despite her size, most men found her remarkably attractive. Rubens would have loved her.

She was a middle-aged forty-eight years old, but no one cared, least of all Olga.

It was Olga Rigele who was to change the nature of the relationship between Hermann Goering and the young Frenchman Paul Stehlin from that of a Reichminister and a foreign, and very junior, diplomat to a much more family-like association.

Toward the end of spring 1937, Ambassador François-Poncet informed his assistant air attaché that his presence would be required at an embassy dinner party that evening. A more important official had dropped out at the last mo-

---

* She was forty-four years old, and this was her first child. But with typical thoroughness, she produced a daughter on June 2, 1938, without any complications. The child was christened Edda and Adolf Hitler stood in as her godfather. The nurse hired by Emmy to look after her turned out not to be a member of the Party, and when the Gestapo reported this to Heinrich Himmler, he rang up to complain. Emmy then pointed out that she wasn't a member of the Party either, and Himmler banged down the telephone in a fury. Goering swiftly arranged for her to join.

ment, and Stehlin was rushed in as a substitute. A few
hours later he found himself sitting next to Frau Olga
Rigele.

Almost immediately, the two of them, after a few polite
asides to their neighbors, concentrated on each other. It
soon became apparent that Olga had a sort of adoration
for her brother, and that he reciprocated with a particularly tender affection toward her. Most of their conversation was about Goering. Stehlin, without dissimulating the
French patriotism which had stayed with him all through
his childhood, described to her his schooldays under German masters in German-occupied Lorraine, and how it was
there he had heard Goering's name used for the first time.†
He went on to tell her how he had read of her brother's
war exploits and determined one day to emulate him as a
flier.

"She was moved quite evidently by my words, even
though I noticed that it did not prevent her appreciating
the perfection of the dinner nor the quality of the wines,"
Stehlin, something of a connoisseur himself, said later.
"She was both touched by the warmth of our contact but
also animated and merry."

She was then taken in hand by more important guests
when they rose from the table, and he saw her only from a
distance. But next afternoon the ambassador called Stehlin
into his office and informed that he was invited to dinner
that night at Frau Rigele's house. Stehlin had been looking
forward that night to an outing with some people of his
own age, and explained that he already had an engagement.

"Then get out of it," said the ambassador crisply. "Be at
Frau Rigele's at eight o'clock."

Cursing his status as a junior diplomat and a bachelor,
always being sent from one dinner party to another to fill
an empty chair, he went off to his apartment that evening
to get dressed. He was convinced that one of Frau Rigele's
guests had dropped out and she had remembered him when
stuck for a replacement. But when, a little later, he arrived
at the house and eventually sat down to dinner, he discov-

† The pupils were fed on German war propaganda, and Goering
was a hero at the time.

ered that they were seven at table and that a place had quite evidently been made especially for him. He sat between Olga and Ilse Goering, and he had a hard time dividing his time between his two neighbors, "trying to please the one while having the pleasure of addressing myself to the other."

Late in the evening, just when he was getting ready to leave, the door opened and in came Hermann Goering. He walked across to Stehlin, took his hand in both of his and greeted him as if he were a long-lost friend. Putting his arm around his shoulder, he drew him to one side and said:

"I know that you see a lot of Bodenschatz and Udet. I'm very happy about that."

Then he began to talk about French and German aviation. "The advantage we have over you," he said, "is that we had to start from scratch. The only collaborators I have taken on are dynamic men with imagination and modern ideas, capable of handling new projects, and using aircraft of the kind one should be using in 1937. I have put on one side those who still live in the past, the ones I think you still have with you—at least, if what I read in the press is true."

Stehlin protested in defense of the French Air Force that it was now in the process of redevelopment, that modern materials were being pressed into service, and that French ideas were being adapted to the present and the near future.

Goering grinned and grabbed him by the arm. "Between what I am doing," he said, "and what you possess, at least so long as you refuse to change the men in charge, there will soon be little in common. Come out into the field, come and see our exercises, look at our factories, I'll hide nothing from you, and you will get a more accurate idea of how it is with the Luftwaffe."

Stehlin accepted this startling invitation, and then asked Goering how the Luftwaffe had managed to build up its numbers in such a short time.

"I've eliminated those who are always trying to do better," he said. "Once a plan has been made and judged reasonable and practical, and once the program of construction has begun, it is necessary to press on and protect it against those who criticize its imperfections. In matters

of strength, numbers count more than quality. It is necessary to accept a compromise between the two."

They were words that would one day rebound on Hermann Goering.

Paul Stehlin went back home that night to write out a
full report for his ambassador and for the Deuxième Bureau in Paris. He was aware that some sort of a milestone
had been passed in his relationship with the Goering family. From that day onward, he was bombarded with invitations from Olga Rigele, and he saw her more and more
frequently, at her home, at the Ministry of Air, at the Haus
der Flieger (a club for aviators), and at Carin Hall. She
wrote him long letters, sent him presents when she was
holidaying in her Bavarian home or on a voyage, and
would telephone to the embassy to inquire about him
whenever he was back in Paris.

"I had never hoped," Stehlin wrote later, "when I arrived
in Berlin that I would learn, merely as a result of simple
and straightforward conversations, in complete intimacy,
what diplomats of high rank were desperately trying to find
out or interpret from events, from interminable interviews,
or from studies of the newspapers."

An association had begun that would continue long after
World War II had turned France and Germany into enemies. But though he didn't realize it at the time, Captain
Paul Stehlin was falling for one of Hermann Goering's
most effective ploys for subjecting the French to Nazi
propaganda.

In the actual discussions which took place at Munich in
1938, when Neville Chamberlain and Edouard Daladier
signed away the Sudetenland of Czechoslovakia to Germany, Hermann Goering played little part. He was on
hand in case Adolf Hitler needed to consult him, and the
statesmen and pressmen assembled for the great sellout
were conscious at all times of his plump figure in sky-blue
uniform, moving swiftly from room to room, chatting with
Chamberlain or Daladier, his arms around Count Ciano,
the Italian Foreign Minister, and always a large, friendly
smile on his round, open face.

But what was there for him to do during the negotiations?

"Actually the whole thing was a cut-and-dried affair," he

said later. "Neither Chamberlain nor Daladier were in the least bit interested in sacrificing or risking anything to save Czechoslovakia. That was clear as day to me. The fate of Czechoslovakia was essentially sealed in three hours. Then they argued four more hours over the word 'guarantee.' Chamberlain kept hedging. Daladier hardly paid any attention at all. He just sat there like this." Goering spread out his legs, slumped down, and bent his head with a bored expression. "All he did was nod approval from time to time. Not the slightest objection to anything. I was simply amazed at how easily the thing was managed by Hitler. After all, they knew that Skoda etc. had munitions plants in the Sudetenland, and Czechoslovakia would be at our mercy. When he suggested that certain armaments which were across the Sudeten border should be brought into the Sudeten territory as soon as we took it over, I thought there would be an explosion. But no—not a peep. We got everything we wanted, just like that." He snapped his fingers. "They didn't insist on consulting the Czechs as a matter of form—nothing. At the end the French delegate to Czechoslovakia said, 'Well, now, I'll have to convey the verdict to the condemned.' That's all there was to it. The question of a guarantee was settled by leaving it up to Hitler to guarantee the rest of Czechoslovakia. Now, they knew perfectly well what that meant."

But in fact he had done all the work beforehand, and if anyone was responsible for the climate of uncertainty and fear in which the British and the French prime ministers came to negotiate at Munich, Hermann Goering could take the credit. It must be admitted that he had had considerable if unwitting aid from his young friend at the French embassy, Captain Paul Stehlin.

In the months which followed the blossoming of his friendship with Goering and his sister, Stehlin had eagerly accepted (with the encouragement of his embassy) all the invitations he received not only to stay with the Goerings, but also to see the airfields, fortifications, factories, and plane performances which were banned to all other foreigners in Germany.

He was taken on a tour of the great system of fortifications, the Siegfried Line, which guarded Germany's westward frontier with France, Belgium, and Luxembourg, and he was deeply impressed.

Karl Bodenschatz, his guide, hastened to assure him that
the Siegfried Line had been built with the most pacific
intentions toward France. It was merely there to prevent
all conflict between the two countries. Goering had ordered
the construction of the Line as part of his duties as Minister in charge of the Four Year Plan.

"The German Government wants to make sure that it
will have complete liberty of action in the east," Bodenschatz said, "first of all by neutralizing the danger of
Czechoslovakia on its flank, and then by eliminating the
Soviet danger further east which menaces all Europe . . . I
repeat that the building of this Line is evidence of our
friendly disposition toward your country. . . . Your mission
is African. You have found overseas what you consider
necessary for your needs. Our mission, our German mission, is European. In eliminating the Soviet danger, we are
contributing to your own security and, from the human
point of view, we are assuring those people who will be
associated with us, as equal citizens, a standard of living
incomparably superior to what they enjoy today."

Stehlin did not know that the Siegfried Line in 1938
(and even a year later) had considerable and vital gaps in
it, for he was not allowed near those areas. He obviously
thought the fortifications impregnable, and was much
taken with Bodenschatz's remarks. He made a report to his
ambassador, who immediately telegraphed its contents to
Paris.

He was also taken around the air factories and a picture
was continually built up for him, by Goering himself, by
Bodenschatz and Udet, of a modern German Air Force of
enormous strength capable of dominating her enemies on
both sides of her frontiers. He so reported and back went
the dispatches to Paris.

So when, in August 1938, the commander-in-chief of the
French Air Force, General Joseph Vuillemin, arrived for
an official visit to the German Air Force, he was well
primed to be scared out of his wits. He was. He was first
taken to the Messerschmitt works at Augsburg to see the
steady production of Me 109s and 110s, and then the
French party went on to the Luftwaffe's Tactical Experi-
ment Center at Barthe, on the shores of the Baltic. Large
numbers of aircraft of all types were put in the air for
them, and bombing raids were carried out, not only by new

heavy bombers but also by the new Stukas, which dove down and smashed up moving vehicles on the ground with devastating effectiveness.

When General Vuillemin eventually left Berlin for Paris "he told General de Geffrier [the chief air attaché] and me of his astonishment and anxiety at all he had seen and heard," Stehlin wrote later. True, when the general at a farewell reception at Carin Hall was asked by Goering what France would do in the event of a German attack on Czechoslovakia, the Frenchman stoutly replied:

"France will remain faithful to her pledges."

But he knew and Stehlin knew that he was frightened, and would convey as much to his government when he got home. As indeed he did.

So when the four-power meeting started at Munich, Goering could be pretty sure that the French, at least, would be desperately afraid to get themselves involved in war, and would grasp at any face-saver to keep them out of it. In fact, at one point in the talks, when an impasse seemed to be reached in the *pourparlers* and the British and French seemed to be standing firm against Germany's demands, the French Premier, Edouard Daladier, called Paul Stehlin aside.

"You are a flier," he said to the young air attaché. You have seen our chief, General Vuillemin. He is terribly disturbed. What is your view?"

For the next fifteen minutes Stehlin talked about the Luftwaffe, "of its great power, the way it could be employed, its close association with the Army, about everything which distinguished it from our own Air Force." Daladier listened with great attention, and then said:

"Do you think, as Vuillemin does, that after a few days' fighting we would have no planes left?"

Stehlin was too embarrassed to reply, and Daladier did not insist. Instead, he went back into the conference hall to join Chamberlain in signing the humiliating terms of the Munich Pact.

As one distinguished Frenchman‡ remarked when a fellow countryman described the agreement as *"un grand soulagement* (a great relief)":

"Ah oui, un soulagement! Comme quand on a merdé

‡ Alexis Léger, an official of the Quai d'Orsay.

dans sa culotte (Oh yes, a relief! Like crapping in your pants)."

Goering would have appreciated that remark.

On November 8, 1938, a Jewish refugee named Herschel Grynspan walked into the German embassy in Paris and shot dead a minor attaché named Ernst vom Rath. He was obviously mentally unbalanced by his own experiences and the sufferings being endured by his parents, and his motivations for the killing were vague. Unfortunately for the Jews, he committed his desperate act on the eve of the anniversary in Munich of the Beer Hall Putsch, and the killing was raw meat to throw to the fanatics of the Nazi old guard.

Hermann Goering had attended the early stages of the celebrations, but nowadays he spent as little time as possible with the veteran Party militants, and a beer hall crammed with them at full belch filled him with distaste. He crept away with Karl Bodenschatz and they boarded their special train which was standing by to take them to Berlin. As they sped through the darkness, they noticed that fires were burning in some of the towns through which they passed, and that in the city of Halle there was a great conflagration. It was only when they reached Berlin that they learned that Goebbels had made a fighting speech rousing the Party against the Jews who, he claimed, were responsible for Vom Rath's murder. Orders had gone out to the Brownshirts and to the SS, and the faithful were now on the rampage, burning buildings, sacking stores, rounding up Jews and taking them off to concentration camps.

The anti-Jewish riots of November 9–10 subsequently known as "Crystal Night" killed thirty Jews, put thousands of them into concentration camps (from which many were allowed to bail themselves out later), and did damage amounting to five million marks. Nearly all the great Jewish stores in Berlin and scores of fashionable shops along the Kurfürstendamm were sacked. Thousands of tons of smashed glass from their windows littered the streets.

Goering was furious, and railed against Goebbels and the Party for the stupidity of it all. At a time of shortage, precious foreign currency would have to be spent buying replacements of glass from abroad, because Germany herself could not cope with the damage. And who would have to pay for all the damage? Why, the insurance companies— German insurance companies.

"Incredible, the problems you have created!" he told Goebbels, angrily. "I'd rather you had killed two hundred Jews than allow all these valuable goods to be destroyed."

When he reached home after a day of irate conferences, he found Emmy waiting for him, and he groaned because she had a paper in her hand, and Goering guessed that it was a list of Jews she wanted him to help. He called in Pilli Koerner and told him to start telephoning the Gestapo for news of Emmy's friends.

"If you go on like this, you're going to turn Himmler into my enemy," he told Emmy.

Next day there was a curt note from the Fuehrer to inform him that his wife had been intervening again on behalf of the Jews. It must stop.

"Now you see," cried Goering. "You are even turning the Fuehrer against me." He shook his head. "Ah, the Jews, the Jews, they'll be the death of me yet!"

Yet for the moment he had no fear that his wife's "sentimentalities," as he was wont to call them, would get him into trouble with the Fuehrer. Things were going too well. And though Hitler would have given credit to his own boldness and political sagacity for the successes Germany was enjoying, Goering was convinced that his own part in the strategy against the democracies had much to do with it.

Goering had no doubt in his mind now that terror worked, and he used the reputed might of the Luftwaffe rather like the U.S. and Russia were to use the atom bomb after World War II—as a great deterrent. He had convinced the French, just before Munich in September 1938, that it was strong enough to wipe out their own Air Force and destroy their cities. In March 1939, he hurried back from a holiday in San Remo, in Italy, at Hitler's behest, and once more rattled his bomber planes in the ears of a terrified statesman.

This time it was the aged President Emil Hácha of the Czech republic who succumbed to the Reichminister's blackmail. He bullied the frail old man with threats of bombs raining down on Prague, and, convinced that even as Goering spoke the death planes were warming up on the airfields, he signed away his country's independence and put Bohemia and Moravia under German occupation. In fact the weather was too bad for air operations, the bomber squadrons were not really ready, and even the German Army tied itself in knots trying to reach Prague in the appalling weather conditions. But no one opposed their entry.

The bluff had worked again. What did it matter if he had made President Hácha faint from sheer terror by his loud-voiced threats? Had he not also called in Hitler's own doctor to revive him? What did an old man's fainting fit matter beside the fact that a war with Czechoslovakia, which might also have meant a war with Russia and with the West, had been avoided?

"Yet curiously enough," said Thomas von Kantzow, who saw him shortly afterward, "Hermann could not get rid of the feeling that he had acted like a cad. 'I agree that it was not a gentlemanly thing to do,' he would keep saying to Emmy. 'I am not a cruel man. I do not get any pleasure out of bullying old people. But why did the Czech people choose such a man of straw in the first place? And think of the terrors I saved the Czech people from by making the old fool sign. His beloved Prague would have been smashed to pieces.' Emmy said: 'But you told me your bombers could not take off. And in any case, I thought you were only bluffing—that you had no intention of at-tacking Prague.' Hermann grinned. 'Yes, but the old man wasn't to know that, was he?' Then he shook his head. 'Still, it wasn't a gentlemanly thing to do.' "

But, almost as if he were doing penance for the sin of arrogance, he then told his wife that he would look through her list of Jews and anti-Nazis, and see what he could do about getting them out of the country. At the same time he called in Karl Bodenschatz and charged him with a mission which astonished him. He was sent to Mu-nich to search out Frau Ilse Ballin and her sister, the two Jewish ladies who had helped to bathe his wound and hide him after the 1923 Munich putsch. Bodenschatz was told to tell them that it was no longer safe for them to remain in Germany, and that they must prepare to leave at once. Meantime, they must go to the Argentine consulate general in Munich and apply for visas, which, they were assured, would be granted. The Ballin sisters left shortly afterward, and, something more unusual, they were allowed to take their money with them.

In the meantime, Baronin Lilli von Epenstein had come to Berlin in a fraught state of nerves. She had been to see her legal adviser in Germany, and had made out a deed transferring Veldenstein Castle to Goering and his daughter immediately. Mauterndorf would follow after her death. But she was mortally afraid of a war beginning, and pleaded with Goering to help her get permission to go away from Europe for a while. He helped her to get an exit permit and she applied for, and was granted, a visa to visit relatives in Chicago.*

"The one thing that haunted Hermann all summer of 1939," said Thomas von Kantzow, "was that the madmen of the Party were going to plunge Germany into a war. He ranted and raved over Ribbentrop's malevolence toward England, but you would never have guessed from the way he talked that Hitler wanted war too. He kept saying: 'There is no need for war—why don't those fools realize it? If only the Fuehrer would leave it to me, I would see that Germany had her place in the sun and peace for a generation—but without war.' "

But at the same time, as commander-in-chief of the Luftwaffe and dictator of German industry, he was determined to get Germany ready for war if it should come, and Thomas von Kantzow, lolling by the lake at Carin Hall, or returning from a walk through the forest, was aware of the almost constant coming and going of large cars. Armed guards stood outside the doors of the conference chamber, and from inside he could hear the low hum of voices, occasionally punctuated by Goering's high-pitched, indignant rasp of annoyance.

One of the most important of these conferences was one he called with the leaders of German industry. He said that the threat of war hung over Europe, and that the Jews were to blame for it. German industry must rise to meet

---

* Unfortunately for her, she did not like America and pined to get back to Mauterndorf. She came back in the summer of 1939, and, on September 1, 1939, while listening to a radio announcement that German troops had invaded Poland, she died of a heart attack.

the challenge. They were still making too many consumer
goods for the home market.

"What does your production for the home market mean
in comparison with the interests of the nation?" he asked.
"Such considerations reveal very small minds. What the
hell does it matter to you whether we produce aircraft
instead of bed chambers—as long as Germany is able to
stand the challenge of battle?"

As he looked around his audience, he noticed that one
face was missing. Fritz Thyssen, the great Ruhr magnate,
was not there, and he missed him. When it was over, he
asked Erhard Milch, who was also there, what had happened to Thyssen, but he didn't know.

That night Goering put in a telephone call to Essen and
spoke to Thyssen, who mumbled some excuse about indis-
position, but Goering, who had known Thyssen for many
years, sensed that something was wrong. On an impulse, he
told the industrialist that he was coming down for a meeting a few days hence at the Essener *Nazional Zeitung*† and
that he would use the opportunity to see him. He made
part of the journey in his new motor yacht, *Carin II*, with
Robert Kropp at the wheel, moored at a small town on the
Rhine, and drove over to the rendezvous. Thyssen was
pale, preoccupied, and nervous, and very evasive. Finally
he blurted out that he did not like the way things were
going. He had sources of information in the French
Government, and what he had learned from them had
disturbed him considerably. Did Goering know that the
German Government, with the apparent approval of Hitler,
was making overtures to Moscow? It seemed unbelievable
that anyone could be thinking of making a pact with the
Reds, but if it was true it would be a tragedy for Germany,
for it would open the floodgates to the forces of Bol-
shevism.

Hermann Goering knew quite well that Thyssen's infor-
mation was correct, for he had supplied it to the French
Government himself. On May 2, 1939, he had primed Karl
Bodenschatz for a meeting with the French assistant air

---

† Goering was one of the main shareholders of the *Zeitung*, which
was his principal mouthpiece in Germany. Fritz Thyssen had fi-
nanced the purchase of his shares, just as he had helped Goering in
money matters ever since he came back to Germany in 1928.

attaché, Paul Stehlin, during which the German had stressed to the Frenchman the significance of Hitler's latest speech—which had been virulently anti-Polish but had contained not a single mention of Soviet Russia.

"The Poles think they can be insolent and arrogant toward Germany," Bodenschatz had said, "because they are relying upon the backing of France and Britain, and that, in the event of war, they will have material support from Russia. They are fooling themselves. Just as the Fuehrer didn't think of solving the Austrian and Czech problems without first securing the agreement of Italy, he does not now contemplate solving the difficulties with Poland without first securing the consent of Russia. . . . There will be no war on two fronts this time."

The point in leaking this information to the Frenchman‡ was once more part of Goering's strategy of the big deterrent. He was pleased that the ploy had worked, and Stehlin had fed the information back to Paris. But there is little doubt that he shared Thyssen's anxiety about this latest diplomatic move on Hitler's part. His suspicion of the Soviets was deeply ingrained and it went against his instincts to make a pact with them. But he was even more suspicious of the man conducting the negotiations that were now in progress, Joachim von Ribbentrop, the Foreign Minister. He suspected that Von Ribbentrop wanted a pact with Russia not to stop a war from starting—which Goering saw as its only justification—but in order to make a quick and devastating victory in one certain.

Goering was later to say that he believed the Russo-German Pact of 1939 would sufficiently terrorize the French that they would refuse to go to war, no matter what their pledges. But he never had that certainty about the British, and was convinced that only reason, and not terror, would persuade them to keep out of war. Neither the threats from the sky from his bomber fleets nor the tie-up with Russia were going to divert the British from their signed agreements, he decided, and it is significant that he never tried to find in the British embassy a young man to act as the British equivalent of Paul Stehlin.

Now he tried to reassure his worried friend, Fritz Thys-

‡ Stehlin later detailed all his conversations with Goering, Bodenschatz, et al. in the official French *Livre Jaune.*

sen, that the Fuehrer knew what he was doing, and that the
negotiations with Russia were simply designed to keep the
world out of war. They dined that night at Thyssen's home,
and Goering once more walked around his house, admiring
his Maillol statues, his Canalettos, his Rembrandts, and his
El Grecos. It never occurred to him that a man with such
wealth and such treasures was on the verge of doing something drastic.

XVIII. LAST HOPES DASHED

Hermann Goering's relations with the other Nazi leaders had never been good, or close, as mentioned above, but now they were going from bad to worse. Himmler was in a constant cold rage over his repeated interference with his anti-Jewish and anti-Nazi purges, and had asked Hitler to warn him against his habit of giving in to his wife's "sentimental weaknesses." Von Ribbentrop suspected (rightly) that Goering did not trust his diplomatic methods, and was eager to show that he could do better. And now the state of unarmed truce between Goering and Goebbels had flared into open enmity.

As was usually the case, it was all because of Josef Goebbels' moral habits. Despite his short stature and his crippled leg, Goebbels had for most of his adult life been a successful stud, and his diaries are dotted with details of his female conquests. He preferred women tall, pretty, and long in the leg (no doubt as a sop to his egoism), and once he became, by virtue of his position as Minister of Propaganda, overlord of the German cinema, different film stars came almost nightly to his casting-office couch.

Adolf Hitler was remarkably tolerant of the sexual peccadilloes of his right-hand men (though he allowed them to bring only their wives to his lunch, tea, dinner and all-night cinema sessions), but Goebbels' activities had become so notorious and the humiliation of his quietly charming wife, Magda, so much talked about, that he had urged the little doctor to show more discretion. Goebbels promised to reform, and was soon going around Berlin with the look on his face of a martyred monk, and sadly proclaiming his respectability.

In fact, however, he was having an even more torrid affair than usual, with a well-known star named Lida Barova, a dark beauty with a pair of the most famous long legs in Germany. He was convinced that he was keeping the whole thing a secret, and he was furious when he discovered that Hermann Goering and Emmy knew all about it.

How could they have found out? Learning all about Goering's telephone-tapping service, he had thought of a way of bypassing it whenever he wanted to speak to his latest love. He had engineers take a line off Emmy Goering's own personal telephone, and used that to conduct long conversations with Lida Barova of an erotic nature steamy in the extreme.

He was furious when he discovered that Emmy Goering had gone to tea with Magda Goebbels and told her all about it. He was even more angry when he discovered that Goering had taken transcripts along to Hitler to see, and that the two men had read out the more titillating portions to each other.

"How could they have found out?" asked Goebbels at the height of one of his rows with his wife. "I took every precaution."

"But didn't you know?" replied Magda Goebbels coolly, "Emmy Goering's telephone is tapped too."

Goebbels was to discover that the Goerings knew something else concerning him of which he was completely ignorant. His secretary of state at the Propaganda Ministry, Karl Hanke, had fallen madly in love with Magda and had all but persuaded her to divorce her faithless husband and marry him. This too Goering told to Hitler, this time in order to prevent a public scandal that would be bad for the Nazi image. Hitler agreed, and he called Magda and Josef Goebbels together and forced them to agree to a reconciliation.

Magda was heartbroken, for she also had to promise never to see Hanke in private again. Goebbels was glad that he was not going to lose his elegant and intelligent wife. But he never forgave Goering for involving Hitler in his private affairs.

That summer of 1939, war came nearer to Europe. Having failed to come to the aid of Czechoslovakia in 1938-39, Britain and France—as if to salve their guilty consciences —had now pledged themselves to come to the aid of Poland if Germany attacked her. Goering searched desperately for some way of outwitting the hated Von Ribbentrop, who wanted war with Britain, and of persuading the British to "see reason."

"He was always asking why the British were so stubborn over Danzig and the Polish Corridor, which was all that Germany wanted from Poland," said Thomas von Kantzow. "Couldn't they see that both were part of Germany, and should never have been taken away? Why, what would the British say if someone took away their Channel Islands —where they didn't even speak English? They would never rest until they got them back, and that went for Hong Kong and Gibraltar too."

It was through Thomas's intervention that Goering finally thought he had found a way of circumventing Ribbentrop and making the British listen. About a year earlier, Goering's stepson had gone to work in Sweden for a Swedish industrialist named Birger Dahlerus. Dahlerus had good connections with some powerful members of the Conservative Party and the business world in Britain, and he also had a slight acquaintance with Goering. It occurred to him during one of the critical months of 1939 that he might be useful as a go-between to bring the two sides together.

He went with Thomas von Kantzow to Carin Hall to discuss the idea, and Goering was taken with it. The upshot was that, with Hitler's permission, it was decided to invite a number of influential Britons to a meeting with Goering in which mutual problems could be frankly discussed. At first it was proposed that the meeting should be in Count von Rosen's medieval castle in Sweden, and Goering was all in favor of that. Peace talks in the place where he had first met his beloved Carin could not help but be fruitful, he felt.

But eventually it was decided that no one could really conceal Hermann Goering's considerable bulk from the Swedish press and news of the talks would inevitably leak out. A rendezvous was made instead at Dahlerus' wife's house in Schleswig-Holstein, in Germany, where security was tighter. Dahlerus came in from Sweden bringing Thomas von Kantzow with him. The British delegation (of big-business men; the British Government at the last moment decided not to send any officials) arrived from England. Hermann Goering came in from the Island of Sylt, where Emmy had a house and beach front where she liked to indulge her passion for nude sunbathing.

Thomas, who was present at the talks, was impressed by his stepfather's performance.

"He always spoke in a quiet, jolly sort of tone, and never got angry, no matter what was said," he recalled later. "I don't think he was very well at the time, and he sweated prodigiously, and he often looked quite distressed when we were alone together. But he made a very good case for Germany, I thought, and I think the British were impressed too, especially since he listened to everything they said and never tried to interrupt or score points off them."

The result of that meeting was several more which stretched on all through August and September. Dahlerus was taken by Goering to see Hitler and then went to London to see both Neville Chamberlain and Lord Halifax, the British Foreign Minister. On several of these trips Thomas von Kantzow went with him.

"I think I was brought along as a sort of stamp of authenticity on Dahlerus' mission," Thomas said later. "Whenever the British had any doubts about what Dahlerus was proposing, I almost always caught them glancing speculatively toward me, as if to say: 'But he must be what he says he is. He's brought Goering's stepson along to prove it.' I stayed in the Strand Palace Hotel when I was in London, and in my spare time I used to walk along to Trafalgar Square and feed the pigeons. When I returned and told Emmy about London—the life and people there, I mean, not politics—I sensed that Hermann was jealous. I knew how much he would love to have been able to go to London himself."

In fact, that was just what Hermann Goering was planning to do. The Dahlerus negotiations had not produced the effect he had hoped upon Neville Chamberlain and the British Government. The British Cabinet (if not Chamberlain himself) was no longer willing to trust any German representative who came to them with "reasonable" proposals for a solution of the situation. The disillusionment produced by the Munich Pact and its aftermath, the occupation of Czechoslovakia, had convinced them that war was inevitable, and that Goering's was simply a siren voice calculated to weaken their resolution.

Goering was, in fact, quite sincere. He did not want war. He considered that the Poles were reckless and unreason-

able and that the Anglo-French guarantee which they had
been given had filled them with arrogance and an eagerness
for a war with Germany which they were convinced they
could win. Goering believed otherwise (only too rightly, as
it turned out), and it was his contention that if only the
British would bring pressure on the Poles to talk instead of
applauding them when they beat their breasts, a conflict
could be avoided. When Dahlerus failed to make the case
with the British, he thought that he might be able to do it
himself.

Around August 19, 1939, he saw Hitler and received
permission to fly to London, providing Chamberlain
agreed, for talks with the Prime Minister and other members of the Cabinet. On the morning of August 21, he telephoned Dahlerus in Stockholm and told him:

"I am going to try something radically different. It's the
only way to break the deadlock, I think."

He hung up without any further explanation. At about
the same time, the British ambassador in Berlin, Nevile
Henderson (who always believed that Goering was the
only "reasonable" man in the Nazi Party) happily sent a
cipher telegram to London saying that Goering was prepared to fly to Britain on August 23 for a talk with Prime
Minister Neville Chamberlain.

The visit was to be made in the greatest secrecy, and it
was therefore impossible for Goering to fly to London.
Instead the Royal Air Force suggested that he land at a
small airfield near Bovingdon, in Herefordshire, from
which he would be driven straight to the Prime Minister's
official country residence, Chequers. Chamberlain's regular
staff would be given leave of absence during the meetings,
and the chores done by the Secret Service.

"All telephones are to be disconnected," Lord Halifax
reported. "It looks as if it is going to be a dramatic inter-
lude, and having laid the plans, we await confirmation
from Germany."

They never got it. On the night of August 21, 1939, the
main German radio service faded out its music and announced:

"The Government of the Greater German Reich and the
Government of the People's Republics of the Soviet Union
have agreed to conclude a mutual nonaggression pact. The

Reich Minister for Foreign Affairs, Von Ribbentrop, will arrive in Moscow on Wednesday, August 23, for the conclusion of the negotiations."

It was Von Ribbentrop's moment of triumph, and he squeezed every drop out of it. He had heard of Goering's Swedish go-between* and of his plan to fly to London himself. Now he pointed out to the Fuehrer that there really was no need to go to such lengths. Why bother to continue "reasoning" with the British? Now they would *have* to back down. Goering did not believe it; he was convinced that the British would stand by their pledge to Poland unless he could find a way out for them. And that could be done only by personal negotiations.

But Hitler no longer seemed to be interested. Like Ribbentrop, he seemed bent on war and confident that it would soon be over.

Shortly after the announcement of the conclusion of the Russo-German Pact, Adolf Hitler called Goering to him in the Reichschancellery. When he got there, he found Hitler pacing up and down his vast study, his face pale and his hands fluttering.

"Your good friend Thyssen—do you know what he has done?" he cried. "He has run out on us. Left Germany for good. And dared to leave this behind!"

He thrust a sheet of paper at Goering, who read it through with growing dismay. It was a message Thyssen had written for publication in the German press, giving his reasons for leaving Germany. It was a spirited attack upon Hitler and all he stood for, and it finished with the words:

"Your policy will terminate in a *finis Germaniae.*"

Goering put the paper down, and said:

"Fritz has been overworked. He must have had an aberration. Leave it to me, I'll get him back."

He put Bodenschatz and Pilli Koerner to work tracking down Thyssen's refuge, but it was his telephone-tapping unit which came up with the industrialist's whereabouts. He was in Paris and they produced his telephone number.

Goering immediately telephoned him, but Thyssen re-

---

* There is good reason for believing that, at one point, he planned to sabotage the plane carrying the Swede to England.

fused to talk to his old friend. Instead, on August 31, he sent a telegram pleading with Goering to get his manifesto printed in the German press. The Reichminister sent a reply asking Thyssen to come back to Germany at once. If he recanted, Goering swore that Hitler would forgive him.

I PREFER TO AWAIT THE END OF NATIONAL SOCIALISM HERE, Thyssen telegraphed back.

By that time, German troops had crossed the frontier into Poland, and World War II had begun.

In the next year Hermann Goering reached the apogee of his career. There had been a coolness between him and the Fuehrer in the days just before and after the attack upon Poland, and though Hitler had publicly (in a speech in the Reichstag) proclaimed him his heir, Goering was gloomily convinced that this was only a sop to the pride of the Air Force, and that other plans had been made behind his back.

But then the victories began in Poland, and the bombs and banshee wails of the dive-bombing Stukas had much to do with the success of the blitzkrieg. In a few days, the Polish Air Force was blown, burned, or strafed out of existence. The campaign was over almost before it had begun, and the Luftwaffe was principally responsible for the victory.

Goering was the hero of the hour, and he savored it. His campaign train trundled across the now-Germanized Polish Corridor into Danzig, where he received the acclamation of the "liberated" citizens. He went on into Poland to see the wrecked cities of Warsaw and Lwow, and dictated the first directives for the seizure of raw materials and the conscription of forced labor to feed the armament factories of the Reich. Jews were rounded up, their art treasures and belongings confiscated; and measures were launched that would, in the next few years, mean the pillage of a whole country and the starvation of millions of people. Goering was afterward to make as his excuse for these draconian decrees that they were only intended to be of short duration, "until the Allies came to their senses and made peace," and that, in any case, "it was either them or us."

That he was still seriously seeking peace is true. On November 9, 1939, at the Munich Beer Hall Putsch anniversary, a bomb exploded where Hitler had been standing a few moments previously. The Nazi Propaganda Ministry blamed the British Secret Service, but the rumor spread that Goering may have been behind it. He had not even bothered to turn up for the anniversary celebration this year, on the grounds that he was unwell, and this was considered suspicious. It wasn't. Goering just didn't like swilling beer with the Party faithful, and, in any case, he was too busy working on schemes to get Britain and France out of the war. But he did say to Emmy in Bodenschatz's hearing that if Hitler had been killed by the bomb, he, as the Fuehrer's successor, would have immediately stopped the fighting, withdrawn troops from all non-German territory, and started peace talks with the Allies.

He certainly did not make his conditions as plain as that when he contacted the British about this time. He had still kept Birger Dahlerus on call as a go-between and on September 10, 1939, he sent Thomas von Kantzow (who had been staying at Carin Hall) to him in Stockholm with letters from two RAF war prisoners who had been shot down while making leaflet raids over Germany. Goering gave his personal assurance that the men would be well looked after, and asked him to convey both the letters and assurance to the British.

Dahlerus went at once to see Sir Edmund Monson, the British Minister to Sweden, and handed over the messages as proof of Goering's good will. He then went beyond his brief by assuring the British Minister that "Herr Hitler's popularity was declining" and that "Goering was the only man possessing everyone's full confidence." He insisted that Goering "in contrast to the rest of the German Government was absolutely trustworthy and would stake his reputation on the observation by the German Government of terms, and any truce negotiated by himself personally. In this he would receive the support of the German people who were tired of war."

Thomas von Kantzow says that Goering never to his knowledge—and he was the courier—gave Dahlerus any indication that he was prepared to go behind Hitler's back to get peace. He was willing to outwit Ribbentrop, but his loyalty to the Fuehrer was as unswerving as ever.

What he did believe was necessary now was the initia-

tion of some sort of negotiations between the British and
the Germans, and for that purpose he believed he was the
most reasonable person to conduct them. He once more
saw himself as the flying emissary of peace, and was seriously contemplating (if the British could be persuaded to
agree) taking a plane to some neutral capital where he
could discuss with the British an agreement for ending the
war.

On September 26, Dahlerus flew to Berlin and was taken
by Goering to see Hitler. The Fuehrer was in an aggressive
mood, full of arrogant satisfaction over the German
Army's tremendous victory in Poland. The British did not
seem to realize that peace terms on the basis of *status quo
ante*, in other words a German withdrawal from defeated
Poland, were now impossible. The Russians had now
moved in to the agreed demarcation line and occupied the
eastern half of Poland. In the unlikely event of Hitler's
agreeing to withdraw from his portion, it would still have
left the Russians in possession of theirs—and, in the circumstances of the time, they would probably not have
delayed very long before mopping up the rest.

So Hitler simply told Dahlerus that the British could
have peace "if they want it," and "if they move with dispatch." He was certainly not willing to withdraw from
Poland, but he was prepared to give assurances that the
neutrality of Holland and Belgium would be respected, that
the West Wall (or Siegfried Line) would be "the unalter-
able western border of Germany," and that "Germany did
not wish any conquests in the West or in the Balkans." As
for Poland, he would incorporate the ethnic German re-
gions of it into Germany and Austria, and use the rest for
resettlement and as an "asylum" for the Jews.

On September 27, Birger Dahlerus left for Holland,
where he was handed a special visa by the British ambassador, Sir Nevile Bland, and given a priority air flight to
London. He could not have come at a more propitious
moment, from Goering's point of view. The British Prime
Minister, Neville Chamberlain, was ripe for peace overtures.

"It won't be by defeat in the field," Chamberlain was
writing about this time, "but by German realisation that
they can't win and that it isn't worth their while to go on

getting thinner and poorer when they might have instant relief and perhaps not have to give up anything they really care about."†

Dahlerus had talks at the Foreign Office with Sir Alexander Cadogan, permanent secretary of state, and told him of Goering's willingness to fly to a neutral capital for peace talks. They would be "soldier to soldier" discussions, Goering suggested, with someone like General Ironside. He also summarized Hitler's "terms" as they had been set out by the Fuehrer at the meeting of September 26. Cadogan was skeptical.

"All of this, or some of it, may be very nice," he said of the proposals, "but we cannot trust the word or the assurance of the present rulers of Germany."

He could trust Goering, Dahlerus insisted. He launched into an impassioned description of his friend's earnest and desperate eagerness to bring "this unnecessary war" to a peaceful conclusion.

"He's like a wasp at a picnic, one can't beat him off," commented Cadogan of Dahlerus' insistence.

He promised to convey the Swede's overtures to the Cabinet. But the Cabinet was divided. Neville Chamberlain and his more intimate friends were hoping Goering would join in one or other of the anti-Hitler plots that were now simmering in Germany, and seemed convinced that the Reich Marshal would be ready to betray the Fuehrer, a complete misreading of his character.‡

"His [Hitler's] entourage must also go," Chamberlain wrote to his sister, in a passage about the need to remove the Fuehrer, "with the possible exception of Goering who might have some ornamental position in a transitional government."

The other faction in the Cabinet (led by Winston Churchill, still one of Chamberlain's subordinates) was determined that Poland must be restored *in toto* by its con-

---

† In a letter to his sister on November 11, 1939.
‡ He was never mixed up in the anti-Hitler plots which were being hatched in Germany at this time, but, ironically enough, if these schemes had come to anything and Hitler had been either assassinated or imprisoned, some of the principal plotters, Canaris (the Abwehr chief), Ulrich von Hassell, and the Kordt brothers among them, considered Goering as the only possible head of the new regime.

querors, and by this time that was manifestly impossible. So Goering's peace efforts, and with them Birger Dahlerus, slowly faded out of the picture. Germany and the Allies settled down to the boredom and delusive calm of the so-called phony war.

Hermann Goering was disillusioned. He had worked hard, and taken many risks, to stop the war from starting, and to bring it to a speedy conclusion once it had begun. But as the British continued to reject each offer he made, and attached impossible conditions to any negotiations in which they agreed to engage, his mood changed. He began to see the British as stubborn, arrogant, in need of a lesson. All right, they would have one—and the Luftwaffe would teach them the folly of failing to see reason.

In this new mood, what Goering now wanted, above everything, was to see the war finished quickly. The three-week Blitzkrieg in Poland had convinced him that a mighty air fleet could not only be used as a deterrent, it could actually do what it threatened. For the moment no one argued against Goering's boasting, and the omnipotence of the Luftwaffe was now generally accepted even in the service itself. Later on, fighter commanders like Adolf Galland would complain that the Messerschmitt 109 was a machine inferior to its counterparts in Britain, Erhard Milch would lament the failure to build heavy bombers for long-range operations, and the Stuka dive-bomber would turn out to be a pricked balloon when matched against good air defenses. But in the aftermath of Poland, no one grumbled. The Luftwaffe was the almighty weapon, and Goering its king.

He went to Hitler repeatedly and pleaded with him to allow the Luftwaffe to switch westward and start the air war against Britain. It was a practical suggestion which could well have borne startling fruit, for Britain was in a far poorer position to defend herself against air attacks in 1939 than seven months later. He had a plan for destroying aircraft, airfields, and factories, and of paralyzing British industry, thus opening up two possibilities, the physical one of an airborne invasion, or the psychological one of yet another and more menacing offer of peace on "reasonable" terms.

But Hitler would not agree. He wanted any Luftwaffe attack to coincide with a land offensive against France and the Low Countries, and the Army High Command repeatedly told him that they were not yet ready for that. They feared the might of the French Army, and did not realize that its ranks were riddled with doubt and dissension.

While he waited for Hitler to make up his mind, Goering spent increasing periods at Carin Hall. He was already contemplating an annex in which to house his art treasures, and making plans with Emmy for the Hermann Goering Museum which he planned to open to the public after the war was over. He did not put it into so many words, but it was to be a rival to a similar institution which Adolf Hitler was projecting in Linz, and Goering was sure that his would be better because his taste in art was so much superior.*

He was at Carin Hall on March 3, 1940, when President Roosevelt's special envoy, Sumner Welles, came to talk to him. Welles had been on a fact-finding mission to the belligerent countries, and Hitler had at first been reluctant to allow him into Germany. Relations with the United States were at this time cool to the point of frigidity. There was no ambassador at the American embassy (he had been withdrawn as a protest against the anti-Jewish excesses on "Crystal Night," 1938); Congress had just rescinded the Neutrality Act, enabling Britain to purchase armaments from the U.S.; and America was quietly co-operating with the Allies in maintaining the blockade of Germany.

The Fuehrer was eventually persuaded to receive the U.S. envoy, but before he arrived he described for Joachim von Ribbentrop and Hermann Goering the lines that their conversations should follow. They should stress that it was Britain and France, and not Germany, which had declared war; that it was Britain which had resisted all overtures for peace Hitler had made "now that the Polish problem is settled"; and that it was Britain which wished to destroy Germany, whereas he (Hitler) had always stood for the support and preservation of the British Empire.

Sumner Welles was not the most flexible nor the most imaginative reporter Roosevelt could have sent to Europe at this time. Paul Schmidt, the official German interpreter, was afterward to describe him as nothing more than "two

---

* They both had a taste for large-breasted ladies, but at least Goering's were painted by better artists.

ears with a pencil between."† He had obviously been
briefed by the President and the State Department to make
no comments on what he heard or open up any negotiations. But in the process of sponging in the information, he
could, at least, have put an amiable front on his passive
role. Instead, he was charmless to the point of being
wooden, and any initiative which a more stimulating character might have aroused in Adolf Hitler was chilled by
this lack-luster man. Von Ribbentrop treated Welles in kind
and jolted him by a reception "without even the trace of a
smile and without a word of greeting." He was afterward
to describe it as "the most astonishing experience of my
whole mission" and even his tough skin was penetrated by
the obvious malevolence shown him by the Nazi Foreign
Minister.

In contrast, Hermann Goering was cordiality itself, and
he made endless efforts to strike some sparks in the U.S.
envoy. He drove him through the Schorfheide and showed
off his wildlife, he handed him a pet lion cub to cuddle,
from which Welles recoiled in some dismay,‡ and they
made a long tour of Carin Hall during which Goering,
speaking at times in halting English, showed off the pictures now mounted one above the other on the walls.

In between, he followed the Party line of preaching
peace, and, in Paul Schmidt's words, "was the most skillful
and the most natural." But even Goering tired of bouncing
his ball off such a consistently dead wall, and he eventually
gave up and indicated to Schmidt that the talks were over.
Welles had obviously expected lunch, for it would be late
afternoon before his party got back to Berlin, but the
Reichminister made no mention of it and sent them back
to the capital, hungry.

It was while he was at Carin Hall that Goering's intercept and intelligence unit picked up news that Hitler was
planning not the attack against England which the Reichminister wanted but an invasion of Scandinavia. He rushed
to Berchtesgaden and, more in sorrow than in anger, asked

† The French diplomat, René Massigli, first used the phrase about
himself.
‡ The Goerings were particularly fond of lion cubs, handing them
on to zoos as they grew too big. A ritual with Emmy and Goering
was to bathe the cubs weekly, in their own bath.

Hitler why he had not been officially informed of the plans. Even Bodenschatz and Milch had been consulted, he complained, but had been told not to worry him about it.

That, the Fuehrer informed him, was because he knew that Goering had been unwell (he was suffering from a swelling of the hands and arm joints), and he wished to see him fully recovered before bothering him. Actually, Hitler knew from Gestapo reports that Goering had recently been in touch with King Gustav of Sweden through his old friend, Count von Rosen, and had assured him that no matter in which direction the war moved, Sweden would be safe, her neutrality personally guaranteed by him. But the plans drawn up by the OKW (the High Command of the Armed Forces) envisioned not only the occupation of Denmark and Norway but also the capture of Sweden, whose supplies of iron ore had now become vital to the German economy.

Goering was too shrewd not to realize this, and a study of the plans which were now handed to him confirmed his fears that his beloved Sweden was the next country on Hitler's list of conquests. For the first time for many years, he found the courage to stand up to the Fuehrer. He had given his word, he said, that Sweden's neutrality would be respected. In return, Sweden had promised to guarantee the regular arrival of iron-ore supplies. What more could Hitler ask? That German troops be allowed to move across the country into Norway? Leave it to him, he would arrange it. He would also see to it that pro-British influences were removed from government and official positions in Sweden. But if the OKW persisted in the invasion of Sweden, he would have to insist that the Fuehrer accept his resignation.

He knew that if Sweden were attacked, she would, like her Scandinavian neighbors, defend herself, and the thought of his ex-brother-in-law, Von Rosen, his stepson, Thomas von Kantzow,* and his other Swedish relatives and friends in arms against him was almost too much to bear. His anguish was so evident that Hitler relented and promised to tell the General Staff to revise the plans so as to exclude Sweden. But he resolutely refused to write a

---

* Who was at that moment in Finland fighting with the Swedish volunteers against Russia.

note to King Gustav backing up Goering's guarantee of peace with Sweden.

"You will just have to go on taking my word for it," Goering wrote to Thomas von Kantzow, "that it [an attack on Sweden] will never happen."

Like many actresses, Emmy Goering was deeply superstitious. One of her bitterest complaints about the execrable coffee which was all that was available in Nazi Germany was the fact that it left no sediment in the cup, and she was therefore unable to read her fortune or the fortunes of her friends from the shape of the dregs. She was an avid teller of the cards and an enthusiast for astrology, and even though she had once met the journalist who did the star charts in her favorite weekly and knew he wrote the forecasts out of his head, she still read and half-believed them.

Sometime in 1938 she began consulting a soothsayer to whom she had been introduced by one of her aristocratic friends. His name was Dr. Augustus Heerman, and he was supposed to have second sight.

"He was a very ordinary-looking man," said Thomas von Kantzow later, "except that he nearly always wore a very deep stiff white collar to his shirt, and whenever he was concentrating on something he would take it off, carefully roll it up and put it in his brief case, and walk up and down with his front and back studs hanging out."

Emmy swore by him. For her his greatest triumph had been the recovery of a gold cigarette case which she had given to Hermann for his birthday. It lay on a table with the other presents during his birthday party, and when they were out of the room for a moment, it disappeared. It had obviously been stolen.

"As I was dressing for dinner I remembered Dr. Heerman," Emmy wrote later. "I telephoned him on the spur of the moment, and told him what had happened. He said: 'Please hold on for about ten minutes and keep the telephone in your hand.' After that time had elapsed he said very slowly: 'The case has been taken by one of the waiters hired for the evening. Your husband will get it back tomorrow morning; it will be found by one of your own staff.'"

During dinner that night, Emmy went on, she said in a deliberately loud voice:

"Hermann, I know who took your cigarette case. Thank goodness it was not one of our own staff."

At which point, she said, one of the hired waiters almost dropped the silver dish and spilled some soup down her sister's dress.

" 'Ahah,' I thought to myself," wrote Emmy. "Next morning when the rooms were being cleaned the cigarette case was found between a cushion and the back of a chair."

What more could you ask of a soothsayer than that? Emmy now used him as a consultant about her sciatica, about Hermann's diet, and about the future of the war.

In January 1940 Emmy persuaded both her husband and Adolf Hitler to put their faith in the omnipotence of Dr. Heerman. A Luftwaffe courier had been told to take to Army Headquarters in Cologne a copy of a top-secret document. It was called "Memorandum and Directive for Conduct of the War in the West" and it went into some detail about German plans to make a simultaneous attack upon Holland and Belgium (both of them then neutral countries) as part of the over-all campaign against Britain and France. The courier was supposed to take the plan with him by train but begged a lift from a colleague aboard a plane. The plane lost course in bad weather and crash-landed in Belgium.

Goering was at his castle at Veldenstein when he was urgently called to Berlin by the Fuehrer and confronted with news of the catastrophe. A copy of the master plan for the invasion was now on Belgian soil—and it contained dates, dispositions, tactics, the lot. The big question was, had it fallen into Belgian hands, or had the courier succeeded in destroying it?

"How can we find out?" asked Goering. "It makes all the difference to what we do in the next few weeks—whether we invade or postpone, whether we continue to pretend that we have no intention of breaching the neutrality of the Low Countries. We are in a terrible dilemma. The Fuehrer is very angry. I have already had to sack General Felmy to help calm him down."†

---

† General Felmy was commander of the German Air Force in the West and had no responsibility for the accident, but a scapegoat had to be found. He was replaced by General Kesselring.

Emmy had no doubt about how to solve the situation. Once more she telephoned Dr. Heerman and beseeched him to put his sixth sense to work.

"After a short pause on the telephone," she wrote later, "he said: 'The man with the documents landed in Belgium.' I caught my breath for I had not mentioned Belgium to him. Dr. Heerman went on slowly: 'Immediately after the forced landing the officer asked a passing peasant for a light for his cigarette. He tried to set fire to the documents with the match but was only partially successful. He asked the peasant for another match but the man had no more. Meanwhile Belgian police arrived on the spot. They took the officer and his friend, the pilot, to the police station, where there was a small iron stove burning. The officer screwed up the documents and threw them into the stove. The policeman jumped forward and pulled them out again. But in the meantime as much of the documents had been burned as to leave legible only about as much as might be covered by a normal hand in the center of a page. There were two documents and they were inside a black briefcase.' "

Emmy waited for Goering to come back from his latest interview with Hitler, and as he stumbled in, bowed from the impact of the Fuehrer's invective, she told him of her conversation with her pet soothsayer. He did not even try to humor her but stormed away to his study, but she followed him in, beseeching him to telephone to Hitler.

In the end, he consented to do so, and presently Hitler arrived at the Leipziger Platz and demanded to know what Frau Emmy was involving herself in this time. She told him her story about Dr. Heerman, and persisted in her contention that he had an extraordinary power of perception. The Fuehrer and Goering both slowly allowed themselves to be convinced.

The picture which Emmy Goering gave of what followed has its choice touches. Here were the two leading men of the National Socialist state, racked with worry that their carefully planned attack in the West was now in jeopardy, slowly being seduced by the superstitions of an old actress.

The original document was fetched from the Reichschancellery and placed on the table. Then one by one they laid their hands across the center of each page, Emmy's plump pink hand, Hitler's trembling pale fingers, Goering's pudgy fist, and one by one they tried to read what their hands failed to conceal.

One can almost hear Emmy's throaty cry of relief as she pointed out that not much was left to be seen except for a disjointed set of words and figures. Goering looked skeptical, Hitler hopeful.

Next they took a sheaf of papers of exactly the same size and type as the secret documents and they went downstairs to the boiler room. There they tossed the papers into the fire, and then pulled them out again, and studied the smudges on the pages.

"You see," Emmy cried, "it is all right. Dr. Heerman is telling us the truth. They can't possibly know what is in the documents."

For a time they comforted themselves with this. Everything was going to be all right. The documents had been half burned, and were practically illegible. Thanks to Dr. Heerman, they could take comfort. The enemy did not have the Plan . . .

It was only after a period of mutual felicitation, that Hitler and Goering came to their senses. The one looked at the other, and they did not need to speak the question that was in both their minds: How could a quack talking over the telephone to a superstitious actress possibly *know* what had been happening to some papers hundreds of miles away?

"I think," said Goering, "we had better alter the plans."

"And when the courier comes back," said Hitler, "have him shot."

Emmy Goering was in tears. She went on believing right until the end that her soothsayer was right, and that it had all happened "just as Dr. Heerman had seen it." In fact, the papers had fallen intact into Belgian hands, as the Belgian ambassador informed the German Government later. The courier committed suicide before he could be sent back to Germany.

And the German attack on the West was once more postponed.

XIX. WHO WON WHAT?

The great German attack in the West finally began on May 10, 1940. Paratroops under Luftwaffe command dropped on Schiphol, Holland's main airport, and captured it on the first morning. Seaplanes landed on the river Maas and captured intact the bridges leading into Rotterdam, and dive-bombers screamed down and wrecked the center of the city. The attack was unnecessary, for Rotterdam was in process of negotiating its surrender at the moment when the planes of the Luftwaffe appeared, but botched lines of communication failed to get the message to them in time for them to hold their bombs. In any case, the Germans were not unmindful of the deterrent effect of such a mass bombing; coming after the smashing of Warsaw, it was calculated to have a salutary influence upon the citizens of other large cities, sapping their will to resist.*

Holland surrendered after five days. The Belgians capitulated without informing Britain or France first. Then the German armored columns, with Goering's planes in close support, outflanked the main French defenders on the Maginot Line and were off into the heart of France. In three weeks it was all over. The French asked for an armistice. A large proportion of the British Army, most of whose members never fired a shot during the campaign, managed to escape to England via Dunkirk, but left the bulk of their arms behind them.

German generals are like generals the world over. They always have good explanations for their defeats, and they are never quite satisfied with their victories; and the blame

---

* The Allies unwittingly helped the German terror propaganda by grossly exaggerating the casualties from the Rotterdam attack. It was widely believed that 25,000 were killed in the raid. In fact 814 people died.

for the first or the shortcomings of the second are invariably placed firmly on the heads of someone else, but never themselves.

In the military post-mortems on the Battle of France published since the end of World War II, Hermann Goering has been strongly criticized for his tactics, and the inference of the generals' strictures is that if it hadn't been for him not only would France have been defeated but Britain too, and the war won. This is because, on May 24, 1940, the German armored divisions were halted on the canal line before Dunkirk on Hitler's direct orders, and stayed there for forty-eight hours. During that time the Luftwaffe was supposed to go in and finish off the British trapped in the Dunkirk pocket. It was only when Goering's planes, because of bad weather and poor visibility, and because of the effective opposition of the Royal Air Force, failed to prevent the evacuation of the British troops that the German tanks were allowed to resume their advance.

The theory is that had they not been halted, they would have driven straight into the British enclave and rounded up the Army once and for all. But what all of the armchair or postwar strategists seem to assume is that the German armor would have scattered and terrorized the British Army in exactly the same way as it had cut through the French Army. In fact the circumstances were quite different. The German tanks had spread havoc among the French because they did not fight but simply scattered and ran. Wherever the French did stop and stand and fight (and a certain Colonel Charles de Gaulle and his division did just that), the Germans suffered severe casualties and were held up in their advance.

At Dunkirk, the British had no option but to fight, for their backs were to the sea. Had the German armor attacked, fewer British troops might have got back to England, but fewer German tanks and soldiers would have lived to fight another day, and the reputation of the panzer forces might well have been severely blunted, the terrors of the blitzkrieg seen in proper perspective.

As it was, the bulk of the British Army got away, and the generals of the OKW, most of whom cordially hated Goering, blamed him for it. It cannot have made them feel any better when neither he nor Adolf Hitler took any notice of them.

On June 5, 1940, after the last of the little ships set sail for England and the German Army finally took over Dunkirk, Hermann Goering held a conference with his Luftwaffe commanders aboard his armored train, which was halted near a convenient tunnel not far from the English Channel. Erhard Milch, Kesselring† and Jeschonnek‡ listened as he outlined the situation, and then told them that, with their approval, he was going to make a proposal to the Fuehrer.

He wanted to advocate an immediate attack upon England. For this purpose, he needed from the Army five divisions to reinforce the existing parachute division of the Luftwaffe, plus five further divisions as a backstop organized into the 6th Division Airborne Corps.

"Irrespective of the question whether to make an invasion [of England] immediately or not," he said later, "the Luftwaffe was to be brought to a state of immediate preparedness, with sufficient fighter planes, bombers and transport planes to invade England at a moment's notice . . . I said to the Fuehrer, if we immediately attack England's Navy, by making use of these parachute and airborne troops, and back them up with all available shipping, then the entire Royal Navy and the entire British Air Force will have to appear over the battlefield and in the Channel."

This would enable him, he said, to use the Luftwaffe to destroy not only the enemy's forces in the air but their formidable force of ships at sea.

"At the end of these decisive battles," Goering said, "both sides would have found themselves without anything left, and then, with our reserves, with a mere handful of the 5th and 6th Airborne Divisions, we would bring about the final decision."

It was certainly the moment (and probably the only moment) to strike across the Channel without the most elaborate and meticulous preparation, and such was the disarray of the British Army and the paucity of England's defenses, especially from attack from the air, that such a plan might well have succeeded. But Adolf Hitler banned any such move on the part of his Luftwaffe commander. He was still in a state of euphoria over the triumph of the

† His commander in the West.
‡ His chief of staff.

German armies, and seemed surprisingly reluctant to do anything which might further humiliate the British. As he had already made clear to his army commanders, he was convinced that the war would now be finished in six weeks.

At a conference which he called with them after the French armistice, he told them "he wished to conclude a reasonable peace with France and then the way would be free for an agreement with Britian." General Guenther Blumentritt, his army commander's chief of staff, said later: "He then astonished us by speaking with admiration of the British Empire, of the necessity for its existence, and of the civilization that Britain had brought into the world . . . He said that all he wanted from Britain was that she would acknowledge Germany's position on the Continent. The return of German colonies would be desirable but not essential . . . He concluded by saying that his aim was to make peace with Britain on a basis that she would regard as compatible with her honor to accept."

Those sentiments must have astonished Hermann Goering. They expressed exactly his own feelings toward England. But, unlike Hitler, he realized only too bitterly that the time had passed when the British could be expected to accept them. The die had been cast. The game was on. And he knew enough about the British to realize that they would not be willing to abandon the game until it was won or lost. It was a time for striking hard, striking quickly, and defeating your opponent at the moment when he was most vulnerable.

But the Fuehrer had adopted this strange, almost Anglophile attitude. He was convinced that the British Empire was "a factor in world equilibrium," and that rubbing her nose in the mud of defeat "would not benefit Germany . . . only Japan, the United States and others."

So the Luftwaffe, poised for the knockout blow, was refused permission to launch the final punch, and the opportunity was never to present itself again. Not even the German generals could blame Goering for that.

Hermann Goering wrote to Thomas von Kantzow from Paris on June 27, 1940, and went into raptures over the beauty of the French capital. It had always been one of Carin Goering's favorite cities (she had lived there before World War I, when her first husband was military attaché at the Swedish embassy), and she had vainly hoped to revisit it one day with Goering.

"Yesterday, in the hush of the early evening," Goering wrote, "I strolled along the Champs Élysées and I felt that your dear Mother's hand was in mine."

Six days previously he had dressed in his full field marshal's uniform, baton in hand, and accompanied Hitler to the clearing in the forest of Compiègne where the armistice was to be signed with the French. The old railway carriage in which the defeated Germans had signed a similar armistice in 1918 had been brought from a museum in Paris, and it now stood beside the memorial block on which the French had chiseled the words:

"Here on the eleventh of November 1918 succumbed the criminal pride of the German Empire—vanquished by the free peoples which it tried to enslave."

Hitler, Goering, Ribbentrop, General Keitel, and Rudolf Hess stood beside it for a moment, and then moved into the railway carriage where the French armistice delegation, headed by General Huntzinger was awaiting them. General Keitel read out the preamble to the armistice conditions:

"After heroic resistance . . . France has been vanquished. Germany does not therefore intend that the armistice conditions should cast any aspersions on so courageous an enemy. The aim of the German demands is to prevent a resumption of hostilities, to give Germany security for the further conduct of the war against England which she has no choice but to continue, and also to create the conditions for a new peace which will repair the injustice inflicted by force on the German Reich."

The text was translated by Dr. Paul Schmidt, and then Hitler, Goering, and the other Nazi leaders rose, bowed to the French, and left the carriage. As they came down the steps, the granite block engraved with the humiliating record of Germany's 1918 defeat was already being pried out of the ground by German soldiers. It was blown to bits three days later, after the French had reluctantly accepted the armistice conditions. The railway carriage was shipped to Berlin to go on public show, a symbol of how Adolf Hitler had avenged Germany's humiliation after World War I.*

---

* It was destroyed by an Allied bomb in 1944.

The Fuehrer departed with Albert Speer on a tourist's trip around Paris, visiting the Louvre, Les Invalides, and all the mandatory three-star buildings and museums. Goering preferred to slip away to the Musée du Jeu de Paume, where Alfred Rosenberg had established a team of experts whose task from now on would be to "acquire" for the Reich the art treasures of occupied Europe. Goering was anxious that the choicest of them should be earmarked for him, and so far as he was concerned the war faded into insignificance as he browsed through the Louvre and the overflowing rooms of the Jeu de Paume, immersed in the delights of Bouchet, Rubens, Fragonard, Chardin, Velasquez and the elder and younger Cranach. In the next twelve months his art collection was to reach truly fabulous proportions, and, as will be seen, he would spend more and more time savoring the sensual pleasures of his pictures, statues and other objets d'art, and forgetting the nagging worries of a war he had never wanted in the first place.

On July 19, 1940, Adolf Hitler celebrated the victories of the German armies and air forces in the West by addressing a meeting of the Reichstag in the Kroll Opera House. The crux of his speech was a peace offer to Britain:

"In this hour I feel it to be my duty before my own conscience to appeal once more to reason and common sense in Great Britain as much as elsewhere. I consider myself in a position to make this appeal since I am not the vanquished begging favors, but the victor speaking in the name of reason. I can see no reason why this war should go on."

It was a gesture which most Germans wanted to be made, and it may have been more for their benefit than for the British that he publicly made his overture to London. William L Shirer, who was in the Kroll Opera House, afterward wrote:

"I mingled with a good many officials and officers at the close of the session and not one of them had the slightest doubt, as they said, that the British would accept what they really believed was a very generous and even magnanimous offer from the Fuehrer."

They were kidding themselves.

"I drove directly to the Rundfunk to make a broadcast

report of the speech to the United States," wrote Shirer later. "I had hardly arrived at Broadcasting House when I picked up a BBC broadcast in German from London. It was giving the British answer to Hitler already—within the hour. It was a determined 'NO!' Junior officers from the High Command and officials from the various ministries were sitting around the room listening with rapt attention. Their faces fell. They could not believe their ears. 'Can you make it out?' one of them shouted to me. He seemed dazed. 'Can you understand those British fools?' he continued to bellow. 'To turn down peace now? They're crazy!' "

What were the Germans going to do now?

For a few hours, at least, Hermann Goering did not bother about how to answer that question. He was too busy admiring himself in his latest uniform and baubles. In the midst of his speech to the Reichstag, Hitler had suddenly broken off to praise "my generals" for their brilliance during the campaign in the West, and he now announced a whole series of promotions. Nine army generals were raised to the rank of field marshal. Three Luftwaffe officers were also made field marshals—Milch, Kesselring, and Sperrle.

But for Goering was reserved the most spectacular promotion of all. Solemnly the Fuehrer read out the citation:

"As a reward for his mighty contribution to victory, I hereby appoint the creator of the Luftwaffe to the rank of Reich Marshal of the Greater German Reich, and award him the Cross of the Iron Cross."

He had been placed above all others and hung with a medal which was awarded to no other soldier during the war. A new uniform had been designed for him. "It has two collar tabs," ran the official description. "On the left are two crossed gold-embroidered marshal batons on a silver brocade base, on the right a gold-embroidered Reich eagle also on a silver brocade base. The collar is lined with gold braid. Color of the uniform and blouse is gray-blue."

To complete this peacock ensemble, there was yet another medal to ornament it, and this one Goering had long yearned for. It came from Italy and the Italian Foreign Minister, Count Galeazzo Ciano, had come from Rome especially to drape it around his ample neck. It was the gold and bejeweled Collar of the Annunziata, and Goering, who had wept a couple of years earlier when Ribbentrop had received it and he had been passed over, now had tears of joy in his eyes.

"We had a very special dinner at the Leipziger Platz that evening," Thomas von Kantzow recalled later. "Hermann had brought back some pâté de foie gras from Paris, and as we ate it we drank toasts with each one a different-colored vodka from Poland. Then we had roast salmon done in the Danzig style with Moselle from a cellar Hermann had purchased in Trier, a goose from the Schorfheide with Château Haut Brion, and then tiny very light Viennese *torte* with Château Yquem."

Goering, Thomas, Pilli Koerner, and Bruno Loerzer drank Napoleon brandy afterward, but Emmy and the wives of the latter two men sipped Danziger goldwasser.† The women were dressed in the latest fashions from Paris, and were liberally sprinkled with French perfume.

"Everyone got quite tipsy," said Thomas, "and I remember Hermann, very red in the face, a happy smile beaming from it, grasping Emmy to him and saying: 'Liebchen, you look just as good as you smell!' It was a very jolly and memorable occasion."

But there was always the morning after, and on the morning after the decision had to be made—what were they going to do next, now that the British had refused to sue for peace?

It was Adolf Galland, one of the great fighter pilots of World War II, who summed up the dilemma of Adolf Hitler and the General Staff in July 1940. He wrote:

"I should not care to say which one of the three following strategic aims was responsible for the order to gain air supremacy [over the British]: the total blockade of the island, the invasion, or the defeat of Britain according to Douhet tactics.‡ I rather doubt if the General Staff knew themselves, because during the course of the Battle of Britain the stress was put on all of them in turn. Such an operation is rarely successful, and it was quite alien to the

---

† Albert Speer reported that later on, when supplies grew scarcer, Goering kept his choice old brandy to himself and served his guests lesser brands.
‡ Douhet, an Italian air force general, believed that attack from the air alone could defeat an opponent and summed up his theory in the words: "Resist on the ground in order to mass in the air."

usual German methods. The only answer I can find is that, taken all in all, the High Command had no clear plans for the further pursuit of the war. Hitler's aims, as before, still lay in the East. The war against Britain was for him merely a necessary evil, with which he had to cope somehow—just how, he was not quite sure."

Hermann Goering partly confirmed that.

"After the rapid collapse of France [Hitler] had not quite decided what to undertake," he said later, "and, strategically whether to make an invasion of England or to push ahead in the Mediterranean theatre of war."

As has been mentioned earlier, Goering had urged an aerial onslaught, plus heavy parachute drops, immediately after the end of the French campaign, when, he felt sure, the British would not have their coastal defenses ready.

But Hitler hesitated, waiting for peace overtures from Britain, and the British in the meantime used the time gained to build coastal defenses, beef up their antiaircraft batteries, and build up reserves of fighter planes. By the time Hitler gave Goering permission to start the aerial war against Britain, conditions had radically changed.

Goering set up his headquarters in Paris and commuted between the French capital and his armored train, parked near a tunnel in a siding near Calais. He had his valet, Robert Kropp, his masseur, Müller, and a brisk female nurse, Christa Gormans, with him to keep him fit for the battle. His paracodeine pill intake had now gone up to some thirty a day, and he sometimes popped two at a time into his mouth when Adolf Hitler was on the telephone, which was often.

The weather, which had been good during the period of procrastination, now turned sour. Days passed without the bombers being able to take off; there were no night bombing operations for the moment, because Goering was demanding pinpoint accuracy in his attacks on seaports, factories, and airfields. The most salutary surprise was the discovery of a defensive air force up in the skies, ready to meet the Luftwaffe. In Poland and against the French, most of the aircraft on the other side had been destroyed on the ground; but now the RAF was in the skies against them, and, as Adolf Galland found, the British Spitfires were more than a match for his Messerschmitt 109s. The infamous Stuka dive-bomber became a weapon no longer to be feared, because it was slow and cumbersome in level flight and squadrons of it were knocked out of the sky like clay pigeons by the sharpshooters of the RAF and by ground defenses. They had to be withdrawn.

"This eliminated about fifteen hundred planes," Goering said, "and they were the best and most exact of the bombing planes . . . I was forced to add bombs to fighter planes, and that is why I created the so-called 'Jobo,' which is a combination of fighter and bombing plane."

Disasters piled up. There was the strategic error of underestimating the efficacy of Britain's radar screen. There was trouble at home in finding replacements for the Messerschmitts that the RAF were bringing down. For the first time the defects in Ernst Udet's technical direction were beginning to show up, and fighter reinforcements were coming out of the factory at the rate of only 375 a month.* There were actually in 1940 more fighter pilots than planes in which they could fly.

Despite these setbacks and defects, the sheer persistence of the Luftwaffe attacks upon the RAF in the sky, on their airfields below, and upon the factories which supplied them and the ports and shipping which kept them and the populace fed, might well have succeeded in bringing Britain to her knees. As if aware in his bones that all that was needed was a last Teutonic straw to break the British camel's back, Goering alternately prodded and praised his pilots, at one moment beating them with a stick and at the next offering them liberal supplies of carrots. He raged at Galland for the lack of aggressive spirit (at one time he called it "cowardice") of his pilots, but two hours later raised hell with the supply depots for not keeping them supplied with good French food and plenty of champagne. He knew in his heart that the pilots were doing their best, at great risk.† But he was now convinced that his tactics were working out, and that given a week or two more, Britain would be on her knees. All his pilots needed was a spur and they would press home the attacks that would bring them vic-

---

* That figure compares with 4,000 a month in 1944, when Albert Speer took over.
† His own favorite nephew, Peter Goering, had already been killed in the battle.

tory. British war leaders, including the RAF commander, Sir Hugh Dowding, were inclined to agree that that was a strong possibility.

And then Adolf Hitler let Britain off the hook. A small group of RAF planes made an attack on the outskirts of Berlin. As a raid it was nothing more than a shake of a pepperpot to make the German public sneeze, but it infuriated Adolf Hitler and persuaded him that his prestige was threatened. The German capital had been attacked. He must reply by hitting London, but ten times as hard. At this moment the Luftwaffe was not only battling the RAF over the Channel but had also begun smashing up airfields and raiding aircraft factories in the Bristol and Southampton areas.

"I believe this plan would have been very successful," Goering said later, "but as a result of the Fuehrer's speech about retribution, in which speech he asked that London be attacked immediately, I had to follow the other course. I wanted to interpret the Fuehrer's speech about attacking London in this way. I wanted to attack the airfields first, thus creating a prerequisite for attacking London. . . . I spoke to the Fuehrer about my plans in order to try to have him agree I should attack the first ring of RAF airfields around London, but he insisted he wanted to have London itself attacked for political reasons, and also for retribution."

The result of that strategic error is well known. The London blitz began and people died and suffered. But Britain was saved.

"I considered the attacks on London useless," said Goering, "and I told the Fuehrer again and again that inasmuch as I knew the English people as well as I did my own people, I could never force them to their knees by attacking London. We might be able to subdue the Dutch people by such measures but not the British."

For propaganda purposes, Hermann Goering went to the cliffs of Cap Gris Nez to be photographed watching the Luftwaffe bombing fleets sweeping across the Channel on their way to London. But after that he went back to Paris. He was disgusted with the new development, and full of forebodings over the outcome of the Battle of Britain. He had begun to suspect that now it could not be won.

The last time Adolf Galland, the fighter pilot commander, had seen Goering during the Battle of Britain they
had had a blazing row. Goering had asked him what he
wanted to make the fight go better and swifter. Galland
had replied by sneeringly asking for a squadron of British
Spitfires. He thought from the anger of Goering's reaction
that he would never be forgiven. He was wrong. That fall,
as the blitz was raging on, Galland came to Berlin to be
invested with the Oak Leaves to his Knight's Cross, which,
apart from Goering's Grand Cross, was the highest military
award in Germany. Afterward, the Reich Marshal invited
him to be his guest at his hunting lodge on Rominten
Heath.

"The Reichsjägerhof was a log cabin made of tree
trunks," Galland wrote later, "with a thatched roof jutting
far over the eaves. Goering came out of the house to meet
me, wearing a green suede hunting jacket over a silk blouse
with long puffed sleeves, high hunting boots and in his belt
a hunting knife in the shape of an old Germanic sword. He
was in the best of humor. Both the disagreeable memory of
our last meeting and his worries about the Luftwaffe in the
Battle of Britain seemed to have been spirited away. We
could hear the stags out on the heath: it was rutting time."

Goering announced that he had secured special permission for Galland to hunt one of the royal stags which were
usually reserved for him, a so-called "Reichsjägermeister
stag."‡ He knew them all and each one had a name; he
watched over them and was loth to part with one of them.

"I promised Moelders,"* Goering said, "to keep you
here for at least three days, so you've got plenty of time."

Galland bagged his deer at ten o'clock the following
morning. "It was really a royal beast, the stag of a lifetime.
There was no further reason to prolong my stay at the
Reichsjägerhof. Yet Goering kept his promise to Moelders
and did not let me go. In the afternoon the latest frontline
reports from Air Fleets 2 and 3 were brought to him. They
were devastating. During a raid on London exceptionally
high losses had been sustained. Goering was shattered. He

‡ Except for the two or three Goering was allowed to shoot an-
nually, royal stags were "protected."
* Moelders was Galland's chief rival for the title of Germany's
champion fighter ace.

simply could not explain how the increasingly painful losses of bombers came about, and I assured him that, in spite of the heavy losses we were inflicting on the enemy fighters, no decisive decrease in their numbers or their fighting efficiency was noticeable."

Goering glumly allowed Galland to go back to his unit, lugging the head of his king stag with him. Hitler's switch of tactics was proving a worse disaster than anyone (except the British, perhaps) had feared.

That autumn Hitler announced to his General Staff that Operation Sea Lion† had been postponed until the spring of 1941. In fact, as Goering well knew, the invasion of Britain had been called off for good.

Adolf Hitler had turned his eyes eastward and was making plans. For twelve uneasy months, the Germans and the Russians had been bound together by the pact they had signed in 1939. But now both sides were beginning to strain against the promises that bound them. The Fuehrer, who had never lost his fear and hatred of the Russians, and had allied himself with them only because he thought it would scare Britain out of making war, was now convinced that the alliance was no longer tenable. There was no room, he believed, for Russian Communism and National Socialism on the same continent—and the time was coming when one must crush the other.

† Code name for the invasion of Britain.

XX. THE COLLECTOR

It was the beginning of 1941 and so far the war had caused no hardship whatsoever to the bulk of the German people. They were, in fact, better off now than they had been at any time since 1914—those who supported the National Socialists, that is. The Jews had almost all been rounded up and herded into the concentration camps, and so had the few remaining opponents of the regime. The Germans were now like the Romans of ancient times, living on the fat of their conquered lands, the slave masters of Europe with Poles, French, Belgians, and Dutch drafted into their factories under forced-labor laws.

In Berlin it would have been hard to tell that there was a war on. The restaurants were packed every night and the menus were rich and full. Night clubs flourished. There was a sort of sexual liberation of young German women that was uncannily like that produced in the 1970s by the birth-control pill. The contention of Heinrich Himmler's SS propagandists was that every German girl's duty was to have a child by a German soldier, and thus produce the population that the Greater Reich would now need to people its conquered lands. There was now no slur on having a baby out of wedlock, and there was a current story that one mother of illegitimate triplets, when asked which soldier to name for her allowance, put down the names of three.

Most of the soldiers who came home on leave brought silks or scents or food from the occupied countries. Hermann Goering preferred art treasures.

The difference between Hitler and Goering so far as the collection of art was concerned was that the Fuehrer did not really appreciate the pictures that came into his hands. He looked at them once, had them stored away for the museum he planned at Linz, and then forgot about them.

To him they were simply part of a collection that would bear his name. On the other hand, thanks to the enthusiasm stirred in him by Carin while she was alive, Goering both loved art and knew something about it. It was true that he had a weakness for pulpy nudes, but he was also a considerable expert on Renaissance painters and the Dutch school. He not only liked looking at pictures for long periods, lost in contemplative delight over them, but it was hard to fool him.*

He now had four stately homes (plus his hunting lodge at Rominten) to house his art acquisitions. There was Carin Hall, where the plans had now been roughly drafted for the Hermann Goering Museum.† There were his two castles, Mauterndorf and Veldenstein. And there was his palace in the Leipziger Platz.

He was constantly on a search for treasures for all of these residences and by this time had art agents in practically every country in Europe on the lookout for him. Walter Andreas Hofer was his chief administrator and kept up the records of the collections, the amount paid for each picture, ornament, sculpture or piece of furniture, and also superintended the "swaps" which Goering frequently made when he badly wanted a painting but was not prepared to pay the going price.

"Hofer was an art dealer by profession," said Goering later, "and he knew all the art dealers in all the countries, and kept in contact with them. In France there was a Dr. Bunjes, who would inform me any time that he heard of some art objects that were for sale or at an auction."

A young art expert named Bruno Lohse was put on Goering's staff and given a Luftwaffe uniform so that he would have freedom of movement inside the occupied countries. One of the first things that Goering told him was "to forget about the racial background of the dealers with whom you come in contact."

"The Reich Marshal explained that a great many of them, especially in Holland, were apt to be Jews," Lohse

---

* Though he was fooled; so were his experts.
† Goering planned to open the collection to the public to celebrate his sixtieth birthday, which would have been in 1953. He chose this date so as not to clash (and have his thunder stolen) by Hitler's rebuilding of the New Berlin, timed for 1950, and the opening of his Linz museum, timed for 1951.

said later, "but I was not to let that affect my attitude. He put me in touch with a dealer in Amsterdam named Katz, who was Jewish. Katz had done us a favor by letting us know about the Goudstikker Collection.‡ He had left behind him a collection of Renaissance pictures and Eastern art conservatively estimated to be worth several million dollars, but the Dutch authorities consented to let us have it for two million guilders, only about a quarter of its value. We were very grateful. We paid him a very good commission. When the anti-Jewish laws were promulgated, we arranged for Katz to get a visa for Switzerland and take his money with him."

Later on, Lohse appealed to Goering for his aid in helping another Dutch Jewish dealer who was about to be victimized by the Nuremberg laws. It was a moment when Goering was in trouble with Hitler owing to Emmy's activities, and he told Lohse over the telephone to Amsterdam that he could not personally intervene.

"But use your initiative," he said.

"I did just that," said Lohse. "I used Goering's name and managed to get the man [his name was Friedländer] a visa for Switzerland. I still have his letter of grateful thanks."

Goering was to maintain later that every art object he acquired was legally paid for, or properly exchanged for a picture or pictures of equivalent value. He once gave 175 paintings in exchange for a Rubens' "Atalanta and Meleager." On the other hand, he was not so generous with his own servants. Robert Kropp recalled how a dealer in Amsterdam gave him a small but valuable picture merely because he had admired it.

"Kropp was astonished but took the picture and later asked Goering whether he had been right to accept it," wrote Manvell and Fraenkel. "Goering just laughed. 'Of course you must keep it,' he said, though, when he saw it, he wanted it for himself. He gave Kropp a large but quite valueless view of Carin Hall in exchange, and did not hide his pleasure at acquiring another small treasure in this way."

He could, of course, afford to pay the price for the paintings he wanted. He estimated his own income around this time at something around a million marks a year—this

‡ Jacques Goudstikker was a Dutch dealer who died in 1940.

calculated by adding his salaries as head of the Luftwaffe, Controller of the German Economy, and Minister of Prussia to his considerable shareholdings in armament firms, plus royalties from his books. In addition, he established an art fund to which most of his industrial friends were expected to subscribe, the accrued sum from which was used to acquire new works. And in the New Year, when presents to the Nazi ministers traditionally flowed in from those who wanted to keep or secure official favor, he always let it be known that he would most appreciate objets d'art. In 1941 a Ruhr industrialist named Friedrich Frick gave him a Van Ruysdael valued at 100,000 marks, and in the same year the city of Berlin bought him a Van Dyck worth 250,000 marks, plus an equally expensive Tintoretto a year later.

There will always be a dealer, even in wartime, however, and even in occupied countries they were not always fazed or overborne by the high-powered Nazi art fanciers who were now sniffing around their galleries. In Holland and in Paris they were soon aware that the market was competitive, because the Rosenberg Commission, Goering, and Hitler himself were all ready to bid against each other for the treasures they wanted.

"It is very unfortunate that this happened," Goering said later. "Many times we did not know about it, and thus the prices went very high with the art dealers . . . I want to tell you, for instance, that if I went to Holland or Paris or Rome I would always find a huge stack of letters awaiting me. There would be letters from private people, princes and princesses, and there were many genuine offers, and many fake offers, and the prices were anywhere from good to improbable, and everybody offered me this stuff to buy . . . However, they did not make these offers to me alone. They would write to all the people who were interested—to the Fuehrer, for instance, and other personalities, and they would inform me of any auctions to be held. I, at various times, visited them in order to get the feel of the market and find out what was happening."

Goering was a shrewd bargainer. He had an eagle eye for a masterpiece, no matter in what dark corner of a gallery it was hidden. He would try every tactic he could think up to make the dealer cut down his price, but if the man firmly stood his ground he would eventually pay.

It seems to be generally accepted that Goering went out of his way to protect the collections in the French national museums, especially the Louvre. He helped the directors to find shelter for their treasures in specially constructed air raid shelters.

"I did exchange two statues and two paintings," he said later, "for one wooden statuette and one painting in the Louvre. I was very fond of the statuette.* I had a long and difficult negotiation with the director in order to obtain them, but they were very firm and at no time did I bring pressure to bear upon them."

The great Jewish collections he dealt with only through Dr. Rosenberg's officially appointed art commission.

"The Jewish properties were exhibited in the Salles du Jeu de Paume," said an official report later, "under the supervision of French and German officials. The most valuable of these were sent, on Hitler's orders, to the royal castles of Neu-Schwanstein and Hohenschwangau, in Bavaria, to the shelters of the Fuehrerbauten in Munich, the Reichschancellery in Berlin, and to Obersalzberg. Their ultimate destination was the new National Museum at Linz."

The remaining works of art exhibited at the Salles du Jeu de Paume were put up for auction, and most of them went to Nazi officials, OKW generals, or French collaborators. Goering bought Teniers' "Adam and Eve in Paradise" from the Rothschild collection and a Boucher "Venus" from the Seligmann collection.†

"[He also] bought some paintings, statues, antique furniture and Gobelin tapestries," the report went on. "In these deals Goering was advised by a French expert, a museum official, and his bids never exceeded the valuation set by this adviser. The only jewelry which he bought was antique. French and German antique dealers were also authorized to take part in these auctions. Goering claims that the Fuehrer demanded photographs of all works of art bought by other amateurs, and that the latter often had to turn over their purchases to Hitler's representative, for eventual shipment to the Linz Museum."

---

* It was the carving known as "La Belle Allemande," and Goering thought it looked like Emmy.
† The money paid over at these auctions went into a special "Jewish Art Fund" which, of course, was never paid out to the Jews.

By rail-car load (once twenty-six of them at a time), the priceless art treasures of the occupied lands went back to Germany to join Goering's collection. There was little doubt of the truth of his claim, which he was to make later, that he was now the possessor of the most valuable art collection in the world. Among the treasures which had come into his possession were:

From Poland

Thirty-one sketches by Albrecht Dürer, taken from the Lemberg Museum. (Though these were later handed on to Hitler, at the Fuehrer's insistence.)

From Holland

Paintings by Franz Hals, Van Dyck, Goya, Van Ruysdael, Jan Steen, several Rembrandts including "Bearded Man" and "Man with a Turban," Velasquez's "Infanta," Rubens' "Resurrection of Lazarus," thirty paintings of the fifteenth-century Flemish School, oriental rugs, swords, and alabaster vases.

From Italy

Memling's "Portrait of a Man," the Spiridon Leda attributed to Leonardo da Vinci (though this was taken from him by Hitler), a vast selection of Renaissance paintings, tapestries, and furniture, the Sterzing Altar (a gift from Mussolini), and a selection of Titians, Van Dycks, and Raphaels, plus antiquities from Pompeii and Herculaneum, which turned out to have been looted by soldiers of Goering's SS Division from the Naples Museum and had to be returned.

From France

Chardin's "Joyeuse de Volant," Fragonard's "Young Girl with Chinese Figure," David's "Mystic Marriage of St. Catherine," four nudes by the older and younger Cranach, a Boucher, a Rubens, Gregor Erhardt's statue known as "La Belle Allemande," tapestries from Beauvais and Gothic hunting scenes, Louis Quatorze and Louis Seize furniture, including a writing desk once the property of Cardinal Mazarin.

Goering also proudly displayed on his walls a Vermeer called "Christ and the Woman Taken in Adultery" which he had bought from the Goudstikker Gallery in Amsterdam. It had been closely examined and certified as genuine both by Goering's expert administrator Andreas Hofer, and by Hofer's wife, who was a professional picture restorer. Goering paid 1,600,000 guilders and also gave several of his pictures as the price for the Vermeer. In fact it was a fake painted by the Dutchman Van Meegeren, whose expert forgeries were revealed after the war.

The sheer plenitude of these great masterpieces was seen by Goering's opponents in the Party not as the gems of his future museum but as vulgar props to his arrogance and pride.

"The halls and rooms of Carin Hall were sheathed with valuable paintings," wrote Albert Speer later, "hung one above the other in three or four tiers. He even had a life-size nude representing Europa mounted above the canopy of his magnificent bed."

Speer sneered that he "dabbled in art dealing." "In the middle of the war, Goering sold [some of his Dutch] pictures to Gauleiters, as he told me with a childlike smile, for many times what he had paid—adding, moreover, an extra something to the price for the glory of the painting having come 'from the famous Goering collection.' "

It was only too true. But with methodical Germanic thoroughness, his administrator Andreas Hofer, and his assistant secretary, Fräulein Gisela Limberger, kept a detailed series of ledgers and photographs of every painting Goering bought and sold, with an exact account of the restoration work which had been performed upon them (by Frau Hofer). Hofer later confirmed that all the money received from the sale of any of the paintings went into the funds of the Hermann Goering Museum for future purchases.

But, of course, the museum was still only a drawing on paper and was not to be built until Germany had won the war. In the meantime, the treasures were there for the personal delectation of Hermann Goering and his guests. At Carin Hall he sometimes dressed with special care when he was making a tour of his acquisitions. He wore velvet knickerbockers, shoes with gold buckles, a colored velvet jacket, and a frilly shirt.

"*Ich bin nun mal ein Renaissanztyp* (After all, I'm a Renaissance type)," he was wont to say, as he strolled past the lush splendor of his overladen walls.

But perhaps he felt best of all nowadays when he was at Veldenstein Castle and in bed. He had taken over the master suite which had once been Ritter von Epenstein's domain when he stayed in the castle, and the bed was the one to which his mistress, Goering's mother, had been nightly bidden. Now the son lay there, with his Gobelin tapestries on the wall opposite, and a Lucas Cranach nude hanging above the canopy of his bed.

It was an experience to savor, and Goering must indeed have felt like a feudal lord of the Renaissance. Or even imagined that he was Ritter von Epenstein himself.

XXI. BARBAROSSA

Despite his infatuation with his art treasures, his preoccupation with the setbacks during the Battle of Britain, and the problems of the labor and raw materials situation, Hermann Goering found time to work on a plan which he was convinced would bring the war (at least against Britain) to an end. It was his brainchild and, during 1941, he tried hard and repeatedly to persuade Adolf Hitler to adopt it.

It was, briefly, a plan for a massive offensive in the Mediterranean. Three army groups were to take part in a vast envelopment operation. One group would go through Spain, capture Gibraltar, move across the Straits to Morocco, and then drive across the North African coast as far as Tunis. A second group would go through Italy and across the Mediterranean to Tripolitania. A third group would go through the Balkans and Greece and capture the Dardanelles, Turkey, and push down through Syria to the Suez Canal.

Upon completion of these operations (always assuming that they succeeded, of course) it was planned to make a peace offer to Britain. The British would already have been presented with the *fait accompli* that the Mediterranean was no longer under their control. They would be allowed to use it again, but *only if they agreed to ally themselves with Germany in the fight against Russia.*

Goering believed that the British would be forced to accept Germany's terms, since otherwise they would be cut off from their Indian and Far Eastern possessions.

In the beginning, Hitler gave the impression of welcoming the plan, and allowed Goering to make the necessary arrangements and dispositions. "Everything was prepared," he said later. He described these preparations as follows:

"Fifteen divisions, including two parachute divisions and

three flak corps, were lined up for this purpose. Approximately 600 eighty-eight millimeter anti-aircraft guns and a number of specially constructed eighty centimeter pieces, plus a number of 'smaller' sixty centimeter artillery pieces were to bombard Gibraltar until it was pulverized. It was felt that no living soul could have remained in the galleries [under the Rock of Gibraltar] under such a bombardment. The new eighty centimeter guns were already mounted on railcars and were ready to roll through Spain. The guns, when in firing position, occupied four railroad tracks. The two parachute divisions would never have been necessary, since the bombardment by all the guns, which was to be an incessant procedure, would have brought the garrison to its knees."

Goering had been working on the Mediterranean Plan ever since he had realized, in the summer of 1940, that the Fuehrer was serious about his intention of attacking Russia. The idea of waging a war with the Red colossus in the East before Britain was disposed of in the West appalled him, for it meant campaigns on two fronts of the very kind which had sapped Germany's strength in World War I. And Hitler had repeatedly warned his generals about this. Why else had he signed the Russo-German Pact in 1939 if it was not to avoid such a calamity?

If Hitler was now changing his mind, it seemed to Goering now that it was even more vital to get Britain out of the war, and since the Luftwaffe was failing to do it over the English Channel, the Mediterranean Plan seemed the only other way. He was considerably perturbed when, at the end of August 1940, the Fuehrer called in his staff planners and indicated that he was thinking of attacking Russia "in the spring of 1941." The OKW thereupon issued a preliminary order called Aufbau Ost which, though it did not mention Russia by name or any intention to attack it, was designed to swing the might of the German armies eastward.

But Goering was still convinced that his own pet operation could be started first. He was therefore shattered when Adolf Hitler suddenly went sour on the Plan. Hitler had worked out in his own mind a confused explanation of why, despite the disasters of 1940, the British had refused to accept Germany's peace overtures. It was because Churchill was hanging on and waiting for Stalin to come into the war. He would still hang on no matter where he was struck next, even through the Mediterranean. So he flatly told Goering to call off his dispositions and abandon the plan.*

Goering was flabbergasted. He felt that the abrupt dismissal of the Mediterranean Plan was a serious error on Hitler's part. But he thought his decision to go ahead with the attack on Russia was even graver, and the depressing effect it had upon the Reich Marshal was to have profound consequences for him and for Germany in the days to come.

"Early one afternoon in the early spring of 1941," said Goering later,† "I was at Berchtesgaden and Hitler called me. I remember it was a very sunny day . . . The Fuehrer explained to me in a two-hour report why he had decided to preclude a Russian attack on Germany by attacking Russia himself. I listened to him, and then I asked the Fuehrer to give me some time, so that I could in turn inform him of my opinion, which happened later that evening."

In the interim, Goering bolstered himself with pills and decided that once and for all the moment had arrived to stand up to the Fuehrer. He appears to have argued long and loudly and, for once, to have ignored Hitler's evident anger over his interference. Goering pointed out that what he was planning to do—to open a second front—was against Hitler's own belief and contrary to what he had written and promised the people in *Mein Kampf*.

But Hitler seemed now to have an obsession (or he may have pretended to have, for Goering's benefit) that Stalin was about to attack Germany. He pointed out that the Russians had suddenly permitted German engineers and officers to inspect their armament factories, where aircraft engines, plane parts, and tanks were manufactured. The

---

* Another factor in his reckoning, of course, may well have been the attitude of the Spanish dictator, General Franco. He had talked with Franco about German troop movements and Gibraltar, and had been asked in return to give Spain—and in writing—a guarantee of a free hand in North Africa. This he had refused.
† Goering couldn't remember the exact date. It was actually August 9, 1940, when the records show that he talked with Hitler about future plans.

report on what these Germans had seen gave him (Hitler) great cause for anxiety. Russia was becoming too strong, and Stalin's attitude was increasingly independent. Germany must move quickly, before it was too late and the Russians struck first.

"We will smash the Russians before winter," he said.

Goering pointed out that even if he succeeded in smashing the Russian Army, the war would not be over. The Russian people would never make peace. The country would never be controlled. He pleaded with Hitler to think of Napoleon.

Hitler crisply replied that Napoleon did not have the greatest tank army and the mightiest air force the world had ever seen.

"This time," said the Fuehrer sarcastically, "it must behave like the mightiest air force, and there will be no mistakes. Then we will have victory before winter arrives!"

With the heaviest forebodings, Goering left the next day for Carin Hall and had a discussion there with Erhard Milch. He told his second-in-command what had been decided. Milch seems to have detected none of the doubts which were obviously filling Goering's heart, and presumed that Goering was as much in favor of the Russian campaign as the Fuehrer. That night Milch confided to his diary that he thought it was the maddest of decisions, and that far from being over before the winter it would not be over in four years' time. It is indicative of his relations with Goering that he did not convey these doubts to him, or guess that he shared them.

Though Hitler had vetoed the Mediterranean Plan, he was forced to put one of its operations into action in the winter of 1940–41, when Italy had to be rescued from its reckless attack upon Greece. The Germans struck first at Yugoslavia, and on April 17, 1941, the Yugoslav Royalist Army capitulated. Shortly afterward the Nazi invasion of Greece began. On May 20, in a co-ordinated air operation, Nazi paratroopers descended on Crete and expelled the British Army and Navy from Cretan territory and waters. In a little over a month, the Germans had captured the Balkans and dipped their jack boots into the Mediterranean. Goering must take the credit for this campaign, and, despite the heavy losses suffered, it was an indication of what might have been achieved had the whole, instead of merely part of his Mediterranean Plan been put into operation.

The victory put Goering into a good humor and shortly after the fall of Crete, when he came to Paris to brief his Luftwaffe unit commanders, he seemed in bouncing good health. He implied in his speech that the capture of Crete had been nothing more than a sort of rehearsal for the imminent invasion of Britain. The battle over the British Isles was the overture to the final subjection of the British enemy. He explained how it was to be effected by increased rearmament of the Luftwaffe and intensification of the U-boat war, and how it would be brought to a conclusion by the actual invasion itself.

"I must say," wrote Adolf Galland later, "that the plans Goering unfolded before us were convincing, and that we took it for granted that the necessary war-industrial capacity was available. At the end of the discussion, Goering took Moelders and myself aside. He beamed, and as he asked us what we thought of his speech, chuckled softly, and rubbed his hands with glee. 'There's not a grain of truth in it,' he said. Under the seal of greatest secrecy, he disclosed to us that the whole discussion was part of a well-planned bluff, whose aim was to hide the real intentions of the German High Command: the imminent invasion of the Soviet Union. It was a paralyzing shock!"

Again, Hermann Goering must have been concealing his true feelings about the forthcoming attack, for Galland wrote later:

"I was stunned by the idea, and did not hide my scruples. But no one shared my opinion. To my amazement, not only Goering but Moelders was excited and enthusiastic. In the east, said Goering, the Luftwaffe would win new laurels. The Red Air Force was numerically strong, but hopelessly inferior in machines and personnel. It would only be necessary to shoot down the leader of a unit for the remaining illiterates to lose themselves on the way home. We would shoot them down like clay pigeons."

Galland asked him what was going to happen to the Battle of Britain, the defeat of England.

"Goering merely waved his hand disdainfully. In two, or at the most three months the Russian colossus would be crushed. Then we would throw against the West all our strength, enriched by the inexhaustible strategic resources of Russia. The Fuehrer, he said, could not wage the war against England with the full weight of our forces as long as his rear was threatened by a power which undoubtedly had offensive and hostile intentions towards us."

From this encounter Galland came away with no inkling whatsoever that Goering also had his forebodings over the Russian plan. So far as the young fighter pilot was concerned, the only Nazi leader who shared his opinion of the folly of the enterprise was Rudolf Hess, the Deputy Fuehrer. On May 10, 1941, Hess suddenly took off from Germany in a purloined Messerschmitt 110 and flew to England. A subsequent communiqué announced that "he harbored the illusion that he could bring about peace between Germany and England by a personal intervention."

Galland decided in his own mind that Hess had heard about the plan to invade Russia, and had made a desperate attempt to prevent the two-front war that would follow.

"Someone had made a last-minute attempt to pull the emergency cord of a fast train speeding over the wrong points," he wrote later.‡

A few days after Goering's Paris meeting with his Luft-waffe unit commanders, he called General Josef Kamm-huber to see him at Veldenstein Castle. Kammhuber, who had served as a regular officer in the German Army during World War I, had transferred to the Luftwaffe in the early thirties and was now commander of the night-fighter squadrons in Holland. RAF bomber raids against north-western Germany had begun to intensify, and his squad-rons were kept busy trying to intercept the increasing number of planes and their fighter escorts.

He drove over to Veldenstein from his headquarters at Zeist and ate lunch with Goering and Pilli Koerner in the vaulted dining hall of the castle. Kammhuber had also been at the Paris meeting, and he now noticed the change for the worse which had taken place in the Reich Marshal's

---

‡ Shortly after Hess's flight, Galland was ordered by Goering to put up his fighters and intercept the Deputy Fuehrer. "The order I received was mad," said Galland. It was impossible to find a plane at that hour, as darkness was falling. "Just as a token, I ordered a takeoff. Each wing commander was to send up one or two planes. I did not tell them why. They must have thought that I had gone off my head." Hess bailed out over Scotland and was made a prisoner-of-war. His peace overtures got nowhere.

appearance in the short time since that event. His face was
very red, there were deep rings under his eyes, and he
seemed tired to the point of exhaustion. He merely picked
at the boiled trout which they were served and hardly
drank any wine, and Kammhuber noticed that the diamond ring which he wore on his fourth finger was so tight
that when he turned his hand palm upward it seemed to be
buried in the flesh.

The night-fighter commander had tried to talk about the
RAF offensive during the meal, but Goering turned the
conversation to music, a subject Kammhuber found con-
genial enough, since he was (and is) a musician himself.
Afterward they came out into the courtyard and Goering
drew deep breaths of air into his lungs, at one point throwing out his hands wide as if to admit as much as the lungs
would hold. The expression on his face was as if he found
something distasteful, and Kammhuber ascribed it to the
fact that the atmosphere was quite heavy with the fumes
from the brewery in Pegnitz village, a few hundred feet
below.

Presently, Koerner was dismissed and the two men went
into Goering's study, where a huge map of Europe was
hung on the wall. Goering stared at it sourly for a few
moments and then said:

"Kammhuber, I have called you here to tell you in the
strictest confidence that my conference in Paris was bluff,
pure bluff. The campaign against England is no longer
important. This is." He flung a pudgy hand in the direction
of Eastern Europe. "The Fuehrer has decided that the time
to attack Russia has arrived. Dispositions are being made
and the requisite forces will now be transferred in readiness
for action. This is where you come in. I want you to begin
the withdrawal at once from Holland of sufficient night
fighters to meet our needs on the Russian front, and for the
protection of Eastern Germany from any Red reprisals
from the air. How many squadrons can you give me?"

Kammhuber was astonished, not so much by the news
about Russia, which he took with the phlegm of a hardened regular soldier, but at Goering's ignorance of the
night-fighter situation.

"But Herr Reich Marshal," he said, "there are not
enough night fighters in Holland to do the job for which
they are needed. RAF attacks are increasing, and we just

do not have enough planes. We need more. We certainly
do not have any to spare for an attack on the Russian
front."

Goering swung around on him angrily.

"Look, Kammhuber," he said. "I do not want this war
against Russia. I am the one who is against it. So far as I
am concerned, it is the worst possible thing we could do. It
is economically mistaken, politically mistaken and militar-
ily mistaken.* But Ribbentrop wants it and Goebbels wants
it, and they have persuaded the Fuehrer to want it. I have
argued against it until my face is blue, but they won't
listen. Now I wash my hands of the whole business—the
whole war! Do what you can. Get half of your night fighters transferred. I just can't be bothered about what happens any more! I'm going upstairs!"

And with that, he turned and almost trotted out of the
room, leaving Kammhuber staring after him in amazement.

On June 22, 1941, the German armies crossed the frontiers of the Soviet Union and Operation Barbarossa began.
Despite all the warnings they had been given, the Russians
were taken by surprise and by nightfall of the first day they
had been overrun. The attack had begun with heavy Luftwaffe raids on sixty Russian airfields and a number of
aircraft factories, and by nightfall 1,800 planes had been
reported destroyed. Eight hundred more were wiped out
the following day, 557 on June 24, 351 on June 25, and
300 on June 26. Nearly all these casualties were inflicted
while the Red machines were still on the ground. Meanwhile, thousands of Nazi tanks began thrusting across the
Russian plains toward Leningrad, Moscow, and the Ukraine.

Everything looked good. Hitler was jubilant, convinced
that his instincts had been right and that all of Russia
would be in his hands before winter. Even Goering felt
better about the campaign, and spent his days in conference with Pilli Koerner and his economic advisers, working
on the scheme with which Hitler had charged him for the
exploitation of the vast manpower, food, and matériel resources of the Soviet Union. Within three weeks, his requi-

* *"Es ist wirkschaftlich falsch, politisch falsch, militärisch falsch."*

sition and recruiting teams were already on their way into Russian territory, for the German armies were now in Smolensk, forty minutes' flying distance from Moscow. They were hammering at the gates of Leningrad, and tank columns were surrounding Kiev, capital of the Ukraine.

The Luftwaffe had done well, both for the Nazi Reich and for Hermann Goering. Did he not stand higher now in the Fuehrer's esteem than ever before? To those ignorant of the inner workings of the Party, it might have seemed so. On June 22, 1941, Adolf Hitler hailed the Reich Marshal as the greatest hero of the National Socialist state, and legally named him as his successor in the event of his death. But despite the Russian successes, relations between Goering and Hitler had been deteriorating ever since the blitz on London and other cities had failed to bring the British to their knees. That Hitler was even more to blame than Goering for the failure of the strategy only exacerbated the Fuehrer's bitterness, and the situation was not helped by the fact that Hitler had a new and dangerous crony at his side. The departure of Rudolf Hess had brought the egregious Martin Bormann a step up in the Nazi hierarchy. When Hitler had asked Goering's advice as to whom he should choose for deputy in Hess's place, he had replied:

"Anyone but Bormann."

Bormann stood for everything that Goering disliked about his National Socialist comrades. He was uncouth, brutal, and immoral, and he had done two things which had shocked Goering profoundly when they were brought to his attention. One was his action in bringing home his mistress and forcing his long-suffering wife to entertain her. The other was his treatment of a stray dog which had dared to attack his mistress's poodle. He had had it soaked with gasoline and then set afire, and had roared with laughter as the unfortunate animal raced screaming down the street.

But Bormann had one virtue, so far as Hitler was concerned, and it was a virtue of which he was to grow increasingly fond. No matter what Hitler asked of him, he would always obey. "If Hitler ordered all gauleiters to address him standing on one leg, Bormann would see that they did it," someone once said. And so far as Bormann was concerned, Hitler was omnipotent, he could do no wrong, and must never be denied. Bormann was, in fact, a slavishly toadying yesman, and his constant flattery was dear to the Fuehrer's heart. Against Goering's advice, Hitler appointed him his deputy anyway, and from that moment on the Reich Marshal had an enemy with his tongue close to Hitler's ear whenever it was not licking his boots.

The result was that Hitler nowadays was often sarcastically critical of Goering's performance not only in private but in the presence of his General Staff and advisers. His comments became so wounding, and caused such titters among Hitler's toadies, that Goering came more and more infrequently to the Fuehrer's daily situation conferences, but sent Bodenschatz instead.

"Where is the Iron Man (*der Eisener*)† today?" Hitler would then ask, looking around the room. "Shooting defenseless deer again instead of British aircraft, I suppose."

On one of Goering's occasional attendances at the conference, however, Hitler greeted him with all the old warmth and friendliness, and then announced that he had a bold new project for the Reich Marshal. If he carried it out successfully, it would not only bring renown to him as leader of the Luftwaffe but it would also solve his problems as the Director of the German Economy.

The project, which had come to Hitler as an inspiration, was to have Goering mount the greatest attack in the history of air warfare. All bomber planes should be recalled at once from France, Scandinavia, and the Mediterranean, and then a series of raids by the full force of the Luftwaffe would begin on both Leningrad and Moscow. The entire cities and their populations would be destroyed and the raids would continue so long as a building stood and a human being moved. This was not, Hitler went on, to be an attack for the purpose of winning the war with Russia. The war was already won in his view (this was September 1941). It was now all over but the cleaning up.

No, declared Hitler, the purpose of the raids was to prepare for peace. When the fighting had stopped, all the food in Russia would be needed for the German people. There would be none to spare to feed the Russians. True,

† The Iron Man was one of the Luftwaffe's nicknames for Goering. Another was Fatty (*der Dicke*).

as the Reich Marshal had once said,‡ it was always possible to let the Russians starve. But that took time. It could cause unrest, and would take manpower to control. Whereas, bombing—a mighty onslaught from the combined airfleets of the Luftwaffe—would simply wipe out a huge portion of the population cleanly, without fuss.

While Bormann loudly made known his enthusiastic approval of this "brilliant inspiration of the Fuehrer," all the generals were looking at Hermann Goering for his reaction.

Bodenschatz was to say later that he was proud of Hermann Goering at that moment. It was one of the last times that he plucked up the courage to fight back against Adolf Hitler.

"He began very politely by saying that while he found the Fuehrer's project worth studying," Bodenschatz said, "his immediate reaction was that it would be a most difficult operation to carry out. When Hitler harshly asked him why, he became bolder and said outright that it would be the height of folly to withdraw the Luftwaffe from all other fronts just for one operation. What about the attacks on London? Had not the Fuehrer demanded that they must be continued with unremitting force? It would be dangerous to stop, because it would give the British people respite. Their factories would open again, their aircraft industries get under way, and before they knew it the British RAF would be as strong as Germany."

Hitler had been listening with a stony expression on his face, and all the original friendliness shown the Reich Marshal had by now disappeared. He suddenly broke in and cried out that he knew why Goering was decrying the plan. The Luftwaffe was afraid. He had suspected it during the attacks on England, and now he knew it was true. They were cowards. They didn't want to attack Leningrad because they were afraid of its antiaircraft defenses.

"Goering could have told him what everyone else in the room knew, that Leningrad's defenses were nothing like as fearsome as London's, over which our fliers had been operating for months," Bodenschatz said. "But instead he said: 'It is impossible, mein Fuehrer. It cannot be done.'

‡ In a report which his experts prepared for the exploitation of Russian resources which was issued just before the invasion of the U.S.S.R. began.

Hitler looked at him coldly for a moment, and then turned his back on him and ignored him for the rest of the conference."

From this incident onward, the relationship between Hitler and his Reich Marshal went from bad to worse.

Not long afterward Goering was involved in another clash with the Fuehrer, this time over the long-term strategy of the war against Soviet Russia.

In his directives for the exploitation of the captured territories which he had written before the opening of the campaign, Hermann Goering had made it coldly clear that what Germany needed from the lands to be conquered was food and raw materials, and that the severity of these demands might well bode ill for the local populations. He laid down certain "civilized methods" to be followed in providing for them, but expected that famine would follow.

"These measures will not avert famine," he had instructed his staff in a directive dated May 23, 1941. "Many tens of millions of people in this area will become redundant or have to emigrate to Siberia. Any attempt to save the population there from death by starvation by importing surpluses from the black-soil zone [of the Ukraine] would be at the expense of supplies to Europe. It would reduce Germany's staying power in the war, and would undermine Germany's and Europe's power to resist the [Allied] blockade. This must be clearly and absolutely understood."

But soon his friend Alfried Krupp, the armaments man from the Ruhr, was persuading him that far from having a surplus population, the captured Ukraine had need of all the labor it could hold onto, and that included Jews. Into Krupp's hands had now come dozens of industrial complexes as a result of the German armies' advances, and he was anxious to begin the immediate exploitation of them. On the whole, the civil population of the Ukraine was disposed to help him keep the factory wheels turning. Many of its leaders, disillusioned with Stalinism, had done a good deal of underground work before the arrival of the German armies in persuading the populace that they came as liberators and not as conquerors, and the first Nazi troops passing through the towns and villages of the Ukraine were, to their astonishment, received with flags and cheers.

Unfortunately, the political commissioner who had been

put in charge of the Ukraine by Hermann Goering was a malevolent and sadistic little upstart named Erich Koch, in whose small, dark, sour-faced frame beat a fierce blond Nazi heart. In an extraordinary outburst of xenophobia, he hastened to jail or execute openly pro-German priests or intellectuals, whom he insisted in regarding as trouble-makers; he drove around the villages brandishing a stock whip and haranguing the natives about their humble future in the development of the Ukraine, which was to be turned into a German state; and he then called in the aid of two even more sinister men to help him "organize" the popula-tion. One was Fritz Sauckel, who had been put in charge of civilian manpower in the occupied territories. Sauckel had described the Ukraine as "that plum of the golden pheasants," and proposed now to pick it clean of its able-bodied workers for reshipment to the Reich. The other was Heinrich Himmler, whose extermination squadrons (*Ein-satzkommandos*) would take care of the rest, including women, children, and Jews.

When these measures were announced by Erich Koch, Alfried Krupp demanded at once to know where his la-borers would come from to man the factories which had come into his hands. He pointed out that many of the key workers in the occupied Russian armament works were Jews, and he had need of them. Heydrich, Himmler's dep-uty, who was at the meeting, dryly pointed out that the Reichminister for the Economy, in other words Goering, had himself once said: "Kill all the men in the Ukraine . . . and then send in the SS stallions," and he had taken that as an order.

Krupp smoothly replied that he needed workers now and could not wait until the SS stallions' foals by the Ukraine's women grew up to manhood. He left the meeting and flew back to see Hermann Goering and outlined the situation for him. As a result, the shipments of Ukrainians to the Reich were halted, and an order was given that all Jewish skilled workers were not to be arrested or molested so long as they were engaged in vital labor.*

* That order gave them a year's respite. After that, whether they were vital or not, the extemination squadrons shipped them to the gas ovens. By that time Goering, who knew what was coming and was determined not to get involved, had divested himself of per-sonal responsibility for the fate of the Jews.

It was from his conversations with Krupp and the reports from Erhard Milch, who had recently made a tour of
Luftwaffe bases in the East, that Goering decided to make
one more attempt to influence the Fuehrer regarding the
Russian war. Krupp was apprehensive that if the German
armies went on pushing deeper and deeper into Russia they
would put their heads into the same noose which had hung
Napoleon, and he counseled a halt before they became too
stretched and too involved. Milch had always believed that
it was madness to think that Russia could be defeated in
the short space of a summer and autumn, and that it would
take at least four years to bring about the Soviet Government's downfall. If the push went on, he prophesied the
worst imaginable disaster. He had practical reasons for his
forecast. He knew, as Goering knew, that despite its victories over the Russian aircraft on the ground, the Luftwaffe was in most dire difficulties. There was a desperate
shortage of planes, of replacements, of fuel. The rebuilding
program at home in Germany had gone hopelessly wrong,
and a crisis was coming.

The Luftwaffe, in short, was in no position to continue
the offensive. Like the armies, it needed to pause and build
up its strength. But the pause which Milch envisioned was
not just for a few months, but for a year, at least, perhaps
even more. Germany needed to digest the enormous booty
it had swallowed.

The result of these conversations was that in November
1941, just when the German armies were beginning to
experience the first rigors of a Russian winter, Goering
went to see Adolf Hitler and asked him to halt the war.

"It would be the best thing to hold onto what we have
got, the Ukraine, and not attempt to penetrate any further," Goering later said he told Hitler. "Let us build an
East Wall [like the Siegfried Line along the French fron-
tier] with all the millions of workers we now have at our
disposal. No Russian army will ever break through, because we have a superior Luftwaffe, and they can never
break the defenses without an effective air force."

But Hitler refused to listen. The snows began to blanket
the Russian steppes. The cold bit into the bodies of German troops not prepared, and not clad, for a Russian winter. Oil froze in the German tanks. Planes would not start

or could not take off. The first great disasters of the Russian campaign struck.

Even so, Adolf Hitler told his generals not to consolidate but to prepare for the resumption of the offensive in the spring.

By that time, the Luftwaffe was in trouble everywhere. And so was Hermann Goering.

XXII. DEATH OF A HERO

Ernst Udet was in trouble too. Not woman trouble or drinking trouble, which were normal with him, but real trouble connected with his job as Supply Chief for the Luftwaffe. There was no doubt that he had fallen down badly. The building program for the German Air Force was in a state of utter confusion, and the constructors were in despair. Not only were insufficient new planes coming through to replace the losses on the eastern front, but the Luftwaffe was now steadily losing its superiority in the West.

In the autumn of 1941, Albert Speer visited the Junkers plant in Dessau to see General Manager Heinrich Koppenberg about the plans he was making for a new aircraft plant.

"After we had worked the matter out," Speer wrote later, "he led me into a locked room and showed me a graph comparing American bomber production for the next several years with ours. I asked him what our leaders had to say about these depressing comparative figures. 'That's just it, they won't believe it,' he said. Whereupon he broke into uncontrollable tears."

They wouldn't believe it (not at first, anyway) because Ernst Udet was deliberately deceiving them, and it took them some time to find out. It was General Hans Jeschonnek, chief of the Luftwaffe General Staff, who first became aware that Udet was "cooking" his books and claiming to be producing many hundreds more planes than were, in fact, reaching the Luftwaffe. He mentioned his suspicions to Field Marshal Erhard Milch and Colonel Berndt von Brauchitsch, since 1940 Goering's chief adjutant. He hoped that between the two of them they would persuade the Reich Marshal to do something drastic about the charming but recklessly unreliable Ernst Udet.

The trouble was, Goering had always been a little in awe of the blond giant who was supposed to be supplying the German Air Force. He had topped his own score in the air battles of World War I, he had always been able to outdrink and outwench him, and whenever he had occasion to call Udet in for a conference and awkward questions came up, the laughing giant would recall some incident from the days of the Richthofen Squadron and take cover behind reminiscences of wartime encounters.

Goering suffered from the same defects as Udet, for both of them were lazy men, and both of them found it absolutely impossible to sack their friends. The Reich Marshal had known for some time that his Supply Director was unsuitable for the job, but he could not find it in his heart to get rid of him. In his turn, Udet had filled his administration with wartime pals with no knowledge whatsoever of the techniques of planning and building planes, and they had turned the Luftwaffe rearmament program into a chaotic mess. But he would not tell them to go.

How could Goering be worked up enough to face the truth and rid himself of his wartime comrade? In the end, Milch decided to speak to him on the morrow of the capture of Crete. From Veldenstein the Reich Marshal had telegraphed Milch his congratulations over the "good news" of Crete's capture, but Milch hastened to see him and pointed out that it had been a costly victory indeed. Did the Reich Marshal realize that 271 precious Junkers 52 bombers had been lost during the operation, and that this was half of the total Ju 52 fleet? Did he realize that the success of the Luftwaffe operations in the forthcoming Russian attack would be endangered, because there would only be 2,770 first-line planes available? Why, even in 1940 against England there had been 2,600 planes.

Goering expressed his astonishment. He reached for the figures on his desk and demonstrated that, according to Udet, at least 1,500 more planes were available.

"Udet is lying," said Milch.

The next day Goering summoned Udet to see him and, for the first time in their association, bitterly attacked him, as a liar, a big-mouth, and an incompetent. But he did not sack him, and Udet did not resign. Instead, Goering announced that he was going on leave to Carin Hall, and that in the future Milch would deal with Udet and superintend his affairs. Then he stalked out of the room.

Ernst Udet took his chastisement badly. But the target of his resentment was not Goering, but Milch. Ernst Heinkel, the aircraft constructor, was with him a few days later and Udet did not conceal the bitterness in his voice when he said:

"Everyone's against me. The Iron Man has gone on leave. He's left me alone with Milch. Milch will now be dealing with the Fuehrer, and he'll be only too anxious to see that every failure or fault I have made will be placed on the Fuehrer's table . . . I can't cope with this persecution any longer."

In the next few months, Ernst Udet saw more of Erhard Milch than he ever had before. He grew to hate him. It was true that Milch was an emotionless man who had no time and no sentiment for incompetents, even if they had once been war heroes. "When Milch pisses, ice comes out," Pilli Koerner had once said. Now he drove Udet constantly. A new plan for Luftwaffe rearmament had been drawn up under Milch's direction and approved by the Reich Marshal and Hitler. It was known as the Goering Program, and it made such demands on available raw materials that Dr. Fritz Todt, who was in charge of the army side of supplies, realized that there would be nothing left for him. He said to Milch in despair:

"I might just as well give up and come in as your assistant."

In the plethora of discussions and factory visits which followed, Ernst Udet took little part. It was just as well, for each inquiry that Milch made uncovered mistakes, neglect, and lack of decision. Things were so bad that new bombers promised for production in 1942 could not possibly be ready before 1944.

A combination of what must have been guilt and resentment drove Udet to the bottle as never before (he was also taking pills), and at the infrequent meetings he attended he could be seen surreptitiously sipping at a flask of schnapps. Adolf Galland saw him about this time and "I hardly recognized him; his spontaneous joie de vivre, his gay humor and attractive warmth had all disappeared." He had begun to complain of a constant headache and noises in his ears.

At the end of August 1941, Goering gave his old comrade permission to go on four weeks' sick leave, and during that period Milch went to work cleaning up some of the mess Udet had created, and getting rid of the "scoundrels" with whom he had surrounded himself. By the time Udet was ready to come out of a nursing home, there was enough evidence to convince even Goering that his old comrade had been tricked and lied to, and, as a result, had produced a lag in aircraft production for the Luftwaffe which would take at least two years to make up.

The showdown came on November 12, 1941, at a conference in the Air Ministry. Officials of the Messerschmitt works produced documents to demonstrate the falsification of figures and the alteration of orders; the sheer incompetence, if not worse, of Udet was plain for all to see. The blond giant, haggard now, his hands trembling, sat in his chair and said nothing as the melancholy history of the disaster was read out.

As they were leaving the hall, Milch caught up with Udet, sensing that he was blaming him for his discomfiture. He said, apparently in all seriousness:

"Udet, I have a feeling that our close friendship has taken a bit of a knock as a result of all this, whether you think it or not. We must get things straight between us—let's go for a couple of days' relaxation in Paris. We both need a breathing space."

Udet agreed. It was arranged that they meet at midday on November 17 at Tempelhof Airport and fly to Paris in Udet's private plane, a Siebel 104.

Milch flew off to Breslau, and Udet went back to his bachelor apartment to spend the weekend with two of his cronies who had been sacked by Milch, and some girls, including his current mistress. There was a very drunken party, which eventually ended in the early hours of Monday morning, when they all left. Later that morning of November 17, 1941, just before nine-thirty, the telephone rang in the apartment of Udet's mistress and she at once recognized Udet's voice at the other end of the line. They had parted bitterly and she pleaded with him to let her come to him. He interrupted her.

"No, it's too late," he said. "Tell Pilli Koerner that he is to look after my will."

She heard a shot over the line, and then silence. When

she and Pilli Koerner finally reached the apartment on the Stallüponer Allee, the housekeeper had already broken into the bedroom. Two empty bottles of brandy and a revolver were on the floor, and Udet's body lay across the bed.

In his last conversation with his girl friend, Udet had told her to look behind the bed. There they found a gray screen on which he had scrawled two messages in red crayon. The first read:

"Iron Man, you have forsaken me!"

The second trailed away but began with the words:

"Why did you put me in the hands of that Jew Milch . . . ?"

Udet's adjutant had now arrived, and Koerner swore him, the girl friend, and the housekeeper to secrecy over what was written on the screen, and the adjutant went into the bathroom for a cloth and washed the words away. Then Koerner opened the safe, and while the adjutant went through the service papers, Koerner took possession of a letter in an open envelope addressed to Hermann Goering. Its words were even more wounding than those on the screen, charging his old comrade with every kind of conspiracy against him and viciously attacking Erhard Milch. It ended with the words:

"It was impossible for me to work together with the Jew Milch."

When Milch reached his office in Berlin on Monday morning—he had come in from Breslau by train—he was told that Udet was dead, and that Goering was on the line. The Reich Marshal sounded deeply shocked by Udet's death, but insisted that not a breath of scandal must leak out about it. A few hours later his adjutant and medical adviser, Dr. von Ondarza, came on the telephone from Carin Hall to dictate to Milch the announcement which Goering wished to have issued to the newspapers. It said:

"The Chief Supply Officer of the Luftwaffe, Major-General Udet, on Monday, November 17, 1941, suffered such a serious accident while testing a new type of plane that he succumbed to his injuries. The Fuehrer has ordered a State funeral for this officer, killed in the execution of his duty."

The following day all flags in Berlin flew at half-mast, and three days later the funeral took place, with Goering walking all the way to the Invalidenfriedhof (the military cemetery) in North Berlin behind the gun-carriage. He was manifestly moved by the death of his old Richthofen comrade.

The most famous holders of the Iron Cross, including Adolf Galland and his friend Moelders, were chosen as the coffin-bearers and guard of honor. Moelders failed to show up, for bad weather had stranded him in Russia, but the others stood by in full dress uniform, steel helmets, and ceremonial swords, while the mourners passed the catafalque. Hitler placed his wreath but did not say a word during the service. Only Goering spoke. With tears in his eyes, he said:

"I can only say that I have lost my best friend."

Germany had lost much more than that, as would soon be discovered.

By the end of 1941, all hopes had died that the war against Russia would be of short duration. The Russians had started to hit back. Their factories had been rebuilt and were rolling once more far behind their lines, out of reach of the Luftwaffe bombers.

In the meantime, the United States was now ranged beside Britain in the war in the West, and the raids upon German cities were beginning in earnest. What the Luftwaffe now needed were long-range bombers to get at the Russian industrial centers, and clouds of fighter-planes to put a protective umbrella over Germany and keep it sheltered from the rain of Allied bombs. But, as Goering and Milch now knew only too well, the aircraft building program was only slowly and painfully being brought back to some semblance of order. The ravages of Udet's maladministration had been monstrous. When Milch took over as Chief Aircraft Supplier after Udet's death, he had groaned and cried:

"One hundred and forty-six thousand unbuilt planes— that's what he's cost us!"

Among the appointments Goering had made toward the end of 1941 was that of Adolf Galland to the post of General-in-Command of Fighters. Galland summed up the situation as he saw it when he took over his job in these words:

"The unforeseen prolongation of the Eastern Campaign threatened to upset the entire strategy of the German Command. Hitler had accepted war on two fronts only on condition that a quick and total victory over the enemy in the east could be achieved. When the German offensive came to a standstill, it meant the end of Hitler's plan of resuming the air offensive against England after a speedy termination of the Eastern Campaign. This failure could not be disguised by the grandiose and far-reaching plans for advancing in the direction of the Caucasus in the coming spring."

Of Goering, he wrote:

"As supreme commander of the Luftwaffe, Goering, of all people, should have realized clearly that he could never regain the temporary loss of air superiority in the west with a force which, already in the Eastern Campaign, had been strained beyond the limits of its capacity. Everything beyond this point could only be described as 'burning the substance.' The German air industry was not equal to a war of such dimensions, nor was the ability to replace personnel. Even if immediate attempts were now made to adapt the Luftwaffe to the increased demands made on it, it was impossible to foresee whether the effect of such changes would make itself felt early enough to prevent a total collapse."

Galland moved his headquarters to a railway carriage attached to the train which served as the Luftwaffe's operations center at Goldap, in East Prussia. It was close to Rominten Heath, where Goering had his personal headquarters, and not far from Rastenburg, where Hitler directed the over-all operations. Shortly after Galland's arrival Hitler decorated him with the so-called Diamonds to the Knight's Cross; he was one of the only two soldiers in Germany to receive it (the other was Moelders). Afterward he was summoned by Goering to a conference, but all they talked about was Galland's decoration. Goering asked to examine it, and the embarrassed Galland, who had fixed the cross around his neck with a girl's fancy garter, passed it across to the chortling Reich Marshal. Goering's face became serious as he looked at the diamonds, and he said:

"These aren't diamonds at all. They're just stones, ordinary stones. The Fuehrer has been swindled over this. He knows a lot about guns, battleships, and tanks, but he hasn't a clue about diamonds. Look here, Galland, I'll get

some for you. Then you'll see what diamonds really are. I
still have a few left."

To Galland's dismay (for Goering had once asked to see
his gold Spanish Cross from the Civil War and never returned it) he held onto the diamonds and only handed
back the fighter pilot's Knight's Cross. But some time later,
Galland was called to Carin Hall, and there Goering,
pleased as a child, was holding two sparkling decorations
in his hands.

"Look here," he said, "these are the Fuehrer's diamonds
and these are the Reich Marshal's. Do you see the difference?"

Galland had to admit he was right. The Reich Marshal's
had a beauty of their own, and compared with them the
Fuehrer's looked very inferior. He set off back to his headquarters with two sets of diamonds—"one for weekday and
one for Sunday wear."*

Galland came away from that meeting convinced that
Hermann Goering was tired of the war. He hardly mentioned it during their conversation. He was too busy talking about the diamonds, breeding programs for his bison,
and the latest acquisitions in his galleries. It was a moment
when Hitler was demanding from Jeschonnek and Bodenschatz (Goering's representatives at the Fuehrer's headquarters) all the aircraft they could find for the Russian
spring offensive. Rommel had come from North Africa to
ask for fighters and Stuka dive-bombers to bolster the
Afrika Korps in its offensive against the British Eighth
Army in Egypt. But there were no planes to spare. They
were needed for the fighter forces hitting at the RAF raiders over Germany. The last reserves were being dipped
into, and they were getting dangerously low. Goering did
not seem to care.

---

* There was a sequel to this incident. Hitler must have heard from
someone about the inferiority of his diamonds, and the next time
Galland was in his presence he said: "Galland I can now give you
the highest German decoration for bravery in the best quality.
Those I gave you before were only temporary. Hand them over."
Unfortunately, Galland was wearing Goering's diamonds, and he
passed them over convinced that Hitler would notice their superior
quality. He didn't. He held them in one hand while dangling new
ones in the other, and said of Goering's stones: "Those are just
ordinary stones I gave you. But these here are real diamonds. Take
them in exchange."

It was just about this time that Dr. Fritz Todt, who had had charge of the army rearmament and building program in Germany, died in a mysterious air crash in Russia, and Goering immediately applied to Hitler for the job, yet another one to add to his string of titles. Hitler refused to give it to him, but instead conferred it upon his architect, Albert Speer. At first cast down by this snub, Goering was soon mollified by Speer, who consented to call himself Minister of War Production under the Four Year Plan (of which Goering was the head). In April 1942, Speer, Milch, and other technicians also formed a Central Planning Board and elected Goering as chairman, for Speer shrewdly calculated that once he had the title, the Reich Marshal would not interfere.

It was a curious period in the Reich Marshal's career, and a sort of petulant boredom would perhaps best describe his condition. It was the beginning of his disillusionment with Adolf Hitler, for he was discovering at last that his hero had feet of clay. As he was to say later, "I was surprised to discover that the Fuehrer was not able to withstand setbacks." He had noticed that Hitler was becoming increasingly ill-tempered and unreasonable, but only with other people, never critical of himself. Yet the mistakes he had made!

As a man of many titles, Goering still signed most of the documents which kept the wheels turning in Germany. The acts and decrees which controlled labor, currency, rationing and the laws against black-marketing—although he was not averse to a little black-marketing himself—all had to be approved by him before they were passed into law. But he didn't begin to care what happened to them afterward. For him, the dynamic seemed to have gone out of the war, and the high patriotism with which he had first embraced National Socialism had been rudely disappointed by the way the Party had used the enthusiasm of the supporters who had brought it to power.

On March 21, 1942, he appointed his assistant, Fritz Sauckel, as Plenipotentiary General for Manpower, and on March 27 he signed an enabling decree which said:

"My manpower sections are hereby abolished. Their duties, recruitment and allocation of manpower, regulations for labor conditions, are taken over by [Sauckel]."

The power of life and death, and of enslavement, thus

passed out of his hands into those of a man who was prepared to use them ruthlessly. Theoretically, Goering was still to be consulted on all major decisions, just as he was to be made cognizant of all steps taken by the Central Planning Board, but in fact he was rarely present at the meetings when the decisions were made, and it was only when public speeches or pep talks were needed that Sauckel, Speer, or Milch asked for his help. So, though it was not because of squeamishness or conscience that he was no longer directly involved, he at least took no active part in the appalling acts of cruelty and murder which now became a commonplace in all parts of occupied Russia and Europe. He had divested himself of power over the Gestapo and the concentration camps in 1934, and now he washed his hands clean of the gas ovens. Now aware that Goering was no longer watching, Sauckel and Koch let themselves go. The trains began to fill with slave labor for the factories as never before, and the order was that the slaves should be worked until they dropped. The Jews in the Russian factories were not even to be given that option, but shipped straight off to the extermination centers.

When Hermann Goering first heard of this, he protested. As a result, for a time Jews were allowed to go on working in particular war industries, and 300,000 Jews were still employed in Polish factories, for instance, up until the end of September 1942. Then, on Hitler's orders, the OKW issued an order on October 12, 1942, that all Jews, no matter what their skills, be replaced by Aryans.

From that moment the gas ovens took over.

In the days before the outbreak of war, Hermann Goering had toured the air-defense zone in the Ruhr and Rhineland and boasted that the measures taken were so effective that "if any enemy plane gets through and bombs our cities, you can call me Meier." It was a remark which was now beginning to haunt him, for Meier was what millions of Germans had begun mockingly to name him. The bombers were getting through.

On the night of May 30–31, 1942, the bomber fleet of the RAF raided the Rhineland city of Cologne and dropped fifteen hundred tons of bombs upon it. The damage was enormous, not only to Cologne but to Hermann Goering's relations with Adolf Hitler.

The next day, at the Fuehrer's situation conference, the naval and military spokesmen took their turns in reporting on the previous day's events—a U-boat raid on an Allied convoy in the Atlantic, the progress of the big battle around Kharkov. Then it came the turn of General Jeschonnek, Goering's Chief of Staff, to read out the Luftwaffe report, and Karl Bodenschatz, who was with him, well understood why the hands that held the sitrep paper were shaking as Jeschonnek held it before him.

Bodenschatz has described the scene that followed, as Jeschonnek began to read the report of the RAF raid, and was at once asked how heavy it was.

"According to preliminary reports," said the general, "we estimate that two hundred enemy aircraft have penetrated our defenses. The damage is heavy . . . we are still waiting for final estimates."

It was at this point, Bodenschatz said later,† that Hitler's temper gave way.

"You are still waiting for final estimates?" he cried. "And the Luftwaffe thinks that there were two hundred enemy aircraft? The Luftwaffe has probably been asleep last night . . . but I have not been asleep. I stay awake when one of my cities is under fire. And I thank the Almighty that I can rely on my gauleiter, even if the Luftwaffe deceives me. Let me tell you what Gauleiter Grobe has to say. Listen, listen. I ask you to listen carefully. *There were a thousand or more English aircraft* . . . Do you hear? *A thousand, twelve hundred* . . . maybe more!"

While Hitler was saying: "Herr Goering, of course, is not here; of course not," pointedly omitting his title, Bodenschatz slipped out of the room and telephoned his chief at Veldenstein, warning him that there was trouble and that he had better come at once.

"When Goering arrived, stretching out his hand to Hitler in greeting, the Fuehrer ignored him," Bodenschatz told Frischauer. "Rudely, in front of junior officers, he cut the Reich Marshal. A stammering, bewildered Goering was lost at the Fuehrer's headquarters, where he had few friends. Jeschonnek, his favorite Jeschonnek, could hardly look him in the eye. The young Luftwaffe general was an ardent Nazi who could not resist the spell which Hitler cast

† In a conversation with Willi Frischauer.

over many members of his entourage. The dispersal of the Luftwaffe, the weakening of the once all-powerful force which he represented, had thrown the Chief of Staff off his balance. Hitler's contemptuous references to the Air Force hurt him deeply. From Goering, who was himself downcast, prostrate, he received little/comfort."‡

The truth was, of course, that Germany was not geared for fighting a defensive war. There was neither the raw material nor the gasoline to keep the huge war machine going, and the succession of victories had stretched rather than eased German resources. For the conquered lands were also short of matériel of the kind Germany needed. The basis of Hitler's strategy had always been the quick surprise attack at his enemy's weakest points, and it had won him the campaigns against Holland, Belgium, Norway, Denmark, Poland, and France. If there were any logic in the world, this strategy should have won him the war, because the British in 1940 would have recognized quickly that they were beaten and sued for peace, and so would the Russians in 1941. That was the trouble. Neither had been prepared to accept the dire facts of their situation, and had insisted on fighting on. And Hermann Goering was well aware what that meant—a long war. And a long war was something Germany could not win.

The Luftwaffe which Goering had created for Adolf Hitler was not designed to protect the German people from enemy bombs. It was not a defensive weapon at all. It was created to strike terror in the enemy, psychologically and physically, and when Adolf Hitler screamed at him for failing to save Cologne from RAF bombs, when Adolf Galland pleaded for more fighters to ward off the British and American raiders, they missed the point. That had never been the Luftwaffe's raison d'être. It had been built to win wars for Germany, and not to save them from defeat. By the end of 1941, Hermann Goering could have told Adolf Hitler, and anyone else who cared to listen, that so far as Germany was concerned the war was over, bar the actual fighting; there would be campaign victories for the German armies, but once Britain had repulsed the peace overtures of 1940 and Russia had withstood the disasters of mid-summer 1941, Germany could not win the

‡ *Goering.* Willi Frischauer.

war, and what happened from now on would be nothing but the reflex actions of a dead man.

"We had an air raid over Carin Hall in the fall of 1942," said Thomas von Kantzow, "and we went down to the tunnel shelters which Hermann had had constructed underneath the house. Emmy was there, and so was Hermann's sister, Olga. She had enrolled herself as a Luftwaffe nurse and had just come back from service in Russia. Her description of the winter conditions there were terrible, and they affected us all. Hermann looked most melancholy. Emmy, who was always the most optimistic and cheerful person, suddenly said: 'When we've won the war, do you know what I'm going to do?' We never discovered what it was, because Hermann interrupted her. In a loud whisper, so that the servants next door shouldn't hear him, he said: 'Why can't you realize that we are not going to win the war? It is already lost—but the Fuehrer refuses to recognize the fact.' Aunt Olga looked quite shocked, and Emmy burst into tears. He immediately rushed over to her, because he hated hurting her, and put his arms around her, and he started crying too. It was a very sad sight and my heart bled for them."

All through the winter of 1942–43 things got worse, for Germany and for Goering. The nation was being hammered day and night by the Anglo-American bomber forces. In the Mediterranean, the Luftwaffe's incessant attacks upon Britain's island base of Malta had been successfully withstood, and at El Alamein the British Eighth Army Commander, General Bernard L. Montgomery had begun his successful assault upon Field Marshal Erwin Rommel's Afrika Korps. In Russia Adolf Hitler had made the fatal error of trying to hold onto Stalingrad and capture the Caucasus at the same time, and now the chickens were coming home to roost. Stalingrad and the German Army inside it were besieged.

Toward the end of 1942, Rommel flew from North Africa to the Fuehrer's headquarters at Rastenburg to make a personal report on the situation, and it was grim. RAF Spitfires and Hurricanes operating out of Malta* had

* They had been flown there from the decks of the U.S. Carrier *Wasp*.

wiped the skies clean and British supply convoys were now once more passing through the Mediterranean. Rommel's own troops had been pushed out of Egypt by the Eighth Army and were falling back into Tripolitania. Meanwhile, the Allies had begun landing troops in Morocco and Algeria. Rommel contended that his Afrika Korps was in danger of being trapped by a giant enemy squeeze play, and he strongly recommended that he should get out with his troops and their arms before they were driven into the sea.

"Abandon Tripoli?" shouted Hitler. "Never, never, never! Not if it costs a hundred thousand lives!"

The following day, a chastened Rommel promised that his troops would fight until the end, but demanded in return that he be furnished with fresh supplies of tanks, guns, and other armaments. Turning to Goering, who had been summoned to the meeting, Hitler curtly told him he had *carte blanche* to give the Afrika Korps commander anything he needed.

"I shall attend to it all myself," Goering said grandly.

In fact, he knew (and Hitler certainly did too, though he would have refused to admit it) that the supplies were simply not there to give. Everything was needed for the Russian front and what few reserves remained were being kept in a state of readiness in case the so-called Second Front against Western Europe was opened by the Allies. He had already committed his own pet troops, the Herman Goering Panzer Division, to the North African campaign,† and there was little more he could do. But instead of talking frankly to Rommel, who was, after all, a man who could look a hard fact in the face, Goering put on an act.

He called for his special train, invited Emmy and Frau Rommel along, and accompanied Field Marshal Rommel to Rome. Rommel was afterward to say that it was one of the most exasperating experiences of his life. Like many another German army general, he cordially disliked Goering for his lordly manner, his foppish clothes and jewelry, his airy way of talking about the war, and his general insouciance. Rommel knew that he faced almost certain

---

† The division was later captured almost intact by the Anglo-American forces in Tunis.

defeat and disaster when he got back to Africa, and he writhed in torment over Goering's incessant conversations about pictures, pottery, animals, etc., anything but the war and the supplies he so desperately needed.

Frau Rommel was even more appalled by Goering's behavior, and by Emmy's slavish devotion to him. She thought of him as a great, fat *poseur* and was disgusted with his ostentation, his emerald tie clip, his watch-case dotted with precious stones, and his enormous diamond ring. "You will be interested in this," he told her proudly, "it is one of the most valuable stones in the world." Later Goering went off on a search around Rome for pictures and when he came back he described how he had beaten down a dealer who had tried to sell him a painting. "They call me the Maecenas of the Third Reich," he said. But he avoided all mention of supplies in his private talk with Rommel. To both the field marshal and his worried wife his "antics" made him seem like a Nero who was fiddling while Tripolitania (if not yet Rome) was burning.

Stalingrad was burning, too. The smoke from fired buildings hung thick in the leaden winter sky as Russian shells and bombs pounded the Sixth Army of General Friedrich Paulus, a force of 300,000 men trapped inside the city. The army had already worked out a breakout plan (code name Thunderclap), but Hitler refused to be convinced that it was necessary; instead, he ordered the Fourth Panzer Army under General Hermann Hoth to go to the rescue of the beleaguered army. Paulus reluctantly agreed and tele-typed a message that he was prepared to hold on. But General Wolfram von Richthofen, whose Fourth Air Fleet would have the job of keeping the Stalingrad army supplied with food and arms, gave it as his opinion that it was not a feasible operation with the planes he had at his disposal.

Unfortunately, there was no one at the Fuehrer's head-quarters strong enough to change Hitler's mind. Goering was at Carin Hall, Milch was on a tour of the factories, and Jeschonnek was too terrified of the great leader's wrath to risk more than a mild expression of doubt. The new Chief of Staff of the German Army, General Kurt Zeitzler, strongly recommended the implementation of Operation Thunderclap, but his views were brushed aside. To Hitler, a breakout was as bad as a defeat and he ordered Paulus to hold on at all costs. By November 22, 1942, there was little else that the Sixth Army could do, for the Russians had locked the ring tightly around Stalingrad and no land army could possibly break out or through.

In many German generals' memoirs, the failure of the Paulus army to escape from Stalingrad has been squarely placed on Hermann Goering's shoulders, and corroborated by Allied historians. Fred Majdalany in *The Fall of Fortress Europe*, for instance, writes:

"The last nail in what was to be the coffin of the doomed Sixth Army was hammered in with characteristic irresponsibility by Reichsmarschall Goering, who finally sabotaged the efforts of Zeitzler to make Hitler see sense by airily assuring him that the Luftwaffe could keep the Sixth Army supplied by air."

In fact, by the time Goering was consulted, it was too late for Paulus to do anything but stand and fight and die. His guilt is a negative one, a sin of omission. He was not at Rastenburg to argue with Hitler when he should have been. But by that time his influence on the Fuehrer had all but waned, and Hitler's mood, in any case, was such that he was developing a desire to see Germans suffer and Germans die.

Now he ordered Goering to his headquarters and demanded information about the state of the Luftwaffe's transport fleets. Goering's experts had already furnished him with technical information about what would be needed if an "air bridge" was established between the German Army proper and the besieged Sixth Army. Three hundred tons of fuel, 30 tons of munitions, and 150 tons of food would have to be flown in every day, enough to fill 800 Ju 52 transports. The Luftwaffe possessed only 750 Ju 52s in all, and 100 of these were supplying Rommel's army in North Africa.‡ He now repeated these figures to Hitler, who immediately asked him whether bombers could be adapted for transport purposes. Goering was very bitter about what happened from that moment on.

"I explained to the Fuehrer," he said later, "that while

‡ "If I must criticize myself," Goering had said, the previous September, "it is for not realizing how important an air transport fleet is." But the building program he had set in motion was producing only sixty planes a month.

bombers could certainly be turned into transport planes, it
was not advisable, and that, in any case, the bombers were
being used for action against Britain. But the Fuehrer insisted. He was determined to be able to say to the German
people that he had saved Stalingrad. I would like to have
done so myself, but I knew it was impossible. I had talked
to [General] von Richthofen [Commander of the Fourth
Air Fleet] and I was in possession of all the facts. But
when he was in a mood of this kind there was no gainsay-
ing him. And certainly we had to do something. We just
couldn't let the men in Stalingrad die. I had my own
friends there and I wanted to help.* But Hitler went too
far."

For some time Goering and Milch between them had
been trying to hold onto a wing of new bombers, Heinkel
177s, which they were reluctant to commit to the rigors of
a Russian winter and were keeping in reserve for the spring
offensive. But someone had tipped off the Fuehrer that the
planes had started coming off the production lines.

"He told me that if we gathered together all available
transport planes, including Lufthansa civil planes, plus
sufficient bombers, we could keep Stalingrad supplied,"
Goering went on. "He looked at me and said: 'I know that
you have a wing of He 177s. I have heard that they are
training for the spring offensive. You can tell them that
spring has already arrived. They can finish their training in
Russia.' I protested. The He 177 was a beautiful plane, our
answer to the American Flying Fortress. It was not built
for carrying milk cans. But he would not listen to me. 'I
want everything, everything, do you hear, committed. If
you use enough planes, we can easily keep Stalingrad supplied until the spring.'"

On November 24, Goering called a meeting of his staff
aboard his armored train, the Asian, parked in a siding to
the northeast of Berlin. When the Reich Marshal entered,
his face was grim and he barely greeted his generals. One
of them (General Wolfgang Vorwald, chief of the technical section) afterward said:

* The Sixth Army under Paulus consisted of twenty German and
two Romanian divisions, plus the Luftwaffe's own 9th Anti-Aircraft
Division. Its commander was Major General Wolfgang Pickert, an
old crony of Goering's.

"When he came in, he told us in stony tones that the Sixth Army would be supplied by the Luftwaffe. Every available transport plane and bomber would be used in the operation. He had already told the courier staff to arrange it."

There was no discussion. No one pointed out the vast difficulties that must be faced flying a shuttle service through Russian flak under the appalling weather conditions now prevailing in Russia. It would not have mattered if they had done so. Goering had already brought up these objections with the Fuehrer, and had been angrily waved aside.

At 5 A.M. on November 25, 1942, Hitler signaled Paulus that the Luftwaffe was coming. Three months later the Russian steppes were littered with the broken, stranded, or burned remnants of 1,200 German bombers and transport planes. They had been hit by Russian flak, shot down by Russian fighters, or immobilized on the ground by the relentless cold of the Russian winter. Meanwhile, in Stalingrad, the Sixth Army (those of them who had not died of wounds, hunger, or frostbite) waited for the end. But still Hitler cracked the whip over Goering and Milch, goading them to keep up the supply flights, and at the same time beseeching Paulus to hold on. He even promoted the general to field marshal in the crazy hope that this would stiffen the backbone of the troops.

"He asked for a miracle, and he thinks one will still happen," wrote Milch in his day book.

By this time Hitler had definitely decided that Goering was not the man who could provide him with his miracle. Each day, as the number of flights into Stalingrad diminished, he ranted and raved at the Reich Marshal, berating him for incompetence and his pilots for cowardice. Goering crept around Rastenburg like a whipped dog, aware that the generals and junior officers alike were sneering at him. Finally, he skulked off to Carin Hall for days at a time, and only came back when Hitler personally or Bodenschatz urgently summoned him back to the presence.

Meanwhile, Hitler had called in Milch and sent him to the Russian front to attempt to put some order into the chaos into which the "air bridge" operation had fallen. But there was little Milch could do, and it was in any case too late. Paulus sent out the last signal that he and his men were surrendering. It was the most crushing defeat of the war for Germany, and there was never any chance afterward that victory could be gained.

There had to be a scapegoat, and, since Hitler was not prepared to blame himself, Goering was the chosen target. So far as the generals were concerned, it was a popular choice. Shortly after the surrender, Field Marshal Milch arrived at the Fuehrer's headquarters and Hitler asked him whether he had done all he could possibly have done to save Stalingrad.

"All and still more," said one of the panzer generals who had been with Milch in Russia. He went on to say that if only the field marshal had arrived earlier, all might have been well.

"Yes," said Hitler grimly. "That's my misfortune."

Milch shook his head. "I didn't fulfill my mission."

"Milch," said Hitler, "you fulfilled your mission but you were called in too late."

Again Milch shook his head. If he had been in Paulus's place, he would have ignored the Fuehrer's orders and broken out of Stalingrad while there was still time.

At this, Hitler's manner changed. He said coldly that if he thought that, he was putting the cart before the horse, meaning that he was putting the lives of the Sixth Army before the needs of Germany.

Milch said: "But my Fuehrer, it would have been worth it. One field marshal less, perhaps, but 300,000 soldiers saved."

Hitler's expression was so evil when he said these words that Milch decided to beat a hasty retreat.

Even Goering now accepted the fact that he had lost all influence with Hitler.

"I certainly got the blame," said Goering later. "From that time on, the relationship between the Fuehrer and myself steadily deteriorated."

XXIII. ELEVENTH HOUR

It must have caused Goering some ironic amusement that no one was more disturbed by the prospect of his imminent eclipse than his erstwhile friend and enemy, Josef Goebbels. Moreover, Albert Speer also manifested sudden alarm when he heard that the Fuehrer was angry with the Reich Marshal. The truth was that both of them realized that, in the present situation, Goering's disappearance from the high councils of the Nazi Party would benefit no one else but Hitler's favorite bootlicker, Martin Bormann.

The Reich Marshal called a meeting of his General Staff on February 22, 1943, the first since the fall of Stalingrad, and announced that all the old types of aircraft which the Luftwaffe had been using must now be cast aside in favor of newer weapons. Germany had need of the big four-motor bombers which the British and Americans were now using.

He was in a chastened mood, and he blamed himself for the way in which the Luftwaffe had slipped behind in its conceptions and its building program.

"I must bear the guilt," he said, "because my trust was so great."

But Milch, who was present at the meeting, got the impression that the heart had gone out of the Reich Marshal and that his mind was no longer engaged with the war. Shortly after the conference broke up, Speer came in for a talk with Milch, who told him his feelings about Goering's lassitude and general air of insouciance. It was the moment when Speer and Goebbels were envisioning the creation of a new Inner War Cabinet to take over the direction of the war, and their idea was to make Hermann Goering its titular head, since they believed that his influence with Hitler was still great enough to make an impact upon the

Fuehrer. Goering was furious with Goebbels at this time because he had closed his favorite restaurant, Horcher's, for austerity reasons, so Speer was sent ahead to prepare the way. He hurried up to Goering's summer house on the Obersalzberg and had a conversation with him. The next day he called Goebbels and warned him that the Reich Marshal was in a "resigned mood." He had greeted Speer in his dressing gown, and played with a handful of jewels throughout their talk.

"Goering was at first somewhat ill-humored and distrustful about a number of things on which he had been misinformed," Goebbels wrote in his diary. "In the course of the afternoon, however, he agreed fully and wholeheartedly to my proposals as transmitted by Speer. He wishes urgently to talk to me before his trip to Italy. I have decided to fly to see him next Monday . . . Speer is very expectant and hopeful . . . If I should succeed in winning Goering over entirely to the new war policy, that would be a positive achievement . . . Let's hope perfect solidarity among the men closest to the Fuehrer will result from our meeting. We shall then be able to place a personal guard of collaboration at the Fuehrer's disposal such as he had only in the greatest periods of our struggle for power."

At 4 P.M. on the afternoon of March 2, 1943, Speer and Goebbels drove up the mountain to Goering's house, passing the Fuehrer's residence on the way. "It seems to be sleeping the sleep of Snow White," Goebbels commented. Goering came out to greet them as they arrived. He was "wearing a somewhat baroque outfit, which, if you didn't know him, one would have found a bit comic. But that's the way he is, and one must put up with his idiosyncrasies. They even have a certain charm . . ."

The visitors quickly found that Goering was extremely pessimistic about the state of the war. He thought that Africa would at any moment fall under the complete domination of the Anglo-Americans (as indeed it shortly did), and that there was no hope of sapping the strength of the Soviet Union, since it seemed to have an inexhaustible supply of weapons and men. In addition, he inveighed against the hated Von Ribbentrop for having got Germany into the war in the first place.

"Goering consistently claims that this war is Ribbentrop's doing," Goebbels wrote, "and that he never made any serious attempt at a modus vivendi with England simply because he has an inferiority complex."

He then attacked the generals at GHQ, the influences around Hitler, and expressed great concern over the Fuehrer's condition.

"He too feels that the Fuehrer has aged fifteen years during three and a half years of war," Goebbels wrote. "It is tragic that the Fuehrer had become such a recluse and leads such an unhealthy life. He never gets out into the fresh air. He never relaxes. He sits in his bunker, worries and broods . . . It is the duty of the Fuehrer's closest friends in time of need to gather about him and form a solid phalanx around his person."

Then came the moment when Goebbels and Speer got down to brass tacks and proposed that in the future the political leadership of the Reich should pass into their joint hands. The chicanery of the Fuehrer's bootlickers, always butting in and making malicious gossip, must be stopped, they said. With Goering's help, it could be done.

"While talking, I gained the impression that Goering was visibly stimulated by what I said," wrote Goebbels in his diary. "He became very enthusiastic about my proposals and immediately asked how we were to proceed specifically. I suggested that he make a number of nominations and I would try to win over the rest. We won't tell them about our real intentions—gradually to freeze out the Committee of Three* and transfer its powers to the Ministerial Council. That would only create unnecessary trouble. We have no other ambition but to support each other and to form a solid phalanx around the Fuehrer."

Goebbels and Speer left Obersalzberg "very happy that a clear basis of mutual trust was established with Goering. I believe that the Fuehrer too will be very happy about this."

Unfortunately for all of them, the RAF chose that night to raid Berlin, and 250 four-motored planes dropped 600 tons of bombs on the capital, destroying 20,000 houses, making 35,000 homeless, and killing 700 citizens. Adolf Hitler was not happy at all.

---

* The Committee of Three, who spent most of their time with Hitler, consisted of Field Marshal Wilhelm Keitel, chief of the Supreme Command of the Wehrmacht, Hans Heinrich Lammers, chief of Hitler's Chancellery for Political Affairs, and Martin Bormann, chief of Hitler's chancellery for Nazi Party affairs.

"Where is the Reich Marshal?" he cried. "What is he doing about a reply to this terror?"

But Goering was not there to answer. He had hurried off to Rome.

When Albert Speer described Goering as being in a "resigned mood" he was badly understating his condition. He was, in fact, moiling in the depths of despair, hating every moment of the war, and desperately frightened about what was going to happen to his family now that defeat was looming ahead for Germany.

Something which Goebbels had said during their meeting must have considerably disturbed him, though the Reich Propaganda Minister did not appear to have noticed. Writing in his diary, Goebbels said:

"Goering realizes perfectly what is in store for all of us if we show any weakness in this war. He has no illusions about that. On the Jewish question, especially, we have taken a position from which there is no escape. That is all to the good. Experience shows that a movement and a people who have burned their bridges fight with much greater determination than those who can still retreat."

But Goering knew that Emmy, at least, had not burned all her bridges. She was still helping her Jewish friends, and so long as Goering's position in the Reich was strong that had been all right. But by now Bormann, Himmler and the SS knew about his quarrels with Hitler, and realized that he was vulnerable. It was no moment to exacerbate the Fuehrer's rage over the weakness of the Luftwaffe by having tattle reaching him about Goering's wife's efforts on behalf of the hated Jews.

"We are now definitely pushing the Jews out of Berlin," wrote Goebbels in his diary about this time (March 2, 1943). "They were suddenly rounded up last Saturday, and are to be carted off to the East as quickly as possible. Unfortunately, our better circles, especially the intellectuals, once again have failed to understand our policy about the Jews and in some cases have even taken their part. As a result our plans were disclosed prematurely, and a lot of Jews slipped through our hands. But we will catch them."

Among those who had evaded the roundup was a certain Rose Korwan, and she was a friend of Emmy Goering. She was a Jewish actress who had first worked with Emmy in their early days in Stuttgart, and they had later shared rooms together in Weimar when they both worked for the National Theater. The friendship had survived their transfer to Berlin and Emmy's marriage to Goering.

"Perhaps because of her evident disappointment with me," Emmy wrote later, "I tried not to lose sight of her and as I tried to stay close to her just precisely because she was a Jewess, our friendship became from then on still closer. Every year, on her birthday, I invited her to come to our palace on the Potsdamer Platz. In agreement with Hermann I offered her presents and later, when her resources were beginning to run out, I made her gifts of money. When Edda was born Rosette gave me the baby's first nappies, which she embroidered with a little rose. Hermann joked about it, recalling the proverb: 'The first nappies should come from a Jew.'"

As conditions for Jews in Berlin became more and more fraught, Emmy tried every way she knew to persuade her friend to leave Germany. But she would not go. What she did not reveal to Emmy was that she was in love with a Jew and would not leave him. Meanwhile, Emmy had arranged to pay Rose Korwan a weekly allowance of fifteen marks, which she provided herself but arranged to have paid out by an official postal order so that the counterfoil, with Goering's name on it, would protect her from interference.

But then, just before the roundup of Jews in Berlin began, Rose came to Emmy and told her the news. She had married her Jewish lover; she now asked protection for both of them. Emmy rang up Goering (who was then at Rominten Heath) to ask his help, and was surprised and hurt when he cut her off in mid-sentence. Shortly afterward, he arrived in Berlin and apologized for his abruptness, but explained that Robert Kropp, the valet, had come to him a few days before with some unpleasant news. Not only was the Gestapo now tapping their telephone line, but Martin Bormann was too. What was more, Kropp had informed him that his personal bodyguard was a Bormann spy.

He groaned when he heard about Emmy's latest entanglement with Rose Korwan, but agreed to have the weekly allowance changed to her new name. He also told her to warn her friends of the anti-Jewish drive that was about to begin, and to suggest that they make themselves scarce until the heat was off.

It was a warning which gave Rose and her husband a few months of respite. But then one day Rose's husband got involved in a quarrel in the street with an SS man, and was taken to Gestapo headquarters. It was discovered that he was a Jew who had committed the heinous offense of not wearing his yellow star of David. Rose Korwan rang up Emmy, who was now at Carin Hall, and asked her in a flood of tears to come once more to the rescue. The indefatigable actress immediately put in a call to Heinrich Himmler.

"The chief of the SS was by no means pleased at my call," she wrote later. " 'You must realize, Frau Goering,' he replied, 'that millions of German women have their husbands at the front and do not know what has happened to them. How can you expect that I can concern myself with the fate of one particular Jew?' I begged and implored him to do me this one personal favor."

He was back on the telephone an hour later. The Jew was a dangerous and deranged man, who needed looking after.

"We will send him to Theresienstadt, which is one of our best camps," he said. "He will be very well off there."

When she heard the news, Rose Korwan cried: "If he is sent to a camp, I want to go with him. Can you at least arrange that for me?"

That evening, when Goering returned to Carin Hall, Emmy told him the story. He went to the telephone and spoke to Himmler.

"After some equivocations, Himmler agreed to send the woman to the camp," Emmy wrote later. "Everything would be all right, he assured us. He would personally see that the couple got a room, and even someone to clean it for them. His promise set both our minds at rest."

She had a coat and a dress made for Rose and bought a complete new set of underwear. Her other actress friend, Jenny, went with the two Jews to the station to see them off. But then she telephoned Emmy in great distress. The train in which they had traveled had not gone in the Theresienstadt direction, but the opposite way.

"I told Hermann, who called Himmler," wrote Emmy. "He could not reach him, but during the evening received a

note informing him that Himmler had telephoned to
Theresienstadt and that Rosette and her husband had arrived there safely."

Of course they had not. They had gone straight to the
gas ovens. But whether Goering was aware of that fact or
not Emmy never discovered. If he was, it would have provided him with one more proof that his stock and influence
in the Third Reich were now seriously diminished.

On the night of July 24–25, 1943, 800 heavy RAF
bombers crossed the North Sea from Britain, passed over
Lübeck, and arrived over Hamburg from the northeast.
Hamburg, with a million inhabitants, was Germany's most
important port. Its docks, central harbor and inner city
were bombed with acute and devastating precision. The
enemy formations flew in close and met hardly any opposition from German flak or night fighters.

The German radar system had been outwitted. For the
first time the British had tried out a simple but effective
trick by dropping bundles of tinfoil from the skies, which,
drifting through the darkness, completely "blinded" the
radar defenses. Then down came 1,500 tons of bombs,
which set Hamburg afire.

The following morning U.S. Air Force bombers swept
in to pound the city, and that night the RAF attacked
again. The "round-the-clock" bombing offensive had
begun, and by the end of a week of it Hamburg was a raging inferno.

"Horror reveals itself in the howling and raging of the
fires," wrote the Hamburg police chief, "in the hellish din
of exploding bombs and in the death-cries of the tormented
people. Words fail before the extent of the terror which
shook the population for ten days and ten nights. The
marks left on the face of the town and of the people can
never be erased."

Neither Hitler nor Goering visited Hamburg† But Karl
Bodenschatz went to see the damage, and came back with
a shattering report.

---

† Hitler never once left his redoubt to see what Allied bombers
were doing to the German cities and people. He was always completely unconcerned with their sufferings. Goering later on, on the
other hand, visited several badly bombed cities.

"In Goering's office at the Fuehrer's HQ, he told us repeatedly that something drastic had to be done, that such a disaster must never happen again," wrote Adolf Galland later. "No objection was raised; nor were there any differences of opinion as to what was to be done now. Problems arising from the raids on Hamburg were discussed in the presence of the Chief of the General Staff [General Günther] Korten, Jeschonnek's successor,‡ the General Chief of Aircraft, Milch . . . and many officers of the Luftwaffe."

It was Goering who summed up the result of the conference. It marked a vital turning point in German thinking. The Luftwaffe, after its offensive phase, in which it had achieved outstanding success, he said, *must now change over to the defense against the West*. It should be possible to stop the Allied raids against the Reich by concentrating all forces and their effects on this one aim.

The most important task of the Luftwaffe now, said Goering, was not only to protect the lives and property of the German people who lived in the threatened cities, but also to preserve the potential of the war industry. Under the protection of increased fighter forces concentrating on air defense, the Luftwaffe would soon recover the strength to attack once more, and then Germany could strike its own counterblows.

"Never before and never again did I witness such determination and agreement among the circle of those responsible for the leadership of the Luftwaffe," wrote Galland later. "It was as though under the impact of the Hamburg catastrophe everyone had put aside either personal or departmental ambitions. There was no conflict between General Staff and war industry, no rivalry between bombers and fighters; only the one common will to do everything in this critical hour for the defense of the Reich and to leave nothing undone to prevent a second national misfortune of this dimension."

Everyone seemed to be impressed by the new vigor and determination of Hermann Goering. To Galland "he seemed to be carried away by the general mood. He left us alone for a while, and went into the Fuehrer's bunker to get the 'go ahead' for the measures we had planned. We

‡ Jeschonnek had blown his brains out in despair over the way the war was going.

remained behind, tense with expectation. In this hour the fate of the Luftwaffe was decided. The Supreme Commander himself realized that our air leadership against the West had taken a wrong course, and like us appeared to be convinced and also determined to put the helm about."

All of the air force leadership now realized that everything depended on the last word which Hitler would have to say. Galland was convinced that he would pass and support the findings of the meeting with the whole weight of his authority.

Then the door of the Fuehrer's bunker opened, and Goering came out followed by Hitler's aide-de-camp. Goering did not look at them or say a word, but marched alone into an adjoining room. The assembled Generals looked at each other in amazement. What had happened?

After a while, Goering called Galland in to see him, and General Dietrich Pelz, commander of the bomber fleets, went with him.

"We were met with a shattering picture," wrote Galland later. "Goering had completely broken down. With his head buried in his arms on the table, he moaned some indistinguishable words. We stood there for some time in embarrassment until at last he pulled himself together and said we were witnessing his deepest moments of despair. The Fuehrer had lost faith in him. All the suggestions from which he had expected a radical change in the situation of the war in the air had been rejected; the Fuehrer had announced that the Luftwaffe had disappointed him too often, and a changeover from offensive to defensive in the air against the West was out of the question."

There it was. Goering looked up at them with tears in his eyes. Then he told them that Hitler had given the Luftwaffe a last chance to restore its prestige by a resumption of the air attacks against England, but this time on a larger scale.

"Now as before," wrote Galland, "the motto was still— attack. Terror could only be smashed by counterterror."

Suddenly, Goering rose and straightened his shoulders. He wiped the tears from his eyes, and stared at his two pilot generals defiantly.

"The Fuehrer has made me realize our mistake," he said. "The Fuehrer is always right. We must deal such mighty blows to our enemy in the West that he will never dare to risk another raid like Hamburg. General Pelz, I herewith appoint you assault leader against England."

Goering hurried off to Rominten Heath. The generals trooped out, whipped-dog expressions on all their faces. The Fuehrer had spoken, and they proposed to obey his orders—even though they realized that nothing could more certainly lose Germany the war.

"But why," asked Emmy Goering of her husband, at one of these moments of crisis, "do you stand it? Why don't you resign?"

Albert Speer had the explanation for that. "There was a time later when I had to tell the Fuehrer that I could not carry out his orders," he said. "I offered to resign. But he would not accept that. He told me to go away on leave, instead. He simply could not stand the possibility of losing face by my resignation. It was even more so with Goering. Goering was still very popular. To have allowed him to resign would have been a slap in the face for Hitler, and he would never have allowed it. But neither would he accept Goering's advice. It was always a difficult situation. One did not know quite what to do."

In Albert Speer's case (but this was in the last weeks of the war) he simply disobeyed Hitler's orders and followed his own policy. But Goering could not do this. He was surrounded by too many generals. In any case, as he was to show more and more in the days to come, it was simply not in him to disobey the Fuehrer. He would prevaricate and procrastinate in order to avoid a confrontation, but once given, Hitler's command was still for Goering the voice of God. He had given his word to serve him, and there was never any doubt in his mind that he would continue to do so until the end.

But to serve him heart and soul was an urge that no longer existed. From now on, he did nothing to kill off the Hitler regime, but neither did he work very hard to keep it alive.

In the months that followed, Hermann Goering played little part in the darkening destiny of the German Reich. Like a suddenly ignited rocket, he would fizz unexpectedly through the sky, scattering sparks and making loud noises, and then he would be seen no more for weeks at a time. He was shooting at Schorfheide when the Allied troops disembarked in Normandy on D-Day June 6, 1944, and he was not present at the Fuehrer's headquarters to hear Hitler's fury boil over at the revelation that Germany had only 327 planes to oppose the landings.

When he met Adolf Galland or Erhard Milch nowadays, he rowed angrily with them. To Galland, he repeated that the German fighter pilots nowadays were a bunch of incompetents and cowards and so enraged the young general that he tore his Knight's Cross from around his neck and flung it to the ground. After his most heated encounter with Milch,* the two of them barely spoke to each other. But when Goering met other officers, he made no secret of what he thought of his second-in-command.

"What is this Milch?" he said one day to his new chief of staff, General Werner Kreipe. "A fart out of my arsehole. First he wanted to play the part of my crown prince, now he wants to be my usurper."

Sometimes, as if galvanized—as he probably was, by an extra dose of pills—he would rush out of Carin Hall or Burg Veldenstein and suddenly appear in Nuremberg or Düsseldorf or Bremen, or some other city which had been visited by the Anglo-American wrath from above. Galland, Milch, Speer, Goebbels, and Himmler, all those whose feelings for him now ranged between resentment and contempt, were piqued to discover that with the general public he was just as popular as ever. The people slapped him on the shoulders and cheered him when he came among them and commiserated over their bomb sufferings. One night Albert Speer came into a Berlin air raid shelter during a raid and saw a crowd sitting around Hermann Goering.

"His face was beaming in the reflection of their evident admiration," Speer said later. "He was only too obviously their great hero. And after he had left them, I heard them saying to each other: 'He's a good fellow, *der Dicke*. He cares. There are others who don't.' It was an obvious refer-

---

* It was over the use of the new German jet-propelled Messerschmitts, now beginning to come off the production lines after long and largely unnecessary delays. Milch (like Galland) wanted the new planes for use as fighters against the Allied bombers. Goering agreed with Hitler that they should be adapted as bombers, a totally stupid misuse of a revolutionary new plane.

ence to Adolf Hitler, for whom it now no longer mattered whether they lived or died."

"They should have been throwing tomatoes at him," said Adolf Galland wrathfully, "and instead they shook him by the hand."

He was at his own headquarters on his armored train, preparing for a forthcoming conference with Mussolini, when, on July 20, 1944, a bomb burst in the bunker at Rastenburg. Staff Colonel Werner von Stauffenberg had placed a primed briefcase near Hitler, intending to blow him to smithereens and launch a military revolt against the regime.

The bomb killed General Schmundt and General Korten, two of the Fuehrer's military aides, and burst Karl Bodenschatz's eardrums and burned his hands. But Hitler lost only one eardrum and injured a hand. In the subsequent Gestapo purge, hundreds of generals were taken out and killed, while others who were national heroes (like Field Marshal Rommel) were given the option of suicide.

One of those rounded up by the SS was Goering's nephew Ernest, the son of his beautiful sister-in-law, Ilse. For the last time, Goering decided that he would use his influence on Hitler and save the young man. He went straight to the Fuehrer's headquarters and, ignoring Bormann, who tried to bar him, rushed in to Hitler's bunker. He came out smiling, and said to Bormann:

"My nephew is to be released at once. It was ridiculous to think that a relative of mine could be mixed up with that *Gesindel*" (mob). A few days later, he was back in Carin Hall, surrounded by his adoring womenfolk, Emmy; his sister, Olga; his sisters-in-law, Elsa Sonnemann and Ilse Goering, basking in the sunshine of their admiration.

They were still there on January 12, 1945, for Hermann Goering's fifty-second birthday, and while the German Empire crumbled about their ears and a crazy man in a Berlin bunker presided over the last days of the Hitler regime, they challenged the coming disaster with a feast. Once more there was caviar from Russia, duck and venison from the Schorfheide forests, Danzig salmon and the last of the French pâté de foie gras. There was vodka and claret and burgundy, and all the champagne and brandy they could drink.

There was one uninvited guest at the birthday celebration, for Field Marshal Erhard Milch had turned up unexpectedly to bring his good wishes to his chief. Goering was unpleasantly surprised to see him and only reluctantly invited him to the table. As if to excuse the lavishness of the feast, he said:

"The Goering family has always enjoyed a good table. This is no time to deny ourselves. We will all be getting a *Genickschuss* (a shot in the neck) very soon now."

At the end of the meal, Goering helped himself to Napoleon brandy (Milch had to be satisfied with ordinary cognac) and rose to his feet.

"Heil Hitler!" he cried. "And God help Germany!"

He left later that day with Milch to return to Berlin, after saying an affectionate good-by to Emmy and his womenfolk.

On January 30, 1945, a Russian scout car passed through the forest of Schorfheide. For Carin Hall the end was near.

XXIV. LAST GASPS

Emmy and the Goering womenfolk were evacuated from Carin Hall on January 31, 1945. She went south to Berchtesgaden, taking with her in four trucks the first of several convoys of art treasures which Goering was moving from his forest home.

The sighted Russian scout car was on reconnaissance for the Red armies now pushing across Prussia for Berlin, but for a short time more Carin Hall remained unmolested. To protect it until the last moment, Goering had flung around it one of his Luftwaffe parachute divisions, and whenever things became too difficult for him to bear in Berlin he continued to slip away to the peace of his beloved Schorfheide.

It was there, in mid-February, that Albert Speer came to see him. As usual when he was at Carin Hall, the Reich Marshal was in his traditional hunting garb, the old curved knife in his belt. He looked tired and ill, but he made Speer welcome. His visitor well understood how he must be feeling.

"For a long time he had been made the scapegoat for all the failures of the Luftwaffe," Speer wrote later. "At the situation conferences Hitler habitually denounced him in the most violent and insulting language before the assembled officers. He must have been even nastier in the scenes he had with Goering privately. Often, waiting in the anteroom, I could hear Hitler shouting at him."

That evening Speer and Goering seemed to find a rapport between each other for the first time. Robert Kropp came in and served them a meal of cold venison which they ate beside the fire and washed down with an excellent Lafite-Rothschild. The Reich Marshal told Kropp that they were not to be disturbed, and as they ate and drank they talked.

Speer described his deep disappointment with Adolf Hitler.

"Just as candidly," wrote Speer later, "Goering replied that he well understood me and that he often felt much the same. However, he said, it was easier for me, since I had joined Hitler a great deal later and could free myself from him all the sooner. He, Goering, had much closer ties with Hitler; many years of common experiences and struggles had bound them together—and he could no longer break loose."

Speer went on to say that he had decided to disobey the Fuehrer. The Ruhr was now cut off from the rest of Germany by the incessant Allied bombing raids, and no more fuel was reaching Berlin and the other great cities. There was only enough fuel left for one of two functions—either it could continue to go to the factories for the manufacture of munitions, or it could be used for bakeries to bake bread and hospitals to succor the bomb victims. But not both.

Hitler, Speer said, had ordered him to give priority to the factories.

"I have decided to disobey him," Speer said, "and give priority instead to the bakeries and the hospitals. It is too late to bother about the factories."

While Goering stared at him, Speer went on:

"Why don't you do the same, Goering? Why do you take any notice any longer of what the Fuehrer says? Why don't you disobey him, too?"

Goering: "Herr Speer, if I were in your place I would go to the Fuehrer and say: 'I am no longer in agreement with what you are doing, mein Fuehrer. Please, allow me to leave your service and I will get out of the country, or I will stay on here but do nothing more for you.' But you can't break your word and go against his orders and sabotage him without going to him first and telling him what you are going to do."

"No," said Speer, "I'm not going to go to him. I'm simply going to disobey his orders."

There was a long silence while the two men sipped their wine, and then Speer said:

"I suppose you are going to tell the Fuehrer about this?"

Goering shook his head and said, more in sorrow than in anger:

"I may be many things, Herr Speer, but a denouncer (*ein Denunziant*) I am not."

Albert Speer went back to Berlin that night. A few days later someone informed Adolf Hitler that Goering was using his paratroops to protect Carin Hall. They were almost immediately called away to man the line south of Berlin, and that meant that the forest mansion was doomed.

Hermann Goering stayed long enough to superintend the packing of his old drinking glasses, his rugs, his tapestries, and his pictures, and saw them aboard a convoy of trucks which would take them to Bavaria. He shot four of his favorite bison, paraded his forest workers and shook hands with each of them, and then climbed into his staff car. Robert Kropp was at the wheel and his two aides, Colonel von Brauchitsch and Captain Klaas, were in the car with him. They set off for Berlin, and Brauchitsch said afterward that Goering did not look back once.

A few hours after their departure, engineers from Goering's paratroop division, who had already mined the house and the mausoleum, pressed the buttons, and Carin Hall and all it stood for went up in a clap of thunder. When the paratroopers drove away, no one would have guessed that here had stood one of the most ornate feudal residences that Germany had ever seen.

Carin Hall was no more. A few days later, when Russian tanks came by on their way to Berlin, the Red soldiers got out and went poking among the rubble. What they found no one will ever know. But what they missed was a skull, buried in the rubble. Someone discovered it many months later.

It was the skull of Carin Goering, in whose memory the great house had been built. It was perhaps appropriate that at least part of her stayed on, after everyone else had departed.

For his birthday on April 20, 1945, Adolf Hitler came up out of the bunker for the last time. Through the dusty, half-wrecked rooms of the Reichschancellery, Hitler wandered as if in a trance out into the garden, where a guard of Hitler Youth was drawn up. He inspected it perfunctorily and then received the expressions of good wishes from his colleagues and aides. As Albert Speer remarked, "No one knew quite what to say." At that moment, the Russians were ringing Berlin and the last attack on the capital was about to begin.

Shortly afterward, the Nazi leaders crowded back into the bunker for Hitler's daily conference before the situation map. Hitler did not seem to notice, but everyone else remarked on the fact that Hermann Goering had changed his uniform. Instead of his gray-blue Reich Marshal's dress he was now clad in an olive-colored uniform which looked (at least to the Germans) remarkably like an American uniform. The gold shoulder tabs had been replaced by simple cloth strips to which his gold Reich Marshal's eagle was simply pinned.

As the discussion began about the impending attack on Berlin, Hitler announced that he had now definitely decided that the battle for the city should be fought street by street. After everyone had gulped down this fact, it was pointed out by several of the generals that regardless of this strategy it was vitally necessary to shift military headquarters south to the Obersalzberg, and that a decision to do so must be made before it was too late.

Goering interjected to say that only a single route from north to south through the Bavarian Forest was still in German hands, and that the last escape route to Berchtesgaden might be cut off at any moment. Hitler swung round to him indignantly.

"How can I call upon the troops to undertake the decisive battle for Berlin if at the same moment I withdraw myself to safety?" he asked. "I shall leave it to fate whether I die in the capital or fly to Obersalzberg at the last moment!"

As soon as the conference was over, Goering turned to Hitler. He seemed "utterly distraught," Speer considered.

"He had urgent tasks awaiting him in South Germany, he said," Speer wrote later. "He would have to leave Berlin this very night. Hitler gazed absently at him. It seemed to me that he was deeply moved by his decision to remain in Berlin and stake his life on the outcome. With a few indifferent words, he shook hands with Goering."

Speer had the sense of being present at a historic moment: "The leadership of the Reich was splitting asunder."

It was General Karl Koller, the last Chief of the General Staff of the Luftwaffe, who informed Goering that Adolf Hitler intended to die in the bunker in Berlin. General Alfred Jodl, Hitler's adviser, called him in and said:

"Hitler said that he is staying and will shoot himself at the last moment . . . When it came to negotiations, the Reich Marshal could do that better."

Koller managed to convey this news to Goering at Obersalzberg over a scratchy line from the German capital, and was at once instructed by Berndt von Brauchitsch, Goering's adjutant, to report personally. With the staff of the Luftwaffe High Command he flew to Bavaria, and reported to Goering at the Reich Marshal's house at Berchtesgaden on April 23, 1945. He wanted to talk to Goering privately but was told that the only other man there, a Party official named Philip Bouhler, was a trusted friend and would remain. Koller reported his conversation with Jodl and Hitler's intention to commit suicide in full detail this time, and he gained the impression that Goering was not surprised by the news.

"Both he and Bouhler commented very adversely on Hitler," he said later. "They regarded his behavior as *eine abgrundtiefe Gemeinheit* (a mean trick). Goering felt in a difficult position. He wanted a report on the military situation, which I gave him with the help of maps. Then he asked me whether I thought that Hitler was still alive or whether he had, perhaps, appointed Martin Bormann as his successor. I told him that Hitler was alive when I left Berlin. There were still one or two escape routes from the city . . . Maybe Hitler had changed his plans."

As they digested his words, he could only add:

"Anyway, it is now up to you to act, Herr Reich Marshal."

But act in what way? Goering was quite obviously not only on the horns of a dilemma but frightened, too. It was Bormann he was afraid of.

"Bormann is my deadly enemy," he said. "He is only waiting to get at me. If I act, he will call me a traitor. If I don't, he will accuse me of having failed at the most difficult hour!"

Goering called for the steel box in which he had locked away the precious decree of June 29, 1941, in which the

Fuehrer had appointed him as his successor. The relevant words Goering now read out loud:

"If I should be restricted in my freedom of action, or if I should be otherwise incapacitated, Reich Marshal Goering is to be my deputy or successor in all offices of State, Party and Wehrmacht."

The directive seemed clear enough. But Goering was still doubtful. Among the Nazi officials who were now crowding into the Obersalzberg redoubt was Hans Heinrich Lammers, chief of Hitler's Chancellery for Political Affairs, and he was called in to study the document. He said:

"The law of June 29, 1941, is in force and legally binding. No new publication is required. The Fuehrer has made no other order. If he had, I would have to know. Without me, he could not have changed the decree legally."

But still Goering was not sure. There was a great conflict going on in his mind. Not only was he anxious not to put a foot wrong and earn the wrath of Bormann, but he was also anxoius that he should have the approval of Adolf Hitler for what he planned to do next, so that, as always, he would be under his orders. Finally, he decided to send a message to Berlin. Goering and Lammers dictated it to Koller and tried to make it as plain as possible that what Goering desired above everything was that Hitler should escape from Berlin and continue the battle in the South. But if not . . .

"Mein Fuehrer," the message said, "since you are determined to remain at your post in Fortress Berlin, do you agree that I as your deputy in accordance with your decree of 29.6.1941 assume immediately total leadership of the Reich with complete freedom of action at home and abroad? If by 2200 hours no answer is forthcoming, I shall assume that you have been deprived of your freedom of action. I will then consider the terms of your decree to have come into force and act accordingly for the good of the people and the Fatherland. You must realize what I feel for you in these most difficult hours of my life, and I am quite unable to find words to express it. God bless you and grant that you may come here after all as soon as possible. Your most loyal *Hermann Goering.*"

Albert Speer was in the bunker in Berlin when the telegram arrived. It had been handed to Martin Bormann, who made haste to falsify its significance.

"Bormann claimed that Goering had launched a coup d'état," Speer wrote later. "Perhaps this was Bormann's last effort to persuade Hitler to fly to Berchtesgaden and take control there."

But Hitler was plunged into a trough of apathy and even Bormann's anger could not rouse him. Shortly afterward, however, another telegram arrived from Goering, addressed this time to Reich Minister Joachim von Ribbentrop. It was merely designed to make sure that Goering's intentions were made clear and their legitimacy stressed. It read:

> TO REICH MINISTER VON RIBBENTROP. I HAVE ASKED THE FUEHRER TO PROVIDE ME WITH INSTRUCTIONS BY 10 P.M. APRIL 23. IF BY THIS TIME IT IS APPARENT THAT THE FUEHRER HAS BEEN DEPRIVED OF HIS FREEDOM OF ACTION TO CONDUCT THE AFFAIRS OF THE REICH, HIS DECREE OF JUNE 29, 1941, BECOMES EFFECTIVE, ACCORDING TO WHICH I AM HEIR TO ALL HIS OFFICES AS HIS DEPUTY. [IF] BY 12 MIDNIGHT APRIL 23, 1945, YOU RECEIVE NO OTHER WORD EITHER FROM THE FUEHRER DIRECTLY OR FROM ME, YOU ARE TO COME TO ME AT ONCE BY AIR. (SIGNED) GOERING, REICH MARSHAL.

Bormann waved the telegram before Hitler.

"Goering is engaged in treason!" he cried. "He's already sending telegrams to members of the government and announcing that on the basis of his powers he will assume your office at twelve tonight, mein Fuehrer."

This at last aroused Hitler from his coma. He immediately stripped Goering of his rights of succession and accused him of treason and betrayal of National Socialism. Bormann wrote out a telegram to that effect. The message ended with a promise that Hitler would exempt him from all further punishment if Goering would promptly resign all his offices for reasons of health.

"Bormann had at last managed to rouse Hitler from his lethargy," wrote Speer, who was watching the scene from a few feet away. "An outburst of wild fury followed in which feelings of bitterness, helplessness, self-pity and despair mingled. With flushed face and staring eyes, Hitler ranted as if he had forgotten the presence of his entourage: 'I've known it all along. I know Goering is lazy. He let the air force go to pot. He was corrupt. His example made corruption possible in our state. Besides, he's been a drug addict for years. I've known it all along.'

"Then, with startling abruptness, he lapsed back into his lethargy.

" 'Well, all right,' he said. 'Let Goering negotiate the surrender. If the war is lost, it doesn't matter who does it.' "

The situation in Germany now was rather like life imitating a bad film. In Obersalzberg, Goering, Koller, and Bouhler, unaware yet of what was happening in Berlin, or that the Fuehrer had stripped Goering of his powers, were closeted together in Goering's study working on the messages which they planned to send to General Eisenhower, the Allied military commander; Winston Churchill; and President Truman. One such message had already been drafted in which the Reich Marshall asked Eisenhower for a meeting, to discuss the "honorable surrender" of the German forces. A light plane was standing by down the mountain, ready to fly Goering to an Allied meeting place. At the same time, Goering had written out a proclamation to the Wehrmacht ringingly calling on them to fight on— but it was merely a ruse, as Goering pointed out with a grin, to deceive the Russians and conceal the fact that he was seeking peace.

General Koller had never seen his chief so animated. "It was as if he had come to life again," he said later. He was full of plans and ideas. Occasionally, Emmy bustled in with tea or sandwiches and beer, and brought him check lists of the trucks which had arrived from Carin Hall laden with his art treasures. Four trucks had been mislaid in Berlin, and they contained some of Goering's most beloved treasures.* But after a groan of agonized disappointment,

---

* One of the trucks, at least, was picked up by Russian soldiers later and taken back to the Soviet Union. It contained among other paintings the Boucher "Venus." The picture turned up again on the London auction market, by way of Russia, Poland, Finland, and Sweden, in 1973.

the Reich Marshal shook off the bad news and got back to his planning. What did a few pictures matter at this moment, when at long last he was taking over the destiny of the Reich?

But meanwhile, back in Berlin, the villain of the melodrama was at work to wreck the plans he was making. Before the final fadeout, Martin Bormann was determined to get Hermann Goering once and for all. When Adolf Hitler had told him to send a telegram to Goering forbidding him to take over, he sent two messages instead of one. The first was sent in the Fuehrer's name and said:

"Decree of 29.6.41 is rescinded by my special instruction. My freedom of action is undisputed. I forbid any move by you in the direction indicated."

But the other went from Bormann himself to the two senior SS commanders in the Obersalzberg region, Frank and Von Bredow, and it ordered them to arrest Goering at once for high treason. In case they might have any hesitation about carrying out this drastic order, Bormann appended the words: "You will be responsible for this with your lives."

That Goering had no intention of committing high treason or flouting Hitler's wishes is indicated by the fact that as soon as the Fuehrer's telegram was in his hands, he immediately halted all his plans and sent out messages to Von Ribbentrop and all other Nazi leaders with whom he had communicated earlier. He signaled them:

FUEHRER INFORMS ME HE STILL HAS FREEDOM OF ACTION. REVOKING TELEGRAM OF TODAY NOON. HEIL HITLER. HERMANN GOERING.

But by that time the SS had surrounded his house and he and his family were cut off from the rest of Berchtesgaden and from the world. When Frank and Von Bredow appeared shortly afterward to put Goering under arrest, he simply refused to believe that they could be serious.

"Everything will be cleared up by tomorrow," he said to Emmy that evening. "It's simply a matter of a misunderstanding. Sleep peacefully, as I am going to do. Can you imagine for a single moment that Adolf Hitler would have me arrested today—I who have followed him through thick and thin for the last twenty-three years? Come now! It's really unthinkable!"

But neither of them passed an easy night. Outdoors, in

the drifting snow, SS troops stood on guard. Goering had been separated from Emmy and his daughter, Edda, and sentries stood outside their doors and warned that they would shoot if either tried to communicate with the other. Next morning, while Emmy and her daughter snatched a fitful sleep, Goering came out onto his balcony in his dressing gown. It was at this moment that RAF bombers came over. They had been given the plum job of the war— to make a precision attack upon Adolf Hitler's mountain stronghold, and their bombs took in Goering's residence at the same time.

Just in time, the family was bundled into the cellar under the house, where Robert Kropp, Elsa Sonnemann, Christa Gormans, Cilly, the maid, and a governess were already huddled. But as the house began to shudder and crack under the explosions, it became obvious that no one would last long if a bomb came anywhere near. The moment a lull came, they were hurried down the hill to a great shelter in the hillside into which most other Nazi officials in Berchtesgaden were crammed with their relatives. The Goerings were kept apart, with an SS guard around them, and were forbidden to talk.

When they came out at last, the proud symbol of Hitler's power, the Eagle's Nest, had been destroyed by the Allied bombs. Goering's own house had been badly blasted, its swimming pool destroyed, its roof torn off, Goering's study completely wrecked.

The sight of it seemed to bring home his plight to Hermann Goering at last. He turned round to the SS leader, Hans Frank, who was standing beside him, and said:

"Send a message to the Fuehrer. Tell him that if he believes I have betrayed him, I am prepared to be shot."

It was a moment when Emmy Goering gave the best performance of her career. She had been scared to the point of screaming by the air raid, and she was terrified of what might be coming now to her husband, her daughter, and herself. But she drew herself up and said to Frank:

"The Fuehrer, on my wedding day, promised to grant me a wish. I want to remind him of his promise. If the Fuehrer orders my husband to be shot, I want him to have Edda and me shot at the same time."

Frank nodded gravely, and told her that the message

would be passed on. In truth, he was beginning to be bewildered by the whole situation. He had received another message from Martin Bormann, who was still determined that whatever else happened he would get Hermann Goering.

"The situation in Berlin is more tense," Bormann's message read. "If Berlin and we should fall, the traitors of April 23 must be exterminated. Men, do your duty. Your life and honor depend on it."

But it must have occurred to Frank that if, indeed, Berlin should fall, and Hitler and Bormann with it, what good would there be in killing Goering too? He was now the only Nazi leader who might help them with the Allies.

At all events, it seems certain that from the moment the SS leaders realized that Bormann and Hitler were on their way out, they put the safety catches back on their revolvers, and the Goerings were in no danger of execution (at least from their Nazi comrades) from now on. Indeed, when Hermann Goering suggested that bombed-out Obersalzberg was now too uncomfortable, and that it might be better for them to retire to Mauterndorf Castle, Frank immediately agreed and ordered a convoy of cars to be made ready to convey Goering, his wife, daughter, and servants, plus an SS escort, across the frontier.

The roads were icy and clogged with retreating troops, and it took them thirty-six hours to make the journey. While they were on their way, there was a broadcast from Radio Hamburg which announced:

"Reich Marshal Hermann Goering is suffering from a heart disease which has now entered an acute stage. He has, therefore, asked to be relieved of the command of the Luftwaffe and all duties connected therewith, because, at this moment, the full harnessing of all strength is needed. The Fuehrer has granted his request. The Fuehrer has appointed Colonel General Ritter von Greim to be the new Commander of the Luftwaffe, promoting him at the same time to the rank of field marshal."

In point of fact, Goering had from the moment he arrived in Mauterndorf completely recovered his nerve and his vigor. With the help of his pills, of course. He had divined that the SS leaders, particularly Frank, were uncertain about him, and while they were not willing to release him, they would certainly not object to a rescue operation. To that end, Emmy's niece, Rosswitha, who was part of the Goering entourage, was sent through the underground passages of Mauterndorf Castle to a spot where they debouched on the outskirts of the village. Goering and his brothers and sisters had often used the passages during their childhood.

In the village Rosswitha found a Luftwaffe lieutenant and told him the news that Goering was being held prisoner in the castle. But he refused to believe her. A few hours later, Emmy Goering herself went through the passage and this time contacted both the lieutenant and a Luftwaffe captain. They promised to visit the castle and make sure of Goering's safety, and said that at the same time they would send a message to the nearest Luftwaffe unit informing its commander of the Reich Marshal's plight.

It took another week before the Goerings were released, and in the meantime the Third Reich died. Adolf Hitler, in a formal message dictated to his secretary, stripped Goering of his titles, his membership of the Party, and appointed Grand Admiral Karl Doenitz as his successor instead. Then he put a gun in his mouth and shot himself.

The Goerings now had a radio in their rooms at Mauterndorf, and they heard the news together on May 1, 1945, of the Fuehrer's death. Goering said:

"Now I'll never be able to convince him that I was loyal to the end."

Emmy collapsed with a heart attack.

But soon both of them had recovered. Goering was all bustle again. A Luftwaffe general, Wolfgang Pickert, limping home past Mauterndorf, was amazed to see the Reich Marshal standing at the gates.

"Listen to my orders," Goering said. "I want full protection. Tell General Koller to act immediately. A general should be sent at once to see General Eisenhower to arrange for me to have a man-to-man, soldier-to-soldier talk. That's the way to deal with the situation."

A few hours later he waved to a troop of Luftwaffe soldiers marching under the walls of the castle, and hurried down. By the time he arrived, they had formed up.

"It was one of the most beautiful moments of my life,"

he said later, "to stand there in front of my troops and see them present arms to their commander-in-chief."

Hermann Goering was free again. For the moment, that is.

In May 1945, there were still leaders of the National Socialist Party who believed that they could secure an honorable peace for Germany, and that all that was needed was for one of them to talk to the Allies, soldier-to-soldier, man-to-man. Admiral Doenitz, Hitler's successor, now operating out of Flensburg, in North Germany, was, it is true, discovering that things were not going to be as easy as all that. But Hermann Goering had no doubt of his own ability to make the situation "more flexible."

On May 6, he sent a message to Doenitz in which he said:

"Are you familiar with the intrigues, dangerous to the security of the State, which Reich Leader Martin Bormann has set in motion to eliminate me? . . . Reich Leader SS Heinrich Himmler can confirm the profound extent of these intrigues. I have just learned that you intend to send [General] Jodl to Eisenhower with a view to negotiating. I think it is important in the interests of our people that, besides the official negotiations of Jodl, I should officially approach Eisenhower, as one Marshal to another. My success in all important negotiations abroad with which the Fuehrer always entrusted me before the war is sufficient guarantee that I can hope to create the personal atmosphere appropriate for Jodl's negotiations. Moreover, both Great Britain and America have proved through their press and radio, and in the declarations of their statesmen over the last few years, that their attitude toward me is more favorable than toward all other political leaders in Germany. I think that at this most difficult hour all should collaborate and that nothing should be neglected which might assure as far as possible the future of Germany. *Goering*, Reich Marshal."

Doenitz never replied to this message. He was already beginning to realize what the Allies meant when they insisted on "unconditional surrender," and the lines along which Goering was still thinking hardly accorded with the realities he was now facing.

But Goering did not bother about the admiral's silence. He was busy making arrangements of his own. General Koller had requisitioned a castle for him at Fischhorn, where the Goering entourage installed themselves while awaiting the arrival of the Americans. Berndt von Brauchitsch and another envoy, armed with white flags and two letters, drove across Bavaria until they reached the first U.S. army unit they could find, and then asked to be taken to headquarters. One of the letters was addressed to the local U.S. commander and asked him to protect Goering from the complots of the Gestapo and SS. The other was for General Eisenhower and proposed "discussions."

It took some time for the envoys to find the Americans and deliver their messages, and when they did not reappear Goering became impatient. To Robert Kropp he said:

"Pack all the luggage, Kropp, and pile it into the trucks."

Wearily, Kropp, who had been packing and unpacking for days now, pulled out the pigskin cases and began to fill them with his master's uniforms, costumes, and haberdashery. Cilly did the same for Emmy's wardrobe.

Goering said to Emmy:

"If the mountain will not come to Mahomet, then Mahomet must go to the mountain."

They laughed together at the joke. Then they set off along the mountain roads, packed with retreating troops, refugees, the flotsam and jetsam of a lost war. Whenever Goering was recognized, the soldiers fired their last ammunition in the air in greeting, or waved and cheered, and Emmy and he acknowledged them with smiles and waves. Often their convoy got stuck in traffic jams, and then the troops jumped down from their carriers to shake hands with the Reich Marshal and question him about the prospects of peace. He reassured them. Was he not the Iron Man? He would see that Germany was justly treated. The soldiers cheered.

"Heil der Dicke!" they cried.

It was in one such traffic jam that U.S. First Lieutenant Jerome N. Shapiro finally found him. He had been to Fischhorn first and found his quarry gone, and had been scouring the country ever since for the most important prize of the war. Now he hurried forward and saluted. The Reich Marshal saluted back. Shapiro was surprised to note that both Goering and his wife seemed delighted to see him. He could hardly be expected to realize that, at this moment, to be in American hands was for them the happy ending to a bad dream—or a bad film. They had escaped from the hands of the villanous Bormann, and now here were the Americans, riding in to the rescue.

In the next few hours, nothing happened to dissuade Hermann Goering from his conviction that he was no mere prisoner of war but a plenipotentiary acting on behalf of the German Reich in armistice discussions with the enemy. Shapiro and his troop of GIs were polite and deferential, and so was Brigadier General Robert J. Stack, the first U.S. officer of field rank whom they encountered. He reached out and warmly shook Goering by the hand, and what could be more friendly than that?

Emmy Goering was living in a dream world. "Very fortunately for us," she wrote later, "General Stack was a man of great tact. He had brought an interpreter with him and although my husband spoke English perfectly he had every word translated, since every detail was so important. I heard everything. Stack had telephoned to General Eisenhower to tell him of Hermann's letter. The American commander-in-chief had said that he was ready to see Hermann and was waiting for him to come next day with General Stack. We were all now under Eisenhower's personal protection and were able to move into the castle of Fischhorn at Bruck, near Zell-am-See until we knew whether Burg Veldenstein, Hermann's house, was still standing. We would then go and live in it. Eisenhower had given his word that my husband would be able to see him and leave again in freedom."

It is doubtful if Goering, even stuffed with pills and in a wild state of euphoria, really believed that this could be true, but he did not do anything to disillusion Emmy and she went on believing. That night Goering had dinner with General Stack and they ate and drank until the early hours of the morning.

"My husband came to see me," Emmy wrote. "He told me that next day he would have breakfast again with General Stack and then leave me for a day or two. In any case, they would let him come back. He read the doubts and anxiety in my eyes. The war was over for Germany but was it for us? What would happen to Hermann? He reassured me: 'General Eisenhower has given his word through General Stack as his intermediary.' "†

Goering was driven next day to the headquarters of the American Seventh Army at Kitzbühel, where, among others, General Carl Spaatz of the USAAF was waiting to greet him, together with photographers and war correspondents. Champagne was brought out. It was a very jolly party, with all the Americans joshing the Reich Marshal and making him laugh. But that night, as army censors began to read correspondents' accounts of the conference, Eisenhower clamped down. The order went out and it was curt: Get Goering away as soon as possible, and henceforward treat him like an ordinary prisoner of war.

He was flown the following day to the Seventh Army interrogation center, at Augsburg. When he got there no officers were on the field to greet him. He was crisply ordered to hand over the two medals he was wearing, the Pour le Mérite and the Grand Cross of the Knight's Cross with Swords and Diamonds, plus his solid gold marshal's baton, his solid gold epaulets and the huge diamond ring on his fourth finger.‡ Since the Augsburg center had several Hungarian displaced persons working for it, it was judged wise to deprive Goering of the means of bribing the help. Perish the thought, he might even try to bribe the GIs.

For the first time, Hermann Goering must have begun to feel naked and afraid. The quarters to which he was taken were in a block of workers' apartments on the outskirts of the town, and consisted of a bedroom, living room, and small kitchen. There was no bath and no lavatory, the latter being at the end of a corridor on the landing and the former in the basement of the building. Colonel Berndt von Brauchitsch, who was still with him, protested vehemently and demanded that the Reich Marshal be given a house of his own, in keeping with the dignity of his rank. When the demand was refused, he burst into tears and cried that the German Army was being insulted. When Robert Kropp arrived later with his master's luggage, he found him "in a state of utter dejection."

---

† Eisenhower had done no such thing. He was already writing out a reprimand for Stack for having shaken Goering's hand.
‡ The baton is now in the U.S. Army Museum in Washington.

LAST GASPS 389

But the next day, he had regained some of his spirits
again, though his mood was one of wary resignation. When
Lieutenant Rolf Wartenberg, one of the interrogators,
came in to see him on May 18, he immediately asked what
had become of his property and, when assured that it was
in safekeeping, shook his head skeptically.

"The way things are going," Goering said, in English, "I
fear that from now on you are going to take the pants off
me."

He gazed gloomily at the half-finished helping of army C
rations on the plate before him, and then suddenly grinned.

"I would love to have seen Horthy's face when you
served him this stuff!" he said. Horthy, Regent of Hungary,
had also recently arrived in the camp as a prisoner. "I've
been eating soldiers' meals all my life. But that one was
served Cordon Bleu cooking as a baby—did he turn green
at the sight of this?"

He looked very much more cheerful when Wartenberg
told him that he was invited to the officers' mess for cock-
tails, and shouted for Kropp to give him a shave for the
occasion. The Augsburg Center had once been rebuked by
the Seventh Army Commander, General Patch, for treating
its POWs too gently, but had produced proof during the
campaign that their kid-glove approach had several times
produced information which had subsequently saved soldiers' lives. The Army now wanted as much information
out of Goering as possible as quickly as they could obtain
it, and the commander of the Augsburg unit, Major Paul
Kubala, estimated that an alternating regime of the stick
and the carrot would be most likely to produce it.

After the harsh unfriendliness of a night in a heavily
guarded, unheated room, Goering immediately thawed in
the matey atmosphere of the officers' mess. He never refused a drink and was delighted with the sandwiches and
salads he was offered. Presently, when one of the officers
sat down to play the piano, he joined in the songs with the
rest of the company and heartily clapped his hands together during the chorus of "Deep in the Heart of Texas."
He then confided to Wartenberg that among the luggage
Robert Kropp had brought with him was, of all things, a
piano accordion which he loved to play. If the lieutenant
would get hold of it from Kropp, he would be delighted to
give the assembled company a few numbers.

The accordion was sent for, and Goering's pudgy fingers were soon moving fleetly across the keyboard as, in a pleasant bathroom baritone, he gave them his favorite renderings of "Ich weiss nicht was soll es bedeuten," "Stille Nacht," "O Star of Eve" and music from *Die Meistersinger*. In between the numbers, he drank and talked freely. When the time came—at 2 A.M.—for him to teeter gently back to his quarters, he seemed happily tipsy.

He had talked a good deal, and the Center interrogators spent the rest of the night writing out their reports. But they were also aware that he had certainly told them nothing that he did not want them to hear. Their report to Army Headquarters the next morning (May 19, 1945) started off with these words:

"[Goering] is by no means the comical figure he has been depicted so many times in newspaper reports. He is neither stupid nor a fool in the Shakespearian sense, but generally cool and calculating. He is able to grasp the fundamental issues under discussion immediately. He is certainly not a man to be underrated. Although he tried to soft-pedal many of the most outrageous crimes committed by Germany, he said enough to show that he is as much responsible for the policies within Germany and for the war itself as anyone in Germany. Goering took great pride in claiming that it was he who was responsible for the planning of the paratroop landing in Crete, that it was he who had drawn up plans for a capture of Gibraltar . . ., that it was he who was responsible for the development of the Luftwaffe. On the other hand, he denied having had anything to do with the racial laws and with the concentration camps, with the SS and the atrocities committed both in Germany and outside. Goering is at all times an actor who does not disappoint his audience. . . ."

The report added:

"The cause for which Goering stood is lost—but the canny Hermann, even now, thinks only of what he can do to salve some of his personal fortune, and to create an advantageous position for himself. He condemns the once-beloved Fuehrer without hesitation. Up to now he has not made a plea for any of his former henchmen, alive or dead. Yet, behind his spirited and often witty conversation, is a constant watchfulness for the opportunity to place himself in a favorable light."

From then on, Goering talked freely to the Center interrogators, and a picture began to build up of the Nazi
regime which was both startling and (as it proved) authen-
tic. In the next three days he elucidated many of the mysteries about Adolf Hitler and the Third Reich which had
been puzzling Allied intelligence agencies for years.

One of the subjects on which he was urgently questioned, on behalf of several nations, was the fate of his art
collections. He explained that not all his paintings, tapestries, and furniture could be evacuated in time, and must
now be in the hands of the Russians. The rest he had last
seen in railway cars inside the unfinished tunnel near the
Berchtesgaden railroad station, and urged the Americans to
race to their rescue without delay, since the last he had
heard of them was that they were being looted by the SS.

He insisted that all the paintings and tapestries in his
possession had been legitimately bought, but agreed that
those from the Musée du Jeu de Paume collection had
been illegally seized from their Jewish owners. These he
undertook to co-operate in locating and returning. He
thereupon wrote out and signed the following document:

"I hereby declare that I am ready to return the art treasures (exhibited at the Jeux de Paume [sic]) which I acquired and bought at auctions of requisitioned property.

"That I will do my utmost to find out about the location
of these articles and that I will give all the pertinent information possible.

"That the greater part of these articles and of my total
property of art collections are packed in several freight
cars in Berchtesgaden. The storage of these articles in air
raid shelters was not possible because of my imprisonment
by Hitler the day after my arrival there.

"That I informed the French liaison officer in charge
about several other places where there could be some less
important works of art.

"That I am convinced that a conference with my former
art consultant, Hofer, in the presence of Allied officers will
lead to a speedy recovery and extensive clarification of all
questions. (Signed) *Hermann Goering*, Reich Marshal."

Nearly all the paintings which he named were subsequently recovered (except for those which were left behind
in Berlin, and fell into Russian hands). To celebrate their
return, Goering was invited to yet another cocktail party in

the officers' mess. This time the drink was the champagne which Seventh Army troops had also found in Goering's freight cars while rescuing the paintings.* They did not tell him this.

They also did not tell him that a unit had visited Emmy Goering at Zell-am-See, where she was still in Fischhorn Castle, waiting for him to come home. They demanded the return of a painting he had mentioned she had. It was a Memling Madonna which he had given her, rolled up, just before leaving her for the last time.

Emmy handed it over to the Americans and burst into tears. It had, in fact, been legitimately bought by Goering from the Corsini family in Italy for several million lire.

The next day, May 21, 1945, Goering was awakened and told that he was about to be moved. He was also informed that from now on, he could have only one military aide to accompany him. He decided to dispense with both of them, and chose Robert Kropp to go with him to his new destination, wherever that might be. Colonel von Brauchitsch and Major Klaas bade him an emotional farewell, and he set off with his valet for the airfield.

None of the Americans shook his hand or waved him good-by, but, in truth, most of the officers of the interrogation center were sorry to see him go. He left his piano accordion behind as a farewell gift for Rolf Wartenberg.†

---

* The SS were so busy raiding this trove of wine and liquors that they did not bother to loot the art treasures.
† He still has it and plays it, "though not as well as Goering."

XXV. THE ROAD TO NUREMBERG

Hermann Goering spent the next four months in a small suite of barely furnished rooms in the Palace Hotel at Mondorf, in Luxembourg. It was known to the American Army as "Ash Can" and it was the chief interrogation center for the captured leaders of the National Socialist Reich. Hitler and Goebbels were, of course, already dead; Martin Bormann had walked out into the inferno of embattled Berlin and disappeared; and Heinrich Himmler had committed suicide. But soon fellow guests like Joachim von Ribbentrop, Admiral Karl Doenitz, Albert Speer, Hjalmar Schacht, and the rest of the surviving leadership arrived to share the austerities of the Palace Hotel, though they were not allowed to communicate with each other.

The last illusion Goering retained that he was regarded as only a temporary prisoner was shattered when into his room one morning came an officer in American uniform, who said in perfect German:

"Good morning, Herr Goering. I wonder if you remember me. It is a long time since we last met."

It was Dr. Robert M. Kempner, once the youngest prosecuting counsel in the Prussian Police Department, whom Goering had sacked in 1933. Now he was interrogator and adviser for the Allies. He was meticulously polite to his old enemy and allowed no hint of prejudice or partiality to color his attitude or his questions, but the realization that henceforward experts of Kempner's caliber and background would be cross-examining him jolted Goering into an acceptance of his true situation. He now had to face up to the fact that position, reputation, charm, and personality were going to get him nowhere, and that his fate was in the hands of his enemies from now on.

The commandant of the Mondorf Interrogation Center (he subsequently became commandant at Nuremberg too) was U.S. Colonel Burton C. Andrus. If a film of Colonel Andrus's life were ever to be made, the title role would undoubtedly have to be played by John Wayne with all the stops pulled out. He was a 200 per cent red-blooded American of a type which doesn't crop up so frequently today as it did in 1945, and he made no secret of his contempt not only for the "bunch of Krauts" who had now come into his care but also for some of the experts whose job it was to interrogate or otherwise examine them.

For Hermann Goering he conceived a particular antipathy and was outraged by his clothes, his ostentation, and his arrogance. He despised him all the more when he found that he was addicted to drugs.

"When Goering came to me at Mondorf," he said later, "he was a simpering slob with two suitcases full of paracodeine. I thought he was a drug salesman. But we took him off his dope and made a man of him."

It was not Colonel Andrus, in fact, who helped to cure Goering of his drug addiction while he was at Mondorf. On the contrary, at one point he almost wrecked the process by a particularly maladroit decision. The man who weaned him away was a U.S. army psychiatrist named Douglas M. Kelley. After all he had heard about Goering's addiction, Kelley was surprised to discover the weakness of the drugs with which he was doping himself.

"Actually these tiny tablets contained only a small amount of paracodeine," he wrote later, "and a hundred of them, Goering's average daily dose, are the equivalent of between three and four grains of morphine. This is not an unusually large dose. It was not enough to have affected his mental processes at any time."

Kelley decided that Goering took his pills in much the same way as people smoke cigarettes—it was a habit as well as an addiction, a need to take them at regular intervals in order to do something with his hands and mouth. He got no particular stimulation from them, but continued with them because when he stopped he developed pains in his legs.

"I can testify that his addiction was not very severe," wrote Kelley. "If it had been, I could never have taken him off the drug in the manner I did, following his capture. I used a simple, straight withdrawal method, cutting down the dosage each day until no more drug was allowed.

Throughout Goering had no special complaint other than occasional pains which were easily relieved with mild sedatives."

The only other "medication" Kelley used was psychological.

"Goering was very proud of his physical prowess and his ability to withstand pain. Consequently, it was simple to suggest to him that while weaker men like Ribbentrop (whom he loathed) would perhaps require doses of medicine should they ever be withdrawn from a drug habit, he, Goering, being strong and forceful, would require nothing. Goering agreed that this was reasonable and co-operated wholeheartedly."

It was while he was in a critical phase of his cure that he clashed with Colonel Andrus. With half of Europe on the verge of starvation, the colonel saw no reason why his prisoners should be fed more than enough to keep their bodies together, nor did he insist that the standard of cooking should be high. One day Goering could stand it no longer and shouted:

"I fed my dogs better than this."

According to Colonel Andrus, a German prisoner who was waiting at table immediately replied:

"If that is so, you fed your dogs better than the German soldiers."

This seems a surprising remark in view of the fact that, until the last days, German army rations were kept up to a remarkably good standard. But, in any case, the colonel was irritated by the incident and his regard for Goering was certainly not increased by it.

A few days later, on June 2, 1945, Robert Kropp came to Goering and said simply: "They are sending me away."

It had been decided that the relationship between the Reich Marshal and his valet was on too personal a basis, and that the tie of affection between them must be broken. Kropp would be sent to another camp, and a German detainee appointed as Goering's servant in his place.

The decision came at a critical moment in Goering's struggle against the paracodeine habit, and there were tears in his eyes as he said good-by to his valet. Kropp's last gift to Goering was a pillow for his bed, because he knew that he slept badly without one; but just before he left the camp, two days later, Kropp learned that it had been taken away again.

"As they marched us away," he said later, "I saw the Reich Marshal standing at the window looking through the wire meshing."

It was June 4, 1945, and Robert Kropp never saw his old master again.

Douglas Kelley not only weaned Hermann Goering away from drugs, he persuaded him to cut down his weight as well. He had weighed 280 pounds when he was captured, and ruefully agreed that it was a bit much for a man of his height and pride in his physical make-up. But he made no real effort until he, and the other prisoners, were informed, in August 1945, that they would appear before an International Tribunal in Nuremberg the following November, charged with war crimes. Goering knew what that meant. That night he wrote a letter to Emmy in which he said:

"My dear Wife,—I am so sincerely thankful to you for all the happiness that you always gave me; for your love and for everything; never let Edda get away from you. I can tell you endlessly what you and Edda mean to me and how my thoughts keep centering on you. I hold you in passionate embrace and kiss your dear sweet face in passionate love. Forever, Your Hermann."

Then he told the doctor that he was going on a diet. He made only one condition—that German prisoners of war should be employed to refit his uniforms as his weight dropped.

"This concession was granted," Kelley wrote later. "Not because we were interested in Goering's appearance but because, without refitting, he would have been unable to keep his trousers up."

By the time Goering was transferred to Nuremberg Jail in September, 1945, he had lost eighty pounds and was down to 200. A steady six-hour-a-day session of interrogations, tasteless army food, and freedom from drugs had all helped to turn him into a healthier man than he had been since the days of World War I. His mental state had improved too. He no longer seemed worried about what was going to happen to him, and his concern now was only for the future of Emmy and the baby. He was convinced that he was going to die and had accepted it. To Emmy he wrote:

"To see your beloved handwriting, to know that your dear hands have rested on this very paper—all that and the contents itself have moved me most deeply and yet made me most happy. Sometimes I think my heart will break with love and longing for you. That would be a beautiful death."

But to Kelley he said:

"Yes, I know I shall hang. You know I shall hang. I am ready."

He was still unwilling to admit that he was a war criminal, that anyone else in his place would have acted differently. He refused to believe that the Allies had any right to try him.

"This is just like going into battle," he said, "and I will show that I cannot only dish it out, but can take it as well. I do not recognize this trial's legal jurisdiction, but since they have the power to enforce their will, I am prepared to tell the truth and face anything that may come. . . . Hermann Goering is a soldier. I made war—that is true. As long as every nation has its selfish interests, you have to be practical. I am a practical man. But I am also convinced that there is a higher power which pushes men around in spite of all their efforts to control their destiny."

Yes, he repeated, he knew he would hang, but he was ready.

"But I am determined to go down in German history as a great man," he added. "If I cannot convince the court, I shall at least convince the German people that all I did was done for the Greater German Reich. In fifty or sixty years there will be statues of Hermann Goering all over Germany."

He paused and then added: "Little statues, maybe, but one in every German home."

For a month before the opening of the trial, the defendants were confined to their cells in the prison wing of the Nuremberg Courthouse, and allowed out only for half an hour's exercise a day plus a twice-weekly shower. All communication between them was strictly forbidden.

Goering was in Cell Number 5. Like all the others, it was 13 feet long by 7 feet wide and seven and a half feet high. Each cell contained a washbowl, a flushing toilet, one standard prison bunk with hair mattress, a chair, a mat, and a table. To reduce the possibility of suicide, the cells had been modified by the removal of all metal projections from the walls, all electrical wiring, and the replacement of glass in the one window with clear plastic material. Everything was arranged so that, except during the act of defecation (when only the legs and possibly the head could be seen) the prisoner was completely visible at all times to the guard at the door, who was charged with keeping him under constant and unremitting vigilance. At night the cell was illuminated by reflected light through a port in the cell door, and the prisoner was not allowed to sleep with his arms inside his blanket, even when he was cold.

At unannounced times, there were spot checks and searches in addition to the regular ones. The door would swing open, in would rush burly troopers of the U.S. 1st Division, and roughly order the prisoner to take off his clothes and stand naked while his room, clothes, belongings and body were thoroughly searched. Colonel Andrus often came to Goering's cell on these occasions to see that the naked Reich Marshal received especially close attention.

Other than these unwelcome visitors and duty officers, the only other people who came to Goering's cell were doctors. There was an elderly German general practitioner named Dr. Ludwig Pfluecker, who had been captured by the Allies in France, who looked after the prisoners' ordinary medical needs. He gave them sleeping pills, and he left a blue capsule of sodium amytal and a red capsule of seconal for Goering each evening to allow him to sleep. Then there was the doctor-psychiatrist (Douglas Kelley) and the psychologist (Dr. G. M. Gilbert). It was not surprising that Goering, like the other bored and brooding prisoners, welcomed the proposal from Dr. Gilbert that they submit themselves to an intelligence test.

Gilbert used a German version of the American Wechsler-Bellevue Adult Intelligence Test, which consisted of:

A. *Verbal tests of memory and use of concepts.*
   1. Memory span for number series of increasing length
   2. Simple arithmetic of increasing difficulty

    3. Common-sense questions
    4. Concept formation by verbal similarities
 B. *Performance tests of observation and sensory motor-co-ordination*
    5. Substitution code test (substituting digits for symbols)
    6. Object assembly (like jigsaw puzzles)
    7. Converting designs on color blocks
    8. Recognizing missing parts of pictures

The results of the tests were as follows:

NAME	IQ
1. Hjalmar Schacht	143
2. Arthur Seyss-Inquart	141
3. Hermann Goering	138
4. Karl Doenitz	138
5. Franz von Papen	134
6. Erich Raeder	134
7. Dr. Hans Frank	130
8. Hans Fritsche	130
9. Baldur von Schirach	130
10. Joachim von Ribbentrop	129
11. Wilhelm Keitel	129
12. Albert Speer	128
13. Alfred Jodl	127
14. Alfred Rosenberg	127
15. Constantin von Neurath	125
16. Walther Funk	124
17. Wilhelm Frick	124
18. Rudolf Hess	120
19. Fritz Sauckel	118
20. Ernst Kaltenbrunner	113
21. Julius Streicher	106

Goering was delighted with the results. The tests proved that, with the exception of Streicher, all the Nazi leaders were above the average in intelligence (IQ 90-110). But not only that. Because of age, Von Papen, Raeder, Schacht, and Streicher had been allowed "weightage" and without this their scores would have been 15-20 points lower, leaving Goering and Seyss-Inquart far and away the most intelligent of the lot.

His small pleasure over this flattering result was, however, dashed by the news that Emmy was under arrest. She
had made her way to Veldenstein Castle and had been
living in the porter's lodge, her only news of her husband
received in the letters (previously quoted) which Dr. Kelley had brought to her. On October 15, 1945, she was
arrested by American troops, ordered to pack a small bag,
and, with her niece, her sister, and Christa Gormans, the
nurse, was taken to Straubing prison. Edda was left behind
in the village to be cared for by the authorities.*

Goering had received a copy of the indictment against
him a few days previously, and it contained 24,000 words
of detailed charges against him of which this preamble is a
summary:

"The defendant *Goering* between 1932–45 was: a member of the Nazi Party, Supreme Leader of the SA, General
in the SS [he crossed this out], a member and President of
the Reichstag, Minister of the Interior of Prussia, Chief of
tne Prussian Police and Prussian Secret State Police, Chief
of the Prussia State Council, Trustee of the Four Year
Plan, Reich Minister for Air, Commander-in-Chief of the
Air Force, President of the Council of Ministers for the
Defense of the Reich, member of the Secret Cabinet Council, head of the Hermann Goering Industrial Combine, and
Successor Designate to Hitler. The defendant *Goering* used
the foregoing positions, his personal influence, and his intimate connection with the Fuehrer in such a manner that:
he promoted the military and economic preparation for
war set forth in Count One of the Indictment; he participated in the preparation and planning of the Nazi conspirators for Wars of Aggression and Wars in Violation of
International Treaties, Agreements and Assurances set
forth in Counts One and Two of the Indictment; and he
authorized, directed and participated in the War Crimes set
forth in Count Three of the Indictment, and the Crimes
against Humanity set forth in Count Four of the Indictment, including a wide variety of crimes against persons
and property."

All this Goering took in his stride. It was pretty much
what he had expected. When Dr. Gilbert, who was starting

* She was later allowed to join her mother in her cell.

a collection, asked him to autograph his copy of the indictment, he wrote across the top:

"Der Sieger wird immer Richter und der Besiegte stets der Angeklagte sein!" (The victor will always be the judge and the vanquished the accused.)

Emmy's arrest outraged him, and to Dr. Kelley he repeatedly said:

"It was the only thing I asked for when I surrendered, that my family be protected and adequately cared for."

Kelley promised to keep in touch with Emmy for him and urged him to take his mind off her plight by getting down to work on his defense. Goering had chosen Dr. Otto Stahmer, a staid, almost prim, seventy-year-old lawyer from Kiel, to lead his case, and the contrast between the two men was sharp; but somehow they complemented each other and established a rapport. With Stahmer and his assistant, Dr. Werner Bross, he began building up his defense against the charges in the indictment. He had few papers to guide him, and no diaries, but his memory was a formidable one and he had almost total recall of his life since his first adherence to National Socialism.

He informed Stahmer, at first to that staid gentleman's stupefaction, but eventually with his approval, that he did not propose to excuse himself in court for having followed Adolf Hitler so blindly, and as the Fuehrer's deputy he would take the blame for all the orders which had been issued in his name. In a way, he seemed to feel that he was taking Hitler's place in the dock and that it was therefore all the more important to make a brave showing before the world.

"It was not cowardly of Hitler to commit suicide," he said to Kelley one day. "After all, he was chief of the German State. It would be absolutely unthinkable to me to have Hitler sitting in a cell like this waiting trial as a war criminal before a foreign tribunal. Though he hated me at the end, he was for me, after all, a symbol of Germany. Even the Japanese insisted upon not bringing their Emperor to trial. No matter how much harder it is to me now, I would still rather suffer any consequence than to have Hitler alive as a prisoner before a foreign court. That is absolutely unthinkable."

On October 24, one of the chief Nazi politicians among

the accused, Robert Ley, strangled himself in his cell. He had made a noose from torn strips of towel which he fastened to the toilet pipe. In a note which he left behind Ley stated that he could not stand the shame of his position any longer.

The news of his suicide was kept secret from the prisoners, and it was not until October 29 that Colonel Andrus sent around a note merely saying that he was dead. But Goering guessed that it had been suicide from the increased vigilance outside his cell from then on, and the frequency of the spot searches. When Dr. Gilbert told him of Ley's death, Goering said:

"It's just as well that he's dead, because I had my doubts about how he would behave at the trial. He's always been so scatterbrained—always making such fantastic and bombastic speeches."

He was now becoming worried about the stability of the other Nazi leaders. "I hope Ribbentrop doesn't break down," he said. "I'm not afraid of the soldiers—they'll behave themselves. But Hess—he's insane. He's been insane for a long time."

Gilbert mentioned the attempt on Hitler's life in 1944 and said he had the impression that the German people now wished it had succeeded, because they were completely disillusioned with the Nazi leadership.

Goering snorted. "Never mind what the German people say *now!* That's the one thing that doesn't interest me a damn bit. I know what they said *before!* I know how they cheered and praised us when things were going well. I know too much about people."

He finished yet another day with Dr. Stahmer, wrestling with the answers to the indictment, and that evening he seemed in a good mood. The talk got around to the international nature of the forthcoming trial, and the nationality of the judges. A twinkle came into his eye, and he said to Kelley:

"If you have one German, you have a fine man; but if you have two Germans, they form a *Bund;* and if you have three Germans they start a war. If you have one Englishman, you have an idiot; two Englishmen immediately form a club; and when you have three Englishmen, they create an Empire. One Italian is always a tenor; two Italians make a duet; three Italians and you have a retreat. As for the Japanese—one Japanese is a mystery; two Japanese is also a mystery; and three Japanese"—he paused here for the punchline—"three Japanese, well, that's a mystery too!"

He wheezed with great gusts of laughter at his own joke.

By this time, Kelley had become fascinated by the personality of the Reich Marshal and a genuine admirer of his quick wit and charm and the attitude he displayed toward the rigors of the trial to come. Finally, he could not resist asking Goering why he had always used his talents to support Hitler, even when he felt he was going wrong, and why he had never opposed him in the wildest of his projects. Why had he and all the rest of Hitler's followers been such abject "yes men"?

Goering agreed that he had been, but then wryly added:

"Please show me a 'no man' in Germany who is not six feet under the ground today."

To Gilbert later, he said:

"As far as this trial is concerned, it's just a cut and dried political affair, and I'm prepared for the consequences. I have no doubt that the press will play a bigger part in the decision than the judges. And I'm sure that the Russian and French judges, at least, already have their instructions. I can answer for anything I've done, and I can't answer for anything I haven't done. But the victors are the judges . . . I know what's in store for me. I'm even writing my farewell letter to my wife today."

And it was in this mood that, on November 20, 1945, he took his place in the dock at Nuremberg to face his trial as a major war criminal.

XXVI. PLATFORM

The International Military Tribunal at Nuremberg was not a trial in the sense that is normally accepted in civilized countries. It had been officially announced before the proceedings began that it would generally follow the practices of British and American courts of law, giving the defendants the right to speak and to cross-examine. But even though the presiding judge, Lord Justice Lawrence, was a venerable British jurist renowned for the impartiality of his judgments, both he and his American, French, and Russian colleagues knew what was expected of them, and that there could be no question of the principal accused winning acquittal. The defendants were doomed before the trial started, no matter what case they made for themselves in court.*

The purpose of the tribunal was not to give the accused a fair trial to the extent that they could introduce all kinds of relevant evidence in justification of their actions. That would have proved embarrassing. Goering, Von Ribbentrop, and Frank, for instance, could almost certainly, and justifiably, have involved the Soviet Union as accomplices in the monstrous crimes against Poland and the Polish-people, in whose subjugation they played a bloodthirsty role. But since two Russians were among the judges and the Russians were co-prosecutors, the defendants and their lawyers were warned that all attempts to implicate the Soviet Union would be disallowed.

What the tribunal set out to do, by meticulous presentation of the Third Reich's own documents, by the evidence of witnesses and victims, by the patient examination of the

---

* It is true that three out of the twenty defendants were, in fact, acquitted. But most reporters at the trial could have guessed their number and names from the start.

acts and motives of the accused themselves, was to draw a picture of Hitler's Germany in the fullest detail possible so that the German people themselves, and the rest of the world, could at least see what a horrendous spectacle it had been.

There are some jurists who still maintain that Nuremberg was a perfectly valid legal process, and they can make a case for it. But in fact it was just as much a political trial as any which had taken place in Russia, even though the motives of most of its organizers were decent and civilized. Hermann Goering himself must have been reminded of the Reichstag Fire Trial, and if so, he might have remembered Dimitrov, the brave Bulgarian who had defied him in the dock. Dimitrov had been acquitted, and Goering had no hope of that; but at least, if he made the most of his appearance, he could write his name in history in the same way as Dimitrov had done, defiant and unvanquished until the last.

It all depended on the quality of his performance.

The trial began with the reading of the indictment on November 20, 1945, and for the next four months American, British, French, and Russian prosecutors came into court to read documents, make impassioned accusations, show films, and take witnesses painstakingly through their unhappy stories. For the first time in the history of jurisprudence, a trial was being conducted with simultaneous translation of all words spoken in court, and it was remarkable what facial expressions or gestures Goering could produce in response to the remarks coming over his earphones. In truth, there was little else he could do except mime and utter *sotto voce* remarks in order to keep alive his interest; for though there were days when films were shown of concentration camps that shocked and subdued him, or days when evidence was given that aroused him to indignation, skepticism, or fury, there were other days when the drone of the translator's voice reciting the long list of Nazi crimes grew monotonous and lost its impact by the sheer weight of its statistical horror.

It was behind the scenes that he really came alive. With the start of the trial, Colonel Andrus decided that the accused should be allowed to speak to each other again, and for the first few days it was like the reunion of an old wartime battalion. But then they began forming up into cliques, according to their rank in the Party as much as their personal inclinations. Only Julius Streicher, the arch Jewbaiter, was generally eschewed by the rest. But otherwise, Hermann Goering was automatically recognized as the titular leader and he bustled around them all, keeping up their spirits, giving advice on how to present their evidence, urging them to keep a united front against their accusers.

In the evenings he would look forward to long talks with Dr. Gilbert, and he would comment on the trial or the day's proceedings.

"You know, the Americans are amateurs at this game," he said one night. "They are so arrogant and naïve. We Germans made the same mistakes. The English are much cleverer about these things. They are older hands at it. There is a proverb, 'The German has a soft heart and a hard hand. The Englishman has a hard heart and a soft hand.' That is how they have kept their power. They beat the Boers then used the soft hand and had them fighting on their side ten years later. They are doing the same now. They say, 'Sure, let the Americans be the jailers and the prosecutors. We just present our case simply. We have a Chief Justice who is impartial and even sticks up for the defendants' rights now and then. Let the Americans take the aggressive part and earn the hatred of the Germans.' "

On January 3, 1946, Goering had a setback. During the evidence being given by one of the Gestapo chiefs, Karl Ohlenburg, who admitted the mass-killing of Jews, the lawyer for Albert Speer rose and asked the witness whether he knew that Speer had tried to assassinate Hitler and had planned to deliver Himmler to the enemy to answer for his crimes.

During the intermission, Goering lunged across at Speer and asked him how dare he make such a treasonable admission. It had shattered their united front! Speer and he argued angrily for several minutes.

That evening Goering, looking tired and depressed, said to Gilbert:

"This was a bad day. Damn that stupid fool, Speer! Did you see how he disgraced himself in court today? *Gott in Himmel! Donnerwetter nochamal!* How could he stoop so low as to do such a rotten thing just to save his lousy neck!

I nearly died of shame. To think that Germans will be so rotten just to prolong this filthy life—to put it bluntly—to piss in front and crap from behind just for a little longer. *Herrgott! Donnerwetter!* Do you think I give that much of a damn about this lousy life."

He faced Gilbert with his eyes blazing. "For myself, I don't give a damn if I get executed, or drown, or crash in a plane, or drink myself to death. But there is still a matter of honor in this damn life. Assassination of Hitler! Ugh! *Gott in Himmel!* I could have sunk through the floor. And do you think I would have handed Himmler over to the enemy, guilty as he was? Dammit, I would have liquidated the bastard myself!"

The next day, Goering was as furious as ever. At the table where he was sitting at lunch with the generals and Baldur von Schirach, Gilbert heard him saying:

"Damn it, I don't care a hoot what the enemy tries to do to us, but it makes me sick to see Germans double-crossing each other." He nodded to Von Schirach and in reference to Speer, said to him: "Go and talk to that fool!"

Schirach went out into the hall and started a deep discussion with Speer, telling him that Goering thought he was disgracing himself and the good name of Germany. Speer rebuffed him.

"I told him Goering should have been furious when Hitler was leading the whole nation straight to destruction," said Speer later. "As the second man in the Reich, he had the responsibility of doing something about it, but then he was too much of a coward. Instead he doped himself with morphine and looted art treasures from all over Europe."

Goering and Speer from now on became bitter enemies, and as the long trial droned on, a battle began between the two of them behind the scenes, with Goering trying to isolate Speer from the rest of the defendants and hold them to the Party line, and Speer determined to break up the united front and smash Goering's influence. Speer had the advantage over Goering in this particular fight, because he was prepared to do something which his adversary would never have contemplated, and ally himself with the enemy in order to bring Goering down. On January 4, he fired his first shot by saying to Gilbert:

"You know, Goering still thinks he's the big shot and is running the show even as a war criminal. He even told me yesterday, 'You didn't even tell me you were going to say that.'† How do you like that?"

Over the weekend of January 12–13, he went a stage further and said to Gilbert:

"You know, it is not a very good idea to let the defendants eat and walk together. That is how Goering keeps whipping them into line. It would be much better if they weren't intimidated from saying what they feel, so that the people will be rid once and for all of the last rotten remains of their illusions about National Socialism."

Gilbert mentioned Speer's remarks to Colonel Andrus, who was much impressed. From that moment onward, not only Gilbert but all other officials who had contact with the prisoners were watching and listening to Goering, and assessing the nature of his influence. Finally, on the evening of February 15, Gilbert assembled the prisoners before they were taken back to their cells and read out a new edict from the commandant. They had been put back into solitary confinement, and had been forbidden to communicate with each other.

"They took it in silent anger," Gilbert commented. Even Hjalmar Schacht, who was no friend of Goering's, was furious over the new ruling.

"He actually screamed as he worked himself into a frenzy over his treatment in prison," wrote Gilbert in his diary. " 'It is disgraceful—*shabby!* The colonel can do with us what he likes, but I do not envy him his power . . . This shows treatment by people who have no tradition and no culture—it is *contemptible!*' "

Goering was depressed, for he guessed, rightly, that his ridiculing, domineering attitude had something to do with the orders for reconfinement.

"Don't you see—all this joking and horseplay is only a comic relief," he said. "Do you think I enjoy sitting there and hearing accusations heaped on our heads from all sides? We've got to let off steam somehow. If I didn't pep them up, a couple of them would simply collapse."

But Albert Speer was pleased with the new regulation. "It comes at a critical time, too," he said, "just when some of them are beginning to become a little uneasy over Goe-

† Implying that Goering should have been told beforehand of the intervention by Speer's lawyer.

ring's dictatorship, and he is beginning to put on the real
pressure. He got hold of Funk in the exercise yard a couple
of days ago, and told him to reconcile himself to the fact
that his life was lost and the only question now was to
stand by him and die a martyr's death . . . Goering knows
his goose is cooked, and needs a retinue of at least 20
lesser heroes for his grand entrance into Valhalla."

On February 18, the solitary confinement came to an
end, but Colonel Andrus had thought up a new way of
isolating Goering. He ordained that henceforward the defendants would be separated at lunchtime into five separate
rooms. There would be what Andrus called (a) the "Youth
Lunchroom" with Speer, Fritsche, Von Schirach, and
Funk ("the purpose," commented Gilbert, "to let Speer
and Fritsche wean the other two away from Goering's
influence"); (b) the "Elders Lunchroom" with Von Papen,
Von Neurath, Schacht, and Doenitz ("the purpose being to
give the old conservatives a chance to denounce Hitler and
Ribbentrop"); (c) Frank, Seyss-Inquart, Keitel and
Sauckel ("the purpose being to take Keitel away from
Goering"); (d) Raeder, Streicher, Hess, and Ribbentrop
("the intractable Nazis who would not be apt to talk to
each other even if allowed, because of Streicher's presence
and Hess's secretiveness, Raeder's security-consciousness,
Ribbentrop's frustration—keeping them neutralized"); (e)
Jodl, Frick, Kaltenbrunner, and Rosenberg ("nothing in
common"); and (f) Hermann Goering on his own.

Albert Speer had won. Goering was isolated.

"Goering was furious over being put in a small room by
himself," Gilbert wrote later, "and complained of the lack
of heat and daylight, though it was obvious that his anger
was really due to his frustration over losing his audience.
Frank was quite pleased by the new arrangement. Schacht
was still indignant but stressed that there were no hard
feelings towards me personally. Speer looked pleased."

On March 9, 1946, news was brought to Goering that
Emmy had been released from Straubing prison, and it
could not have come at a better time to stir his flagging
spirits. The previous day the case for his defense had
begun, and it had started badly. The first witness on his
behalf was Karl Bodenschatz, who had loyally testified
about his chief's unremitting efforts to negotiate peace

with England behind Hitler's back, to his work in rescuing
victims from concentration camps, and to his over-all
image as a peace-loving man. His testimony was, unfortunately, torn to pieces by a polemical attack from the U.S.
chief prosecutor, Mr. Justice Robert H. Jackson, who
overwhelmed the unfortunate Bodenschatz by tripping
him up in a maze of contradictory statements and admissions.

Schacht was delighted at Goering's discomfiture. "The
fat one is sure taking a beating so far," he told Gilbert.
"Your prosecutor Jackson is certainly a brilliant cross-
examiner. Even when he is not sure what he will find, he
beats on each bush to see if a rabbit jumps out—and
sometimes it does."

All Goering said was: "Wait until he [Jackson] starts
on me—he won't have any nervous Bodenschatz to deal
with."

In the next few days Milch, Berndt von Brauchitsch, and
Paul Koerner, his former secretary of state,‡ all testified in
Goering's favor, and nothing could shake their firm statements that he had worked for peace, had treated his enemies decently, and had tried to ameliorate the lot of those
who had found themselves captured or placed in concentration camps. Mr. Justice Jackson appeared to be considerably disturbed by this.

On the morning of March 13, 1946, it was Hermann
Goering's turn to take the stand. He had waited a long time
for his day in court, and he was nervous.

"I still don't recognize the authority of the court," he
said to Gilbert, before the session began. "I can say, like
Maria Stuart, that I can be tried only by a court of peers."
He grinned as he said this. Then he shrugged his shoulders.
"Bringing the heads of a foreign state before a foreign
court is a presumptuousness which is unique in history."

But when the moment came, he was ready for it. In the
next four days, he was taken carefully, meticulously, and
patiently through the history of the National Socialist
Party and of his relations with Adolf Hitler as he had lived
them and experienced them. Even his enemies admitted
that it was quite a performance. Goering's total recall of all

‡ There was only one old friend missing. To Goering's stupefaction
his lifelong comrade, Bruno Loerzer, refused to testify.

that had happened to him stood him in good stead at this moment, and he gave to every incident he described and every interview in which he was involved a color and a verisimilitude which was impressive. The courtroom settled into a tense and then into a pregnant hush as he spoke, and for the first time a sense of drama and history tingled in the heavy air.

At the end of the first day of his testimony, even his enemy Albert Speer was ready to admit that it had been a moving performance. It seemed to symbolize, for him, the tragedy of the German people, and he said:

"Seeing him [Goering] so serious and stripped of his diamonds and decorations, making a final defense before a tribunal, after all the power, pomp and bombast—it was really *erschütternd* (gripping)."

Goering himself said: "You must realize that after being imprisoned for almost a year, and sitting through this trial for 5 months, without saying a word in court, it was really a strain for me—especially the first ten minutes. The one thing that annoyed me, dammit, is that I could not keep my hand from shaking." He held it out. "There, you see, it is steadier now."

He went on the next day, and the next, and whenever there was a break in the session he would bounce up to Gilbert (he was not allowed to speak to his fellow accused) and say:

"Well, how was it? You cannot say I was cowardly, can you?"

It was a formidable performance, and he knew he was making a good impression. He did not flinch from responsibility.

"I should like to emphasize," he said at one point, "that although I received oral and written orders and commands from the Fuehrer to issue and carry out these laws, I assume full responsibility for them. They bear my signature. I issued them. And consequently, I am responsible and do not propose to hide in any way behind the Fuehrer's order."

He justified the existence of the National Socialist state: "I upheld this principle and I still uphold it positively and consciously. One must not make the mistake of forgetting the political structure in different countries has different origins, different developments. Something which suits one country extremely well would, perhaps, fail completely in another. Germany, through long centuries of monarchy, has always had a leadership principle." He paused, and then added: "It is the same principle as that on which the Roman Catholic Church and the Government of the U.S.S.R. are both based."

He denied that he had condoned Gestapo and SS excesses. "At the time when I was still directly connected with the Gestapo such excesses did, as I have openly stated, take place. In order to punish them, one naturally had to find out about them. Punishments were administered. The officials knew that if they did such things they ran the risk of being punished. A large number of them were punished. I cannot say what the practice was later."

And of Hitler's failure to take advice from him or from the generals: "How on earth can a state be led if, during a war or before a war which has been decided upon by the leaders, the individual general could vote whether he was going to fight or not, whether his army corps was going to stay at home or not. . . . That privilege would have to be afforded the ordinary soldier too. Perhaps this would be the way to avoid wars in future, if one asks every soldier whether he wants to go home or not. Possibly—but not in a 'Fuehrer' state."

At last his testimony was over, and, tired from the strain, he came back to his cell, asked that the light through the door porthole be dimmed, and "brooded over his destiny . . . and his role in history," as Gilbert put it.

Speer had now begun to worry a little over Goering's performance, and told Gilbert that he was anxious to have the Reich Marshal's "heroic pose of loyalty and integrity stripped to its corrupt reality."

"A corrupt coward like Goering—I could tell you about his private air raid shelters, and the soft life he led while Germany was in agony—a coward like that wants to play the hero," Speer said. "That's what burns me up."

He told Gilbert that he assumed Mr. Justice Jackson would reveal Goering in his true colors when the cross-examination started.

Much was hoped for from Justice Jackson's cross-examination, and not only by Albert Speer. The Allies were worried too by the effectiveness of Goering's performance.

One of those officiating at the trial was a famous English jurist, Sir Norman (later Lord) Birkett, who was alternate judge to Lord Justice Lawrence. He kept notes throughout the trial, and at this point he wrote:

"Goering is the man who has really dominated the proceedings, and that, remarkable enough, without ever uttering a word in public up to the moment he went into the witness box. That in itself is a very remarkable achievement and illuminates much that was obscure in the past few years. He has followed the evidence with great intentness when the evidence required attention, and has slept like a child when it did not; and it has been obvious that a personality of outstanding, though possibly evil qualities, was seated there in the dock."

Birkett was surprised to discover that no one had anticipated the intelligence and resourcefulness of Goering.

"Nobody seems to have been quite prepared for his immense ability and knowledge," he wrote, "and his thorough mastery and understanding of the detail of the captured documents. He has obviously studied them with the greatest care and appreciated the matters which might assume the deadliest form."

He summed up Goering at this point in the trial as: "Suave, shrewd, adroit, capable, resourceful, he quickly saw the elements of the situation, and as his self confidence grew, his mastery became more apparent. His self control, too, was remarkable and to all the other qualities manifested in his evidence he added the resonant tones of his speaking voice, and the eloquent but restrained use of gesture."

This was quite a tribute, given the source it came from, and the anxiety between the lines was obvious. No one on the Allied side wanted to see Goering emerge as the hero of the trial. It was the hope of everyone that Mr. Justice Jackson would cut him down to size.

But this was certainly not what happened. Those who watched the duel between the chief U.S. prosecutor and the leading living personality of the German Reich were soon uncomfortably aware that it was no match. Mr. Justice Jackson was not in the same class as Hermann Goering. It was not so much that Jackson had not read his brief as that he had not done his homework about German history. He was shaky on his facts. He gave Goering repeated opportunities to correct him—which he did with an air of great courtesy and mock-humble helpfulness. His questions were so framed that time and again Goering was able to launch upon a long dissertation, and it was hard to bring him to a halt.

Soon Jackson was irritated and had lost his way, and Goering made a great show of trying to help him. From the cross-examination from which so much had been expected, all that emerged was that Goering had done his best for peace, had tried to help the Jews, was against the war with Russia, had not set fire to the Reichstag, and had, despite his faults, always remained loyal to the Fuehrer. As Birkett commented later:

"Goering reveals himself as a very able man who perceives the intention of every question almost as soon as it is framed and uttered. He has considerable knowledge, too, and has an advantage over the Prosecution in this respect, for he is always on familiar ground. He has knowledge which many others belonging to the Prosecution and the Tribunal have not. He has therefore quite maintained his ground and the Prosecution has not really advanced its case at all. Certainly there has been no dramatic destruction of Goering as had been anticipated or prophesied."

So far as Goering was concerned, the clash really came to an end when Mr. Justice Jackson flung down his earphones in a rage at one of Goering's long and persuasive replies, and an embarrassed Lord Justice Lawrence called for an adjournment of the court. There was more cross-examination to come, from Jackson, and from the French, British, and Russian prosecutors, but none of them really made a dent in the image Goering had created of himself.*

Goering came out of court when it was over and called to the others:

"If you all handle yourselves half as well as I did, you will do all right. You have to be careful. Every other word can be twisted around."

Speer seemed to think that Mr. Justice Jackson had, in

---

* Though the effect he had hoped to create by the appearance of Birger Dahlerus as a defense witness was nullified by the collapse of the Swede under the devastating cross-examination of Britain's Sir David Maxwell-Fyfe, who, rather than see him bolster up Goering as a peacemaker, crushed him like a fly.

spite of appearances, succeeded in piercing Goering's armor. But he could not help adding:

"It is remarkable how [Goering] held up under the strain. Your prison discipline has certainly had a sobering effect on him. You should have seen him in the old days. A lazy, selfish, corrupt, irresponsible dope addict. Now he cuts a dashing figure, and the people admire his nerve. I hear from my attorney that they are saying, 'That Goering is quite a guy (*Mordskerl*).' But you should have seen him before. They were all corrupt cowards in the country's hour of crisis. Why do you suppose Goering wasn't in Berlin to stand by his beloved Fuehrer? Because it was too hot in Berlin when the Russians closed in. The same with Himmler . . . No, none of them must go down in history as the least bit worthy of respect. Let the whole damn Nazi system and all who participated in it, including myself, go down with the ignominy and disgrace it deserves. And let the people forget and start to build a new life on some sensible democratic basis."

Hermann Goering's testimony and cross-examination were finished by March 22, 1946, and the concluding speeches for the prosecution did not begin until four months later, on July 26. During that time, the defendants sat in court by day, and squabbled or tattled with each other, and with Dr. Gilbert by night. Goering had steadfastly refused to allow Emmy to come to Nuremberg and testify on his behalf, and he had also told Dr. Stahmer to inform Thomas von Kantzow that he would not allow him to take the stand as a defense witness.†

The euphoria which Goering had felt following his performance in the witness box gradually wilted; its heroic effect had slowly been chipped away by the testimonies which had followed. He got no lift from the concluding speech in his defense which Dr. Stahmer made, which ascribed all his ills to his loyalty to the Fuehrer, "this loyalty which has been his disaster."

† On March 13, 1946, Thomas had written a long letter (a copy of which is now in the author's possession) giving details of Goering's efforts on behalf of Jews and other Gestapo victims, and offering his services as a witness.

He looked as weary of the trial as most people were everywhere. It had now lasted nine months, and in the outside world people were already worried about other things.

Mr. Justice Jackson summed up for the Americans, and made up in his eloquent speech for the ham-handed way he had handled Goering's cross-examination. Of Goering he said:

"[He] was half militarist and half gangster. He stuck a pudgy finger in every pie . . . He was equally adept at massacring opponents and at framing scandals to get rid of stubborn generals. He built up the Luftwaffe and hurled it at his defenseless neighbors. He was among the foremost in harrying the Jews out of the land."

And of all the accused, he cried:

"If you were to say of these men that they are not guilty, it would be as true to say that there has been no war, there are no slain, there has been no crime."

Sir Hartley Shawcross, for Britain, said:

"Goering's responsibility in all these matters is scarcely to be denied. Behind his spurious air of bonhomie, he was as great an architect as any in this satanic system. Who, apart from Hitler, had more knowledge of what was going on, or greater influence to affect its course . . . Years ago Goethe said of the German people that some day fate would strike them, 'would strike them because they betrayed themselves and did not want to be what they are. It is sad that they do not know the charm of truth, detestable that mist, smoke and berserk immoderation are so dear to them, pathetic that they ingenuously submit to any mad scoundrel who appeals to their lowest instincts, who confirms them in their vices and teaches them to conceive nationalism as isolation and brutality.' "

Sir Hartley paused, looked toward the dock and hard at Goering, and said:

"With what a voice of prophecy he spoke—for these are the mad scoundrels who did these very things."

Passing out of the courtroom at the end of the session, Goering said to Ribbentrop:

"There, you see, it's just as if we hadn't made any defense at all."

"Yes, it was a waste of time," Ribbentrop agreed.

The prisoners were allowed to make a final speech before the proceedings came to a close, and on August 31, 1946, Hermann Goering quietly but eloquently denied the prosecution's charges against him.

"I never decreed the murder of a single individual at any time, nor decreed any other atrocities, nor tolerated them while I had the power and the knowledge to prevent them," he said. "I did not want war nor did I bring it about. I did everything to prevent it by negotiation. After it had broken out, I did everything to assure victory . . . The only motive which guided me was my ardent love for my people and my desire for their happiness and freedom. And for this I call on the Almighty and my German people as witnesses."

A month passed by while the judges considered their verdicts. In that period the restrictions on Hermann Goering were relaxed so that he could once more mix freely with his fellow prisoners, but now that the shadow of the verdict was falling across all of them, each man was retreating into his shell, brooding over the bleakness of his prospects. When they did talk together they bickered about the past, blaming each other for the sins of the regime. And because Goering seemed the most undisturbed by the future, so outwardly untroubled by the imminent verdict, they would flare at him.

"Who in the world is responsible for all this destruction, if not *you?*" cried an infuriated Franz von Papen one day. "You were the second man in the State. Is *no one* responsible for any of this?" He pointed through the lunchroom windows at the ruins of Nuremberg beyond.

Goering said: "Well, why don't you take the responsibility, then? You were Vice-Chancellor."

"I am taking my share of the responsibility!" Von Papen retorted. "But what about you? You haven't taken the least responsibility for anything. All you do is make bombastic speeches. It is disgraceful."

Goering laughed at him. And it was just this manner which seemed to stir anger in the others. Waiting as they were for news of their fate, they simmered with rage at a man who could wait so calmly, who refused to give way to his innermost fears, who was challenging his accusers just as strongly now as he had done at the beginning of the trial, ten months before.

On September 15, 1946, it was announced that the wives of the prisoners would now be allowed to visit them daily. With some difficulty, Emmy made her way from Sackdilling, near Neuhaus, where she was now living, to Nuremberg. Life had been difficult for her over the past few months, and she was a sick woman, racked with severe sciatic pains. She and her daughter Edda had been living in a primitive shack in the woods with no running water and few resources. Ironically enough, the most help she had received was from Dr. Robert M. Kempner, her husband's old enemy from Berlin, who had visited her several times, bringing food, and chocolate for Edda, and taking back news of them to Goering.

The woman who had once been the first lady of the Third Reich now had one dress, one hat, and an old pair of shoes left. But Goering did not notice her appearance. After seventeen months of separation, it was enough to see her again. They could not touch, because a wire-mesh grill separated them from each other, and Emmy was inhibited in what she said by the presence of a huge U.S. military policeman standing beside her husband as he faced her. But during the next few days, it became easier for her to talk.

The verdict had been expected on September 23, but it was announced that it would be postponed for a week. Emmy, who had been staying in two rooms allotted to her by Dr. Stahmer, Goering's lawyer, arranged for Edda to come from Sackdilling to join her. When she came into the interview room with Edda holding her hand, Goering broke down for the first time. And then suddenly he began grinning through his tears, for the first words Edda said to him were:

"Daddy, when you come home, will you please wear your medals in the bath—like people say you do? I've never seen them all covered with soap. Do they tickle?"

The next day Emmy shared her visiting session with Goering's sister Pauli, and toward the end of it asked her husband whether he would sign a testimonial for his valet, Robert Kropp. In order to get a job, he had to be able to prove that he had never been a member of the Nazi Party. Goering wrote out the required declarations. He got a wry amusement out of the fact that one in his position could still affect a man's future in the outside world.

Emmy always avoided talking about the forthcoming
verdicts, but on this particular day Goering himself mentioned that soon the fate of all of them would be decided.

"But don't worry," he said to her. "Whatever happens, I
won't hang."

On September 30, 1946, the defendants were brought
back into the courtroom to hear the verdicts. Goering had
seen Emmy the day before for what he believed was the
last time, and their brief farewell had shaken him. But he
was quite calm in court as he listened to the judges, each in
turn, reading out his judgment. It was one long recital of
Nazi crimes and it went on all day, a chilling accumulation
of planned aggressions, broken promises, savagery, brutality, and murder. By the time the judges had finished, it was
afternoon and the individual verdicts were still to come.
The prisoners filed back to their cells for another night of
waiting.

The next morning, October 1, Hermann Goering was the
first to be called and he stood before Lord Justice Lawrence, his vivid blue eyes staring straight ahead to nowhere,
as the verdict was read out:

"From the moment he joined the Party in 1922 and took
command of the street fighting organization, the SA, Goering was the adviser, the active agent of Hitler and one of
the prime leaders of the Nazi movement. As Hitler's political deputy he was largely instrumental in bringing the National Socialists to power in 1933, and was charged with
consolidating this power and expanding German armed
might. He developed the Gestapo and created the first concentration camps, relinquishing them to Himmler in 1934;
conducted the Roehm purge in that year and engineered
the sordid proceedings which resulted in the removal of
von Blomberg and von Fritsch from the army . . . In the
Austrian Anschluss he was, indeed, the central figure, the
ring-leader . . . The night before the invasion of Czechoslovakia and the absorption of Bohemia and Moravia, at a
conference with Hitler and President Hácha he threatened
to bomb Prague if Hácha did not submit . . . He commanded the Luftwaffe in the attack on Poland and
throughout the aggressive wars which followed . . . The
record is filled with Goering's admissions of his complicity
in the use of slave labour . . . He made plans for the

spoliation of Soviet territory long before the war on the
Soviet Union.

"Goering persecuted the Jews, particularly after the November, 1938 riots, and not only in Germany, where he
raised the billion mark fine‡ as stated elsewhere, but in the
conquered territories as well. His own utterances, then and
in his testimony, show his interest was primarily economic
—how to get their property and how to force them out of
the economic life of Europe . . . Although their extermination was in Himmler's hands, Goering was far from disin-
terested or inactive despite his protestations from the witness box . . .

"There is nothing to be said in mitigation. For Goering
was often, indeed almost always, the moving force, second
only to his Leader. He was the leading war aggressor, both
as political and military leader; he was director of the slave
labour programme and the creator of the oppressive programme against the Jews and other races, at home and
abroad. All these crimes he has frankly admitted. On some
specific cases there may be conflict of testimony, but in
terms of the broad outline his own admissions are more
than sufficiently wide to be conclusive of his guilt. His guilt
is unique in its enormity. The record discloses no excuses
for this man. We find him guilty on all four counts of the
indictment."

Goering sat quite still, expressionless, while the rest of
the verdicts were read out. There were three acquittals:
Hjalmar Schacht, Franz von Papen, and Hans Fritsche,
and no one looked more surprised at their escape than they
did themselves. The rest were all found guilty on one or
more of the counts.

But still they did not yet know their fate. After reading
out the verdicts, Lord Justice Lawrence called the luncheon adjournment. The sentences would be given afterward.

In the afternoon, Hermann Goering was once more the
first to be brought into the dock. He stood between a guard
of GIs and adjusted his earphones. Lord Justice Lawrence
began to read the verdict.

"Hermann Wilhelm Goering," he began, when he no-

---

‡ A reference to the fine which Goering imposed on the Jewish
community in Germany—who had, in fact, been the victims—after
the Kristallnacht riots.

ticed that Goering was fiddling with the earphones and indicating that they were working improperly. The whole court waited in a heavy silence, prisoner and judge staring at each other, while mechanics mended the defect. Then they began again.

"Hermann Wilhelm Goering," said Lord Justice Lawrence, "on the counts of the indictment on which you have been convicted, the International Military Tribunal sentences you to death by hanging."

Goering absorbed the words, slowly took off the earphones, let them fall to the desk, and turned and left the court without a word.

It was Dr. Gilbert's duty to meet each prisoner after he had heard his sentence. Hermann Goering came down and went to his cell.

"His face was pale and frozen, his eyes popping," Gilbert wrote in his diary later. " 'Death!' he said as he dropped on his cot and reached for a book. His hand was trembling in spite of his attempt to be nonchalant. His eyes were moist and he was panting, fighting back an emotional breakdown. He asked me in an unsteady voice to leave him alone for a while."

The next day Hermann Goering wrote to the International Military Tribunal formally requesting that, as a serving officer in the German armed forces, he be executed not by hanging but by firing squad.

"At least I should be spared the ignominy of the noose," he said to Gilbert. "I am a soldier. I have been a soldier all my life, always ready to die by another soldier's bullet. Why shouldn't a firing squad of my enemies dispatch me now? Is that too much to ask?"

It was. The request was refused.

Now there was nothing more to do but wait for the hangman.

XXVII. FINAL GESTURE

Colonel Burton C. Andrus, the commandant of Nuremberg Jail, was resolved that none of the convicted war criminals in his charge who had been sentenced to hang was going to cheat the gallows. And, he was convinced that the security precautions he had taken completely precluded any possibility that they would be able to do so.

"We allowed the prisoners to have no weapons whatsoever," he said later, "nor any article that we believed could possibly be used for offense against themselves or anyone else. Glass was removed from the windows. They were denied belts, shoe laces. Eye glasses, fountain pens, watches with crystals were all taken away from them at night, and anything else with which they could harm themselves. They were under constant surveillance, and while they were in their cells were kept in constant view. Their rooms were thoroughly searched when they went to court. Food was brought to them by people who were themselves prisoners in the jail and had no contact with the outside world except by mail, and that was censored. When they went to court, they were accompanied by an escort guard. They were not allowed to speak to each other, and were allowed contact only with my prison staff, the doctor, dentist, chaplain. Their clothes were brought to them for court after they had passed examination. Their cells were subjected to search, and besides there were periodic shakedowns, when their cells and they were searched together. They were thoroughly searched when they were bathed, which was twice a week. A few times some articles that were considered contraband were found—bits of glass, nails, wire, string. I have always thought that the searches were thorough and that no one could keep anything concealed with which he could take his life."

Yet Hermann Goering was determined that, somehow,

he would kill himself before the time came to take him to the gallows. It was to be his last gesture of defiance, and the final proof that he was the special one among the Nazis, who could not, and would not, be treated like the others.

On October 7, 1946, Emmy Goering received an unexpected call at Sackdilling from Dr. Otto Stahmer to tell her that she was to be allowed one last visit to her husband in Nuremberg Jail. It took her some time to arrange transport, but eventually a shopkeeper in Auerbach who had a car which ran on wood alcohol gave her a lift to the city. She went directly to the jail and reported to Lieutenant Schwartz, the duty officer, but it was several hours before she was finally shown into the interview room. As usual, Goering was closely guarded and they were separated from each other by a wire and glass partition.

Goering's first words were to ask her whether Edda had been told about his sentence, and she nodded. She had always sworn to tell the truth to the child.

Goering said: "Dear little Edda. Let's hope life won't be too hard for her. Death would be a deliverance for me if only I could protect you. Would you like me to appeal for mercy?"*

Emmy shook her head. "No, Hermann. You can die peacefully after having done all you could at Nuremberg . . . I shall think that you died for Germany."

"Thank you for your words," Emmy quotes her husband as saying. "You have no idea what good they do me. Don't be afraid that they will hang me. They'll keep a bullet for me. Moreover, I must tell you that these foreigners may murder me but they haven't the right to judge me."

"Do you really think they will shoot you?" Emmy asked.

"You may be sure of one thing," Emmy quotes Goering as saying, "they won't hang me . . . No, they won't hang me."

From that moment on, she was to say later, she knew what Goering was going to do.

All the Nazi leaders carried poison around with them in the last days of the war, and it was with the regulation tube

---

* In fact it was already too late. The prisoners were allowed to appeal for clemency within four days of their sentence. Goering had refused to do so.

of cyanide that Heinrich Himmler had killed himself after his capture by the British in the last days of the conflict. Goering, like the rest, carried a dosage. When he first arrived at Mondorf interrogation center, he had been thoroughly searched, and a brass tube was found containing cyanide. It was hidden in a can of American-type coffee extract, and he showed evident signs of consternation when it was discovered and taken away from him.

At Nuremberg, after he had been weaned off his paracodeine pills, the only drug he was allowed to have were the nightly sleeping pills prescribed by Dr. Ludwig Pfluecker. Dr. Pfluecker had the job of looking after the day-to-day ailments of the accused Nazi leaders, and he had co-operated with Dr. Kelley during Goering's drug cure.

He prescribed a blue and a red sleeping pill to take away the withdrawal pains, and this treatment had been continued right to the last. The German doctor was under curfew and therefore had to make his calls on his Nazi patients before ten-thirty each night, but he handed the pills over to the duty officer, U.S. Lieutenant Charles J. Roska, who then turned them over to Goering nightly at eleven. The doctor later explained that Goering would have liked to take his pills earlier, but that the guard in the corridor outside his cell changed at ten-thirty each night and made such a row that even a pill-induced sleep was broken by it.

Once, while the trial was still on, Pfluecker said to Goering:

"Never try to conceal anything I give you, will you? It would be great trouble for me."

Goering smiled and said: "Doctor, I will never bring you any trouble."

In any case, no one was very worried about these pills. Even a great many of them swallowed at one time would only have produced a very deep sleep, and a stomach pump and shock treatment could have brought a man back easily from the effects.

So Colonel Andrus, though he would not breathe easy until the executions were over, was confident that all necessary precautions had been taken to keep the prisoners from cheating the hangman. In the gymnasium of the courthouse, three gallows had been erected and Master

Sergeant John C. Woods, of San Antonio, Texas, the chief executioner, was standing by.

The executions were planned for 2 A.M. on October 16, 1946, but this was supposed to be kept a secret from both the prisoners and the press. Nevertheless, on the evening of October 15, the buzz spread through Nuremberg that the time had come for the condemned men, and slowly groups of correspondents and cameramen began to gather outside the prison.†

Inside the prison, the sound of the hammering from the gymnasium, the brightness of the lights (they were usually dimmed in the cell block in the evening), and the noise of cars arriving outside all alerted the inmates to the fact that this was going to be execution night. In Cell No. 9 Goering's erstwhile administrator of the occupied territories, Fritz Sauckel, began his nightly bout of sobbing and moaning and shouting for mercy, a noisy display of terror which put everyone's nerves on edge.

Hermann Goering was in a bitter mood. He had said good-by the previous evening to the prison psychologist, Dr. Gilbert, who had found him "nervous and depressed and perhaps a little more bitter than usual." The reason for it was the Control Council's steadfast refusal to allow him, or the other prisoners, a different method of execution from hanging.

The bitterness remained. The prison chaplain, Captain Henry F. Gerecke, visited Goering between seven-thirty and seven forty-five on the evening of October 15.

"He seemed lower than other days," the chaplain noted later, "which to me was not surprising in view of things to come. We spoke about the others and he asked about Sauckel. Complained that he couldn't see poor Sauckel. Assured me he could help him through these days. Was again critical of the method of execution. Called it most dishonorable for him because of his former position with the German people. Then there was a silence. I broke in to ask him once more about his complete surrender of heart and soul to his Saviour. Again he claimed he was a Christian but couldn't accept the teachings of Christ. On yesterday's visit I refused him the Lord's Supper because he denied the Divinity of Christ who instituted this Sacra-

† There was a curfew for German citizens.

ment. He furthermore denied all fundamentals of the
Christian church yet claimed he was a Christian because he
never stepped out of the church. He became more dis-
couraged because I insisted he couldn't meet Edda, his
daughter, in Heaven if he refused the Lord's way of salvation. Goering was a rationalist, materialist, and modernist
of the first class. I hoped he could rest this evening. He
said he felt at ease."

When the chaplain had left, Lieutenant John W. West of
the U.S. guard came into Cell No. 5 for the nightly inspection and search.

"All his personal effects were searched, his bedding removed from bed and shaken," West reported, "the mattress
turned over. No contraband was found."

West said that Goering now seemed "very happy and
talked a great deal," but that otherwise all was normal.

The minutes slowly ticked away. The sound of more
cars could be heard arriving. In the officers' mess, Master
Sergeant Woods was having his supper. So were a U.S.
civilian male nurse who had been summoned from Paris
and an army captain whose job it would be to handle the
bodies of the condemned men once they had been hanged.
Colonel Andrus, who would be the official U.S. witness,
was already in the jail, but the others—representatives of
the Allied nations, press correspondents and two specially
invited German officials—had not yet arrived. The hangings were not due until two in the morning, and that was
four and a half hours away.

At nine-thirty, Dr. Pfluecker arrived at Goering's cell
and went inside, accompanied by Lieutenant Arthur J.
McLinden. Like almost all other members of the U.S.
prison guard, Lieutenant McLinden spoke no German, and
so he could not understand what Pfluecker said to Goering.
He watched the doctor hand Goering a pill which he took
while they were there. Then he took Goering's pulse and
spoke to him for about three minutes in German. After
which he shook his hand and they left.

Pfluecker and McLinden were Goering's last visitors,
and when the door of Cell No. 5 swung shut behind them,
Pfc Gordon Bingham of Company C, 26th Infantry, took
up his vigil at the porthole in the door. Goering was already in his nightshirt and had stayed in bed throughout
the visit with the doctor and the lieutenant.

"Then I locked the cell and looked in," Pfc Bingham said later, "and Goering was looking at me with his body close to the port and lifted off the bed a little, and then laid on his back with his arms at his side above the covers. From the time Goering sat up in bed when the doctor came into his cell to the time he laid his hands to his side, I could not see his left hand. He laid like that for about 15 minutes, then folded his hands on his chest, turning his head a little to the left. I then accidentally knocked the light aside and had to readjust it. When I looked in he was looking at me and pointing his fingers at me with his right hand. He then brought his hand down to his side on top of the covers. He then laid in that way for about 15 to 20 minutes, then laced his hands on his chest and kept them there for a few minutes; then, with his hands laced, put them over his eyes. Kept them there for a few minutes, then put them on his chest and then laid there for a short time; unlaced his hands and laid them to his side and brought them up and put his right hand under his armpit close to his eyes; then brought his arms to his sides; then laid there for about 10 minutes; then looked at me and turned away. Then my relief came in and caused a bit of noise. This made Goering look back at me again. Then I moved away as I was relieved."

Pfc Harold F. Johnson of Company C, 26th Infantry, took over from Bingham promptly at ten-thirty. He did not know it then, but there were just sixteen minutes to go.

"I came on duty as a member of the second relief on Goering's cell at 2230," Johnson said later. "At that time he was lying flat on his back with his hands stretched out along his sides above the blankets. He stayed in that position for about five minutes without so much as moving. Then he lifted his left hand clenched, as if to shield his eyes from the light, then he let it fall back down to his side above the covers. He lay perfectly motionless till about 2240 when he brought his hands across his chest with his fingers laced and turned his head to the wall."

It must have been at this exact moment that Hermann Goering cheated the hangman.

"He lay that way for about 2 or 3 minutes," Pfc Johnson went on, "and then placed his hands back along his sides. That was at 2244 exactly, as I looked at my watch to check the time. About two to three minutes later he seemed to stiffen and made a blowing, choking sound through his lips."

Johnson shouted out for the sergeant who was the so-called Corporal of the Relief that evening, and he came clattering down from the tier of cells on the second floor.

"I told him that there was something wrong with Goe-ring," said Johnson, "so he took off to the Prison Office on the double. He came back in a few seconds with Lieuten-ant Cromer, the Prison Officer, and Chaplain Gerecke. Lieutenant Cromer looked in the cell and then I opened the door and Lieutenant Cromer and the Chaplain went in. I followed them in, holding the light."

Hermann Goering's right hand was hanging down over the side of the bed. Chaplain Gerecke took hold of it and felt the pulse.

"Good Lord," he said, "this man is dead."

Ever since Hermann Goering killed himself on the night of his execution, people have speculated about the way in which he did it. Who passed him the poison?

In fact, the answer was really quite simple. He brought it into Nuremberg Jail himself. As Albert Speer said later, Nuremberg Jail was never really as secure as Colonel An-drus thought it was.

"I had a tube of toothpaste with poison in it all the time I was in Nuremberg," he said, "and took it on with me to Spandau Jail.‡ No one ever thought of looking inside it."

Hermann Goering was so sure that his own poison would not be discovered that four days before he killed himself, he wrote a letter to Colonel Andrus telling him all about it. It was one of the three letters and one envelope which were found under the blanket of his bed.

The envelope contained an empty vial of cyanide poison. The first letter was a long proclamation, addressed to the German people, justifying his actions and rebutting the Allied charges against him. The second was a short and affectionate letter of farewell to Emmy and Edda Goering.

The proclamation was seized by the Allies and has never since been released for publication. The farewell letter was passed on to Emmy. The third was as follows:

‡ Where he served a sentence of twenty years.

Nürnberg, 11 October 1946

To the Commandant:

I have always had the capsule of poison with me from the time that I became a prisoner. When taken to Mondorf I had *three* capsules. The *first* I left in my clothes so that it would be found when a search was made. The *second* I placed under the clothesrack on undressing and took it to me again on dressing. I did this in Mondorf and here in the cell so well that despite the *frequent* and *thorough searches* it could not be found. During the court sessions I had it on my person in my high riding boots. The *third* capsule is *still* in my small suitcase in the round box of skin cream, hidden in the cream. I could have taken this twice to me in Mondorf if I had needed it. None of those charged with searching me is to be blamed for it was practically *impossible* to find the capsule. It would have been pure *accident*.

(signed) Hermann Goering.

P.S. Dr. Gilbert informed me that the control Board has refused the petition to change the method of execution to shooting.

At 2 A.M. on October 16, 1946, Joachim von Ribbentrop took Goering's place as the first Nazi leader to die on the gallows in the gymnasium of Nuremberg Jail. Wilhelm Keitel followed, and then Kaltenbrunner, Rosenberg, Frank, Frick, Streicher, Jodl, and Seyss-Inquart. At 3:15 A.M. it was all over.

The bodies were taken into a canvas-screened chamber, where they were viewed by officers of all the powers who signed death certificates. Photographs were taken of each body, fully clothed and then naked. Each body was placed inside a mattress cover, along with the garments last worn, and the rope used in the hanging, and then placed in a casket. The caskets were then sealed.

When the other bodies had been dealt with, Goering's was brought in on a stretcher under an army blanket. He was dressed in a pale blue pajama coat and black trousers.

At 4 A.M. the caskets were loaded into a number of 2½-ton trucks waiting in the prison yard, covered with tarpaulin, and then driven away with an army escort. A U.S.

civilian and an army captain rode in the lead car, followed
by a French and an American general in a sedan. Behind
came the trucks and, guarding them, a jeep filled with
picked guards and a machine gun. The convoy turned and
twisted through Nuremberg, and then made off for Erlan-
gen to the south. Newsmen who tried to follow were dissuaded with the machine gun.

It was a misty, rainy morning and as the convoy raced
southward the guard was changed four times. No one
asked what was in the trucks. It was dawn when the party
reached Munich, and it made straight for a crematorium
on the outskirts of the town, where the undertakers had
been warned to await the arrival of the bodies of "fourteen
American soldiers." In fact, there were only eleven bodies,
but that was said to lull any suspicions the crematorium
employees might have.

Once there the crematorium was surrounded and radio
liaison made with surrounding units and armored columns,
just in case there was any disturbance. Anyone who came
to the crematorium was not allowed to leave again until the
end of the following day.

Now the caskets were unsealed and the bodies examined
by the American, British, French, and Russian officers who
had witnessed the executions, to make sure there had been
no body switches en route. The cremations began immediately and continued all day.

When they were finished, a car drew up at the crematorium and a container with the ashes in it was placed
aboard. It was still raining.

The car set off into the countryside. An hour later, on
the bend of an anonymous lane, the charred remains of the
lords of the Third Reich, Hermann Goering's among them,
were poured out into the muddy gutter.

Epilogue

Just before he killed himself at Nuremberg, Hermann Wilhelm Goering forecast that in fifty years' time he would have made his mark in history as a great man, because the German people by then would have realized that everything he did in his lifetime was done for the Greater German Reich.

There are still twenty-two years to go before the fiftieth anniversary of his death, and Germany and the world may have changed considerably by that time. So far, however, there are no signs that statues are being raised in Goering's honor, or squares and streets named after him. Yet there is one development which I, and many other observers, find interesting. In the time since Germans have been able to read the truth about the Third Reich, and of what manner of men were those who led it, there is a certain difference of tone which they adopt when they talk of Goering compared with those other "monsters" of the regime, Hitler, Himmler, Goebbels, and the rest of the *galère*. The younger generation refer to him with a mixture of shame that a man of such background and instincts could ever have got himself involved with such a gang, and rueful regret that he did not shape them into something more decent and far-seeing. The wartime generation still regard him with a certain affection, respect, and admiration.

Their attitude was typified for me by a certain German actor who was called upon, not long ago, to play the part of Hermann Goering in a film about the 1940 air war called *The Battle of Britain*, with which I was associated. The director went up to him one day and suggested that he "ham it up a bit" and turn the character of the Reich Marshal into a figure of fun. The actor said he would rather walk out on the film than do so. When the other German players heard about it, they also threatened to withdraw if Hermann Goering was made into a comic character.

It was not that they were old Nazis or neo-Nazis. They were Germans of all ages, some playing Luftwaffe pilots, others senior officers, yet others airmen and NCOs. Their outlooks and political ideas in private life were vastly different from one another's. Yet they seemed to have a common agreement that, of all the Nazi leaders, Goering was not the one to be mocked but rather to be taken deadly seriously, because of the fascinatingly different aspects of his make-up and the end to which his ideals and ambitions finally led him.

How will history judge him?

I believe now that all the facts about him are available, no one will any longer be able to think of him as a clown, an overdressed fop, a drug addict, a war criminal, or just another Nazi. He was all those things, and yet so very much more that his life becomes one of the great tragedies of modern times.

It is a tragedy because Hermann Goering had human qualities which could have made him a great, progressive, and enlightened leader in the turbulent Germany of the interwar years. His civilized instincts had been hardened by his experiences over the Western Front in World War I, when ally and enemy alike recognized his bravery, his chivalry and his qualities of leadership. He had superb energy, drive, and administrative ability. He had, above all, a great love for his native country and a determination to see it rise again from the painful humiliations of defeat. And there is no doubt that when he first joined Adolf Hitler in the early nineteen twenties, it was a burning idealism which motivated him.

How then did he allow himself to be drawn into the squalid plots, racial persecutions, and bestial horrors which became the everyday program of the National Socialists from the nineteen thirties onward? He had no quarrel with the Jews, and he knew that the profiteers who exploited Germany's postwar misery belonged to no one race, yet he went along without protest with Hitler's brutish anti-Semitism. He was a kind and generous man, and he would have given his life to protect a child or an animal, yet he condoned the appalling cruelties against millions of people, and looked the other way when his conscience smote him.

History will no doubt recognize that he was a man of extraordinary talents and considerable achievements. He played a large part in restoring the self-respect of the German people and forcing the world to pay attention to them. He built up the German Luftwaffe into a formidable force which might have won World War II for Germany in 1940 had it been used the way he planned. He worked hard, and at considerable risk, to prevent the war in the West from starting in 1939 and the war in Russia in 1941. He was an extremely brave man, and faced manfully up to the challenges of war, of pain, and, at the end, of death without flinching.

No future historian will be able to avoid conceding that at the International Military Tribunal at Nuremberg, with a poor case to fight, he challenged his enemies and won. His supreme victory was to cheat them in the end of his body dangling from their gallows.

But, for all his fearlessness and defiance, there is one vice from which Hermann Goering suffered which will prevent any history book from accepting him as a great man. It was not the vice of vanity, from which, when all's said and done, many great men have suffered. It was not his hard-driving and ruthless ambition, for that has carried many a great leader to the top in times gone by. It was not his flamboyance, which outraged so many of his contemporaries, but would be unnoticed on Carnaby Street or Sunset Boulevard today. It was not even his Nero-like capacity for fiddling while Rome was burning, or, rather, playing with his jewels and drooling over his pictures while Germany was sinking into defeat, because what else was there to do?

The vice from which Goering suffered, and for which the history books will undoubtedly blame him, was his moral cowardice. It was his great crime. All through his association with Adolf Hitler, there were moments when he might have changed the course of National Socialism and Germany's race to perdition—by arguing with and persuading the Fuehrer to begin with, by usurping him when that was no longer possible.

Dr. Douglas M. Kelley, the psychiatrist at Nuremberg, was talking to Goering one day when the Reich Marshal recounted how he and Ernst Roehm had built up the Brownshirt Army between them.

"It was evident," Kelley noted at the time, "that Roehm and Goering were more than brothers in arms, they were friends."

Then Goering went on to tell how he and Roehm became rivals for Hitler's favor, and how he finally arranged for Roehm to be shot during the purge. Kelley broke in to ask him how he could have brought himself to arrange for the killing of a friend.

"Goering stopped talking and stared at me, puzzled, as if I were not quite bright," Kelley noted. "Then he shrugged his great shoulders, turned up his palms and said slowly, in simple, one-syllable words: 'But he was in my way . . .' "

There came a time when Adolf Hitler was in his way too, and when his elimination would not only have resulted in the apotheosis of Hermann Goering but in the re-emergence of sanity in Germany. But it turned out that the man who was not afraid of anything else, danger or death, was afraid of Adolf Hitler. Rather than challenge him in a last mortal combat and finish him off, for Germany's sake, as well as for the world, he opted out of the struggle.

It is that failure to show his abhorrence, to take a stand, to oust Hitler before it was too late, for which history will not forgive him.

Notes

I

Background for this chapter on Hermann Goering's childhood, parents, family and influences comes from several unpublished and published sources. So far as Heinrich Goering and Ritter von Epenstein are concerned, I was fortunate enough to be able to talk to the late General Paul von Lettow-Vorbeck and make copies of his records at his home in Hamburg-Altona before he died (see the author's book, *Duel for Kilimanjaro*). He knew both of them well and followed them into German Southwest Africa; and in subsequent years he frequently saw and consulted them. He was on friendly terms with Fanny Goering and her family, and when, in 1920, Lettow-Vorbeck was imprisoned for his part in the Kapp Putsch, Hermann Goering visited him. It was probably he who suggested to Hitler that the general should become National Socialism's first ambassador to Britain—an offer which Lettow-Vorbeck refused.

I have made use of the records in Vienna of the late Professor Hans Thirring; talked to some of the older inhabitants of Neuhaus and Mauterndorf, where the Goering family spent their early years; utilized the memories of Frau Olga Rigele, Goering's favorite elder sister, and the stories of his childhood told by Goering to his wife Emmy, and his stepson, Thomas von Kantzow; and also consulted Goering's official biography by Erich Gritzbach, though this work, despite having been written in collaboration with its subject, leaves out some facts and falsifies others.

pp. 16–17
Details of the colonial experiences of Heinrich Goering and Von Epenstein come from Lettow-Vorbeck and also from German documents, including: *Das Kolonialreich*, Vol. 1. (Bibliographisches Institut, Leipzig and Vienna, 1909), *Geschichte der Deutschen Kolonialpolitik* (Mittler, Berlin, 1914), and Schnee's *Deutsche Koloniallexicon*, 3 vols. (1920).

p. 17
The confident prediction about Hermann's eyes was subsequently repeated to her daughter Olga, who remembered it later.

p. 18
Frau Graf, who looked after Hermann during his mother's absence, was a friend of the Goering family. Her two daughters, Franny and Erna, died in the late 1960s.

p. 18
Goering's remarks about children torn from their mothers was made in a note he wrote during World War II opposing a proposal to conscript married women into factories and farm out their children to crèches.

pp. 20–22
Professor Thirring is the main source for details of Fanny Goering's affair with Von Epenstein, though it was also known to Von Lettow-Vorbeck, and Professor Carl J. Burckhardt, the Swiss historian, told the author that he was once told about it by Party leaders during his term as High Commissioner for Danzig. Professor Thirring and his brother were both godsons of Von Epenstein, who was one of their father's closest friends. It was Thirring senior who found Mauterndorf Castle and completed the arrangement for its purchase.

pp. 22–23
Erich Gritzbach, who wrote the official biography, writes that Hermann left Ansbach because he was disciplined for leading a strike against the poor quality of the school food, and that he paid his fare home by selling his violin to a fellow pupil. This version was told both by Olga Rigele and by Emmy Goering.

pp. 24–25
Facts about Goering's early military career are taken from German Army records and from Gritzbach.

pp. 26–27
The story of Lilli von Epenstein's arrival in Von Epenstein's life was told to the author by Thomas von Kantzow, who heard it from his mother, Goering's first wife, Carin.

II

For the general information about the air war over the Western Front in World War I, which is used in this and the following two chapters, I must acknowledge my debt to several books,

notably: *The Great Air War* by Aaron Norman (The Mac-
millan Company, New York, 1968); *An Aviator's Field Book*
by Oswald Boelcke (National Military Publishing Co., New
York, 1917); *Flying Dutchman* by Anthony H. G. Fokker and
Bruce Gould (Holt, New York, 1931); *The Red Knight of
Germany* by Floyd Gibbons (Doubleday, Garden City, New
York, 1927); *Udet: A Man's Life* by Hans Herlin (Mac-
donald, London, 1960); *Ace of the Black Cross* by Ernst
Udet (Newnes, London, 1935); *Richthofen and the Flying
Circus* by H. J. Nowarra and Kimbrough S. Brown (Letch-
ford, Harleyford, 1959); *The Red Air Fighter* by Baron
Manfred von Richthofen (The Aeroplane Publishing Company,
London, 1918); *Jagd im Flanders Himmel* by Karl Boden-
schatz (Verlag Knorr und Hirth, Munich, 1935).

Details of Goering's activities in the Army in the early
stages of the war are taken from Gritzbach's biography, from
contemporary accounts, and German army records.

pp. 32–36
The facts herein are based on Gritzbach's account and also
on conversations with General Karl Bodenschatz and Bruno
Loerzer.

p. 37
The revolution wrought by the French flier Roland Garros, is
graphically described in Aaron Norman's *The Great Air War*.

p. 38
The remark by Fokker comes from his autobiography, *Flying
Dutchman*.

pp. 38–40
The account is based on the account in Fokker's *Flying Dutchman*.

p. 41
Aaron Norman's comment is quoted from *The Great Air War*.

pp. 41–42
Based on the account in Gritzbach.

pp. 43–44
The information comes from the Thirring family, Frau Olga
Rigele, and Thomas von Kantzow, who says his mother mentioned that Goering had shown her a picture of his wartime
fiancée. She pretended to be jealous and he tore it up in front
of her.

III

For the sources used in this chapter, see the preamble to the
previous chapter. For the general situation over the air front
in the West during this period, I am indebted to Aaron
Norman's *The Great Air War*, and to Nowarra and Brown's
Richthofen and the Flying Circus for the account of his death.
Richthofen's own remarks come from *The Red Air Fighter*.
Goering's activities are dealt with by Gritzbach, by Karl
Bodenschatz in *Jadg im Flanders Himmel* and from conversa-
tions with Bodenschatz and Bruno Loerzer.

IV

Like the two previous chapters, this one has made use of many
of the authoritative books on the air war over the Western
Front. In its detailed account of the activities of the Richthofen
Flying Circus after Hermann Goering took it over, I have
made use of Gritzbach, Bodenschatz's *Jagd im Flanders Himmel* and conversations with him, as well as documents in the
German military archives at Freiburg.

p. 55
The quotations come respectively from *Jagd im Flanders
Himmel* and *The Great Air War*.

pp. 55–56
The scene and speech were recalled by Bodenschatz.

pp. 56–58
The report is quoted in *Jagd im Flanders Himmel*, and the
remarks and events were recalled by Bodenschatz.

p. 59
The exchange between Herr Mauser and Goering is quoted
from *Hermann Goering* by Roger Manvell and Heinrich
Fraenkel (Heinemann, London, 1962).

p. 60
The message from the German Government is quoted in *The
Kings Depart* by Richard M. Watt (Weidenfeld, London,
1969).

pp. 61–66
This account of the final days of the Richthofen Squadron is
based on *Jagd im Flanders Himmel* and the recollections of
Bodenschatz.

pp. 66–68
The incident in the Berlin Philharmonic Hall is based on contemporary accounts and on Gritzbach.

V

For the re-creation of the atmosphere in Munich in the days immediately after the end of World War I, I must acknowledge my debt to General Josef Kammhuber, who later became commander of the night-fighter squadrons of the Luftwaffe under Goering during World War II. Kammhuber, a native of Munich, returned to the city after the armistice after service in the Army on the Western Front. He stayed on as a regular officer and was stationed in the barracks in the Schwindstrasse opposite the apartment where he now lives; and he was there all through the Bavarian revolution and commune, and the abortive Munich Beer Hall Putsch of 1923. A keen student of the theater and music, he was able to give a vivid picture of life in the Bavarian capital during the fraught years immediately after the end of hostilities.

I am also grateful to a highly readable and closely documented account of these years in a book called *The Kings Depart* by Richard M. Watt (Weidenfeld, 1969), which gives the best description I have found of the chaotic conditions in Germany that followed the end of the war.

pp. 69–70
The quotation comes from *The Kings Depart*.

pp. 72–73
The description of Eisner's assassination and the events which followed come from *The Kings Depart*.

p. 73
Goering's experiences are described by Gritzbach, and his appeal to Captain Frank Beaumont was recounted by Kammhuber who had heard it from Goering himself.

pp. 73–76
The events here are based on Gritzbach and Bodenschatz.

pp. 76–78
The events recounted in these pages are based on conversations with Thomas von Kantzow and the quotations come from his aunt's privately printed memoir of his mother, *Carin Goering*, by Fanny Countess von Wilamowitz-Moellendorff, written in German and printed by Verlag von Martin Warneck, Berlin, 1940.

pp. 78–83
This account of Carin's affair and marriage is based on conversations with her son, Thomas von Kantzow, together with letters and documents which he provided.

VI

One of the best detailed studies of the abortive Munich putsch has been written by Professor Harold J. Gordon, Jr., in *Adolf Hitler and the Beer Hall Putsch* (Princeton University Press, 1972). I have also made a close study of the researches of Professor Werner Maser of Munich University, whose documentation on Adolf Hitler's activities is now unsurpassed. (See his *Adolf Hitler: Legende, Mythose, Wirklichkeit* [Bechtle, Munich, 1971] and *Hitlers Briefe und Notizen* [Econ Verlag, Düsseldorf, 1973]).

pp. 85–86
The account of the Munich "Patriotic Societies" and the quotations in these pages come from *Adolf Hitler and the Beer Hall Putsch*.

pp. 87–89
Based upon Gritzbach and Goering's own evidence before the International Military Tribunal at Nuremberg (Trial of German War Criminals, Vol. IX). The quotations are from the statements Goering made at the trial.

p. 89
The quotation is from *Adolf Hitler and the Beer Hall Putsch*.

pp. 90–91
The Goering quotations come from his statement to the IMT at Nuremberg (Vol. IX).

p. 91
Captain Truman Smith's statement is quoted from *Adolf Hitler and the Beer Hall Putsch* and the full text is available in the National Archives, Washington, D.C.

pp. 91–93
The quotations and figures used in this section are taken from the Bayerisches Hauptstaatsarchiv (Bavarian State Archives) documents.

pp. 93–94
The letter from Carin Goering was shown to the author by Thomas von Kantzow.

pp. 94–95

The description of the Goering house is from *Carin Goering*.

p. 97

General Ludendorff's remarks are quoted from his book, *Vom Feldherrn zum Weltrevolutionaer und Wegbereiter Deutscher Volksschöpfung: 1919–1925* (Munich, 1940).

p. 100

The Von Lossow remark is quoted from *Adolf Hitler and the Beer Hall Putsch*.

p. 102

The remark by the SA leader is in the Bayerisches Hauptstaatsarchiv.

p. 102

The conversation between Carin and Hermann Goering comes from *Carin Goering*.

pp. 103–5

The account is based on contemporary records, documents in the Bayerisches Hauptstaatsarchiv, *Adolf Hitler and the Beer Hall Putsch*, and other sources. Adolf Hitler's remark (p. 105) was made at his subsequent trial.

pp. 105–6

The eyewitness account comes from *Im Wandel Einer Zeit* by Karl-Alexander Müller (Süddeutscher Press, Munich, 1938). Adolf Hitler's remark is to be found in the Bayerisches Hauptstaatsarchiv.

pp. 107–9

The account is based on *Adolf Hitler and the Beer Hall Putsch*, contemporary accounts, Gritzbach, and Bayerisches Hauptstaatsarchiv.

p. 109

The officer's remark was made by Captain Johann Salbey and is to be found in the Bayerisches Hauptstaatsarchiv.

pp. 110–13

The description of the march and clash is based on contemporary accounts, Gritzbach, Werner Maser, and *Adolf Hitler and the Beer Hall Putsch*.

VII

This chapter is based almost entirely upon the letters of Carin
Goering to her parents and sister, and permission to quote
from them was given to the author by her son, Thomas von
Kantzow. The quotations on pp. 114–15 are from *Carin
Goering*.

VIII

The story of Hermann Goering's morphine addiction and cure
in Stockholm, and of his incarceration in Langbro Asylum,
was pieced together from conversations with Carin Goering's
son Thomas, from documents in his possession. We also
talked at length about the domestic situation at the Goering
apartment at this time and his relations with them, of which
he retained memories that were only too vivid.

p. 129
The quotation is from *Carin Goering*.

p. 130
Thomas von Kantzow's remark was made to the author, and
he also supplied details of the litigation in which his father
and mother now became involved.

pp. 131–32
The quotation is from *Carin Goering*.

p. 134
For further details of Hindenburg's activities at this time, see
Wooden Titan by John W. Wheeler-Bennett (Archon Books,
London, 1936, reprinted 1963) from which the quotation on
p. 134 is taken.

p. 135
The quotation is from *Carin Goering*.

IX

There have been graphic descriptions of what life was like in
Berlin in the late twenties and early thirties, just before the
Nazis came to power, and none catches the atmosphere better
than the novels by Christopher Isherwood, *Goodbye to Berlin*
and *Mr. Norris Changes Trains*. A series of vivid sketches
have also been painted by the late Count Harry Kessler in his
The Diaries of a Cosmopolitan 1918–1937 (Weidenfeld and
Nicolson, London, 1971).

pp. 138–39
The description of Berlin comes from contemporary accounts, diaries and reminiscences.

pp. 140–44
Copies of Carin Goering's correspondence, from which this account is taken, were given to the author by her son, Thomas von Kantzow.

pp. 144–45
The remarks of Erhard Milch are quoted in *Die Tragoedie der Deutschen Luftwaffe* by David Irving, not yet available in English but published in Germany (Ullstein Verlag, Frankfurt, 1970).

pp. 145–46
Carin Goering's correspondence.

X

pp. 149–54
This account of the fortunes of Goering and the Nazi Party is based on many sources, including documents in the German government archives at Coblenz, the Institut für Zeitgeschichte at Munich, evidence at the IM Tribunal at Nuremberg, etc. See also *The Rise and Fall of the Third Reich* by William Shirer (Simon & Schuster, New York, 1960), *I Knew Hitler* by Kurt G. W. Ludecke (Jarrold, London, 1938), etc.

pp. 155–56
Carin Goering's correspondence.

pp. 158–59
The quotations are from Count Harry Kessler's *The Diaries of a Cosmopolitan*.

p. 159
The account of Stennes' meeting is from contemporary newspaper reports. See also *I Knew Hitler*.

p. 160
Carin Goering's remarks are reported in her sister's biography, *Carin Goering*.

pp. 162–63
The description of the motoring holiday comes from *Carin Goering*.

pp. 164–66
The description of Carin's last hours was given to the author by her son Thomas.

pp. 166–67
There are many accounts of the meeting with Hindenburg, including that in *The Wooden Titan*.

p. 168
Reports of the election battles and casualties are cited in Shirer's *The Rise and Fall of the Third Reich*.

p. 169
The quotation comes from *The Wooden Titan*.

p. 170
Goering's remark was later repeated by Otto Meissner to Franz von Papen and used by him in his *Memoirs* (Deutsch, London, 1952).

p. 170
The exchange between Goebbels and Planck is in Josef Goebbels' diaries, which are now deposited in the German archives at Coblenz.

p. 171
Otto Meissner's remarks were made in his evidence before the IMT at Nuremberg.

XI

The author first met Emmy Goering, both in Berlin and at Carin Hall, when he was a correspondent there in 1939. His first postwar encounter with her was during the trials of the major war criminals at Nuremberg (IMT) through Hermann Goering's lawyer, Dr. Otto Stahmer, and he talked with her at some length about her life with Goering during and after her appearance before a denazification tribunal at Garmisch in 1948. He saw her again in 1954, when she talked freely, and in 1963 when she hinted strongly that old Nazis and neo-Nazis were putting pressure on her to keep silent about her life under National Socialism. (Similar pressures were being put upon Goering's close friend General Karl Bodenschatz, the safety of whose wife was threatened, and upon Goering's valet, Robert Kropp, then working at a U.S. leave center at Berchtesgaden.) The author last spoke to her in Munich in 1973 just after she had celebrated with a number

of friends, but no ex-Nazis, her eightieth birthday at a party
at the Hotel Vierjahreszeiten. Thomas von Kantzow, Carin
Goering's son, for whom Emmy had become a second mother,
had come down specially from Stockholm for the occasion,
though he was seriously ill of a lung complaint. Emmy was in
good spirits but poor health, and shortly afterward she was
taken to the nursing home in which she died. In 1967 she wrote
an account of her personal life with Hermann Goering (*An
der Seite Meines Mannes* by Emmy Goering, Verlag K. W.
Schütz KG, Oldendorf, 1967) which is naïve, unpolitical, and
as the late Sam Goldwyn might have remarked, full of gaps.
Thomas von Kantzow believed that several portions were held
back at the urgent behest of old Nazis.

pp. 174–75
The information in these pages was pieced together from
several sources and from conversations with Thomas von
Kantzow and Emmy Goering.

pp. 176–79
The quotations are from *An der Seite Meines Mannes*.

p. 180
The exchange between Goering and Torgler, which was a
story going the diplomatic rounds at the time, and later repeated to the author by Erich Kordt, an official in the Foreign
Office, cannot be further documented. But Von Papen refers
in his *Memoirs* to Goering's sabotage of his decrees, including
the banning of the Red Banner, and he had regular meetings
with Torgler about tactics in the Reichstag.

p. 181
The quotation is from Goering's evidence at the IMT.

p. 182
The quotation is from Von Papen's *Memoirs*.

p. 183
Goebbels' remarks are in his diaries, now in the German
archives.

p. 183
Goering's telephone call was described by Emmy Goering.

p. 185
Emmy Goering's remark is from *An der Seite Meines Mannes*.

pp. 185–86
Goering's radio talk was reported in contemporary newspapers.

p. 186
Emmy Goering told the story of her return to Weimar.

p. 188
Goering's interview with Dr. Robert Kempner has been described by Dr. Kempner, later an interrogator and prosecutor at IMT.

pp. 189–90
The quotations are from Gritzbach and contemporary newspaper reports.

p. 191
The meeting with German industrialists was used in evidence at IMT, as was the statement issued by the Prussian government after the raid on the Karl Liebknecht Haus.

XII

For background details of the Reichstag fire I am grateful to the documentary help of the Institut für Zeitgeschichte in Munich, and also to Hermann Goering's valet, Robert Kropp. Kropp, who now lives in retirement near Königssee, in Bavaria, has lately been subjected to pressure to talk less about his life with his master, but was much more forthcoming during earlier interviews the author had with him.

p. 197
The statement by Goering was made during his interrogation at Nuremberg by Dr. Robert Kempner.

p. 198
Count Harry Kessler's diary entries are quoted from *The Diaries of a Cosmopolitan*.

pp. 198–99
Goering's remarks on these pages were made during interrogation at Nuremberg by Dr. Robert Kempner.

p. 199
The quotations are from *An der Seite Meines Mannes*.

pp. 203–4
The incident with Thaelmann was mentioned during his interrogation at Obersalzberg by Dr. Kempner of Paul (Pilli) Koerner, Goering's secretary of state.

p. 205
Goering's remarks were recalled by Emily Goering.

pp. 206–7
The circumstances surrounding Bodenschatz's appointment and Goering's remarks to him are quoted in *Goering* by Willi Frischauer (Odhams Press, London, 1951).

p. 207–8
Milch's adherence to the Air Ministry and Hitler's remarks to him (pp. 207–8) are recounted in Irving, *Die Tragoedie der Deutschen Luftwaffe* and are taken from the Milch Papers which are now in the German military archives at Freiburg.

pp. 208–9
In the account given in *Die Tragoedie der Deutschen Luftwaffe*, the author, David Irving, who had access to the Milch Papers, implies that Milch was actually born out of wedlock and that his certificate of non-Jewishness was therefore no stratagem. This is contrary to most non-Nazi historians' information, and according to Emmy Goering, her husband never had any doubt that he was half-Jewish.

pp. 209–10
The account of the meeting at the Aero Club comes from Gritzbach.

XIII

pp. 211–13
Information about Hermann Goering's activities on Emmy's behalf come from Emmy Goering, and of his state of health and eating habits from Emmy Goering and Robert Kropp.

p. 214
The story of his disastrous flight back from Rome is told by Erhard Milch in the Milch Papers and quoted in Irving, *Die Tragoedie der Deutschen Luftwaffe*. Gritzbach has a different version of this misadventure in which, in a driving hailstorm, Goering took over the controls from the disoriented pilot and guided the Junker 52 safely home.

pp. 214–19
The accounts of the Reichstag fire trial come from eyewitness accounts and contemporary newspaper reports.

p. 220
The full text of the letter to Roehm was published in the Party newspaper, *Voelkischer Beobachter*, on January 2, 1934.

XIV

The descriptions of Carin Hall in this chapter come from the author's personal observations as, a correspondent, several· eye-witness accounts, and from Gritzbach, whose remarks are quoted on p. 224.

p. 225
The dispatch from Sir Eric Phipps on which this description is based appears in *Documents on British Foreign Policy 1919– 1939*, Vol. VI, pp. 749–51.

pp. 227–28
The descriptions of Carin's interment come from Thomas von Kantzow and *Carin Goering* (from which the quotations on pp. 227–28 are taken).

p. 229
The quotation is from *An der Seite Meines Mannes*.

p. 230
The quotation is from *Inside the Third Reich* by Albert Speer (Weidenfeld and Nicolson, London, 1970, and The Macmillan Company, New York, 1970).

p. 231
Quotations from *Inside the Third Reich*.

pp. 231–34
Hermann Goering's intercept service has been dealt with at some length in *Breach of Security* edited by David Irving (William Kimber, London, 1968) and *Codeword Barbarossa* by Burton Whaley (MIT Press, Cambridge, Massachusetts, 1973), though the latter concentrates on its work leading up to the attack on the U.S.S.R. The documents quoted are in the political archives of the Auswärtiges Amt in Bonn, and the Institut für Zeitgeschichte has produced an invaluable guide to the activities of the Goering organization under the heading: *Forschungsamt* by Dr. Martin Broszat.

pp. 235–36
See above.

pp. 237–42
The description of the 1934 blood purge is based on many
sources including documents in the Institut für Zeitgeschichte,
Munich, the Forschungsstelle zur Geschichte des Nationals-
zialismus, Hamburg, the transcription of the IMT Nuremberg
(Sitzungsprotokolle, Baden-Baden, 1947–49), the trials of Josef
Dietrich and Michael Lippert at Munich, May 6–14, 1967, *La
Nuit des Longs Couteaux* (Collection Archives, Paris, 1964)
by Charles Bloch and *La Nuit des Longs Couteaux* (Laffont,
Paris, 1970) by Max Gallo.

XV

p. 244
Goering's proposal was described by Emmy Goering (see also
her *An der Seite Meines Mannes*).

pp. 245–46
Sir Eric Phipps's dispatch is to be found in *Documents on
British Foreign Policy*, Vol. XII, telegram No. 285.

p. 249
The quotations by Galland are from *The First and the Last*
by Adolf Galland (Methuen, London, 1955).

p. 250
Schacht's views are based on *Account Settled* by Hjalmar
Schacht (Weidenfeld and Nicolson, London, 1948).

p. 251
Text of the "Guns Before Butter" speech is taken from contemporary newspaper accounts.

pp. 251–53
The description of Udet's development of the Stuka comes
from documents in the German military archives at Freiburg,
the Milch Papers quoted in Irving, *Die Tragoedie der
Deutschen Luftwaffe*.

pp. 253–55
This account is based on conversations with General Paul
Stehlin. See also his *Temoignage pour l'Histoire* (Laffont,
Paris, 1964).

pp. 255–59
The description of the Olympic Games comes from Thomas von Kantzow and contemporary newspaper reports.

XVI

p. 263
The account given by Professor Hugo Blaschke of Goering's experiences in the dental chair was recounted to Dr. Robert Kempner during the course of an interrogation for the IMT in 1945.

pp. 266–67
The background to the Von Blomberg and Von Fritsch scandals is taken from a series of interrogations which Dr. Robert Kempner had with Goering, the diary of General Jodl in the archives at Freiburg, *The Sword and the Swastika* by Telford Taylor (Simon & Schuster, New York, 1952).

pp. 269–70
The incidents are based on stories from Emmy Goering.

p. 270
Goering's remark was made in his evidence to the IMT Nuremberg and his speech reported in the local newspapers. The missing sentence was sent by dispatch to Washington and is included in the whole speech to be found in the National Archives in Washington.

XVII

pp. 273–76
Emmy Goering tells the full story of the birth of her child in *An der Seite Meines Mannes*. The background to Paul Stehlin's association with Olga Rigele was given to the author in conversations with Stehlin. The quotations from Stehlin are from his *Témoignage pour l'Histoire*.

pp. 276–77
Goering's remarks were made in the course of a conversation in Nuremberg Jail with U.S. Captain G. M. Gilbert, M.D., the prison psychologist. See *Nuremberg Diary* (Eyre and Spottiswood, London, 1948).

p. 278
Bodenschatz's remarks are quoted in Stehlin, *Témoignage pour l'Histoire*.

pp. 278–80
The description of Vuillemin's visit and Daladier's questions
come from Stehlin.

pp. 280–81
The incident and remarks were remembered by Emmy Goering.

p. 282
Thomas von Kantzow related the conversation to the author.

pp. 284–85
For more about Thyssen, see *I Paid Hitler* by Fritz Thyssen
(Hodder and Stoughton, London, 1941).

p. 285
Bodenschatz's remarks were later incorporated by Stehlin into
the official French government publication, *Livre Jaune*, published in 1939.

XVIII

pp. 287–88
This incident in Dr. Josef Goebbels' stormy love life was told
by Emmy Goering. Albert Speer deals with other facets of it
in *Inside the Third Reich*.

pp. 289–91
The story of Goering's use of Birger Dahlerus as his go-
between is based on conversations with Thomas von Kantzow,
Dahlerus' evidence before IMT, where he was a witness on
Goering's behalf, and his own book, *The Last Attempt*, by
Birger Dahlerus (Hutchinson, London, 1948).

p. 291
Lord Halifax's remark is in *Documents on British Foreign
Policy*, Vol. VII.

pp. 292–93
See Thyssen, *I Paid Hitler*.

pp. 294–97
Dahlerus' further activities are described in the German Foreign Office documents at Coblenz, in *The Diaries of Sir
Alexander Cadogan* edited by David Dilkes (Cassell, London,
1971).

p. 296
Chamberlain's letters to his sister are in *Neville Chamberlain*
by Iain Macleod (Muller, London, 1961).

pp. 298–99
The visit of Sumner Welles is described in the German Foreign
Office documents at Coblenz, in Welles's own book, *The Time
for Decision* by Sumner Welles (Harper, New York, 1944),
and in *Hitler's Interpreter* by Paul Schmidt (Heinemann,
London, 1951).

pp. 301–4
Emmy Goering's experiments with the fortuneteller are described in *An der Seite Meines Mannes.*

XIX

p. 307
The meeting between Goering and his staff is described in
Irving, *Die Tragoedie der Deutschen Luftwaffe.* The quota-
tions on p. 307 are from Goering's evidence before the IMT.

p. 308
General Blumentritt's remarks are in the German army records
at Freiburg.

pp. 308–9
Thomas von Kantzow showed the author Goering's letter.

p. 310
The transcript of Hitler's speech is from contemporary press
reports.

pp. 310–11
The quotations are from Shirer, *The Rise and Fall of the Third
Reich.*

pp. 312–13
Thomas van Kantzow described the dinner celebration. The
quotation from Galland is in his *The First and the Last.*

p. 313
Goering's remark was made during his evidence at the IMT.

p. 314
Goering's IMT evidence. The air-production figures are from
Irving, *Die Tragoedie der Deutschen Luftwaffe.*

p. 315
Goering's IMT evidence.

pp. 316–17
The description and quotations are taken from Galland, *The First and the Last*.

XX

The art treasures looted by the National Socialists during World War II have been dealt with in several reports and books, the most useful among the latter being *Le Front de l'Art* by Rose Valland (Plon, Paris, 1961) and *Salt Mines and Castles* by Thomas C. Howe (Bobbs-Merrill, New York, 1946). The documentation department of the War Institute, Defense Department, Holland, has also printed a lengthy report on Nazi requisitions and "purchases" in which a section is devoted to the acquirements of Hermann Goering, and the U.S. Office of Strategic Services (OSS) also compiled a report on art looting which is in the National Archives in Washington. Some of Hermann Goering's collection disappeared in the last days of the war, when one or two truckloads being evacuated from Carin Hall to Berchtesgaden were lost or captured in Berlin. At least one painting, a Boucher "Venus," has turned up recently in London after having been sent for auction from Sweden. Before that it appears to have been in Poland. It seems likely that there are many others adorning the walls of Party officials or authorized dealers in Eastern Europe and the U.S.S.R.

p. 319
The plans of the Hermann Goering Museum are in the German archives at Coblenz.

p. 319
The quotation from Goering was made during his interrogation shortly after capture at Augsburg, the U.S. interrogation center.

pp. 319–20
The statement by Bruno Lohse was made during interrogation in preparation for the case against Goering at the IMT Nuremberg.

p. 320
The story of Robert Kropp's picture is told in *Hermann Goering* by Roger Manvell and Heinrich Fraenkel (Heinemann, London, 1962).

p. 321
Goering's statement was made while under interrogation at
Augsburg.

p. 322
Goering made this statement at Augsburg.

p. 322
The report on the art treasures was written by interrogators
at the U.S. interrogation center at Augsburg after questioning
Goering and other captured Nazi officials.

p. 323
One of Goering's passions was for the nudes of the older and
younger Cranach. For one of her childhood birthdays, the
City of Cologne gave a Lucas Cranach to his daughter, Edda,
and after the war tried to get it back through the courts.
Edda Goering fought the case and eventually was allowed to
keep the painting, on the grounds that it was given to her and
not to her "war criminal" father.

p. 324
The Speer quotations come from *Inside the Third Reich.*

XXI

pp. 326–29
Hermann Goering gave details of his so-called Mediterranean
Plan both to his interrogators at Augsburg and during his
evidence at the IMT. He described his meeting with Hitler when
he was told of the Russian campaign during his Augsburg
interrogation.

pp. 330–31
The Galland remarks are quoted from *The First and the Last.*

pp. 331–33
The meeting between Kammhuber and Goering was described
to the author by General Kammhuber.

p. 334
Goering's antipathy to Bormann was described by Karl
Bodenschatz and Emmy Goering.

p. 335
Hitler's remark was recalled by Bodenschatz.

pp. 335–36
Hitler's plan and Goering's reaction to it was described by
Bodenschatz. There is also reference to it in Irving, *Die
Tragoedie der Deutschen Luftwaffe.*

p. 337
The full memorandum can be found in IMT documents PS
2718, 1743, and U.S.S.R. 10.

p. 339
Goering's conversation with Hitler was recounted during his
interrogation at Augsburg.

XXII

p. 341
The Speer quotation is from *Inside the Third Reich.*

pp. 342–43
The Milch-Goering exchange is recounted in the Milch Papers.
Udet's comment to Heinkel is quoted in Irving, *Die Tragoedie
der Deutschen Luftwaffe.*

pp. 344–45
Udet's last hours are described in the Milch Papers, in the
interrogation of Paul Koerner in preparation of the IMT case
against Goering, and in Irving, *Die Tragoedie der Deutschen
Luftwaffe.*

p. 346
Milch wrote the comment in his diary, now with the Milch
Papers.

pp. 347–48
General Adolf Galland's relationship with Goering was explained to the author in a succession of stories which Galland
related to the author over several months of discussions in
Germany, Spain, and Britain. At his home near Bonn, he
showed the Knight's Cross and the Pour le Mérite which are
all that survived of his war decorations. The others were
destroyed. He never did get back his gold Spanish cross from
Goering. The quotation on p. 286 is from *The First and the
Last.*

p. 349
The enabling decree referred to and matters pertaining to it
are quoted in IMT documents PS 1666 and 1183.

pp. 350
The activities of the extermination brigades in the East and
Goering's connection with them are referred to in *Anatomy
of the SS State* by Helmuth Krausnick, Hans Buchheim, Martin Broszat and Hans-Adolf Jacobsen (Collins, London, 1968).

pp. 351–52
Bodenschatz's description of the scene at the Fuehrer's headquarters is to be found in *Goering* by Willi Frischauer.

p. 353
Thomas von Kantzow recalled the scene for the author.

pp. 353–55
The incidents with Rommel are described in *The Rommel
Papers* (Collins, London, 1953) and *Rommel* by Desmond
Young (Collins, 1950).

p. 356
Fred Majdalany's *The Fall of Fortress Europe* is published by
Hodder and Stoughton, London, 1968.

pp. 355–58
There are many books and much documentation of the
Stalingrad battle, too many to cite here. Milch has told of his
own part in the operation (to his own credit, not unnaturally)
in the Milch Papers. The quotations by Goering are from part
of his interrogation by Major Paul Kubala and Captain Rolf
Wartenberg, U.S. Military Intelligence, at the Augsburg interrogation center.

p. 359
The exchanges between Milch and Hitler are quoted in Irving,
Die Tragoedie der Deutschen Luftwaffe.

XXIII

p. 360
The meeting was described by Milch in his diary.

pp. 361–62
The meeting between Goering, Speer, and Goebbels is de-
scribed in Speer, *Inside the Third Reich.* The quotations from
Goebbels are in the Goebbels diaries. See *The Goebbels
Diaries*, edited by Louis Lochner (Hamish Hamilton, London,
1948).

p. 363
Hitler's remark was recalled by Karl Bodenschatz.

p. 363
See Lochner, *The Goebbels Diaries*.

pp. 364–66
The story of Rose Korwan was recounted by Emmy Goering and included in her case before the denazification court at Garmisch Partenkirchen, when she was acquitted. It was during this case that several refugees came forward to testify on her behalf. The quotations are from Emmy Goering's *An der Seite Meines Mannes*.

pp. 367–68
Adolf Galland described to the author the atmosphere prevailing in the Fuehrer's bunker at this time. The quotation on p. 368 is from *The First and the Last*.

p. 369
The remark by Albert Speer was made to the author.

p. 370
The remark about Milch by Goering was repeated to him and included in the Milch Papers. The description by Speer of Goering was recalled by Speer during a conversation with the author.

pp. 371–72
The party at Carin Hall was recalled by Emmy Goering.

XXIV

p. 373
The quotation from Speer is from *Inside the Third Reich*.

pp. 373–74
The description of the Goering-Speer dinner at Carin Hall was given to the author by Speer.

p. 375
The last hours of Carin Hall were described by Goering and Berndt von Brauchitsch in conversation with Captain Rolf Wartenberg at the Augsburg interrogation center. Madame Rose Valland, the French art expert, engaged in tracking down stolen French art treasures, was one of the first from the West to reach the ruined hall, and she claims to have

found what must have been Carin's skull in the rubble. She
said a prayer over it and left it where it lay. Whether it was
then buried once more in the debris, crushed by a Russian
tank, or spirited away by one of Goering's old huntsmen, no
one will ever know. It simply disappeared.

p. 377
There have been many books on Hitler's last hours in the
Berlin bunker. The quotations here are from Speer's *Inside
the Third Reich.*

pp. 377–80
The account of Goering's activities in these last hours of
Hitler's life are based on several sources, including the diaries
of General Karl Koller, published as *Der Letzte Monat*
(Wohlgemuth Verlag, Mannheim, 1949), his interrogation at
the Augsburg center, as well as his subsequent statements. The
quotation on p. 377 is from *Goering* by Willi Frischauer, and
Speer's remarks are from *Inside the Third Reich.*

pp. 380–84
The events here were described by Emmy Goering. See also
her *An der Seite Meines Mannes.*

pp. 385–87
The description of these events comes from Emmy Goering
and Robert Kropp.

pp. 387–88
The quotations are from Emmy Goering's *An der Seite
Meines Mannes.*

pp. 388–90
The description of Goering's stay at Augsburg was given to
the author by Rolf Wartenberg, who also showed him the
accordion which Goering gave him as a farewell present. The
report on p. 390 was made by interrogators at the Augsburg center.

p. 391
The document signed by Goering was effected at the Augsburg
center.

XXV

For the descriptions of Hermann Goering's imprisonment first
at Mondorf and then in Nuremberg Jail, I am grateful to
many people. During the IMT in Nuremberg I talked at

considerable length with Dr. Douglas M. Kelley, the psychiatrist, and to a lesser extent with Dr. G. M. Gilbert, the psychologist. They both kept copious notes of their experiences and of their conversations with the major war criminals in their care, and the full transcripts of these have been deposited with the National Archives in Washington, some portions of them still classified. But both Drs. Kelley and Gilbert were allowed to make public part of their reports and observations, and though for the moment both their books are out of print, it is to be hoped that they will soon be republished, for they are of considerable psychological as well as historical interest. The books are: *22 Cells in Nuremberg* by Douglas M. Kelley, M.D. (Greenberg, New York, 1947) and *Nuremberg Diary* by G. M. Gilbert, Ph.D. (Farrar, Straus, New York, 1947). I hope I have made good use of their studies.

I have also talked to a large number of ex-members of the United States forces who were on the staff either of the interrogation centers through which Goering passed or of Nuremberg Jail, and they have helped me to fill in the details of what happened to the Reich Marshal in the twilight weeks of his life. Mr. Rolf Wartenberg, now a United States citizen and a successful shipper in New York, escaped from his native Berlin after Kristallnacht, 1938, and became a U.S. Army Intelligence officer in Germany during World War II. He was the first to greet Hermann Goering on his arrival at the Augsburg interrogation center, and he saw him frequently thereafter in Nuremberg when, after demobilization, he joined the U.S. prosecution staff as a civilian during the IMT. Mr. Howard Triest, also now a U.S. citizen, lives near Detroit. Born in Munich, he did not leave Germany with his father, mother, and sister until 1939. He was separated from the rest of his family after the Germans attacked in the West in 1940 (the Triests had taken refuge in Luxembourg) and he made it to the United States, his sister reached Switzerland, but his parents were turned over to the Gestapo and ended up in the gas ovens. Howard Triest was a U.S. Army interpreter on the Staff at Nuremberg and attended the interrogations of most of the major war criminals. One of the ironies of his situation was that, though Jewish, he looks typically Bavarian, and was treated as such by the accused men. That arch Jew-baiter, Julius Streicher, who claimed to be able to detect a Jew by the shape of his face and his ears and to be quite infallible, used to greet Triest with the remark: "Thank God to be seeing a good German, after all those Jews they're always sending in to see me." It is a measure of Triest's stature that he did not allow what had happened to himself and his parents to affect in any way his outward attitude to the Nazi prisoners.

I have also talked or corresponded with many of the interrogators who questioned Goering during his imprisonment.
These include that remarkable man Dr. Robert Kempner, for
whom Hermann Goering, in one way, did a good turn when
he sacked him during the purge of the Prussian Department
of Justice in 1933. Dr. Kempner has since become a famous
international lawyer who now divides his life between his
home in Pennsylvania and his legal office in Frankfurt, from
which he emerges to fight doughtily and skillfully for the
rights of Nazi victims in the German courts. Mr. Walter H.
Rapp, who now lives near Washington, D.C., talked to me at
length about his lengthy sessions with Hermann Goering. And
Mr. Morton E. Rome, now a lawyer in Baltimore, Maryland,
provided me with some invaluable information about Goering,
with whom he conducted several interrogations.

XXVI

For the source of the description of what went on inside
Nuremberg Jail during the trial, see above. Details of the
trial itself are taken from the official transcript, backed by the
author's own observations at the time.

pp. 413–14
The late Lord Birkett's comments are taken from *Lord Birkett*,
the authorized biography by Montgomery Hyde. Copyright ©
Montgomery Hyde 1964. Hamish Hamilton, London.

pp. 418–19
The description of Emmy Goering's prison visits come from
herself, and from her *An der Seite Meines Mannes*.

XXVII

The detailed account of Hermann Goering's last hours and
the circumstances in which he committed suicide are based on
the full transcript of the Report of Board of Proceedings in
Case of Hermann Goering (Suicide) October 1946, which is
in the National Archives in Washington (German Documents
Section) and has now been declassified. All the statements
made by Colonel Burton C. Andrus and members of his staff
in Nuremberg Jail are taken from this report.

p. 423
This interview between Goering and his family is described in
Emmy Goering's *An der Seite Meines Mannes*.

p. 428
Albert Speer's statement was made to the author.

pp. 429–30
The description of the executions and the disposal of the bodies comes from an anonymous report. The name is still classified. I am grateful to Mr. Owen Cunningham, now an attorney-at-law in Des Moines, Iowa, for helping me to fill in the details of what happened after Hermann Goering died.

Index